The Other War of 1812

New Perspectives on the History of the South

Florida A&M University, Tallahassee
Florida Atlantic University, Boca Raton
Florida Gulf Coast University, Ft. Myers
Florida International University, Miami
Florida State University, Tallahassee
University of Central Florida, Orlando
University of Florida, Gainesville
University of North Florida, Jacksonville
University of South Florida, Tampa
University of West Florida, Pensacola

The Other War of 1812

The Patriot War and the American Invasion of Spanish East Florida

James G. Cusick

Foreword by John David Smith, Series Editor

University Press of Florida
Gainesville · Tallahassee · Tampa · Boca Raton
Pensacola · Orlando · Miami · Jacksonville · Ft. Myers

08 07 06 05 04 03   6 5 4 3 2 1

Library of Congress Cataloging-in-Publication Data
Cusick, James G.
The other War of 1812: the Patriot War and the American invasion
of Spanish East Florida / James G. Cusick; foreword by John David Smith.
p. cm. — (New perspectives on the history of the South)
Includes bibliographical references and index.
ISBN 0-8130-2648-2
1. Florida—History—War of 1812—Campaigns. 2. United States—
History—War of 1812—Campaigns. 3. United States—Territorial expansion.
4. Florida—History—Spanish colony, 1784–1821. 5. Mathews, George, 1739–
1812. 6. Filibusters—Florida—History—19th century. 7. Madison, James,
1751–1836. 8. United States—Military relations—Spain. 9. Spain—
Military relations—United States. I. Title. II. Series.
E359.5.F6C87 2003
973.5′23′09759—dc21 2003042632

The University Press of Florida is the scholarly publishing agency
for the State University System of Florida, comprising Florida A&M
University, Florida Atlantic University, Florida Gulf Coast University, Florida
International University, Florida State University, University of Central
Florida, University of Florida, University of North Florida, University
of South Florida, and University of West Florida.

University Press of Florida
15 Northwest 15th Street
Gainesville, FL 32611–2079
http://www.upf.com

Contents

Figures

Foreword

Between 1763 and 1821, no part of the South's expanding frontier experienced more transition than colonial Florida. In 1763, following the end of the French and Indian War, Britain acquired the province from Spain only to cede it back to the Spanish Crown in 1783 after the Peace of Paris granted independence to the United States. To administer Florida, England had divided the vast territory into East Florida (encompassing the entire peninsula east of the Apalachicola River, with its capital in St. Augustine) and West Florida (extending far west of the Apalachicola into the present states of Louisiana, Mississippi, and Alabama, with its capital at Pensacola). Under Spanish control, the Floridas suffered from colonial benign neglect and, after 1808, when Spain and England became allies, from the imperialistic gaze of their maturing neighbor to the North, the United States.

In *The Other War of 1812*, James Cusick brings to life a gripping but little known episode in southern history—Florida's Patriot War of 1812–14. Drawing heavily upon colonial records of Spanish East Florida and a wealth of other primary sources, Cusick provides the first modern narrative and analysis of the American invasion of Spanish Florida in March 1812 and its place in the expansionist foreign policy of President James Madison and Secretary of State James Monroe. Determined to drive Spain from the Gulf Coast and the Florida peninsula, Madison and Monroe were equally committed to denying England control over this corner of America's evolving frontier.

In 1810, for example, after American settlers in the Baton Rouge District of West Florida staged a coup, Madison immediately declared West Florida (except for the Mobile District) part of Louisiana Territory, which the United States had acquired in 1803. Convinced that East Florida would succumb as easily, Madison appointed General George Mathews, former governor of Georgia, as a U.S. commissioner and authorized him to lead a filibuster expedition into the vulnerable and valuable Spanish province. American leaders justified their scheme by alleging that U.S. forces were assisting a local revolt against Spanish oppression and against smugglers, British spies, and rebellious Indians and runaway slaves who threatened their security. According to Cusick, the resulting filibuster "miscarried into military invasion, embarrassing President Madison, complicating American strategy during the War of 1812, and plunging the southern frontier into a lengthy and destructive blood feud."

Sponsored by the U.S. government, Mathews outfitted a private army along the Georgia-Florida border. The "Patriots" consisted largely of disenfranchised frontiersmen from both sides of the border as well as Georgia militiamen. Supported by American naval and military forces, Mathews's band of filibusters invaded Florida and easily captured Fernandina on Amelia Island in the name of the United States. Buoyed by their success, the Patriots moved southward, overwhelming Spanish outposts, and set their sights on capturing St. Augustine. The Patriots' "rebellion" escalated quickly into a "war," as American forces subjected the East Florida capital to a long siege.

White southerners, especially Georgians along the Florida border, celebrated the incursion into Spanish territory. They "spoke of the Dons with contempt, resentful of a people who mustered black soldiers into their provincial militias—a direct challenge to southern fears about slave uprisings—and who forged worrisome alliances with the Creeks, Miccosukees, and Seminoles. To beat down black troops, humble the red foe, and open up Spanish-controlled lands for settlement, such goals received complete approbation from citizens in Milledgeville, Savannah, Augusta, Temple, Colerain, and St. Marys." President Madison's enemies, however, including northern Federalists, condemned what they considered the administration's brazen invasion of a neutral colony and the plundering of its people and their property.

In his pathbreaking book, Cusick accurately contextualizes the Patriot War within southern history, the early history of American expansion, and the clash of frontier cultures. He unravels a complex story of bloody border conflict between Patriots and Spaniards and of the impact of the war on planters, farmers, slaves, free blacks, and Indians. As Cusick notes, "the Patriot War is an important historical bridge leading from the American Revolution to the Seminole Wars in the Southeast. The destruction of the Negro Fort at Apalachicola (1816), the First Seminole War (1817–18), the cession of Florida to the United States (1819–21), and even the Second Seminole War (1835–42) were outgrowths of the disruptions and lingering hostilities that the Patriot War generated in the region."

While the Patriots' incursion into East Florida ultimately failed, the Patriot War, along with losses in West Florida, nevertheless persuaded Spain to withdraw from the Southeast. The Adams-Onís Treaty of 1819 (finalized in 1821) ceded Florida to the United States. Ironically, the Patriot War accomplished the one thing that other campaigns in the War of 1812 had failed to do: It brought new territory into the United States.

John David Smith
Series Editor

Acknowledgments

Most of my friends and family have been involved in one way or another with the production of this book. Dan Schafer, professor of history at the University of North Florida, prompted me to attempt it after hearing a short talk I gave on the subject at the Florida Historical Society meetings. "Are you writing a book about the Patriot War?" he asked me. "No, I don't think so," I said. So he rephrased the question. "You are writing a history of the Patriot War, aren't you?" And, truthfully, that is how the book had its inception.

At the time I began it, I had a few dozen newspaper articles that had never made it into Rembert Patrick's *Florida Fiasco*, I had my knowledge of the East Florida papers, and I had the daunting shadow of Patrick himself, for I thought it was an act of pure cheek and effrontery to even attempt a retelling of *Fiasco*. I hope I have extended and updated his history.

Much of the research for this book was accumulated with the aid of several institutions. I am extremely grateful to the Jay I. Kislak Foundation, the Winterthur Library and Museum, the John Carter Brown Library, the National Endowment for the Humanities, the St. Augustine Historical Society, and the University of Florida for the assistance they have rendered.

I am also indebted to Canter Brown for providing me with a title for this work, "The Other War of 1812," which also helped me to refine my interpretation of the Patriot War.

Scholars working in Florida are lucky to be part of one of the friendliest and most helpful congregations of people to be found anywhere. Charles Tingley and Jean Parker Waterbury both provided me with the benefits of their insights and knowledge by reading portions of this book in manuscript. I am also grateful to the peer reviewers and to my editors, Meredith

Morris-Babb and Judy Goffman, and the staff of the University Press of Florida for their help and advice. Dan Schafer generously provided material for the work, including the episode of Anna Kingsley and Laurel Grove, and took me on a memorable tour of important locations associated with the Patriot War. Nat Millett, in the course of his own dissertation research on the Negro Fort at Apalachicola, pointed me toward important British sources. In addition, all scholars of this period owe a great debt to Frank Marotti of Cheney University and Wayne de Cesar of the National Archives, for unearthing the Treasury Department's records on the Patriot War Claims, a discovery that will prove to be a windfall for Florida history. Patricia Griffin, Susan Parker, Jane Landers, Sherry Johnson, John Worth, Larry Rivers, John Mahon, Michael Gannon, Samuel Proctor, Kevin McCarthy, Jim Miller, Jerald Milanich, Kathleen Deagan, Larry Harris, and my fellow board members of the St. Augustine Archaeological Association and the Seminole Wars Historic Foundation have all carried me through various stages of this work with encouragement and assistance.

I also note the kind assistance of a number of individuals at the following libraries and archives: Taryn Rodríguez-Boette and the staff of the St. Augustine Historical Society, Debra Wynne and Craig Friend at the Florida Historical Society, Arthur Dunkelman at the Jay I. Kislak Foundation, Ron Kurtz and the Amelia Island Museum of History, Linda McCurdy at Duke University, Laura Bullion at the Western Historical Manuscript Collection, Dean DeBolt at the University of West Florida, and the staffs of the Bryan-Lang Library, the New-York Historical Society, the Georgia Division of Archives and History, the Archivo General de Indias, the Public Record Office, the Library of Congress, and the National Archives. My own colleagues at the Department of Special Collections, George A. Smathers Libraries, University of Florida, have graciously tolerated all the time I spent on this project. Bruce Chappell aided me, as so many others, with research assistance and editorial comments. For the graphics in this book, I am indebted to John Knaub, J. R. Hermsdorfer, and Susan G. Duser of the Office of Academic Technologies.

Finally, I acknowledge with gratitude my parents and family, including uncles, aunts, and cousins, who have always helped me through a long career in the world of academia and who make the whole endeavor worthwhile.

Time Line for the Patriot War

September 23, 1810—American settlers begin an uprising in Baton Rouge, Spanish West Florida, prompting American intervention.

January 15, 1811—Congress passes a secret act for the acquisition and occupation of the Spanish Floridas. General George Mathews and Colonel John McKee are appointed U.S. commissioners to carry out the act's provisions.

July 23, 1811—Spanish officials in East Florida receive the first definite news of a plot to seize the province.

September 5, 1811—The Spanish and British consuls make a formal protest to the Madison administration regarding Mathews's activities on the Georgia border.

October 30, 1811—Secretary of State James Monroe responds to the protests and states the case for American rights to East Florida.

March 17, 1812—The Patriots take possession of Fernandina and Amelia Island, aided by gunboats of the U.S. Navy.

March 18, 1812—George Mathews and John Houston McIntosh formally cede Amelia Island to the United States. This begins the American occupation.

March 25, 1812—The Patriots reach St. Augustine and begin a siege.

April 4, 1812—The Madison administration rescinds George Mathews's commission and repudiates the seizure of East Florida.

April 10, 1812—Continuing a secret policy, the Madison administration appoints Governor David Brydie Mitchell of Georgia to succeed Mathews and instructs him to play for time in East Florida.

May 7, 1812—Governor Juan José de Estrada sends a sortie against the Patriots at San Pablo.

May 16, 1812—Estrada's forces attack Colonel Thomas Adam Smith's contingent at Fort Mose, north of St. Augustine.

June 11, 1812—Governor Sebastián Kindelán y O'Regan arrives with reinforcements to take command of Spanish forces in East Florida.

June 18, 1812—The United States declares war on Great Britain.

June 19, 1812—The Senate refuses to endorse a military seizure of East Florida.

July 26, 1812—The Patriot government is transformed into the government for the territory of East Florida. The Seminoles enter the conflict.

August 4, 1812—Privateer attacks on Spanish shipping begin.

September 12, 1812—Skirmish at Twelve Mile Swamp. American forces are compelled to retreat. The siege is lifted.

September 24, 1812—Colonel Daniel Newnan leads an expedition into north-central Florida to attack the Seminoles.

February 2, 1813—The Senate, for the second time, rejects a bill authorizing a military seizure of East Florida.

February 3, 1813—Tennessee and Georgia militia join Smith's regulars on a second expedition against the Seminoles.

April 26, 1813—American forces begin an evacuation of East Florida and burn the homesteads of settlers loyal to the Spanish cause.

August 8, 1813—Patriots and Spanish loyalists clash at Waterman's Bluff.

November 22, 1813—Laurel Grove destroyed.

April 19, 1814—The Madison administration refuses to support the Republic of East Florida formed by the Patriots in the Alachua District.

May 5, 1814—The Seminoles ambush and kill General Buckner Harris, leading to the final collapse of the Patriot movement.

Americans vs. Spaniards

A Different View of the War of 1812

For the people of Spanish East Florida, the War of 1812 had little to do with animosities between the United States and England. Even while these two countries battled one another over questions of national sovereignty, Floridians were fighting another kind of conflict, a rearguard action against American expansionism, inflamed by old disputes with the state of Georgia and by secret American plans to destroy Spanish power in the Southeast and seize Spanish territory. Much of the trouble for Spanish interests in the region began in 1810, when American agents succeeded in destabilizing parts of Spanish West Florida and Texas. In that same year, signs first arose that East Florida might be ripe for the picking. Five prominent inhabitants of Spanish East Florida, worried about the future of their province, conspired to rebel against king and Crown. Intent on securing their short-term interests, they toyed with the idea of selling out both their loyalties and their colony to the United States.

It is unlikely that any of the five fully understood the dangers they were embracing or the havoc that would result. Perhaps they counted on their influence to shield them. John Houston McIntosh, for instance, was an affluent planter whose ancestors and kin had helped to build the state of Georgia. He had lived quietly in Spanish East Florida for seven years, amassing lands, slaves, and money on his cotton plantations. George Fleming was another wealthy planter with an estate along the St. Johns River. Don Fernando de la Maza Arredondo came from the vicinity of Santander, Spain. As a youth of eighteen, he had immigrated to East Florida via Havana, Cuba, supporting himself as an intern in the military hospital, and had gradually acquired both riches and power. Andrew Atkinson, of Irish descent, was formerly a merchant of South Carolina and Georgia, who had substantial commercial investments in East Florida. The fifth man, Lieutenant Justo Lopez, was the Spanish military commandant at Fernandina and one of Atkinson's business partners.[1]

Why would five such well-to-do men flirt with treason? In some ways, they believed they had no choice. Though they came from different backgrounds, they shared a common concern. Spain's empire, of which their province formed a minuscule part, was in anarchy. The French emperor, Napoleon Bonaparte, through a series of devious political machinations, had forced Charles IV and his son, Ferdinand VII, to relinquish their claims to the Spanish Crown and had installed his brother, Joseph, as king in their place. Ever since 1808, Spaniards had been fighting to reverse this coup d'état, seeking to oust Joseph and restore King Ferdinand, but the effort did not go well. Ferdinand was a French prisoner. A Regency government, ruling in his name, found it impossible to drive French armies out of central and eastern Spain. Meanwhile, the empire was beginning to fracture. Rumors had reached East Florida that colonists in Caracas, Puerto Rico, Cuba, and Mexico were all thinking of breaking away from Spain and declaring independence. American settlers in nearby Spanish West Florida had taken up arms against Crown officials and were clamoring to join the United States. Under the pressure of these circumstances, the conspirators were willing to contemplate drastic action. They did not want East Florida to become a French colony under Napoleon. They did not want it to become an English colony. And if East Florida had to shake off its allegiance to Spain, then they wanted to be the men in charge.[2]

Sometime in 1810, the group met with a sixth man, the one who controlled their fate. General George Mathews, an American citizen, a veteran of the American Revolution, and a former governor of Georgia, listened eagerly to the conspirators' apprehensions. He was ready to assist their rebellion, to bring them American help, and to annex their colony to the American republic. Having spoken with them at length, he concluded that the overthrow of Spanish rule in East Florida would be an easy matter and was soon passing this joyous news along to congressmen, cabinet officials, and President James Madison.

Yet by the time Mathews filed his report, his dreams of success were already dead. The conspirators lost their nerve and abandoned their plot.

The panic about Spain's survival passed, the mood of the moment vanished, and they quickly changed their minds, deciding that American intervention in East Florida would be both unwelcome and undesirable. But that would not stop General Mathews. Although it would require two more years of organization, he would move ahead with his plans to seize East Florida. In 1812 he would spearhead a rebellion that no one wanted and would drag the United States into an odd and destructive debacle that later became known as the Patriot War.[3]

Most people, when they think of 1812, do not envision it as a year in which Americans fought Spaniards. Rather, it was the year of Napoleon's ill-fated invasion of Russia, of the Peninsular War in Spain and Portugal, and of the War of 1812 between the United States and England. However, along the southern borders of the United States, a place where American citizens and Spanish subjects lived side by side, another arena of conflict was heating up. George Mathews was far from alone in his ambitions to annex the lands of Spain. Southern frontiersmen, residing just a few days' march from Spanish territory, also nursed hopes of conquest. Already, their young republic had absorbed the vast Louisiana Territory, once the keystone of Spain's northern borderlands. Now attention was being focused on the Floridas—Spanish West Florida, a narrow province stretching along the Gulf Coast and encompassing Pensacola, Mobile, and Baton Rouge; and Spanish East Florida, comprising the long peninsula with its ancient capital at St. Augustine (see fig. 1). These two colonies, which controlled the southeast corner of the American continent, including the mouths of several important waterways, had become a troublesome inconvenience to settlers in the southern and western portions of the United States, especially to the people of Kentucky, Georgia, and the Mississippi Territory. In an era fraught with warfare, it was almost inevitable that tensions in the borderlands would escalate into disputes and disputes into conflict.[4]

The ambitions of American leaders only increased the likelihood of conflict. President James Madison favored an acquisition of the Floridas from Spain. Ever since the Louisiana Purchase of 1803, he had endorsed the idea of negotiating with Spain for the colonies, something he had espoused during his years in office as secretary of state to President Thomas Jefferson and hoped to conclude in his capacity as president. Like Jefferson, he eschewed the use of military force to achieve his ends, yet in 1810, by a combination of good fortune and clever espionage, portions of Spanish territory fell suddenly within his grasp. American agents succeeded in promoting an internal rebellion in Baton Rouge, a district of Spanish West Florida immediately adjacent to Louisiana. Using this disturbance as a pretext for intervention, President Madison mobilized U.S. troops, ordered them to restore order and protect American lives in Baton Rouge, and marched them across the border. At the same time, he informed Spanish diplomats that the United States was taking possession of all of West Florida between the Perdido and Mississippi Rivers and that he expected Spain to acknowledge American sovereignty there. He also pressed the Spanish government to accept the inevitable and to cede the districts around Mobile and Pensacola to the United States before they, too, resorted to revolt.[5]

This filibuster at Baton Rouge, accomplished at little risk, emboldened the president to widen American efforts at espionage and to employ George Mathews as his agent against Spanish East Florida. When General Mathews proposed a plan to sabotage Spanish rule there, Madison agreed to support it, inaugurating a scheme to seduce Spanish officials at St. Augustine into surrendering East Florida or, barring their cooperation, to assist in a rebellion that would topple them from power. Far from being an easy triumph, however, this second filibuster miscarried into military invasion, embarrassing President Madison, complicating American strategy during the War of 1812, and plunging the southern frontier into a lengthy and destructive blood feud. From the Georgia-Florida border, Mathews sent back report after report to Washington, outlining his plans to aid an insurrection. When no word came to desist, he fitted out and financed a private volunteer army composed largely of frontiersmen from Georgia, placed a few rebellious Florida settlers at the head of it, and dubbed his contingent "the Patriots." Reinforced by U.S. naval gunboats and with a further promise of support from the U.S. Army, these insurgents crossed into East Florida on March 12, 1812, declared themselves in revolt against Spain, and—in less than a week—forced the capitulation of Fernandina, a bustling Spanish entrepôt on the St. Marys and Amelia Rivers. Having turned this town over to the United States, the Patriots proceeded to seize more Spanish outposts and forts with little opposition in pursuit of their ultimate goal, the expulsion of the colonial government and the Spanish military garrison at St. Augustine. At their heels, under orders to invest and pacify the province, came detachments of U.S. riflemen, infantry, and marines. By April, American forces had reached the defenses of St. Augustine and had sent emissaries into the Indian territory of the Florida interior. Then they encountered their first difficulties. The governor and the townspeople, holed up inside the capital and cut off from almost all hope of rescue, steadfastly refused to surrender.

This surprise attack on East Florida stunned national and international sensibilities, awakening the interests of the press, and within weeks a public debate was raging about the rightness or wrongness of American actions. In nearby Georgia, for instance, the march on St. Augustine was wildly popular. Border families of Camden County nurtured many grievances against settlers in East Florida, anchored in thefts, shootings, duels, pursuit of fugitive slaves, and various other causes of enmity. Elsewhere in Georgia, people spoke of the Dons with contempt, resentful of a nationality that mustered black soldiers into its provincial militias—a direct challenge to southern fears about slave uprisings—and that forged worrisome alliances with the Creeks, Miccosukees, and Seminoles. To beat down black troops, humble the red foe, and open up Spanish-controlled lands for settlement—such goals received complete approbation from citizens in Milledgeville, Savannah, Augusta, Temple, Colerain, and St. Marys. "We rejoice to learn that active operations have commenced against the Floridas," observed the editor of Georgia's *Savannah Republican* when he heard about the capture of Fernandina. "Better late than never."[6]

In other sections of the United States, however, enthusiasm and acquiescence were not so pronounced. The flimsy excuse masking General Mathews's actions—that U.S. forces were aiding a local rebellion against Spanish tyranny—was at once rejected in favor of the patently obvious: that American interests had engineered an uprising in East Florida and were brazenly taking advantage of it. What had at first seemed a trifling affair blossomed into scandal. Spanish diplomats threatened the Madison administration with reprisals and called upon their British allies to do the same. Congress refused to condone further military action. Northern and Federalist newspapers wanted to know why the U.S. Army had invaded a neutral Spanish border colony in the first place. "We await some kind of explanation," said the mystified editor of the *New York Evening Post*. Ultimately, the Patriots' unprovoked attack, emanating from the American side of the St. Marys River, bore the stamp of flagrant invasion, and President Madison hastened to disavow his involvement and revoke assurances of aid.[7]

Here the matter might have ended, but when the United States declared war on England on June 18, 1812, affairs in East Florida once more took on a serious aspect. Madison's military advisers, watching their campaigns against the British in Canada go amiss, counseled him to leave a strong force in Spanish East Florida and suppress any potential danger that might arise from that direction. The Spanish and British governments were allies in Europe, fighting against Napoleon, and although the Spanish Regency claimed it would not take sides in hostilities between England and the United States, neither Secretary of State James Monroe nor former president Thomas Jefferson nor any other man close to Madison thought the pledge could be trusted. It was commonly believed that the Spaniards might provide the British Navy with a base of operations on the Florida coast, something that would place the entire American South in peril. "Should Florida be in the hands of Spain or England on a declaration of war," warned an editorial in the *Augusta Chronicle*, "[we can bid] adieu to our extensive, weak and disaffected territory of Mississippi. It cannot be defended—and will become easy conquest to whoever attacks it."[8]

David Brydie Mitchell, the tough, tactically minded governor of Georgia, also opposed withdrawing American troops from East Florida. Aside from averting the danger of English intervention in the area, he was determined to prevent the Seminoles from threatening the frontier and also told Spanish authorities point blank to disarm any black soldiers or black militiamen they had in their service. "Your certain knowledge of the peculiar situation of the southern section of the Union in respect to that description of people, one might have supposed, would have induced you to abstain from introducing them into the province, or of organizing such as were already in it," he said. "I may venture to assure you that the United States will never tolerate their remaining." With tacit support from Georgia's representatives in Washington and from the president and secretary of state, Mitchell mustered companies of militia and dispatched them over the border to assist in the capture of St. Augustine.[9]

Thus began a contest of wills. Far from giving in to American pressure,

Spanish officials in East Florida redoubled their resistance, furious at these further signs of military occupation. The vast majority of Florida's settlers viewed the presence of foreign troops on their soil as a blatant act of aggression. Americans were not assisting a rebellion against Spanish tyranny, they repeatedly informed the American press. Rather, the United States was trying to impose a coup d'état on an unwilling people. Governor Sebastián Kindelán y O'Regan, responding to anger in Georgia over his use of black militiamen, blasted back: "Retrace your steps, withdraw from our country, and you have nothing to fear from our Negro troops. ... The province of East-Florida may be invaded in time of profound peace, the planters ruined, and the population of the capital starved, and, according to your doctrine, all is fair."[10]

One of Kindelán's aides, the talented polemicist Benigo García, expressed Spanish outrage even more forcefully. His acerbic essay, "History of the Invasion of East-Florida," appeared on the front page of Baltimore's *Federal Republican and Commercial Gazette* when the conflict was still in its early stages. "For upwards of six months," García informed the American public,

the peaceable and unoffending inhabitants of East Florida have been exposed to all the horrors of war, because it pleased the president of the United States to suppose that the Spanish authorities might be bribed or terrified into a dereliction of their duty. . . . United States' troops have continued encamped within a few miles of St. Augustine, and as the garrison was inadequate to the task of expelling them from the province, the whole country has been . . . the prey of the banditti calling themselves patriots. The trade has been totally suspended, the crops have been lost, the negroes scattered, and the stock amounting to some thousand head, destroyed or driven off to Georgia. What excuse Madison and his party can offer for such wide ruin . . . it is difficult to conjecture, nor is it easy to conceive by what arts the indignation of an enlightened people has been lulled a sleep.[11]

And so the Patriots' rebellion grew and expanded into the Patriot War, a bedeviling two-year conflict that slowly merged with the War of 1812. Caught in the middle of the conflict were thousands of people—American, English, Spanish, black, white, and Indian. From 1812, when Fernandina surrendered, until 1814, when the last Patriots left Florida soil, military engagements spiraled out of control, generating a siege, an Indian war, and a long series of punitive raids and skirmishes. Spanish subjects in East Florida, like their distant counterparts in Madrid and Cádiz, soon found themselves fighting a desperate battle for survival. "Such be the sons of Spain, and strange her fate!" Lord Byron once wrote. "They fight for freedom who were never free / A Kingless people for a nerveless state / Her vassals combat when their chieftains flee / Back to the struggle, baffled in the strife / War, war is still the cry, 'War even to the Knife!'" The Patriot War was indeed a form of "war even to the knife," one that gradually degenerated into acts of terror, ambush, and scorched-earth tactics.[12]

The nature of the engagements did not help matters. Nothing could be worse for the morale or morality of soldiers than a long-term stalemate under harsh conditions, and this was exactly what the Patriot War became. American troops invaded East Florida anticipating a quick victory. Instead, with the United States distracted by war with England, they found themselves virtually abandoned in hostile territory, having no popular mandate either to proceed with or to withdraw from their mission. They sat and stewed before the fortifications of St. Augustine while the Spanish garrison and most of the province's settlers sat and stewed inside. In an attempt to starve St. Augustine into submission, American military officers sanctioned the slaughter of herds of cattle and protected the Patriots' rebel government as it launched privateer raids against Spanish shipping and issued cavalier orders for arrests, confiscations, and burnings.

In response, the Spaniards instigated bloody Indian reprisals against small American contingents, and resorted to guerrilla-style ambushes to frighten and demoralize the invaders. By the middle of 1813, warfare had devolved into vendetta. Practically every plantation and farmstead between the Georgia border and Cape Canaveral was looted or consigned to flames, the damages amounting to some $1.2 million in compensation claims. Commenting on the devastation in later years, Judge J. H. Bronson observed, "So far as the destruction of property of every kind was concerned, the desolation of the Carnatic by Hyder Ali was not more terrible and complete." Similar sentiments were expressed during the course of the war. "After the plunder we have occasioned, the murders we have tolerated, and the universal ruin we have brought on the inhabitants," wrote one observer to the *New York Evening Post*, "we must, if ever we obtain possession of the Province, be looked upon by them with detestation and abhorrence, as sneaking midnight ruffians."[13]

Eventually, the Patriot War assumed so ugly and vindictive a cast and was so hampered by contradictory directives from Washington that even American commanders began to question its purpose. "All the sin of direct invasion rests on the shoulders of the Government or its agents," commented Major General John Floyd, of the Georgia militia, "and too against a weak defenseless unoffending neighbor."[14]

"Is it intended that I remain here and permit myself to be insulted with impunity?" Colonel Thomas Adam Smith demanded of the War Department. "If so I must insist on being relieved in the command."[15]

"This is not only war—but offensive war," protested Senator William Hunter of Rhode Island in a speech to Congress. "Not only an offensive but an unjust war. It is a wicked war. It is robbery."[16]

As these brief excerpts indicate, the tale of the war is an exciting chronicle of drama and turmoil between Spaniards and Americans on the southern frontiers in 1812. Some may wonder, though, why such a small-scale conflict—featuring no decisive battles and no great generals—merits the attention of a book. There are, in fact, several good reasons to tell and interpret the story. In the first place, the campaigns in East Florida remain largely overlooked, not only in works about the early American republic but even within the smaller compilation of studies about the War of 1812. The last book-length treatment of the Patriot War, Rembert Patrick's *Florida Fiasco*, appeared almost fifty years ago and has long been out of print. About half the text of the present book is based on research in Spanish sources and in later court depositions about the war that were absent from Patrick's narrative. Hence, it is both a recapitulation and an expansion of his work, correcting a few errors in fact and bringing greater balance to the American and Spanish view of events.[17]

The Patriot War also deserves consideration as an illustration of the nature of southern warfare during early American history. Readers of Christopher Hibbert's *Redcoats and Rebels* and Walter B. Edgar's *Partisans and Redcoats* will have some appreciation for the internecine feuding that accompanied the American Revolution in Georgia and other parts of the South during the 1770s and 1780s. Tempers ran hot in the South for a variety of reasons—grudges between rebels and Tories, dread of Indian attack, and fears that the British would arm the slaves and draft them as troops. All of these old enmities resurfaced during the Patriot War. Once again, patriots in Georgia meted out vengeance against southern Tories (who had returned to the Southeast as subjects of the Spanish Crown). Once again, frontiersmen fought furiously against bands of Indians. And once again, southerners lashed out in ire at a foreign power that tried to employ black soldiers against them. In this respect, the Patriot War is an important historical bridge leading from the American Revolution to the Seminole Wars in the Southeast. The destruction of the Negro Fort at Apalachicola (1816), the First Seminole War (1817–18), the cession of Florida to the United States (1819–21), and even the Second Seminole War (1835–42) were outgrowths of the disruptions and lingering hostilities that the Patriot War generated in the region.

The war also represents a major turning point in the expansionist policies that were promoted by Thomas Jefferson when he came to the presidency in 1800 and that were subsequently pursued by his successors James Madison and James Monroe. Frank L. Owsley Jr. and Gene A. Smith, in *Filibusters and Expansionists*, an analysis of Jefferson's doctrines regarding American expansion, have described his policies as "to conquer without war." He became expert, they note, in the use of nonmilitary tactics—diplomacy, negotiation, bribery, and filibustering—to push the boundaries of the United States to the south and west. Under the direction of James Madison, however, such tactics miscarried into military operations and presaged the era of manifest destiny and the Monroe Doctrine, when coercion, as well as guile, would become a tool for expansion.[18]

Finally, the origins and progress of the Patriot War invite a reevaluation of standard precepts about the American republic and the War of 1812. With a few notable exceptions, such as John K. Mahon and Robert Remini, historians have frequently balked at calling the War of 1812 a war of aggression and have downplayed American desires for territorial conquest as a factor in the war, focusing instead on such issues as protection of maritime trade and injuries to national pride. Harry L. Coles, in his 1965 work on the subject, set forth the interpretation that has governed most historical analyses. A new generation of Americans—so his argument ran—thought the British were trying to return the United States and its people to colonial status. The actions of the Royal Navy seemed to exemplify such a design, for British warships routinely intercepted and seized American vessels trading with France, impressed seamen, and (in two instances) engaged in skirmishes with American ships. Attempts to satisfy national honor by negotiation, or by nonmilitary options, only made matters worse. A series of trade embargoes—the Embargo Act, the Non-Intercourse Act, Macon's Bill #2—ended up doing greater harm to the American economy than to British overseas trade. Thus, Americans slowly came to the conclusion that self-preservation demanded a call to arms and a new confrontation with the old English foe. Other issues, such as a desire to annex parts of Canada and to crush British influence among the western Indian tribes, were acknowledged as ancillary reasons for a declaration of war.[19]

While this thesis holds true when one looks at the war from the perspective of debates in Congress or events in the northern states, it is not especially convincing when one considers the South. Southerners had more regional and sectarian reasons for supporting a war effort in 1812. Significantly, while public opinion in Georgia and the Mississippi Territory clamored loudly for war with England, the first combats in the South were directed not against the English but against more familiar foes—the southern Indian tribes and the Spanish.[20]

The Patriot War was therefore one facet of what might be called the South's War of 1812, or the "other war of 1812." A central tenet of this book is that expansionist ambitions, fear of Indians and blacks, and resentment of Spanish political and commercial policies in East Florida played a much greater role in inciting trouble at the Georgia border in 1812 than did grievances against Great Britain. Works that have informed and influenced this one include Julius Pratt's *The Expansionists of 1812*, Billy Lee Akins's "Georgians and the War of 1812," John K. Mahon's *The War of 1812*, and two important studies of the origins and ramifications of the Creek War (1813–14), Frank L. Owsley Jr.'s *Struggle for the Gulf Borderlands* and J. Leitch Wright Jr.'s *Creeks and Seminoles*. Southern antipathy toward the existence of black troops in East Florida has been ably summarized in Jane Landers's *Black Society in Spanish Florida*. Readers should also consult Robert Remini's *Battle of New Orleans* for examples of the vengeful nature of southern war; his *Andrew Jackson and His Indian Wars* for a treatment of southern expansion as it affected U.S. Indian policy and American relations with the Spanish borderlands; and *Filibusters and Expansionists*, by Owsley and Smith, for the influence of Jeffersonian philosophy on southern expansion. These books have become essential supplements to Donald R. Hickey's *The War of 1812: A Forgotten Conflict* and J.C.A. Stagg's *Mr. Madison's War*, the standard political histories of the war. *The Encyclopedia of the War of 1812*, edited by David S. Heidler and Jeanne T. Heidler, is also a useful reference work with regard to the southern campaigns.

It is scarcely possible to interpret the Patriot War without first telling its story, and much of this book is dedicated to narrative history, although I attempt at all times to place the Patriot War in historical context and to link it to broader events. Background information on relations between the United States and Spain in the years prior to 1812 is included in the first chapter, while analysis of the Patriot War's impact and significance is confined largely to the concluding chapter. Whenever possible, the narrative relies directly on the words and recollections of eyewitnesses. The reader will soon become acquainted with the principal historical figures in the struggle: the Americans—General Mathews, Major Laval, Commodore Campbell, Lieutenant Colonel Smith, Colonel Newnan, and Governor Mitchell; the prominent Patriots—John Houston McIntosh, Lodowick Ashley, Daniel Delany, Buckner Harris, James Dell, and William Cone; and the Spanish officials and subjects—Justo Lopez, Governors Estrada and Kindelán, the Clarkes, the Solanas, the Arredondos, the Maestres, the Pellicers, the Atkinsons, and many more. This is their story, often told in their own words, the story of a people who little suspected what lay in wait for them as the year 1811 commenced its cycle and the fateful year of 1812 approached.

1

Mr. Madison's Worries

Though he is generally associated with the drafting of the Constitution and with the struggles of the United States during the War of 1812, James Madison also expended much of his thought and energies in the cause of American expansion. Never as fervent or effusive on this topic as Thomas Jefferson and James Monroe, he nevertheless presided over the Louisiana Purchase of 1803 as Jefferson's secretary of state, and in the following years he consistently advocated the acquisition of the Spanish Floridas as a major goal of American foreign policy. There were, however, limits to the price he was willing to pay. When Jefferson proposed forging an alliance with England in 1805 to pave the way for American encroachments into Texas and the Floridas, Madison counseled against it. England, he said, would expect too much from the United States in return for assistance against Spain. She would require Americans "to join her in the war [on France] or to do what she will accept as equivalent to such an obligation." Then, too, he had a lingering suspicion of the British, whom he regarded as the inveterate political adversaries and chief commercial competitors of the young American republic. He advised Jefferson to pursue a different course of action, a negotiated purchase of the Floridas. The United States should buy them from Spain for $5 million and link the final payments to a settlement of other outstanding disputes between the two countries.[1]

In 1809, when Madison became president, this ambition was as yet unfulfilled. The Floridas were still in Spanish hands, and they became part of the unfinished business that he brought with him into his first term in office. If his abiding interest in the Floridas is sometimes overlooked, this is not surprising, for he brought other unfinished business to the Executive Mansion as well. Madison frequently had to disengage himself from problems with Spain—generally stemming from disagreements over the boundaries of the United States and the nearby Spanish border colonies—to face the major foreign policy issue of the early 1800s, the growing crisis in American relations with England and France. These two powers, locked in a life-and-death struggle for the survival of their respective empires, were fighting a "total war." France was conscripting men into its armies and toppling the monarchies of Europe. England was raiding American shipping to impress seamen into its navy, protector of British supremacy on the high seas. Besides this, both nations had begun to prey upon the maritime trade of noncombatants. Soon they were taking American prizes throughout the Atlantic—in the French and British Caribbean, along the coasts of Europe, even at the limits of the United States's own territorial waters. The motives behind these campaigns were complex, but their effect was singularly clear. Americans took little interest in who presided over Europe—George III and his ministers or Napoleon Bonaparte and his generals. Yet they cared deeply about their own overseas trade and were prepared to resort to war rather than endure the national insults and the losses of cargo and vessels that a distant European conflict was inflicting upon them.[2]

Here, then, were the twin dilemmas confronting President Madison. Convinced that the United States could preserve its national honor and secure its maritime rights by skillful use of embargoes and other commercial sanctions against France and England, he was hesitant to embrace war. Yet, if it came, it would almost certainly fall against England, a nation with 600 warships at sea and 250,000 men under arms. Against this, the United States had a navy of 16 ships and a standing army of 6,000 men. As reluctant as he was to take military action, the president had to face a disquieting reality. In 1808, while Madison was serving out his final year in the Jefferson administration, Napoleon Bonaparte had overthrown the Spanish monarchy and placed Spain under military occupation. In response, the Spanish Regency government allied itself with England. This extraordinary alliance between two traditional enemies held grave implications for the security of the southern frontiers of the United States. The Spanish border colonies, including the Floridas, represented the "back door" into the heartland of the American South and the Mississippi River Valley. In a war with England, Americans had only the slim guarantee of Spanish neutrality to protect them from a British land and sea invasion of the South.[3]

It was, in the opinion of most Americans, a poor guarantee—and they had other reasons for wishing to gain the Floridas. Possession of West Florida would give the United States control over the important port of Mobile, while East Florida dominated much of the Gulf of Mexico and (for the more ambitious) pointed the way to Cuba. Throughout 1810, the Madison administration received reports from its special agents on the frontiers, conveying intelligence about the sentiments of the populations in the Mississippi Territory, Louisiana, and even within the Spanish provinces. It had long seemed likely that American settlers in Spanish West Florida would begin to agitate against Spanish rule, especially if they received secret encouragement. In the fall of 1810, unrest in the Baton Rouge District of this colony produced exactly the outcome President Madison hoped to see.[4]

American residents, frustrated that they had not joined the United States as part of the Louisiana Territory, called a convention to air their grievances against Spain and to adopt procedures for choosing their own elected representatives. Then, in the early morning hours of September 23, under cover of darkness, some of the residents distributed weapons, organized themselves into a mixed party of infantry and cavalry, and stormed Baton Rouge's decrepit Spanish fort. Eighty men shouting "Hurrah, Washington!" overwhelmed a sleepy Spanish garrison, killed the commander and one soldier, and wounded two others. As news of the uprising spread, delegates for the rebels sent urgent appeals to President Madison, asking him to guarantee Baton Rouge's independence or to place it under the protection of the American confederation.[5]

The chance to assert American rights to Baton Rouge was too good to miss. No American feared Spain, and many, including President Madison, thought Baton Rouge should have come to the United States as part of the Louisiana Purchase. How could it be wrong, then, to take what the country had already bought and that Spain had never relinquished? Without making a public announcement, the president issued an executive order to Governor William C. C. Claiborne at New Orleans, instructing him to move troops into Baton Rouge and assume responsibility for law and order there. Unsure of his constitutional authority to employ armed force and wishing to consult with the members of Congress when they opened their session in November, Madison took no further action. Yet the reticent and pallid scholar from Montpelier was opening the door to military intervention in the Spanish borderlands—something his predecessors in office had never been willing to risk. Once opened, the door could not be easily closed. And so, in a short while, President Madison—the unlikeliest of military adventurers—would step through the door in pursuit of the colony of Spanish East Florida and into the quagmire of the Patriot War.[6]

James Madison's thoughts and opinions about American rights to Spanish territory owed much to his long association with Thomas Jefferson and, to a lesser extent, with James Monroe. The years that brought all three of these men to the presidency have been described as the era of early American expansionism. Terms like "manifest destiny" and "the Monroe Doctrine" are often assigned to this period of history, though they were in fact later creations. Terminology aside, however, the so-called Jeffersonians did espouse a coherent set of principles and ideals about American sovereignty that guided their policies in diplomacy and foreign affairs. They hoped to maintain American neutrality with the European powers, so that the Republic could grow into a great and thriving nation of commerce without becoming ensnared in risky and arbitrary wars. They believed that the American people, by their natural increase, were the chosen heirs to the continent of North America and would eventually possess it. Moreover, they felt the American Revolution had nullified European pretensions to ownership of the Western Hemisphere. Above all else, American leaders had an obligation to stop foreign powers from building colonial empires on the borders of the United States and from interfering with the domestic tranquility of its citizens.[7]

This political philosophy was not a formal written doctrine but took shape gradually between 1783 and 1812, influenced in part by the United States's rather turbulent relations with proud and ancient Spain. Although the two countries came out of the American Revolution as friendly powers, their amity did not persist for long. The Spanish Crown had assisted Americans to their independence primarily as a means of achieving its own goals. When the Revolutionary War ended in 1783, Spain had humbled England, retained its Louisiana colony (which it had gained from France in 1763), and won back other possessions, including the Floridas and the Mediterranean island of Minorca, previously lost to the British. At the same time, it faced new hazards. The creation of the United States meant that, in the future, Spain had to defend its colonies not just against France and England but also against a vigorous American republic that seemed destined to grow. The Conde de Aranda, arguably Spain's wisest and ablest minister of the late eighteenth century, made an early and fairly accurate prediction about the pressure the United States would apply to the border territories. "The day will come," he warned, "when it will grow into a giant, even a fearsome colossus in the hemisphere. Then it will forget the assistance it received from [us] and will think only of its own exaltation. The first step of this Power . . . will be to seize upon the Floridas, in order to dominate the Gulf of Mexico."[8]

Spain's difficulties in Europe only worsened Aranda's prognosis. Throughout much of the eighteenth century, Spain had offset threats from England by allying itself with France. The French Revolution in 1789 terminated this balance of power. Although the Spanish government at first seemed willing to reach an accord with the revolutionaries in France, the execution of King Louis XVI in 1793 forced it into a policy of war. Despite aid from England, battles against the French went badly, and Spain's armies suffered defeat after defeat. By the late 1790s, the Crown had to withdraw from the conflict, and shortly afterward changed sides, abandoning the English to resume a connection with France under Napoleon.[9]

This decline in Spain's military and political fortunes—to the status of a weak satellite of either France or England—played havoc with its autonomy and also had a generally deleterious effect on its relations with the United States. Americans—young, brash, and confident—had little esteem for the Spanish and were eager to break through the arc of Spanish colonies (Louisiana, Texas, West Florida, and East Florida) that hemmed them in on two extensive frontiers. Through its possession of the Louisiana Territory, Spain blocked westward expansion of the American republic and wielded an unwelcome amount of control over commerce on the Mississippi River. The fact that other important southern rivers emptied into the Gulf of Mexico through Spanish East Florida and Spanish West Florida also engendered resentments. Settlers moving into Tennessee, Kentucky, and Illinois did not want a foreign empire regulating their access to the sea. Their misgivings diminished somewhat in 1795 when the Spanish Crown acceded to the Treaty of San Lorenzo. Under its terms, the monarchy made various concessions to the American government in an effort to foster friendly relations. It accepted stipulations that the northern boundary for Spanish West Florida should be the thirty-first parallel, opened the Mississippi River to American shipping, and reduced tariffs at New Orleans so that American merchantmen could enter and clear the port at low cost. However, Spanish actions during the Quasi-War (1797–

1800), a naval combat between the United States and France, shattered whatever goodwill had been previously gained. Although Spain proclaimed itself neutral in the conflict, the Crown allowed French privateers to bring 168 captured American vessels into Spanish ports, while Spanish privateers seized more than 100 American ships. Merchants in New England and the southern states screamed with outrage and insisted that Spain compensate them for their losses at sea, which they eventually assessed at $5 million in damages. When no restitution was forthcoming, American diplomats began to suggest that perhaps Spain should give the United States its colony of East Florida as a form of collateral against a final settlement.[10]

Before any progress was made in this direction, however, the Louisiana Purchase created additional strains in relations between Spain and the United States. In 1800, the Spanish Crown, in an effort to appease Napoleon, secretly ceded its province of Louisiana back to France. Learning of the cession and sensing an opportunity to acquire essential territory for the United States, President Jefferson began negotiations with Napoleon's government to buy Louisiana. In 1803, in the face of Spanish protests, the deal went through at a cost of $15 million, doubling the size of the United States and driving a wedge of American settlement between the Spanish Floridas and Spanish Texas. King Charles IV's ministers objected bitterly to the purchase and were soon growing incensed over other American presumptions. Jefferson, far from trying to mollify Spanish feelings, insisted that the purchase included not only Louisiana but the adjacent district of Baton Rouge, which the Spanish Crown considered to be part of West Florida. American envoys pressured the Spanish to cede West Florida and to surrender East Florida as well, arguing that this would compensate the United States for the seizure of American vessels during the Quasi-War.

Disputes about where Louisiana began and ended, and who owned what, continued into 1804, 1805, and 1806, leading to acrimonious threats and counterthreats. Ultimately, however, the Jefferson administration was forced to drop the issue. Other concerns suddenly reared up to distract American attention. On June 22, 1807, a British warship, the fifty-gun Fourth Rate H.M.S. *Leopard*, nearly started a war between the United States and England by firing upon the American frigate U.S.S. *Chesapeake* off the coast of Norfolk, Virginia. The captain of the *Leopard* tried to carry out his orders to forcibly detain and search American ships for

British deserters. When the commander of the *Chesapeake* refused a boarding party, the *Leopard* responded by firing several broadsides into the vessel, killing three men and wounding eighteen others. There were cries for war on both sides of the Atlantic (indeed, it was a near thing that England and the United States did not fight the War of 1807 instead of the War of 1812). Trying to avert a collapse in relations with England, President Jefferson concluded that the United States could no longer afford to antagonize Spain and ceased demands for territorial concessions.[11]

Although disputes with Spain about the Floridas were postponed in 1807, they were not resolved, and they began to resurface as James Madison took the presidential oath of office in 1809. Events in Europe once again played a role, for Spain was facing the worst crisis it had seen since the days of the Moorish invasions in the Middle Ages. In 1808, Napoleon, though still an ally of the Spanish Crown, struck against the royal family and betrayed them. Preferring Spanish subservience to Spanish alliance, he forced King Charles IV and his son, Ferdinand, to abdicate their rights to the throne. French troops crossed the border and occupied Madrid and other key locations in the Iberian Peninsula, and Joseph Bonaparte, Napoleon's brother, was proclaimed as the new king. This coup d'état plunged Spain into anarchy. Spaniards refused to accept King Joseph and cried out instead for the restoration of Ferdinand, who was under house arrest in France. Members of the Spanish Cortes fled from Madrid to the heavily fortified port city of Cádiz, where they set up a Regency government in Ferdinand's name. The crisis in Spain prompted action by the British government as well. Seeing a chance to challenge Napoleon's stranglehold on Europe, the English sent Sir Arthur Wellesley, the future Duke of Wellington, to mobilize Portuguese, Spanish, and English forces against French troops in Spain and to liberate the nation from military occupation.[12]

Americans watched these events from a distance and largely with an eye to the opportunities they presented. No one was sure how long the people of Spain could maintain their fragile independence. They seemed destined to fall helplessly under either French or British domination, and then the Spanish empire would become the spoils of whatever nation could take it. Henry Clay, speaking in the U.S. Congress, voiced the ambitions of many American expansionists at the time. "I am not, Sir, in favor of cherishing the passion of conquest," he said, "but I must be permitted to conclude by declaring my hope to see, ere long, the new United States (if you will allow me the expression) embracing not only the old thirteen States, but the entire east of the Mississippi, including East Florida, and some of the territories to the north of us also."[13]

British support for the Spanish Regency also had Americans worried. Some twenty-five years after the Revolution, people in the United States still looked upon England as a vengeful power, embittered by American independence and committed to harassing its former colonies. Many thought Spain would try to curry favor with England by allowing the British to station troops and ships in Spanish America, giving them a series of footholds in Cuba, in Mexico, and even in the colonies on the southern frontiers of the United States. Under these circumstances, southern leaders in Congress favored a preemptive strike against East and West Florida. President Madison was also coming to the conclusion that annexation of the Floridas might be in the country's best interests. He shared Jefferson's belief that Americans, from their previous grievances against Spain, had as good a right to East and West Florida as did the Spanish Crown and certainly a better one than either France or England. Indeed, he had long believed that a cession of the Floridas was in both Spain's and the United States's best interests: "What is it Spain dreads?" he once inquired of James Monroe. "She dreads . . . the growing power of this country, and the direction of it against her possessions within its reach. Can she annihilate this power? No. Can she sensibly retard its growth? No." The conclusion was obvious. The territories of West and East Florida, Madison felt certain, were destined to become part of the American confederation "either by purchase or by conquest."[14]

Hence, late in 1810, as Americans awakened to the fact that the president had moved troops into Baton Rouge, the problems and dangers of war entered once again into the deliberations of the national government. The Eleventh Congress of the United States, meeting for its third session between November 1810 and February 1811, commenced floor debates on the two crucial issues of the day: whether to declare war on England and France and whether to challenge Spanish sovereignty in East and West Florida. Of these, relations with France and England attracted most attention. For four years, these nations had made the United States an unwilling partner in their hostilities through their attacks on American shipping in European waters and on the high seas. Americans were, of course, well acquainted with the wartime tactic of blockade—the practice of stationing warships off a harbor mouth to intercept vessels of trade. They had seen the British employ blockades against Boston, New York, and Charleston during the Revolution. To their dismay, however, the Napoleonic Wars introduced a new and unwelcome application of this principle—one that was taking a heavy toll on the economic life of the United States. In 1806 and 1807, the French (under the provisions of the Berlin Decree) and the British (through the Orders in Council) had extended the concept of blockade over the entire ocean and began stopping and searching commercial vessels and merchantmen on the high seas, even when those ships were registered to a neutral country. If a ship was carrying the enemy's goods or seemed destined for one of the enemy's ports, it was seized. "The whole world is thus laid under an interdict by these two nations," Thomas Jefferson had complained, "and our vessels, their cargoes and crews, are to be taken by the one or the other, for whatever place they may be destined, out of our own limits."

By 1811, some 900 American merchant vessels had been confiscated as French or British prizes of war. Other abuses of naval power were also causing American tempers to burn short. The British seemed unwilling to accept the fact that their former colonies were truly independent, an attitude exemplified, in American eyes, by the behavior of the Royal Navy. Besides harassing American commerce, English warships routinely cruised in the Republic's territorial waters and boarded American vessels to search for sailors who had deserted from British service—a policy that had led to the confrontation between the H.M.S. *Leopard* and the U.S.S. *Chesapeake*. Increasingly, Americans believed England was using its war with France as an excuse to lash out against the United States and its commerce. The infuriating humiliations that American vessels and crews had to endure—stopped at sea, searched, pressured to give up crew members—seemed to be part of an English policy to assert mastery over the oceans and to keep American merchants away from important British markets in the West Indies and Spanish America. This, at least, was the president's opinion—that England was engaging in an unofficial war on American commerce—and many others agreed with him.[15]

Faced with these violations of maritime rights, previous Congresses had tried to retaliate with economic reprisals, adopting and subsequently casting aside a whole series of sanctions designed to intimidate France and England while avoiding war. The sanctions were wholly economic in nature. To begin with, in 1807 the Ninth Congress had banned imports from England. Then the Tenth Congress resolved upon a more drastic step—the

Embargo Act. Implemented between 1807 and 1809, the embargo was a nonexportation measure that prohibited American ships from leaving the coastal waters of the United States. Based on the faulty belief that England needed essential raw materials from the United States (the British quickly found alternative sources of supply in Canada and the Baltic), the embargo raised little concern in Europe while having the catastrophic side effect of shutting down American foreign trade. It bit deeply into American revenue, eliminating overseas markets for manufactures and agricultural products, bottling up American shipping in a self-made prison, and plunging the nation into economic depression. New Englanders, in particular, had cursed the embargo—the "O-grab-me"—as they called it by reversing its letters. In the House of Representatives, John Randolph described it as an attempt "to cure corns by cutting off the toes." Senator James Bayard of Delaware, pointing to the alarming decline in American trade, observed, "It is ourselves who are the victims of this miserable experiment."[16]

Two unhappy years of this policy accomplished nothing, and, with public protest mounting, Congress finally had no choice but to rescind the embargo, revoking it just as Jefferson was leaving office and as Madison took over. Yet attacks on American trade had not ceased, and so James Madison's administration tried two other forms of economic sanction. In 1809, the Tenth Congress passed the Non-Intercourse Act, banning imports and exports with the belligerent powers. In 1810, it tried yet another tactic, Macon's Bill #2. By this measure, Congress reopened trade with England and France but added a proviso: if either country stopped its attacks on American shipping, the United States would demonstrate its appreciation by reimposing trade restrictions against the rival nation.[17]

None of these measures produced results, and seizures of American ships by French and British vessels continued unabated. Yet in the eyes of Americans, the British seemed much the greater villains. Wrath against England was fast approaching the flashpoint of explosion it had reached during the Revolution. In the meantime, the government was running out of options. The Eleventh Congress, still reluctant to put the nation at risk in a conflict, resorted to yet another ban on English imports, not in any real belief that it would work but to buy time. Both inside and outside the capital, a growing number of Americans were calling for stronger action. More and more, they were agitating for war.

With such momentous issues before the nation, relations between the

American republic and the Spanish empire garnered less attention. Even so, Americans could never completely ignore the Spanish colonies that shared their hemisphere. Cuba and Mexico were major markets for American goods. The Floridas and Texas touched U.S. borders, and their proximity, along with their sparse population, encouraged many proposals for attaching them to the American Union. Assumptions that this was inevitable found frequent expression in the American press, as, for example, in the comments of the *Freeman's Journal* of Philadelphia—"At all events, Florida must one day be a part of the United States. Nature has ordained the event"—or those of the *New York Evening Post*—"The idea of an independent state of West Florida is preposterous, and should Great Britain and France get a foothold in it, they would be very troublesome neighbors."[18]

Hence, even as the Eleventh Congress argued for and against the wisdom of mounting a war effort, the question of relations with Spain and the mobilization of U.S. troops at Baton Rouge also came before the members. In his annual address, President Madison made his first public statements about the American military occupation of Baton Rouge. Reiterating arguments that Jefferson had used in 1805 and 1806, he exonerated his actions, asserting that Baton Rouge was encompassed within the provisions of the Louisiana Purchase and that Spain should have conceded it (and other portions of West Florida such as Mobile) long ago. Then, too, the United States had a right to protect Americans living outside the nation's borders if they were threatened by the disorders of an uprising. The time had come, Madison said, to extend American sovereignty over all the lands along the northern Gulf Coast: "The Spanish authority was subverted and a situation produced exposing the country to *ulterior events* which might essentially affect the rights and welfare of the Union."[19]

The president's reference to "ulterior events" became clear a few weeks later. On January 3, 1811, Madison sent further communications to the U.S. Senate while the body met in a secret closed-door session. Included in his message was a letter from Don Vicente Folch, the governor of Spanish West Florida at Pensacola, which contained an offer to surrender the entire colony to the United States. If the government acted quickly, Madison noted, it could secure its possession of Baton Rouge and also gain Mobile and Pensacola. The chief obstacles were the English, who might defend Spanish rights and oppose American efforts to obtain the colony or even land forces there themselves. The United States could never countenance a British presence along the Gulf Coast. Therefore, Madison urged, Congress should officially annex Baton Rouge, press American claims to the rest of Spanish West Florida, and make provisions to reinforce American military detachments in the Louisiana and the Mississippi Territories, so that U.S. forces could occupy Mobile and Pensacola if circumstances warranted it.[20]

In these statements, the president focused attention exclusively on the colony of West Florida. He made only an allusion to Spanish East Florida. "The wisdom of Congress," he said, would dictate how the government should proceed there. His silence did not signify disinterest, however. Already, he was seeking a pretext that might justify action in that direction as well.[21]

In the wake of the president's address, Congress commenced a heated debate on the issue of the Floridas, which quickly exposed the strengths and weaknesses of Madison's support in the legislature. Although his party—the Democratic Republicans—had a virtual lock on the House and Senate, the president did not enjoy overwhelming party loyalty. The machinations of various political cliques—the "malcontents" or "Invisibles" (so-called from their habit of working behind the scenes), the Clintonians, and the "War Hawks"—complicated policy-making and denied the president the unanimity he needed for his initiatives. Besides, the president had numerous enemies in Congress, men who disliked him for personal reasons, or because he had abandoned federalism to become a Republican, or because they suspected him of being a secret Federalist. As a result, his requests and recommendations became mired in the partisan wrangling and anti-Madison cabals that were ever-present within the Capitol.[22]

Things were little better in his cabinet. Robert Smith caused many headaches as secretary of state. He was the brother of one of Madison's rivals in Congress and was foisted on the president as part of a backroom deal to approve Albert Gallatin as head of the Treasury. Hoping to run for president himself, Smith took little interest in Madison's diplomatic initiatives and was so lax in his duties that the president had to handle most of the State Department's responsibilities. Other cabinet members, notably Secretary of War William Eustis and Secretary of the Navy Paul Hamilton, have come down through history's prism as men of moderate talent who added neither foresight nor lustre to Madison's body of advisers.[23]

The question of the Spanish border territories proved a perfect example of how a divided government could enmesh the president in problems. There was no consensus on how to deal with American claims to the Floridas. The cabinet was split on the issue. In Congress, the question pitted expansion-minded individuals from the West and South against their nemeses, the more conservative members from the North. The War Hawks—who would later spearhead calls for war with England—vociferously endorsed the use of American troops to occupy Baton Rouge and favored further actions to obtain Spanish territory. Their number included Henry Clay of Kentucky (a senator, but soon to be Speaker of the House), his compatriot Richard M. Johnson, Felix Grundy of Tennessee, Langdon Cheeves, William Lowndes, and John C. Calhoun (all from South Carolina), and George M. Troup of Georgia. These men, a fervent new breed of patriots, wanted the president to adopt a more defiant attitude in dealing with the European powers.[24]

Opposing the policies of the War Hawks were the Federalists. This party could no longer claim the national prominence it possessed when it put George Washington and John Adams into the executive office. Instead, it was fast becoming a regional party, with much of its constituency in New England and the Mid-Atlantic states. The mercantile classes of these northern states, with their busy factories and seaports, had suffered heavily under the Embargo Act and wanted a restoration of friendly relations with England and France.[25]

By January 1811, members with opposite political leanings were hammering away at each other in floor debates about the Floridas. The stormiest sessions occurred in the Senate, where Henry Clay became the spokesperson for keeping and annexing Baton Rouge, as well as any other Spanish territory whose people wanted to join the United States. Although he was absent from the first day of debate, his written arguments, comprising one of his early classic speeches, were forcefully delivered by fellow Kentuckian John Pope. France was going to vanquish Spain and destroy its Regency government, Clay asserted. After that, it would be England or France that ruled the Spanish colonies, and Congress should take steps to prepare for this eventuality. The Spanish border territories had already caused enough problems. Slaves ran away to hide in Florida.

The Spaniards were charging exorbitant duties on commercial traffic passing through the port of Mobile. Given the importance of the Gulf of Mexico to American trade and to national security, the government should, with the consent of the local inhabitants, acquire "not only West but East Florida, Cuba, or any other province which we shall deem it expedient to connect with the United States."[26]

Clay's eagerness to incorporate Spanish territory brought angry rebuttals from leading Federalists. Such acts, they said, would only provoke war with Spain and retaliation against American business in Cuba and Spanish America. Distribution of political power also affected their thinking. Many Federalists had opposed the Louisiana Purchase, fearing the southern and western portions of the country, as their populations grew, would come to dominate the national government. Hence, they had little sympathy for adding the Floridas to the Republic and hoped instead that expansion, if it took place, would be toward Canada. Timothy Pickering of Massachusetts embarrassed his colleagues by producing French documents denying that West Florida had ever been a part of the Louisiana Purchase. His revelation cut the ground from President Madison's statement that the United States could claim Baton Rouge through previous negotiations. Outerbridge Horsey of Delaware challenged the Democratic Republicans on the same issue, adding that annexation of Baton Rouge risked war with Spain and Britain and would inevitably drag the United States into further military actions in the Floridas.[27]

The following day, Clay struck back hard at these objections, praising the president for sending troops to occupy West Florida. If Madison had failed to secure Baton Rouge, "he would have been criminally inattentive to the nearest interests of his country." Make no mistake, Clay bristled, France and Britain both had designs on the Gulf Coast. "Are you prepared," he demanded of Horsey, "to see a foreign power seize what belongs to us?"[28]

Even former president Jefferson felt compelled to voice an opinion, privately warning Democratic Republicans to support Madison. They should confirm American claims to Baton Rouge and the rest of West Florida, and they should authorize the president to move against East Florida. Otherwise, England, seeing West Florida succumb to the United States, would jerk the strings of its Spanish puppets and send its own soldiers into the Florida peninsula. It was both of the Floridas or neither of them, said Jefferson: "There never was a case, where the adage was more true, 'in for a penny, in for a pound.'"[29]

While this debate raged in Congress, President Madison had to gauge the depth of his own commitment for employing force and coercion in the Floridas. Secretary of State Robert Smith, soon to be dismissed in favor of James Monroe, had already received protests from two Spanish officials—Juan Bautista Bernaben, Spanish consul at Baltimore, and Don Luis de Onís, the unrecognized minister plenipotentiary from the Spanish Regency—as well as from J. P. Morier, the British chargé d'affaires. The allied governments regarded the seizure of Baton Rouge "as an act of open hostility against Spain." American assistance to the rebel settlers in the colony was merely a "pretext for wresting a province from a friendly power, and that in the time of her adversity." The British chargé d'affaires was so disgusted with American opportunism and cupidity that he advised his home government to teach the United States a lesson. Foreshadowing English strategy in the War of 1812, he called on Lord Wellesley to hamstring American military adventures by blockading the Mississippi River and inciting a slave uprising in the American South. "In the event of war," he said, "England should take New Orleans. . . . Another very vulnerable Point is in Georgia and South Carolina and the Mississippi Territory, by means of the Black population, to whom the Spaniards might send their Black Regiments from the Havannah, to assist them in asserting their Independence."[30]

Preoccupied with other matters, Madison paid little heed to the protests of these diplomats and was, in any case, listening intently to voices that heightened, rather than dampened, his conviction that the Floridas could be easily acquired. Throughout November, December, and January, the president had received regular reports from Judge Harry Toulmin of the Tombigbee District in the Mississippi Territory. Toulmin kept his ear focused attentively on public opinion in Mobile and other parts of Spanish West Florida. There was no doubt, he said, that the inhabitants, by a large majority, favored a union with the American republic. More important, Governor Vicente Folch in Pensacola seemed ready to come to terms and had forwarded a statement to Spain, advising the Regency to commence negotiations for a cession of West Florida to the United States.[31]

With this news, Madison and Secretary of State Smith began to amass and evaluate the intelligence they had collected on Don Vicente Folch. The loss of Baton Rouge had apparently shaken the Spanish governor's confidence that he could defend his province. Three times he had suggested a cession of West Florida: once to his own superiors, once to Governor David Holmes of the Mississippi Territory, and then directly to the Madison administration. His intentions seemed clear enough, based on his statement to Holmes: "I have made a representation to His Excellency the Captain Marquis de Someruelos who resides in the Havanna, the purport of which is that he will please address himself to the U.S. in order to treat with the Executive authority of the same relative to the delivery of Florida in trust until the conclusion of a treaty." On December 2, Folch had conveyed the same idea to Colonel John McKee, the American agent to the Choctaws, and had reiterated it yet again in a letter that McKee delivered to Secretary of State Smith. "I have thought of addressing myself directly to the Executive power of the United States," Folch said, "proposing to treat for the delivery of the province . . . because, as our difficulties every day increase, the necessity of hastening their conclusion increases also." This was the letter that Madison had revealed to Congress on January 3.[32]

Seeking further information, the president met with Colonel McKee, who was only too happy to elaborate on his conversations with the Spanish governor. Folch, he said, had given up on retaking Baton Rouge and was facing possible revolts at Mobile, led by Reuben Kemper, an old adversary of the Spaniards, and on the Pascagoula River, led by Sterling Duprée. Without aid from Cuba or Mexico, he was doomed. From what McKee could gather, Folch would surrender the entire province of West Florida on condition that the United States cede back an equivalent amount of land to Spain in some other part of North America, perhaps on the borders of Texas. Quick action was required because Folch might revoke the offer if his superiors sent him military aid.[33]

While ruminating on this news, Madison learned through Senator William Crawford of Georgia that another American agent had just come north. General George Mathews had spent much of 1810 on the borders of both East and West Florida. He had important information to relay. Mathews, Crawford said, was willing to negotiate with Folch to arrange a cession of West Florida. In addition, Mathews claimed he could deliver Spanish East Florida into Madison's hands. Was the president interested in seeing him?

A Plot Thickens

It was a cold day in mid-January when George Mathews, the man who would figure so largely in the Patriot War, arrived at the Executive Mansion for his appointment with the president. Amid the mansion's rich decor—the bright yellow draperies and upholstery of Dolley Madison's parlor, the red velvet and Grecian ornamentation of the Oval Drawing Room, and the imposing portrait of George Washington that hung on the wall of the State Dining Room—the elderly Mathews was an incongruent, even outlandish figure. Like the president, he had been born in Virginia, but there the similarities in their upbringing ended. The son of an Irish immigrant, Mathews had grown up as something of a fighter and brawler and had first drawn attention to himself for killing nine Shawnee warriors in the Battle of Point Pleasant in 1774. Wounded at the Battle of Germantown during the American Revolution, he spent two years as a captive aboard a British prison hulk before rejoining the cause in the southern campaigns of General Nathaniel Greene and witnessing the surrender of General Cornwallis at Yorktown. Even in 1811, at the respectably advanced age of seventy-one, he emanated energy, retaining the reddish hair and sharp blue eyes of his frontier youth, the Irish lilt of his ancestry, and the old-fashioned dress of his war years—long coat, ruffled shirt, knee breeches, stockings, buckled shoes, and tricornered hat—a quaint and antiquated garb that cloaked him in the glorious mystique of 1776.[1]

Mathews had spent almost all of his adult life in Georgia, first as a planter in Oglethorpe County, then as governor (1787), as Georgia's representative in the First U.S. Congress (1789–91), and once again as governor (1793). The infamous Yazoo Act of 1795 and its attendant land fraud scandals had severely blemished his reputation, and in 1796 a once-admiring electorate threw him out of office along with many other politicians tainted by Yazoo. Even with such an abrupt end to his political career he continued to be a person of influence, and Senator William Crawford, a long-time friend, thought his talents and experience might prove useful in matters related to East and West Florida.[2]

The plot that precipitated the Patriot War was developed in secret and, being covert in nature, can only be reconstructed in its details from the few documents that openly refer to it. For example, neither the president nor General Mathews kept notes about their strategizing session. Even the exact day of their meeting is uncertain. The substance of what was said comes from hints and inferences in other writings. Colonel Ralph Isaacs, who would serve Mathews faithfully as personal secretary throughout 1811 and 1812 and was privy to his councils, asserted that their talk focused first on Spanish West Florida and included provisions to bribe Governor Vicente Folch. Mathews had met with Folch at Mobile in 1810 and believed him sufficiently venal and ambitious to strike a private bargain with the United States. Folch would not oppose a cession of West Florida, Mathews said, if he received a consideration and if it forestalled any chance of the French or British acquiring the colony.[3]

Since the president already knew much about the situation in West Florida, discussion quickly turned to East Florida, a subject on which Mathews had even more to impart. Aspects of what he wished to say were summarized in a report he had submitted to the State Department entitled "Affairs of E. & W. Florida," and he probably went over the main points again. He had visited the borders of East Florida in 1810 and was convinced that the settlers, like those of Baton Rouge, were ready to take up arms against Spain. He was dismally wrong in this assessment, and yet his report, based on his communications with just a few men, exuded his convictions:

> I persued [sic] my journey to East Florida, [and] I found the people there in expectations of soon declareing [sic] for themselves. They appeared only to be waiting to hear the fate of Cádiz. A large majority of them are disposed to become a part of the United States but they will expect some arrangements on the part of our Government with respect to debts due to individuals from the Government of Spain. The Officers & Soldiers will likewise expect, if they become a part of the United States that the debts due them will be paid, and [that] some provision in land for each family [will be made]. How far these expectations are Just, our government will determine. The Military

force of East Florida consists of about two hundred and fifty Soldiers, [almost] the whole of which are stationed at Augusteen [*sic*]. Should the people declare for themselves, those who will be foremost in it expect to get possession of the fort by surprise. To those most favourable to our government, it would be grateful to see some Military force of ours on that frontier. It would have a tendency to awe what British influence there is in the province and give confidence to those friendly to us.[4]

In order to gauge "friendly" sentiments in the colony, Mathews conducted secret meetings with five prominent East Florida settlers. Although he had promised not to commit their names to paper, he was "at liberty to mention them in a conference with the president." The five men in question were John Houston McIntosh, a wealthy planter closely connected to Georgia; Don Fernando de la Maza Arredondo, the wealthiest Spaniard in the colony; George Fleming, another affluent planter; Andrew Atkinson, originally a merchant from South Carolina and Georgia who had planting and commercial interests in East Florida; and Don Justo Lopez, a close friend of Atkinson's and the military commander of the thriving border town of Fernandina on Amelia Island. These men were worried about the colony's future, especially if the French succeeded in destroying Spain's embattled Regency government. The entire political apparatus of the Regency was concentrated at Cádiz, and Cádiz was under siege. If the city fell, Spain's legitimate government would disappear, and there would be little hope of ever reviving it or of placing Ferdinand VII back on the throne. The settlers of East Florida, Mathews's informants hinted, would rather join the American Union than live as vassals of Napoleon Bonaparte.[5]

Hearing their concerns, Mathews suggested broaching the matter with Henry White, the Irish-born officer who governed East Florida, in order to discover his loyalties. Andrew Atkinson vehemently rejected the idea. White was not the type of man who would listen to proposals for independence or annexation to the United States, he warned. "As sure as you open your mouth to White on the subject, you will die in chains in Moro Castle, and all the devils in hell can't save you."[6]

This was all the substance that Mathews wanted to convey to the president: that there was little chance of negotiating any kind of settlement with Governor White; that at least some of the colonists in East Florida, apprehensive about the course of war in Spain, were ready for drastic action; that there was a dangerous British faction in East Florida; and that the key to success depended upon a rapid capture of St. Augustine, the capital, and its formidable Castillo de San Marcos. At some point, the president apparently asked for recommendations regarding a territorial governor for Florida, and Mathews suggested Major General John Floyd of the Georgia militia. He probably also apprised the president of his previous experiences with East Florida, especially from his years as Georgia's governor. Once before, in 1795, a portion of the colony's settlers had risen in revolt. It was an abortive affair, poorly supported and quickly suppressed. Inspiring a new rebellion in East Florida would therefore require great discretion. Governor White was watching for signs of sedition. He had recently banished one person, a Dr. James Hall, for acts of espionage.[7]

Shortly after this interview, Mathews and Colonel John McKee both received appointments as U.S. commissioners, with the various powers that Mathews had requested, including authority to settle Spanish debts and to draw on military forces along the frontier. Even as Secretary of State Smith pushed through their paperwork, Congress was completing the legal underpinnings for a campaign of intrigue against East and West Florida. "The President has certainly manifested proper energy in relation to [this]," observed Henry Clay, who was strongly in favor of a filibustering effort. On January 15, 1811, the House and Senate passed a joint resolution endorsing the United States's right to take temporary possession of the Floridas "under certain contingencies." A bill drafted by Clay, in collaboration with William Crawford and other senators, set out the specifics that would trigger American action. President Madison could "take possession of and occupy all or any part" of the Floridas if he received a cession of the territories or if he had evidence that a foreign power, such as Great Britain, intended to occupy them. The crucial first section of this bill read: "That the President of the U. States be and he is hereby authorized to take possession of, and occupy, all or any part of the territory lying east of the river Perdido, and south of the State of Georgia and the Mississippi Territory, in case an arrangement has been, or shall be, made with the local authority of the said territory, for delivering up the possession of the same, or any part thereof, to the United States, or in the event of an attempt to occupy the said territory, or any part thereof, by any foreign government." Sections 2 and 3 provided for an allocation of $100,000 to defray expenses and granted the president authority to create a territorial government in the Floridas after they came under American jurisdiction. The provinces would be retained by the United States pending subsequent negotiations with Spain. This bill was approved and enacted into law on January 15, the same day as the joint resolution. To keep it secret, Congress prohibited its publication.[8]

With this legislation in hand, and with General Mathews and Colonel McKee ready to return to the southern frontiers, the president and Secretary of State Smith began to translate plans into reality. Smith briefed the commissioners on the goals of their assignment. Some of his instructions, as befitted a clandestine operation, were not committed to paper. Again, the exact substance remains unknown. Ralph Isaacs later referred to them as "back stairs instructions and approbation." Based on Mathews's future actions and his assertion that everything he did had the authorization of the government, it appears that Smith advised something of the following: He said that the government was resolved upon acquiring the Floridas and would accept the cession from either the Spanish authorities or, if that proved impossible, from other local authorities. The term *local authorities*, Smith made clear, referred to rival or rebel governments that might rise up to oppose the Spaniards, as had happened at Baton Rouge. McKee and Mathews were expected to assist in the creation of a rebel leadership if none was already in place. To shield the president from complicity, they were to recruit rebels in secret, offering inducements, such as lands and offices, to sweeten enthusiasm for the cause. All of this had to be done inconspicuously, so that the hands of the administration were hidden from view.[9]

Smith also provided explicit written instructions, which reminded the commissioners that their goals and purposes were confidential. In their embassy to West Florida, the administration wanted them to reach an amicable agreement with Governor Folch resulting in a cession of the colony to the United States. They could draw funds for expenses from New Orleans or Savannah at the rate of $8 per day. It was inadvisable, the instructions noted, to discuss compensating Spain for loss of territory. Such questions could be left to a future settlement. However, the commissioners could assume, on behalf of the United States, any debts the Spanish government owed to its subjects in West Florida and could confirm land titles, affirm the legality of Spanish laws, guarantee offices for Spanish functionaries, and advance money for the removal of Spanish troops. If they received a cession of Mobile, they were to communicate immediately with Governor William Claiborne of the Louisiana Territory and tell him to occupy it with a detachment of troops.[10]

As for Spanish East Florida, the commissioners' instructions were open-ended, since no one knew what they might encounter: "The conduct you are to pursue in regard to East Florida, must be regulated by the dictates of your own judgments in a close and accurate knowledge of the precise state of things there and of the real dispositions of the Spanish Governor." Significantly, the wording in this set of instructions departed slightly from the text of the original congressional act, saying: "Should you discover an inclination *in the governor of East Florida, or in the existing local authority*, amicably to surrender that province . . . you are to accept it on the same terms that are prescribed by these instructions in relation to West Florida." It was this phrase, with its implication that the "existing local authority" might be something different from the governor and his council, that embraced the possibility of dealing with a friendly rebel government in East Florida.[11]

Above all, the commissioners were to prevent any British move against the Floridas. They had authority to call on nearby U.S. military installations for help. If the British showed any signs of stationing troops in Spanish territory, McKee and Mathews were "to preoccupy *by force* the territory to the entire exclusion of any armament that may be advancing to take possession of it."[12]

Even as the commissioners received these instructions, Secretary of War William Eustis and Secretary of the Navy Paul Hamilton were busily transferring men, munitions, and equipment to points where they could be used against Spanish East and West Florida, as circumstances required. On January 24, 1811, Eustis sent out confidential instructions to General Wade Hampton, commanding U.S. troops in the Mississippi Territory, and to Colonel Thomas P. Cushing, who commanded Fort Stoddert above Mobile. Governor Folch, he told them, might deliver West Florida to the United States. They must have troops ready to occupy the territory. At the same time, he transferred Lieutenant Colonel Thomas Adam Smith and a body of infantry from Colerain, Georgia, to Point Peter, a military post on the St. Marys River close to the populated areas of Spanish East Florida. Smith was told to place himself completely at the disposal of McKee or Mathews. The secretary quoted their commission from the president, noting that they had authority to treat with the "local authorities" for the surrender of any lands "lying east of the River Perdido and south of the

State of Georgia, and the Mississippi Territory. . . . You are hereby authorized and directed, on the request of those gentlemen or either of them,
stating that an arrangement has been made as aforesaid, to march with the
troops, under your command, and to take possession of such posts within
the territory aforesaid, as may be so agreed to be surrendered, and to hold
and defend the same."[13]

Orders from the secretary of the navy were more ambiguous but of the
same intent. Commanders of war ships at New Orleans were notified of
McKee's and Mathews's mission and told to assist, if requested. Meanwhile, Hugh Campbell, the senior naval officer at Charleston Station, received instructions to transfer five gunboats to the St. Marys River and to
procure twenty barrels of gun powder and 500 pounds of lead and send
these munitions south to Lieutenant Colonel Smith at Point Peter as
quickly as possible.[14]

All these preparations having been made, in the last week of January
Mathews and McKee headed south, the old Revolutionary War veteran
merrily regaling his younger companion with tales of his life and adventures on the southern frontiers. Despite the seeming urgency of affairs to
the west, Mathews decided against an immediate visit to Pensacola. Instead, he sent his secretary, Colonel Isaacs, to speak with Governor Folch,
while he and McKee headed for the borders of Spanish East Florida. On
February 25, they arrived at St. Marys, a boisterous frontier settlement in
Camden County, Georgia. From here and the nearby post at Point Peter,
Mathews intended to devise and organize a rebellion that would bring the
southern tip of the Atlantic seaboard into the confederation of American
states.[15]

Mathews was already well known at St. Marys, having spent much of
1810 in its vicinity, and his return aroused considerable excitement. The
town, founded in 1788, had originally been called both St. Patricks and
Newton before adopting the name of the river that gave it life. In 1811, St.
Marys was a small but rapidly growing trading post, with 349 white inhabitants and a slave population of 236. It was a typical river port, flush
with profits from smuggling, packed with sailors and grogshops. Ships of
seventeen-foot draught could find safe harbor there, and through the
town passed pelts, beef, corn, potatoes, cotton, rice, and all manner of naval
stores. "Very few of the streets were built upon and the whole town only
had fifty or sixty houses, and those built near the river," noted one visitor.
"They were built of wood without much regard for comfort or beauty.

With the forest so near the houses, the town had the appearance of being buried in the woods."[16]

Immediately upon his arrival, Mathews sought out two local confidants, James Seagrove, the former U.S. Indian agent to the Creeks, and Archibald Clark, a wealthy lumber merchant. During his tenure as governor of Georgia in the 1790s, Mathews had frequently called on Seagrove's services, sending him, among other things, to negotiate for the return of fugitive slaves from East Florida. Clark was more of a protégé. At twenty-eight years of age, he was a mere youngster against the other two men, but his influence at Colerain, where he owned the largest sawmill, and his dislike of Spanish rule in Florida made him a promising ally.[17]

These two men knew the general's mind regarding East Florida and listened with relish to his account of his stay in Washington. Yet their fervor was tempered with caution. It would not be easy, they told him, to rouse Spanish subjects to rebellion. Indeed, they had already tried to do so and had failed. In early January, shortly before Mathews's arrival, Seagrove had sent a small party of armed rabble-rousers across the border. The leader was another close acquaintance, Dr. James Hall—the same man who had been thrown out of East Florida in 1810 for intriguing against the Spanish government and had subsequently taken up residence in Colerain. Unfortunately, Seagrove said, several East Florida border residents—Abner Broadway and William Dell among them—discovered Hall's plans. Within days, George J. F. Clarke of Fernandina, in the role of local magistrate, had hunted down Hall at his camp and confronted him. This discovery had preempted any chance of instigating a successful revolt, and, in any case, it soon became clear that Hall would attract few adherents. East Florida was extremely prosperous—more so than many parts of Georgia—and settlers had no desire to risk their affluence in the uncertain tumult of an insurrection. Their business with England was booming—the economic sanctions curtailing British trade with the United States had only served to benefit the inhabitants of Spanish Florida. They were getting an astonishing 50 to 75 cents a pound for sea island cotton, $1.25 a bushel for corn, and $15 to $25 a head for cattle and were happy with their profits. Without inducements and a guarantee of their property, Floridians would dismiss Mathews's overtures just as they had dismissed Hall's. Much would depend, as well, on affairs in Spain. Cádiz, to everyone's surprise, had withstood French assault, and there was a British army in Portugal, gathering strength to oppose the French. People were no longer so pessimistic about the chances for the Spanish Regency's survival, and this had revived a local sense of patriotism.[18]

Other circumstances also precluded action. No troops had arrived to reinforce Point Peter, Mathews observed in a report to Secretary of State Smith, and there was no sign of any gunboats. "From this cause," he concluded, "it is thought not proper to attempt anything at present."[19]

Taking everything into account, Mathews decided to defer on his mission to East Florida and try his luck in West Florida. Bidding his friends adieu, the general resumed his travels with McKee.

Their trip across Georgia to West Florida, however, resulted in more wasted effort. Since communicating with the president in January, Governor Folch had received both aid and orders from his superiors in Cuba. He was determined to resist the growing American military presence around West Florida, and the captain general of Cuba, angered at the American seizure of Baton Rouge, had issued directives to stop any further American incursions. Isaacs, McKee, and Mathews spent almost ten weeks trying to dissuade Folch from this course, but he was adamant. Gradually, even Mathews's spirit for intrigue began to falter, and he turned his attention back to Spanish East Florida. Twice thwarted, he finally heard news that he hoped might change his fortunes. Governor Henry White was dead, and a new man, Juan José de Estrada, had assumed command in the province. Wondering if this change in leadership would aid his plans, in June 1811 Mathews said his farewells to McKee and, traveling in company with Ralph Isaacs, journeyed back east.[20]

Georgia and Spanish East Florida, a Clash of Cultures

While Americans braced for possible war with England in 1811, Spain's subjects were already in the thick of combat against Napoleonic France. In Spain itself, the Regency government at Cádiz was struggling to survive in the face of a French siege maintained by Marshal Soult. In nearby Portugal, Marshal Masséna, capitalizing on his capture of Ciudad de Rodrigo, was in hot pursuit of Sir Arthur Wellesley and a combined Spanish, Portuguese, and British army of 68,000 men. At Torres Vedras, Wellesley struck back, halting and reversing the French advance and forcing Masséna to retreat with an overall loss of 43,000 casualties in dead, wounded, and sick. It was the first major allied victory of the Peninsular War. Overseas, however, the news was not so bright. With Spain in disarray, tremors of unrest and revolt were undulating through the American colonies. In Mexico near Guadalajara, the army of General Félix María Callega was about to confront the peasant forces of Father Miguel Hidalgo y Costilla. Ripples of this insurrection were spreading into Texas, where José Bernardo Maximiliano Guitiérrez de Lara was planning his own rebellion against Spanish rule. On the island of Cuba, the great city of Havana—a place of "mud and palaces, dried beef and opera," as one historian phrased it—was fast becoming a hub of foreign intrigue. Every week British and American agents sought audiences with the marquis de Someruelos, the captain general of the island. Always they asked the same question: If war should break out between the United States and Great Britain, which side would the Cubans support?[1]

So far, these tumults and turmoils had made little impression upon the colony of Spanish East Florida, nestled somewhat innocuously on its sandy peninsula between the United States and the Caribbean. Along

Florida's beaches, Minorcan fishermen sang songs in Catalán as they dragged the coastal currents with seine nets; residents of St. Augustine reveled in masquerades on Catholic feast days; schooners and brigs shipped cargos of rice, cotton, beef, and oranges; soldiers gambled at dice and cockfighting; officers wagered at *ombre* and billiards; and Indian traders bartered for pelts and cattle. At the governor's house, officials scrutinized American newspapers brought back by local merchants from Charleston, South Carolina, and Savannah, Georgia, keeping abreast of the debates in the U.S. Congress and the military situation in Spain. At the same time, they began to hear vague rumors about a plot inside Georgia to stir up dissension in their province.

Such rumors were always a cause for worry. Relations with Georgia and other parts of the American South had never been good. During the early 1700s, Florida had been "a land of living war," embroiled in power struggles with the southernmost British American colonies. In 1702, for example, James Moore, at the head of colonial militia from the Carolinas, had invaded Florida and burned St. Augustine. Even more infamous in local annals was a 1740 expedition led by James Edward Oglethorpe of Georgia. After ransacking the free black settlement of Gracia Real de Santa Teresa de Mose, just north of St. Augustine, Oglethorpe's troops had besieged and bombarded the capital during an attack that lasted six weeks. Only the timely arrival of a Spanish fleet carrying relief troops compelled Oglethorpe's men to withdraw.[2]

Rivalry continued even as the Southeast underwent major changes. In 1763, at the close of the Seven Years' War (1756–63), Spain had temporarily forfeited possession of the Florida peninsula. Unsuccessful in its war effort, the Spanish Crown was forced to make a trade—giving Florida to the British as a kind of ransom for Havana, Cuba, which an English army had captured and occupied and which Spain could not afford to lose. Over the next twenty years, from 1763 until 1783, the British tried to stabilize and develop their acquisition. They divided Florida into two territories: British West Florida, with a capital at Pensacola, and British East Florida, which retained St. Augustine as its capital. However, at the close of the American Revolution, the English were obliged to cede these colonies back to Spain. The change from Spanish to British and then back to Spanish sovereignty caused considerable disruption and displacement in the population. In 1763, after the first transfer, Spanish settlers had evacuated the area, signing away their homes and properties to a land agent, while British and British American settlers arrived to take their place. In 1783 and 1784, the situation was reversed. English and British American families forsook their homes and properties, and Spanish and Cuban families came back to reclaim the lands they had previously lost. A few European settlers also decided to stay in the province, as did a large group of former indentured servants from Greece, Italy, and the Balearic Islands of Minorca, Mallorca, and Ibiza. Thus was Spanish East Florida born, a colony that was Spanish in name and allegiance but diverse in its composition.[3]

Although Spaniards returned to East Florida with enthusiastic plans to revive their fortunes, reasserting a Spanish presence in the Southeast was difficult. American settlers also wanted to dominate the region and were in a far better position to do so. By the 1780s, the population of Georgia was many times greater than East Florida's, and the existence of a rapidly growing American state next to a barely sustainable Spanish border territory ensured there would be a contest of wills along the frontier. Georgians were avid proponents of territorial expansion, their politics and public policies shaped by constant calls to acquire more land from nearby Indian tribes (mainly the Creeks and the Cherokees). As far as they were concerned, the Spaniards were only marginally preferable as neighbors to the British Tories who had preceded them. A 1794 editorial in the *Augusta Chronicle and Gazette of the State* voiced a common sentiment when it suggested driving the Indians and the Spaniards out of the Southeast. It would be wise, the editor said, for Georgians to push the Creeks beyond the Mississippi River, "and it would not be very difficult to send the Spaniards of East Florida a-packing with them, for the frontier people are highly exasperated against them."[4]

With the population and economy of the United States growing by leaps and bounds in the years after the Revolution, Americans confidently forecasted their ascendancy over the nearby colonies of Spain. Some predicted that Cuba and Mexico would join the American confederation. At any rate, the fate of the borderlands—Texas, Louisiana, and the Floridas—seemed sealed. "Because of their situation and small population and agricultural deficiencies," said one newspaper editorial, "[they] must in time fall under the dominion of the American States." Sheer force of numbers reinforced this attitude. For example, at the taking of the first U.S. census in 1790, the state of Georgia had a population of 82,540 people; over the next ten years this total nearly doubled to 161,667. By 1810, there were more than a quarter million people in Georgia, of whom 147,215 were whites and 105,218 were black slaves. This population, fed by constant immigration, placed great pressure on available lands, and settlers looked southward and westward for additional places to homestead.[5]

The Spanish borderlands could not rival such growth. Spanish East Florida greeted the nineteenth century as a province virtually devoid of people, a place rich in land and poor in inhabitants. In the 1780s, the colony's settlers, slaves, and soldiers, far from numbering in the tens of thousands, barely amounted to 2,000 persons, whom local census-takers described according to categories they deemed significant: 450 men in St. Augustine's military garrison; 216 civilians from Spain, Cuba, and other Spanish possessions; 459 settlers from the Balearics, Italy, and Greece; 217 settlers from Europe and the United States; 100 free persons of color; and some 550 slaves brought from Africa or from other colonies. By 1811, although the population had doubled in size, East Florida still sheltered a mere 3,690 persons. Fernandina and St. Augustine, both coastal ports, were the only towns. The former, with a population of 600, had grown into a modest center of shipping and was named in honor of Ferdinand VII, Spain's captive king. St. Augustine, lacking Fernandina's prosperous trade, could still claim preeminence as the larger of the two towns, the colonial capital, and (with a founding date of 1565) the oldest settlement on the Atlantic seaboard. It supported a population of 1,500 and was the center of political, social, and religious life in East Florida.[6]

The rest of Florida's habitations and enterprises were rural in nature, made up of a scattering of forts, cotton and rice plantations, citrus groves, farms, cattle-ranching operations, sawmills, and lumber camps (see figs. 1 and 2). Colonial land holdings stretched along all the major and secondary waterways that were a prominent feature of north Florida's landscape: the St. Marys, Nassau, and St. Johns Rivers, winding out of the hinterlands, and the tributaries and coastal rivers, San Pablo Creek, the Trout River, Julington Creek, and the Guana, North, Matanzas, and Halifax Rivers. Other major landmarks (important during the Patriot War) included San Vicente de Ferrer, a lookout station and depot on the bluff above the St. Johns River; Fort San Nicolás, guarding the Cowford, where the King's Road between St. Augustine and Colerain intersected with the St. Johns River; and Forts Picolata and Pupo, facing each other across the middle stretches of the St. Johns, where a garrison kept watch on river traffic and guarded the routes into Indian country.[7]

The emptiness and apparent vulnerability of the Florida wilderness fostered many plots for conquest. By 1811, officials in East Florida had already discovered and defeated three separate intrigues aimed at overthrowing Spanish rule: one fomented by French agents in 1794, another instigated by the ambitious Georgian war hero Elijah Clarke in 1797, and a third undertaken by the charismatic English adventurer William Augustus Bowles in 1801.[8]

Differences between the societies that grew up in Georgia and East Florida also contributed to strained relations along their mutual frontier. Between 1790 and 1811, Georgia was well on its way to becoming the classic three-tiered society of the antebellum South, dominated by rich planters, professional men, and shipping magnates, with a supporting population of artisans and yeoman farmers and a large labor pool of enslaved blacks. Land was the key to power, to inherited wealth, and to profits in speculation and investment. Like the United States in general ("two thirds of the landless white men of Virginia moved west in the 1790s"), Georgia was a restless state, with a high influx of immigrants who looked to land lotteries as a means of securing homes and acreage. Settlement concentrated in the eastern portion of the state, in the thirty-seven counties bounded by the Savannah River and the Atlantic Ocean on the east, the Ocmulgee and Altamaha Rivers on the west, and the St. Marys River on the south. By the 1790s, settlers were moving south from the densest areas of habitation, near South Carolina, into Glynn, Wayne, and Camden Counties. At the border with East Florida, they founded the enclaves of Trader's Hill, Colerain, and St. Marys, while the U.S. military secured the frontier with a cantonment at Point Peter and a marine installation on Cumberland Island. Western sectors of Georgia—those beyond the Altamaha River—were at this time still governed as Indian territories, and although settlers migrated into them, they were largely controlled by the Cherokees in the northwest and by the Creeks along the tributaries of the Alabama, Flint, and Chattahoochee Rivers. The Chattahoochee River marked Georgia's boundary with the Mississippi Territory (see figs. 1 and 2).[9]

A flourishing economy helped to speed the rapidity of Georgia's expansion. Savannah, the largest city and a bustling port of call, had a population of 5,000. State revenues amounted to a respectable $70,000 per annum, based on poll taxes and on taxes on agricultural lands and urban real estate. In 1795, the Yazoo land fraud scandal cost the state its far western claims of territory and had the effect of augmenting an already-prevalent hunger for land. Over the next ten years, state officials put great pressure on the Creeks to cede all of their lands east of the Ocmulgee River. Once acquired, these newly opened lands quickly attracted investors and settlers, as the state's plantation economy continued to grow.[10]

In 1807, however, Georgia was shaken by economic woes. Congress's implementation of the Embargo Act wrought tremendous harm in the South, as it did in other sectors of the United States. Encouraged by good markets for tobacco and cotton, many of Georgia's planters had risked going into debt in order to enlarge their operations, purchase more slaves, and bring more fields into cultivation. The coming of the embargo struck them a severe blow. It shut down access to markets in England and France and glutted the domestic market with a surplus of agricultural products that could not be absorbed. Demand collapsed and prices dropped precipitously. Cotton, selling at twenty-eight cents per pound in 1807, fell to just six cents per pound a year later. State exports, valued at $3.7 million in 1807, plummeted to a mere $24,000 in 1808. In 1809, 1810, and 1811, Georgia managed only a partial recovery from the shock of this economic distress, and exports remained depressed to about a third of their pre-embargo level. Bankruptcy and foreclosure threatened so many citizens that the Georgia Assembly had to pass special legislation, the Alleviating Act, to give debtors greater protection and extra time to repay their outstanding loans.[11]

The man who had to shepherd Georgia through these difficult times was forty-five-year-old David Brydie Mitchell, a Scottish immigrant who had steadily advanced in Georgia's military and political circles, becoming a major general in the militia, a member of the assembly, a solicitor general in the superior court, and mayor of Savannah. In 1809, the state legislature had elected him governor by a vote of sixty-one to forty-one over incumbent Jared Irwin. An intelligent, quick-tempered, and energetic man, Mitchell enjoyed the support of two other noted Georgians, William H. Crawford of the U.S. Senate and George M. Troup of the U.S. House of Representatives, and he also had the regard of Major General John Floyd of the militia. Convinced that war between the United States and England was inevitable, he spent his first years in office stockpiling arms and ammunition in state arsenals and pushed through construction of a line of forts along the western frontier. Coastal defenses were also high on his list of priorities, and he listened intently to his constituents' concerns about future relations with the Creeks, the British, and the Spanish.[12]

In contrast to burgeoning and expanding Georgia, Spanish East Florida was a small, somewhat self-contained world, one in which Spanish officials had to carefully balance Crown prerogatives against local needs and had to defend Spanish interests with limited resources. Political life revolved entirely around the governor in his dealings with various factions of settlers. Juan José de Estrada, the man who succeeded to the governorship after the death of Henry White (April 13, 1811), exemplified what Spaniards admired as *capaz* and *hidalguía*, or efficiency and nobility. Forty-three years old, married, and a Cuban by birth, Lieutenant Colonel Estrada was a professional soldier and the ranking officer of the Third Infantry Battalion of Cuba, the military detachment that garrisoned St. Augustine. Since East Florida was a sparsely populated province and did not merit a complicated local bureaucracy, the governor was the equivalent of a big fish in a little pond. Aside from an advisory council made up of other royal functionaries, all prerogatives rested with him. He was not only the supreme political and military commander of the province, but he also presided over trials; oversaw collection of duties and taxes; approved all minor appointments, public contracts, and awards of land; and otherwise enforced Crown rights. Though he represented royal authority, he had to court favor with the province's leading Spanish, Cuban, Minorcan, and English families, who wielded great influence over both the public purse strings and public opinion.[13]

All governors who took office in East Florida soon ran up against the basic shortcoming of the province—it was a colony that cost Spain money and survived as a necessary expense rather than as a boon to the Treasury. East Florida suffered from an impoverished tax base, and its expenses almost always outstripped its income. To alleviate this dilemma, it received an annual subsidy, called the *situado*, which was levied against the Treasury of Mexico and was used to pay for salaries, military expenses, and repairs to government property. The *situado*, however, did not always arrive on time. In 1811, it was 200,000 pesos in arrears. The local Real Hacienda, or Royal Treasury, had a second source of income in the import and export duties levied against shipping at Fernandina and St. Augustine (at the rate of 15 percent of value on imports and 6 percent on exports). Yet even these funds could not fully balance the ledgers, and so civil and military officials resorted to purchasing supplies on credit. They preferred to buy from American suppliers (who charged less than those in Cuba) and often went into short-term debt with merchant houses in Savannah or Charleston for such items as foodstuffs, cloth, and other basic goods. These debts were settled with *libranzas*, a type of promissory note that could be redeemed against the *situado* or directly against the treasuries of Cuba and Mexico.[14]

Given such financial straits, both public and private interests in East Florida had a stake in promoting trade. By the 1790s, restrictions on commerce had been set aside in favor of open trade with the United States, and by 1808, when England and Spain became allies, trade with English ports was also thriving. While Mexico and Cuba underwrote the costs of East Florida, the colony provided a good living to many settlers. Cotton plantations along the barrier islands and on the coastal rivers were yielding their owners an annual income greater than 25 percent of initial investment. Long-staple cotton, the principal export crop, garnered a price ranging from fifty to seventy-five cents a pound, and the cultivation and ginning of cotton capped a seasonal round that also encompassed rice planting, citrus growing, ranching, timber cutting, and farming, as well as a pelt trade and a slave trade. During the period of the Napoleonic Wars (roughly 1797–1815), about 40 percent of East Florida's exports went to the United States, 43 percent to England, and 13.5 percent to Spain or Spanish possessions. By contrast, East Florida imported 90 percent of its textiles, household goods, farming equipment, and nonlocal foodstuffs from the United States. The Embargo Act and other American economic sanctions had little impact on this trade, for the sanctions did not apply to commerce with Spanish America.[15]

It was East Florida's prosperous economy, and the profits to be made from it, that softened various other strictures of Spanish rule. Religion, for example, was a delicate matter. The only acknowledged faith in the colony was Catholicism, and no other form of worship could take place publicly, although many settlers—close to a third—were Protestants. Governor Estrada and the Catholic clergy, seeking to avoid confrontations regarding faith, did not inquire too thoroughly into private forms of worships, while Protestant settlers, loath to do anything that would jeopardize their land holdings, quietly went to Georgia or the Bahamas when they required rites within their own faith. In other respects, Spanish East Florida reflected many aspects of frontier society. It had a flexible social structure that allowed for upward mobility. The Minorcan settlers, having first arrived in the colony under British rule as indentured servants, exploited opportunities to acquire property. Under the Spanish, most became landowners, and some entered the ranks of the colonial elite. Free people of color also acquired land, the men sometimes gaining land grants in acknowledgment of their military service. For wealthy immigrants, East Florida afforded many inducements—land, commerce, and low taxes. Social mores—at least for the rich—were also flexible. It was fairly common for affluent white planters and merchants to raise families with wives or mistresses who were women of color. Their children's social status was determined not by their skin color but by money and family influence.[16]

The causes of antipathy between Georgia and East Florida were many and various, stemming in part from a basic conflict of interests and in part from a frontier environment at the border, where law and justice were often enforced by private retaliation. Always suspicious of southern frontiersmen, whom they described as "nomadic like Arabs," officials in East Florida took whatever precautions they could to stave off encroachments on Spanish territory. In particular, they competed with their Georgia counterparts to win the goodwill of the Florida Indians—the Creeks and Miccosukees in the northwestern part of the peninsula and the Seminoles in the north-central area. These tribes could put hundreds of warriors in the field in times of war and controlled a lucrative trade in pelts, cattle, and horses. Each year the Spaniards sent gifts to the chiefs of the major Indian towns, which they identified by the tribal names Chowchate, Oguilibaja, Oulaschuche, Mosquitos, Quinapaja, Oitomosca, Lachua, Guacapote, and Canajarque.

In their parleys with Indian leaders, Spanish officials drew attention to the lax hand of the Crown in its dealings with native peoples compared to the belligerence of American pioneers. "If you go to treat with those Georgians," a local Indian trader once warned the Lower Creeks, "I'd advise you to do it at the head of Six Thousand Warriors." The Indians, for their part, tended to use the threat of an alliance with the Spaniards as a form of leverage when dealing with representatives of the American government. All in all, a Spanish-Indian alliance in Florida worked to Georgia's detriment. In times of peace, it blocked American Indian traders from making contact with the Seminoles (who traded almost exclusively through a Scottish firm, the Panton, Leslie Company, later Forbes and Company, that had a special Spanish license to operate throughout the Floridas). In times of war, on the other hand, fear of Indian raids put all the western and southern counties of Georgia in a state of alarm. "Will you be so good as to inquire what the commanding officer of the Federal troops in Georgia has been doing . . . with the very fine troops of Calvary at Fort Wilkinson," a resident of St. Marys asked the Savannah press during one episode of Indian hostilities. "I am of the opinion they would be much better and more usefully employed on this frontier."[17]

Differences with regard to slaves, runaways, and free people of color also contributed to tensions. Conscious of the American South's dependence on slave labor, Spanish officials had at times employed various contrivances to discomfit southern plantation owners. In the eighteenth century, obeying the directives of the Crown, they had encouraged slaves to desert from their masters in Georgia and the Carolinas and to flee into Florida, where they could secure freedom by converting to Catholicism and assisting in defense. This long-standing policy of sanctuary for runaways was finally rescinded in 1790—largely because of an upwelling of resentment against it in southern quarters of the United States. Even without a formal policy, however, slaves continued to escape into East Florida, often heading for Indian territory. "The Negroes uniformly testify to the kind treatment they receive from their Indian masters," said one witness. "They dress and live pretty much like the Indians, each having a gun, and hunting a portion of his time. Like the Indians, they plant in common, and farm an Indian field apart, which they attend together." Serving as military auxiliaries, laborers, and interpreters, few slaves wanted to exchange their relatively light servitude among the tribes for the chattel slavery they had experienced in the South. This early version of an "underground railroad" generated constant fear among whites on the Georgia frontiers. For slave owners, no treaty or agreement could fully dampen apprehensions about living within easy reach of ex-slaves who could move freely through the Florida wilderness.[18]

Dread of blacks under arms would become so central to the Patriot War that it deserves some discussion. The size of East Florida's slave population—or its free black population, for that matter—was not what principally concerned whites in Georgia. Altogether, the number of slaves in East Florida was small when compared to southern states, even taking into account the 1,500 to 2,000 slaves belonging to settlers, the maroon community among the Indians (number unknown but hardly larger), and the temporary arrivals of recently captured Africans who were disembarked at the port of Fernandina as part of the slave trade. Southern planters feared these groups not so much because of their size in numbers but because they perceived them as loosely controlled and as potential leaders of a slave revolt that would burst out of Florida and engulf Georgia, South Carolina, and the Mississippi Territory. Concerns about slave uprisings had been growing in the South ever since a bloody insurrection swept through the French colony of Saint Domingue in the 1790s. In 1810, when rumors circulated about an alleged slave conspiracy in Georgia, the repercussions were felt on both sides of the border. East Florida's governor sent out the militia to confiscate all weapons found at slave quarters, despite the protests of some planters, and even some slaves, that the seizures were unwarranted and that weapons were needed for hunting and for protection from bandits.

In this one instance, the government of East Florida acted in a manner that calmed the fears of southern whites. Usually, however, people in Georgia voiced many misgivings about Spanish attitudes toward slavery. The issue of runaways was a constant provocation—in any given month, notices about fugitive slaves published in the Georgia press were apt to contain phrases such as "believed to have gone to St. Augustine." East Florida was regarded as a magnet that enticed slaves to flee from their masters, knowing that slave catchers had little hope of pursuing them into Spanish territory. Then, too, residents in St. Marys and Colerain were uneasy with the existence of the African slave trade at nearby Fernandina. Although England and the United States had banned the trade from their territories in 1808, Spanish colonies still offered safe harbor for the practice. The town of Fernandina on Amelia Island was deeply involved in the importation and sale of slaves, and this meant disembarking hundreds of recently captured—and presumably dangerous—African prisoners each year.

Differences in American and Spanish slave codes also caused concern among southern whites. Grounded in Roman and medieval precedents, Spanish codes accorded limited rights to slaves, including the right to own property, testify in court, petition for relief from an abusive master, and negotiate for manumission or liberty. The enforcement of Crown authority also demanded that officials investigate serious breaches in the codes, such as cases in which a slave died at a master's hand. Governor Estrada was prosecuting two such cases in 1811. Domingo Fernández of Fernandina was charged with contributing to the death of a sickly field hand, while William Braddock of the Lanceford Creek area faced indictment for flogging a slave to death. While some East Florida settlers argued that paternalism over slaves and adjudication of their rights was the best way to keep them in a state of servitude, slave owners inside and outside Florida typically had little use for Spanish interference in how masters treated their laborers. The sentiments of most southern frontiersmen were aptly expressed by William Dell, a planter of East Florida with close family ties to Camden County, Georgia. In 1810, he stood accused before the Spanish authorities for whipping the slave of another settler and then chasing him into a river, saying he would teach him to respect whites. The planter scoffed at the idea that he had committed a crime. When he was informed that his actions might have caused the slave to drown, he allegedly responded, "If he was in the United States, he [Dell] did not care if he did drown."[19]

Just as damning in the eyes of Georgians were Spanish policies regarding the arming of free men of color. The presence of black citizen-soldiers in East Florida's militia aroused the same fears as the presence of maroons among the Indians—namely, that they would use their military training to incite a slave revolt. Free blacks occupied a low-to-middling stratum in the province's social hierarchy, working as artisans, sailors, lumber cutters, cow punches, shopkeepers, domestics, traders, and farmers. Together with all other adult males, men of color were obligated under Spanish law to serve in the militia. St. Augustine's black militia unit was made up of about fifty men, some of them with extensive training and field experience. At various times, *pardo* and *moreno* soldiers from other parts of the Spanish empire also arrived in the colony to augment provincial defense. The training and deployment of black troops, even volunteer militia, were viewed almost as a kind of devilry in Georgia. During the Patriot War, southern leaders would repeatedly condemn the Spaniards for raising up a "Negro Army" on the borders of the American republic.[20]

Besides these general tensions between the people of East Florida and southern Georgia, another event contributed significantly to the creation and perpetuation of enmity along the border. In 1794 and 1795, the area exploded in violence when an abortive revolt against Spanish rule shook northern Florida and Camden County. At the center of the revolt was a cadre of U.S. citizens—all recent immigrants to East Florida. When their insurrection failed and they escaped punishment by fleeing into Georgia, they created a community of exiles who ever afterward remained bitterly opposed to the Spaniards. The 1795 rebellion was a precursor of the Patriot War and in some ways its progenitor.

The roots of the rebellion rested in Crown immigration policies adopted in the 1790s, which allowed dozens of families from the southern United States to establish themselves on generous head right grants in East Florida. Spanish officials, initially at least, were inclined to trust these new settlers, believing the lure of land would encourage them to be good and obedient subjects. Their hopes proved ill founded. By 1794, several men among the immigrants were conspiring with a Savannah merchant and Indian trader by the name of Abner Hammond to stage an uprising. Hammond's associates included John McIntosh, a Revolutionary War hero from a prominent Camden County family, and several other recent arrivals from the southern states, Richard Lang, William Plowden, and John Peter Wagnon. When word of their activities leaked out, Governor Juan Nepumuceno de Quesada ordered the arrest of McIntosh and Hammond. Charged with collusion to commit treason, they were turned over to the Cuban authorities and sent to languish in the dungeons of the fortress of El Moro in Havana. The detention of these two men—one a citizen of Georgia and the other a war veteran and an acquaintance of President George Washington—riveted the attention of the American public on East Florida.

In the meantime, Governor Quesada, determined to stamp out sedition, acted against the advice of his own council and began to employ harsh measures to deter other would-be rebels. Suspecting that settlers living in north Florida would seek aid from the United States, he ordered an evacuation of the East Florida border area, instructing people to abandon their lodgings and plantations and to move south of the St. Johns River. To stop any rebel force from seeking succor or provisions at the border plantations, he also dispatched troops north to enforce his orders with a scorched-earth policy. The burning and razing of homesteads, including those of some loyal settlers, only stirred up greater anger in the province. The harassment of McIntosh's wife and family also drew public notice.

In the end, despite Quesada's measures, revolt came anyway. Having won release from Cuba in 1795, John McIntosh returned to East Florida to exact retribution. He joined Richard Lang, Elijah Clarke, and other associates at the head of about a hundred armed men and attacked Spanish outposts, capturing Fort Juana on the Trout River and Fort San Nicolás on the

St. Johns River. Unable to hold these posts against a strong detachment of Spanish troops sent to retake them, he and the other rebel leaders gave up their insurrection and fled across the border to seek refuge in Georgia.[21]

The consequences of this short-lived uprising were far more damaging than the revolt itself. Loyal settlers who lost their homes to Quesada's scorched-earth tactics turned against him. By 1796, some sixty-eight residents of East Florida were under indictment on a variety of charges. Of these, thirty-five were charged in absentia, having escaped into Georgia, while four others had died in prison. Those deemed to be traitors, including all the rebel leaders, suffered a traitor's fate: their property was inventoried and confiscated as forfeit to the Crown. In Georgia, bitterness over the confiscations ran deep. John McIntosh vowed to punish the Spaniards for the affronts to his family and the loss of 1,700 acres of land he had owned in East Florida. Two other rebels grew so incensed about their fate that they broke back in to the colony seeking revenge. William Ashley and William Downes took out their anger by terrorizing their former neighbor, Daniel Plummer, whom they suspected of informing on them. They forced their way into Plummer's house and held him captive, laughing at his wife and threatening to shoot him in front of her. Then they rifled his belongings, stole the family silverware, and made off with three slaves. Other exiles satisfied their anger by venting their contempt for the Spanish, one of them proclaiming that Governor Quesada "might kiss his ass, for he did not value him and that he could whip him at a fair fite."[22]

Spanish military responses to the revolt also sparked outrage throughout Georgia. Pressed for soldiers, Governor Quesada mobilized St. Augustine's black militia unit, issuing orders to "arm all the free Negroes and Mulattoes in the province, for, being fugitives from the state of Georgia, they will be loyal and will defend themselves to the death in order not to return to their former slavery." More black troops arrived as part of reinforcements from Mexico under the command of Colonel Sebastián Kindelán y O'Regan. The presence of these men in East Florida created panic along the Georgia frontier, as word spread that the Spaniards were going to attack the town of Temple "with about five or six hundred troops of different services and colors."[23]

By the middle of 1795, the administration of President George Washington, already angry about other problems in the state of Georgia, demanded that state officials take action to restore order along the frontier. George Mathews, serving his last term as governor, had little choice but to comply. Though certainly no friend to Spanish interests, he feared that Georgia would come out the worse in a conflict, especially as the Spaniards already had reinforcements in place and could call on the Seminoles and Creeks to join them in alliance. Through a series of negotiations with Spanish officials, he managed to calm tensions and to draw the frontier area back from the brink of war.[24]

Desires for vengeance against the Spaniards never completely died away, however, and the 1795 rebellion bequeathed a legacy of lingering acrimony to the Georgia-Florida border. Two years passed before the area lapsed into an uneasy truce, and it took the more liberal and even-handed administration of Henry White (1796–1811) to restore tranquility inside East Florida. Aversion to the Spaniards remained strong throughout Georgia. In 1798, when Spanish privateers were engaged in their raids on American shipping during the Quasi-War, a mob in Savannah retaliated by attacking a schooner from St. Augustine that put into port. Marching down to the wharfs at midnight, a crowd of men boarded the Spanish vessel and, as local papers reported, "maltreated in the most outrageous manner the crew, then unmoored and carried her about a mile up the river, where she was set fire to, and entirely consumed."[25]

At the border itself, Spanish subjects and citizens of Camden County vied against one another in feuds that set local official against local official. In one notorious case, Henry O'Neill, a magistrate of East Florida, traveled into Georgia to arrest Nathaniel Ashley, a prominent settler of the town of St. Marys, whom he suspected of stealing cattle from Spanish territory. Ashley (himself a sheriff) defied O'Neill and then, in a fury over his accusations, followed him back across the border and shot him, "not having the fear of God before his eyes, but being moved and seduced by the instigation of the Devil." O'Neill subsequently died of his wounds, and Ashley was indicted for murder in Georgia, though not convicted. Sometime after this, Governor White of East Florida found it necessary to send a formal protest to his Georgia counterpart, Governor Jared Irwin, objecting to the presence of American bounty hunters on Spanish soil. "It is always an abuse of authority in them to enter foreign territory, weapon in hand, to apprehend fugitives . . . or for any other purpose," he wrote angrily to Irwin. "This is to usurp a jurisdiction that is not theirs, and to 'lord it' over an independent country."

Pursuit of runaway slaves also provoked flare-ups. On one occasion, White sent an emissary to St. Marys to hold discussions about resolving problems with runaways. Far from welcoming the Spanish envoy, the town officials grabbed him, threw him in jail, and refused to release him until they had extracted a bond of 2,000 pesos. In another case, Archibald Clark, of Colerain, Georgia, crossed over the border to Amelia Island and beat and threatened a Spanish subject, whom he claimed had stolen one of his slaves.[26]

The years following the Louisiana Purchase saw a further heightening of such border tensions, as American and Spanish diplomats argued heatedly over what the purchase had encompassed. Dr. Daniel Turner, a Rhode Island physician, writing to friends from the town of St. Marys in 1806, commented on the eagerness to invade East Florida. "Our inhabitants are expecting war with Spain," he said, "and appear to be very desirous of it. . . . No opposition would be made to American troops marching in that province, till they arrived at Augustine, & five days siege with a thousand man would carry that place."[27]

If the citizens of Camden County required any further incentive for a showdown with the Dons, they only had to look as far as Fernandina, on the Spanish side of the St. Marys River, to see everything they most hated about the colony. Besides its unsettling association with the African slave trade, the port was largely financed by wealthy English merchants, some of them former Tories from the American Revolution who were residing in East Florida as Spanish subjects. Anger against activities at Fernandina ran especially high during the years of the Embargo Act (1807–9). Exempt from the provisions of the embargo because of its status as a Spanish American port, the town capitalized on the suspension of trade between the United States and England. Ships from Liverpool, Portsmouth, and London were invited into harbor to pick up products they could no longer obtain from the United States. British demand for cotton, rice, beef, sailcloth, timber, naval stores, and other commodities soon turned Fernandina into a boomtown, even as nearby St. Marys and more distant Savannah saw their shipping arrivals and departures steadily drop.

The plethora of commerce at Fernandina infuriated George M. Troup, one of Georgia's congressmen. What good was it, he asked the U.S. House of Representatives, to stop American exports to England, or ban imports, if English merchants could conduct normal business, and obtain whatever they required, just outside the limits of American jurisdiction? "There is at this moment twenty sail of British vessels in waters falling into the St. Marys River," he railed in 1809, "all of them loading with timber, naval stores, cotton, and provisions. . . . If some method cannot be found to put a stop to this smuggling trade, there is no use in keeping the Embargo on." Spanish subjects were profiteering off the embargo, he said, taking advantage of the situation to supplant southern commerce with England. Indeed, so many British vessels were entering Spanish East Florida's waters that "the fish, who never saw anything larger than an eight-oared canoe, are in vast consternation!"[28] Governor Mitchell was also disgusted with how easily Spanish, British, and even American merchants violated the spirit of U.S. trade sanctions at Fernandina, and he solemnly promised his constituents to "prevent, as far at least as depends on Georgia, a repetition of their schemes."[29]

By 1811, then, even as anger in Georgia mounted against the British, grievances against Spain also began to resurface. Hugh McCall's *History of Georgia*, published in Savannah in that year, chronicled the circumstances that had led Carolinians and Georgians to attack Spanish Florida in 1702 and 1740. Newspapers focused on more recent problems. In January and February, both the *Georgia Journal* and the *Georgia Argus* began to publish lengthy narratives about the anti-Spanish revolts taking place in West Florida and the advantages that would accrue to annexing the Floridas to the United States. The *Journal* had previously endorsed this idea, "one of the most popular topics of conversation." "The possessors of Florida may at pleasure obstruct that portion of our commerce which must necessarily be wafted down the Mobile," said the editor, referring to West Florida. "The pusillanimous Spaniards have not scrupled to exact an oppressive duty on all the exports and imports of our citizens through this Territory—we have been compelled to purchase the use of 'nature's highway,' and to pay for navigating those waters which arise out of our own country." Besides obstructing American river traffic, the editor continued, the Spaniards had to be closely watched, to make sure they did not invite the British into the Southeast. "We suspect there is great danger that Britain will possess herself of the Floridas," he warned. "The Spaniards are not very pleasant neighbors—we should have little cause to be pleased with the change, if the British should supply their place."[30]

Georgia's leaders shared these sentiments. In their eyes, the Floridas were becoming what James Madison had always predicted they would be, "at all times a source of irritation and ill blood with the United States." Though Senator Crawford expressed doubts about the efficacy of aiding revolts, preferring to negotiate with Spain for a cession of the provinces,

Congressman Troup had no such quibbles. "In case of war [with England]," he said, "I am of the opinion that it would be a wise measure in the United States to take immediate possession of the Floridas, to prevent the British having a footing there." These were the stormy attitudes that prevailed along the southern frontier as General Mathews endeavored to reverse the verdict of 1795 and to launch a rebellion in East Florida that would triumph where the previous one had failed.[31]

4

Intrigues and Discoveries

Even as the mission to Spanish West Florida faltered in 1811, impediments to an American seizure of East Florida were dropping away. In March, President Madison dismissed Robert Smith as secretary of state and replaced him with James Monroe, an accomplished diplomat and protégé of Thomas Jefferson, who had served as Jefferson's envoy to Paris and Madrid during the negotiations for the Louisiana Purchase. This appointment resolved several difficulties for the president. It freed him of Smith, who had become something of a political liability; it brought a first-rate statesman into the administration; and it partially healed an emerging breach among the Democratic Republicans, for Monroe, contrary to expectations, had run against Madison in the presidential race of 1808. Although Madison had won the election by a handsome margin, the challenge from his junior had produced some hard feelings, and the two men were on somewhat distant terms even as Monroe joined the cabinet. Besides this, Monroe had publicly criticized the administration's foreign policy, especially Madison's attempt to befriend Napoleon Bonaparte as a lever to use against the English. Yet despite the fact that Monroe was "his own man," the gains for the president and his administration were worthwhile.[1]

At fifty-three years of age, James Monroe was a well-rounded politician with impressive experience. He had fought with the Continental Army as a teenager, had suffered through the terrible winter at Valley Forge with George Washington, and had faced British fire at the battles of Manhattan, Trenton, and Monmouth. Popular in his home state of Virginia and among "Old Republicans," he was elected to both state and federal positions and was serving as governor of Virginia when called to the cabinet. His most valuable background, however, was as an overseas diplomat. He had spent several years at the British and French courts, and also in Spain, crossing wits with some of the cleverest and most cunning courtiers and ministers that Europe could produce. Like Jefferson and Madison, he believed the United States had a legitimate claim on West Florida through the terms of the Louisiana Purchase and that Spain should forfeit East Florida as a settlement for the raiding of its privateers in the 1790s. Though he was considered an Anglophile who wanted to see an improvement of relations with Britain, he also advocated taking a harder line with the ever-warring countries of Europe: "Without an aspect of menace, and an evident ability," he had once counseled, "nothing will be gained from any of them, not even of Spain, the most feeble and vulnerable of Powers."[2]

Among the tasks that Monroe immediately took over was the supervision of Mathews and McKee. Conceding that chances for success in West Florida were vanishing and that nothing further would be gained from discussions with Governor Folch, he thanked the commissioners for their services and suspended their powers, turning future negotiations over to Governor Claiborne. At the same time, he told General Mathews to continue with efforts to secure East Florida. "The letter written this day to Col. McKee and yourself is not intended to interfere with the state of things relating to East Florida, esp. if you entertain any reasonable hope of success there," said Monroe. "It will be very satisfactory to receive information from you on the subject."[3]

For the elderly General Mathews, waiting anxiously to hear from the administration, the journey from Fort Stoddert back to the borders of Spanish East Florida proved a stressful one. During the trip, he fell ill with what he called "a bilious complaint," probably a recurrence of the malaria that at times incapacitated him. Upon his arrival in St. Marys on June 9, though eager to prosecute his mission, he had no choice but to take to bed, and there he remained, passing several weeks in frustrating idleness as he recovered his energies. Ralph Isaacs proved invaluable to him. He served as both secretary and amanuensis (Mathews was a poor hand at writing and spelling) and made visits and undertook meetings on the general's behalf.[4]

With the death of Henry White, Mathews hoped to find a more amenable governor installed in East Florida, one who could be persuaded to surrender the colony quickly and quietly to the United States. His friends in St. Marys soon disabused him of this idea. Juan José de Estrada, they said, was as much a fire-breather as White had ever been and would never act against Spanish interests. Besides this, British and Spanish victories against the French in Spain had roused a latent patriotism in many subjects of East Florida.

Mathews refused to be daunted, informing Monroe that affairs in Florida were "in a very unsettled and discordant situation." There was a rumor going about, he said, that the British might try to prop up Spanish rule in East Florida by landing a regiment of black troops from Jamaica, something that would stir up local fears of slave rebellion and cause a major breach in the peace. "The best class of inhabitants [here] view it with just and dreadful apprehensions, and in the event would flock to the American standard, and acquit themselves in a manner becoming the legitimate defenders and asserters of our country's rights."[5]

During his convalescence, Mathews returned to a consideration of his greater scheme, to subvert Spanish rule and establish a local rebel government that could, with at least the appearance of legality, deliver up the colony. Even from his sickbed, he matured his plans. While Archibald Clark and James Seagrove canvassed for recruits among fellow Georgians, he wrestled with his main problem, finding someone to lead a revolt. His own role in fomenting discontent had to remain hidden, at least until such time when secrecy no longer mattered. He therefore required a collaborator, a bona fide resident of Spanish East Florida, preferably someone with status, recognition, and military experience who could articulate grievances against Spain. Such a man also had to be prepared to run risks, to place the interests of the United States above his own oath of loyalty to Spain, even, perhaps, to underwrite expenses out of his own finances.[6]

Eventually, the name "McIntosh" came to mind. The McIntoshes had a distinguished if somewhat unfortunate heritage as enemies of the Spaniards in East Florida. In 1740, during the War of Jenkin's Ear, John Mohr McIntosh, one of the family patriarchs, had joined the expeditionary force that James Oglethorpe launched against the province. He had taken part in the unsuccessful siege of St. Augustine, where he was captured by the Spaniards and sent to Spain with other prisoners of war. Mathews's first instinct was to seek out Mohr's grandson, John McIntosh, one of the men who had led the 1795 rebellion in East Florida. He was now a major general in the Georgia militia and still seethed with hatred for the Spaniards. However, he had long ago forsaken his East Florida properties, confiscated after he turned rebel, and was no longer a subject of the Spanish Crown.[7]

The alternative was John Houston McIntosh, another grandson of John Mohr McIntosh and the younger cousin of Major General McIntosh. John Houston McIntosh was not a soldier. His interests were concentrated for the most part on commerce, to a lesser degree on politics, and not at all on bearing arms. In other respects, though, he fit Mathews's requirements: he was suave and well educated, respectable, with large plantations in both Georgia and Florida, and he resided in East Florida as a Spanish subject. He also had the necessary capital to finance a rebellion: his Florida estates alone were worth more than $28,000. Mathews had conferred with John Houston McIntosh in 1810 and had listed him among his possible allies. All in all, he seemed a good prospect, one that Mathews intended to pursue.[8]

Meanwhile, there was always the possibility that British or Spanish activities in East Florida might provide a suitable pretext for an American show of force. A British deployment of Jamaican troops in the province would have greatly simplified matters for Mathews. He had explicit instructions to advance into the colony with regular U.S. forces if Great Britain established any military presence there. However, the report of British intervention turned out to be one of many false rumors circulating along the frontier, and by August Mathews had committed himself heart and soul to staging an uprising. The rebels would create a rival government, as was done in Baton Rouge. Then they could claim the status of "local authorities," complying with Mathews's written instructions from the State Department, and cede whatever portion of East Florida they could hold to the United States. Everything would have the veneer of legality, to undermine Spanish protests, and the presence of American troops would prevent any sort of armed escapade to retake the colony. As soon as it became clear that Spanish officials were powerless to suppress a rebellion, all the local residents, even the reluctant ones, would happily transfer their loyalties to the United States. The fact that he had neither leader nor rebels in hand did not prevent Mathews from writing confidently again to Monroe: "The inhabitants of the province are ripe for revolt. They are, however, incompetent to effect a thorough revolution without external aid." For this reason, he was submitting an immediate requisition for "two hundred stand of arms and fifty horsemen's swords." Later, he said, the government should stand ready to send on a company of artillery with large siege cannons, sappers, and breaching equipment to destroy the fortifications at St. Augustine. The plan of the campaign was to bypass East Florida's northern outposts and strike directly into the heart of the colony with a night assault against the capital. Once St. Augustine had fallen, the minor fortifications and outlying settlements would be eager to give up.[9]

Certain that success was merely a matter of time, Mathews thrashed out his strategy with Seagrove and Clark and outlined some of it to Lieutenant Colonel Thomas Adam Smith, the commander at the cantonment of Point Peter. Slowly, he incorporated other people into the plot. Buckner Harris, an officer in the Georgia militia, and the Ashley family, long-time residents of St. Marys, were early converts. Harris had been spying on St. Augustine and was often across the border cutting timber illegally in Florida's stands of yellow pine and live oak. William Ashley had ties to the 1795 rebellion in East Florida and had been banished because of them. His mother still resided in the colony, having retained her lands by virtually disowning her eldest son. Lodowick, William's younger brother, was also a Spanish subject and made his living in the lumber trade. He was a member of the East Florida militia, with a solid knowledge of local geography, and his plantation near Rose's Bluff on the St. Marys River would afford a useful headquarters for the rebels on the Spanish side of the border.[10]

Having taken these men into his confidence, Mathews deliberately avoided opening his mind to one other man. Major Jacint Laval, Smith's second-in-command at Point Peter, was, like Mathews, a veteran of the American Revolution. He was also the general's host. The two men were sharing quarters in the major's private cottage on the grounds of the military cantonment. Notwithstanding this close daily contact, they had no liking for one another. Laval was a somewhat refined and effete French émigré—not at all the kind of officer to appeal to Mathews's rough-and-tumble pioneer upbringing, nor one he would trust. So Mathews excluded the major from all of his initial plans for East Florida. It would prove to be a costly mistake.[11]

While Mathews pondered and dreamed, various dangers to his plans were mounting in the form of rumors and gossip about his activities. Residents of St. Marys welcomed news of a possible expedition against East Florida, and local men were soon making inquiries regarding terms of recruitment. These would-be adherents came from backgrounds as struggling frontiersmen or ambitious but poor-to-middling farmers, and they harbored an almost instinctive hostility toward the individuals who symbolized Spanish hegemony in East Florida—the haughty Dons, the privileged and wealthy merchants of Amelia Island, and a disconcerting mixture of other settlers who seemed to be drawn from all corners of the Spanish empire. In Camden County, Georgia, recruits formed a potent but talkative group, and their enthusiasm for Mathews's project placed it in jeopardy. People openly discussed his comings and goings. It was only a matter of time before word of his intrigues leaked to St. Augustine—and it happened much sooner than Mathews anticipated.

When writing to Monroe in August, Mathews emphasized the need for secrecy in all matters regarding East Florida. He admitted that it was difficult for him to escape notice or cover his tracks in the small, intimate community of the border. Nevertheless, he was taking precautions to conceal the true nature of his mission and to hide the involvement of the American government. "I shall use the most discreet management to prevent the United States being committed," he said.[12]

These caveats about discretion proved to be too little, too late. Even as Mathews wrote to his superiors, Governor Estrada was sending out his own report to Captain General Someruelos in Havana and to Don Luis de Onís in Philadelphia. Far from being ignorant of the general's purposes, the Spaniards possessed a detailed knowledge of his mission and his future plans. Their principal source of information was John Houston McIntosh—the very man Mathews was considering as leader for his rebellion.

For much of the spring of 1811, Estrada had been unaware of the trouble brewing along the edges of his colony. He was adjusting to his role as governor and attending to routine internal affairs. Lieutenant Justo Lopez, his subordinate at Fernandina, warned him that more and more interlopers were cutting timber illegally in East Florida, seeking to cash in on the booming lumber trade. Besides this, there seemed to be an increase in American military activity and troop movements at Point Peter and on Cumberland Island. Other matters at the border also claimed much of Estrada's time. In 1810, Governor White, upset that Fernandina was growing without rhyme or reason, had ordered the surveyor general, George J. F. Clarke, to replat the town in accordance with Spanish edicts for the arrangement of streets and lots. Fernandina would have a plaza, like St. Augustine, and a grid of streets intersecting at right angles, with space allocated for a church and for defensive gates and walls. Estrada had inherited the burdensome task of completing this project, made all the more difficult because many of Fernandina's timber-frame structures were already standing and would have to be disassembled and relocated to comply with the new layout.[13]

From another subordinate, William Craig, an Irish-born settler who served as magistrate for the St. Johns River district, Estrada learned about problems in the rural settlements. Craig was worried, for example, about the security of the ferry station at the Cowford. The ferry was a key transit point in the overland journey from East Florida to Georgia, standing roughly at the halfway point of the King's Road, the main artery for horse and cart traffic that ran from the gates of St. Augustine to a junction with the St. Johns River and then on to Colerain (see fig. 2). Despite the ferry's importance, it was poorly guarded and badly run. A small garrison at nearby Fort San Nicolás provided the only protection, and the ferry operator, according to Craig, was "an old widow woman of upward of eighty years of age, who can neither read nor write, and, who, having no white man on the place, cannot possibly be compelled to pay the attention to the ferry or obedience to the orders of Your Excellency, which the King's interest and the Good of Society requires."[14]

These trying but mundane administrative matters were swept suddenly aside in late July when John Houston McIntosh sent Craig an alarming report from Camden County. He had just relocated his wife and family there, moving them from his Fort George Island estate in East Florida to the town of St. Marys so that his children could attend an American school. Upon arriving in town, he said, he found the streets lively with talk about a move against the Spaniards.

> General Mathews is now at that place, in the capacity of a Commissioner of the United States Government, and is ordered to treat with the constituted powers of East Florida, for the possession of the Province. He says that he is authorized to give every white man fifty acres of land, insure them the enjoyment of their religion, the protection of their private property, and to pay up all arrears of the [Spanish] Government, and also to assure the [Spanish] Officers and soldiers that they shall be sent to any quarter of the world they please, or be enlisted if they wish it, in the service of the United States.

McIntosh advised Craig to forward his letter to the governor but also implored him to safeguard his identity as the informant. "This information, I did not throw myself in the way to receive," he told Craig.

I conceive it a duty I owe the [Spanish] Government to give all the information I get in this way. Indeed unless my information be obtained accidentally, I never should receive any at all, for I never would consent to act as a spy for any Government. Let me, however, Sir, request, that if you communicate to our Government the information I have given to you, that you would enjoin on them not to mention my name. My family living at St. Marys, it may be attended with some inconvenience, were it known there, that I had given to you the above mentioned information.[15]

At almost the same time, McIntosh sent a letter directly to Governor Estrada. The two men were in the middle of a quarrel about McIntosh's decision to remove his family from the province. Estrada wanted to know why McIntosh had rented lodgings in Georgia. He reminded McIntosh that the Crown did not want absentee landlords and that if he intended to reside outside the province, he might have to forfeit title to the lands he held in East Florida. This was not the first time they had exchanged words. Shortly after taking office as governor, Estrada had met with McIntosh in St. Augustine. He had questioned him closely about his association with General Mathews in 1810 and had warned him to stay away from the general in the future. McIntosh now tried to allay the governor's mistrust in a long letter in which his tone was both offended and contrite:

I think that I may with confidence assure your Excellency that I have never been wanting at any time in duty and attachment to my Country. I discovered when in its embryo, that some men in Georgia were uniting to attack our happy Country. I immediately wrote to some of my friends, whom I knew had an influence in that part of [Georgia] where this was contemplated, and as I have heard nothing more of it since, I have reason to believe, I was instrumental in preventing it. Had it assumed anything like a serious appearance, I should have lost no time in giving my Government information of it. Shortly after this, the United States Troops arrived on the St. Marys River, and being informed that their intention was to attack us, providing any other foreign power should attempt it, I wrote to my friend Mr. Craig and informed him of it. He being an officer of the Government and on [the] St. Johns, I conceive it my duty to convey to him any information I may receive, and he of course will give the Government information of the same, in an official form. These instances of my fidelity, my general good conduct, the large property I hold in the Province, the warm affection I have for my family and quiet domestic life, and my perfect obedience to our Excellency's commands, will I flatter myself give me a claim to your Excellency's protection and good opinion.[16]

More information about affairs on the border soon arrived. On August 5, Craig wrote to Estrada concerning everything that could be discovered or surmised about American intrigues. Referring to the debates of the Eleventh Congress, which had been extensively covered in the American press, Craig predicted that the Madison administration would try to instigate an insurrection in East Florida and then use the rebellion as an excuse to station troops in the province. The 1810 rebellion at Baton Rouge was clearly the wellspring for the idea, he told Estrada, but this time the Americans were not going to wait for a genuine rebellion. They were going to stage one.

Yet it hardly seemed plausible that such a scheme could succeed.

Although the Majority of [Congress] are of [the] opinion that they ought to have possession of both the Floridas, yet their situation with respect to England, as well as the Divisions among themselves, prevents them authorizing any coercive measures for that purpose. . . . It is however highly probable that Mathews is secretly encouraged by some Influential character in Congress, to excite an Insurrection among the Inhabitants in order to serve as a pretext for their Interfering as was done in West Florida last year. For this purpose, we find him on the St. Marys last winter offering (as was reported) arms, ammunition, men, and money to the Inhabitants on this side, on Condition of their Declaring themselves Independent.

Such attempts to create trouble were common, Craig argued, and did not need to be handled with undue alarm. He reminded Estrada that Governor White had quashed a similar anti-Spanish conspiracy in 1810. Dr. James Hall, a resident of East Florida with a plantation on the middle section of the St. Johns River, had been implicated as working for the American government. "Letters were written and circulated by the said Hall, stating that Several Officers both Civil and Military of this Province, had made overtures to the American Government to Declare themselves Independent, and join the U. States, on condition of being permitted to retain their respective commissions." When White found out about the letters, he banished the doctor. More recently, Hall had tried to lead an armed expedition into the province but had been discovered and turned back.

Mathews's agitations, Craig concluded, would also amount to nothing. The general's attempts at espionage were too public to carry forward. "With respect to the great Body of the Inhabitants in this Quarter, I believe they are firmly and decidedly attached to the present Government and are fully sensible of their enjoying greater and more Fair advantages (as your Excellency very justly assumes) than are to be possessed under any Government (I may venture to say) either on this or the other side of the Atlantic." The true threat to East Florida, Craig said, was the possibility of war between England and the United States, which would almost certainly ignite conflicts in the Spanish colonies. "In that event, it is publickly said (I think with strong grounds for belief) that an attempt would immediately be made by the Americans to take possession of the Province, under the pretext of preventing the English from doing so." This concise and well-reasoned appraisal of the situation proved surprisingly accurate. Craig had given Estrada a complete résumé of how and why Americans would invade East Florida. His one error was in underestimating George Mathews.[17]

Estrada summarized the situation in a confidential report to the captain general of Cuba, enclosing Spanish translations of McIntosh's letters. He sent these dispatches by the next available courier, requesting instructions and additional funds to augment defenses in the province. While he awaited a reply, he received additional intelligence from Justo Lopez in Fernandina, saying the French were fomenting plans to launch a naval strike against Amelia Island. Then, in late August, Don Luis de Onís, the Spanish Regency's minister plenipotentiary to the United States at Philadelphia, confirmed Craig's speculations about an American plot. The Madison administration had designs on East Florida, Onís said, and was pressuring Congress to approve a military campaign. Even the British were alarmed, seeing a seizure of East Florida as the first step in a larger war directed against them.[18]

All of this provided Estrada with plenty on which to brood. French threats to Florida he dismissed as exaggerated. However, a war between England and the United States would certainly place the province at risk. For the English, East Florida would provide an inviting tactical foothold on the Georgia frontier and a base of operations for the British fleet.

Americans, on the other hand, had even more to gain by seizing the colony. In one blow, they could eliminate foreign threats to the southern states, open up thousands of square miles of Indian lands to pioneers, and obtain a valuable staging ground for any future endeavors to capture Cuba or portions of Mexico. It was a tempting prospect, the governor realized. But would Americans risk war to achieve it?

The Diplomacy of Deception

Throughout the summer of 1811, the murky world of George Mathews's intrigue continued to befuddle both its creator and its intended victims. The general's pleas for support were being totally ignored in East Florida. Of the five men identified as potential collaborators—McIntosh, Arredondo, Fleming, Atkinson, and Lopez—one had already betrayed his confidences to the Spanish, and the other four showed no interest in resuming their communications. Their brush with conspiracy and treason had emanated from events in 1810—a year when Spanish fortunes were at a low ebb, blighted by French victories on the Iberian Peninsula, the Hidalgo Revolt in Mexico, and the West Florida revolution at Baton Rouge. Fear that the Spanish empire might utterly collapse had made annexation to the United States an acceptable course of action. In 1811, however, conditions were different. The province was prosperous, Spain's Regency government was holding its own against the French, and there was talk of establishing a new constitution, one that would limit the power of the monarchy and give the colonies representation in the Cortes. Under these circumstances, the vast majority of East Florida's settlers had no desire to trade a Spanish affiliation for an American one.[1]

It was at this point that John Houston McIntosh made a surprising decision that would haunt him the rest of his life—the decision to turn rebel. At thirty-eight years of age, he, like other affluent men in the colony, seemed too far set in his ways and too secure in his fortune to risk his neck on insurrection. A shrewd and hard-nosed businessman, narrow eyed and sharp featured, he was indulgent to his wife and children, cold to outsiders, and always attentive to his finances. He had immigrated into East Florida in 1803 specifically to expand his commercial enterprises and, in addition to his Georgia estate (the Refuge, on the Satilla River), was the proprietor of two plantations in Florida—the old McQueen holdings on

Fort George Island and the Ortega estate on the west bank of the St. Johns River. With his beautiful young wife, Eliza Bayard McIntosh, and their growing family, he had completed all the requirements stipulated for new settlers by Spanish law, taking up permanent residence in East Florida, swearing an oath of fealty to the Crown, and making improvements to his lands, which were worked by a labor force of nearly 250 slaves.[2]

For eight years he had led a prosperous and quiet life in the colony, keeping largely to himself. In contrast to his earlier public career in Georgia, where he held some minor positions, he remained isolated and aloof from East Florida's social and political life, neither asking for nor receiving any local office. Even in the militia musters he was listed merely as "soldier." George J. F. Clarke, a resident of considerable reputation, once characterized McIntosh succinctly as "not influential with the government or people."[3]

His loyalty, however, seemed well attested. Though his grandfather and cousin had both fought against the Spanish in the past, prominent men in East Florida regarded him as a man who worked for Spanish interests, Craig and Arredondo both calling him a friend of the Crown. Governor Estrada had written him a complimentary note, thanking him for the intelligence he had provided on Mathews.[4]

Despite all of this, McIntosh was far more heavily involved in subterfuge than appeared on the surface. He had spoken at length with General Mathews in 1810 about the prospects for a revolt in East Florida and, more important, about the prospects for American aid. "I had been for some time living occasionally in the town of St. Marys, and [the General] frequently visited and assured me 'that his government would be friendly to any party in Florida, who would depose the Spanish authorities, and declare themselves as desirous of becoming citizens of the United States.'" At first, McIntosh was pessimistic about the chances for success. "I told the General, that there would be great difficulties attending an attempt to bring about a revolt . . . that the population was much spread, and composed of men of various political opinions." The merchant and planting classes, the lumber interests and cattle ranchers, he had explained, viewed their enterprises in the province as highly profitable and satisfactory. "In a pecuniary point of view, they were for the most part doing well." McIntosh himself took in $56,000 in 1810 from his cotton and lumber exports. Growing rich on the proceeds from his Georgia and Florida estates, he had ultimately dismissed the idea of a revolt as premature and ill advised.[5]

Other factors had also influenced him. Rebels, he had told Mathews, could not hope to capture St. Augustine and its fort. Such an endeavor required an army. It was therefore only when Mathews returned to the border as a U.S. commissioner in 1811 that McIntosh began to take a more sober view of things. Sometime after July, he ceased to report on Mathews's activities and began to listen to what the general had to offer. Hence, having at first colluded with the general and then betrayed him, the planter switched allegiances once again. He was impressed with Mathews's assertions that President Madison supported plans for a revolt. Besides this, "a report existed . . . that the British intended to occupy the country. The fair prospect held out . . . of placing our property and persons under the protection of the United States, and the dangers of anarchy . . . among ourselves, were circumstances so weighty that it was impossible to resist the impulse that they gave." Nor did McIntosh have any qualms with secret conspiracies or with using force to liberate East Florida from Spanish rule. "Finally, after frequent interviews with Gen. Mathews, I engaged to excite an insurrection." As he would later explain: "They who think that the most just and honorable government is not sometimes obliged to make use of very objectionable means to accomplish a good and a great end, know little of governments, and less of mankind."[6]

As McIntosh contemplated treason, Spain and England were focusing their attention on affairs in the southern borderlands. The Spanish and British governments were by no means reconciled to President Madison's use of troops to assert American authority in Baton Rouge or to the various menaces and pressures being brought to bear on the rest of Spanish West Florida. From Baltimore, Juan Bautista Bernaben sent a harshly worded letter to Secretary of State Monroe. Spain, he reminded Monroe, freely opened its ports to American trade. Spain had spilled blood to assist American independence. Spain was the first nation that had recognized the new republic. Yet "Spain notwithstanding this conduct is treated by the United States as an Enemy, her frontiers in this quarter of the World are invaded without any other reason or motive . . . saving the convenience of the acquisition."[7]

American relations with England were running equally hot, aggravated by an incident in mid-1811 when an American frigate opened fire on a British vessel. On May 16, 1811, Commodore John Rodgers, commanding the U.S.S. *President*, was hunting for two British warships, the H.M.S. *Melampus* and the H.M.S. *Guerrière*, that had been interfering with shipping off the coast of New York. In poor visibility, determined to intercept them, he ran down an unidentified vessel that he believed was the *Guerrière* and engaged it. Instead of the *Guerrière*, however, the other ship turned out to be a small, twenty-gun British corvette, *Little Belt*—no match at all for the larger and more heavily armed *President*. After forty-five minutes of battle, the *Little Belt* limped away with thirty-two men dead.[8]

The naval combat reawakened war fever on both sides of the Atlantic and shattered efforts to defuse tensions. A new British consul had just been dispatched to Washington with orders to settle outstanding griev-ances about the *Chesapeake* affair of 1807. Augustus John Foster, an af-fable and experienced diplomat, disembarked on American soil only to find history repeating itself, this time with his own government angrily demanding redress for an insult to its flag. The fury stirred up over what was rapidly becoming known as the *Little Belt* incident destroyed Foster's rather fragile chances for opening a new dialogue on British-American relations. Although Secretary of State Monroe hoped to reach an accord over rights of neutral trade, the two men had barely begun to discuss matters before they were quarreling over the confrontation between the *President* and the *Little Belt*, Foster maintaining that Commodore Rodgers had fired without provocation, and Monroe rejoining that the presence of British warships in American waters was provocation enough.

As Monroe would later confide to friends, it was during these weeks of fruitless bickering that he finally abandoned his belief that England and the United States could settle their differences amicably. "War, dreadful as the alternative is, could not do us more injury than the present state of things, and would certainly be more honorable to the nation, and gratify-ing to the publick feelings," he told an English acquaintance. Foster, for his part, grew disenchanted almost as quickly. He spent much of his time vis-iting his Federalist friends in the U.S. Congress, and his correspondence often reflected their contemptuous assessments of the president and his advisers. It became clear, as well, that the Foreign Office had given him no powers to negotiate with respect to the Orders in Council—the nub of American grievances with English policies at sea—and so President Madi-son and Secretary of State Monroe soon dismissed him as merely a token envoy.[9]

It was in this atmosphere, with tempers already frayed, that Foster car-ried out his instructions to broach the subject of American military actions in Baton Rouge, which he characterized as a transgression against Spanish rights and "the ungenerous and unprovoked seizure of a foreign colony." When his written comments drew only a chilly silence from Monroe, he repeated the charge in a personal interview. The American government, he said, was taking advantage of Spain's weakness "to despoil her of a distant and unprotected province, to which the [United States] seemed to have at best a very doubtful claim."[10]

Monroe showed no hesitancy to answer and did so coldly and unapologetically. If the United States exerted itself to calm a revolt at Baton Rouge—a revolt the Spaniards had shown they were incapable of suppressing—what cause did Spain have for complaint? he asked Foster. And why should the matter concern the British? His remarks surprised and flustered the consul. Taken off-guard, Foster accidentally blurted out questions he had meant to keep in reserve. He asked Monroe directly "if the United States was not acting on letters from Governor Folch to surrender the territory [of West Florida] and if Congress had not also approved a move against East Florida, in case any traitors were to be found base enough to sell the territory of their lawful sovereign?" Monroe made denial after denial, watching in apparent amusement as Foster tried to sound him out about government policy. After the meeting, the angry British consul shot off a report to his own government requesting permission to threaten the Madison administration directly "if they presume to invade East Florida." "They seem to imagine," he told Lord Wellesley, "that we will bear any usage from them rather than go to war."[11]

Monroe, for his part, began to believe there was little point in concealing American aims in the Floridas. Certain that neither Spain nor Britain had the stomach to oppose American expansion by force of arms, he cared little about their protests and found the president to be of the same mind. In August, at an informal soiree that Foster attended, the secretary of state spoke with complete candor, saying the administration would act as it thought best to protect the national interest. As Foster reported, both Monroe and Secretary of War Eustis stated frankly "(though of course neither of them [did so] officially) that when they shall seize on East Florida, it will be done at once, and the reasons given afterwards."[12]

Not long after this, Foster and Don Luis de Onís received confirmation that General Mathews was down on the borders of Spanish East Florida trying to incite the settlers to rebel. The time had come, they decided, to lodge a joint protest. On September 5, Onís sent a terse letter to Monroe on behalf of the Spanish Regency, repeating almost word for word the information obtained from John Houston McIntosh and William Craig in East Florida. General Mathews, he said, was endeavoring to foment an insurrection there, under an appointment from the president, and was offering a series of inducements to encourage revolt. The Madison administration, at the very least, ought to disavow Mathews's purposes, suspend his activities, and arrest him. Otherwise, "the Spanish Nation at large will view this conduct with the utmost indignation, and cannot be accountable for the fatal consequences that must inevitably result."[13]

On the same day, Foster submitted a protest from the British government and again sent a letter to his own superiors recommending that they take steps to intervene, for "there cannot be any doubt that [the United States] if they can find an opportunity and any sort of plea for such an attempt will endeavor to occupy East Florida."[14]

These protests, like their predecessors, brought no reaction from the Madison administration. Indeed, the president and the secretary of state were not even present in Washington to receive them. Taking the customary summer hiatus, the two men had departed the humidity and discomforts of the capital to rejoin their families at their Virginia estates. There, during the course of August, the president, Monroe, and Thomas Jefferson spent the evenings debating foreign policy at Madison's Montpelier estate. All three men agreed that negotiations with the English on neutral trade were proving fruitless and that war now seemed the only option. They had come to the conclusion that the English were too arrogant to compromise and too sure of themselves to worry about fighting their former colonies. Thinking ahead to the next session of Congress, Madison began to outline how and when a declaration of war ought to be made. This, rather than concerns about the Floridas, occupied all of his attention.[15]

The issue of East Florida therefore remained in abeyance until Monroe and Foster faced each other once again on October 30. By this time, the secretary of state had thought the matter through and had his response in hand. Referring to the old issue of Spain's privateer attacks on American shipping in the 1790s, he told Foster "in very plain language that he had been of the opinion that the United States should have seized on that country [East Florida] long ago and held it as a pledge for the payment of the debt due by Spain for illegal captures." He expanded on this in his official reply to Onís and Foster. Passing over all their questions regarding

Mathews, whom he did not even mention, he set forth numerous justifications for American rights to East Florida. The territory of East Florida must serve as a surety against payment of the old privateer claims, he told Onís, for compensation had been too long in coming. In the meantime, the United States was entitled to hold the province as a form of collateral. To Foster, he was even more brusque. What was England's interest in East Florida? he asked. Perhaps the British hoped to gain the territory for themselves. If so, Foster and Onís should know that the U.S. government would never allow it. "Situated as East Florida is, cut off from the other possessions of Spain, and surrounded in a great measure by the territory of the United States," he said, "and having also an important bearing on our commerce, no other power could think of taking possession of it, with other than hostile views."[16]

Thus, the die was cast. With all chance for secrecy spoiled, Monroe took the bold step of admitting American desires for East Florida. He stopped short, however, of acknowledging any government complicity in Mathews's activities. Having sent out this answer, Monroe published his entire correspondence with Foster in the *National Intelligencer*, the official mouthpiece for the administration. American policy thus became a matter of record: he had advanced a plausible claim against East Florida, one that had been used in the past, and had obliquely warned the British not to interfere.[17]

Monroe's indifference to possible war with Spain was consistent with his long-established predilections regarding American foreign policy. Though he was hardly a warmonger, he had, ever since the 1790s, advocated taking an aggressive stance with the European powers. His recommendations found little favor during the administrations of Washington, Adams, and Jefferson. By 1811, though, under Madison, they were finally beginning to carry weight.[18]

Far from being alarmed by his exposure as a secret government agent, Mathews was elated. The revelation, which appeared in the text of Foster's letters as published in the newspapers, solved numerous problems for him. For one thing, he had been growing increasingly uneasy at the Madison administration's failure to issue instructions or advice regarding the progress of his mission. Although he wrote to Monroe on a regular basis, describing in detail his undertakings, he never received replies. He assumed the secretary of state was behaving discreetly, leaving no written evidence of the administration's affiliation with the scheme. Still, Mathews and those at St. Marys who had so far agreed to follow him wanted verification of official support before they assumed any more risks. In mid-October, after recuperating from another bout of fever, he traveled to Oglethorpe County, Georgia, where he met with Senator William Crawford and voiced his concerns. The likelihood of war with England made East Florida indispensable to the American cause, he said. The government ought to expedite his requests for weapons and munitions. He would also need the support of some gunboats on the St. Marys River. "The present aggregate force at St. Augustine," he said, "consists of 150 men, ninety of whom only are effective and fit for active duty, and even these would be easily subdued, as they are destitute of good ammunition, and their fort . . . at present is in a weak and decayed state."[19]

Crawford promised to communicate all of the general's information and requests to the president and the Senate as soon as he returned to Washington. Mollified, Mathews returned south. Yet when Congress opened its sessions and the president gave his annual address, no word came back concerning East Florida, neither instructions to proceed nor an order to desist.[20]

The publication of the Foster-Monroe correspondence in November therefore proved to be the watershed in Mathews's arrangements. Here was a clear defense of American claims to East Florida, entered into the public record with Monroe's own approval. Mathews freely displayed the published transcripts of the letters when they appeared in the southern press. This, he told his colleagues, was ample proof that the government would approve their actions and support their efforts.[21]

The correspondence also went a long way toward convincing John Houston McIntosh to support Mathews. McIntosh studied the Foster-Monroe letters and carefully reread Mathews's commission and the act of Congress setting forth the circumstances that would allow President Madison to use armed force in East Florida. His previous misgivings began to slip away. He felt no pangs of conscience about betraying his oath to the Spanish Crown, he said, because King Ferdinand was a prisoner of the Bonapartes, and he owed no loyalty to either a French dictator or a captive king. He also did not wish to see the British intervene in the colony. Other inducements may have enlivened his enthusiasm for the cause. It seems likely that Mathews dangled the office of territorial governor before McIntosh's eyes. At least, he later suggested such an appointment in a letter to Secretary of State Monroe. In addition, he offered personal assurances to the planter, promising that no harm would come to him or the other rebels and that private monies paid out to support the revolt would be fully reimbursed by the American government. Listening to these persuasions, McIntosh found it "impossible to resist the impulse they gave."[22]

Having forged an alliance, Mathews and McIntosh rapidly hammered down the details for an attack against Spanish forces and government officials. They dubbed their revolutionary party as the "Patriots." Once the rebels gained control of East Florida, McIntosh would transform this group into the "constituted local authorities" of Mathews's instructions, and the ad hoc Patriot government could then cede the colony to the United States. From a military standpoint, the Patriots' first priority would be to capture St. Augustine and its fortifications. This had to be done quickly and by surprise, McIntosh insisted, before the Spanish could rally their militia or obtain reinforcements from Cuba. Mathews, in complete agreement with this strategy, was already encompassing methods to achieve it.[23]

By the end of 1811, then, Mathews had his rebel leader and his band of revolutionary supporters. From Georgia, he could count on the help of James Seagrove and Archibald Clark. John Boog, McIntosh's overseer at the Refuge plantation, also figured in the plot. From East Florida and the border, Mathews secured the support of Gabriel Priest, who ran McIntosh's lumber-cutting business on the St. Marys River, and several other residents of the border area—George Cook, William Kelly, Benjamin Sands, and Francis Young. Lodowick Ashley was appointed as chief field officer for the Patriots, a role for which he was well suited. With little formal schooling and a hard road in life, he shared the harsh values of southern frontiersmen: desire for land, fear of marauding Indians and blacks, and distrust of the Spaniards. He was also descended from one of Camden County's founding families, and the rank and file, drawn predominantly from Georgia, would regard him as one of its own.[24]

To supplement the rebels, Mathews was counting on support from American military officers on the border. Commodore Hugh Campbell seemed willing to assist, and Lieutenant Colonel Thomas Adam Smith, in charge of the cantonment at Point Peter, was under orders from the secretary of war to cooperate. Smith's junior officers—Captain Abraham Massias, Captain Joseph Woodruff, and Lieutenant Daniel Appling of the riflemen and Captain Fiedler Ridgeway and Lieutenant Elias Stallings of the infantry—also endorsed a move against East Florida. To these, Mathews could add the support of Major General John Floyd of the Georgia militia and Colonel Ralph Isaacs, his personal secretary.

All in all, it was a tight-knit group of men. Floyd, McIntosh, and the Ashleys were all major landowners on Georgia's Satilla River. They were well acquainted with one another and, like Seagrove and Clark, had close ties to Camden County. Only Major Jacint Laval continued to be excluded from Mathews's otherwise cozy circle. Although Mathews and Laval still shared quarters near Point Peter, they rarely conversed. Mathews saw no reason to cultivate Laval's friendship or to seek his cooperation in the mission, as he expected the major to obey whatever orders Lieutenant Colonel Smith issued.[25]

Having squared away the Patriot leadership, Mathews resumed efforts to amass the foot soldiers for his revolution. He promised fifty acres of land to any volunteer who would take up arms for the cause. This offer was aimed chiefly at disenfranchised laborers and artisans who were eager for property. Other guarantees sought to reassure Spanish subjects about their future as American citizens. The United States, Mathews said, would uphold freedom of religion and honor all existing rights, deeds, and titles. It would pay the outstanding debts of the Spanish government, confirm civil authorities in their jobs and salaries, and allow Spanish troops to join the American army, with full arrears of pay, or to freely depart for the nearest Spanish post. This was the message he wanted to spread among East Florida's settlers.

While Mathews and McIntosh forged ahead with their plot, Governor Estrada was playing a desperate game of catch-up. He had not been idle during the summer and fall, but he faced great difficulties in overcoming the normal bureaucratic inertia of imperial administration. Justo Lopez continued to keep watch on the border area, submitting brief reports on the movements of Mathews and on an American military buildup.[26]

The amount of news Estrada received was not matched by any aid. On September 12, 1811, the marquis de Someruelos wrote from Havana, telling Estrada to reject any British offers to garrison Florida. Direct aid from the British would only provoke the Americans and give them a pretext for an assault. He also sent along 12,000 pesos, a ridiculously insufficient sum of money to upgrade defenses and buy munitions. Estrada, angry at this meager help, wrote directly to the viceroy of Mexico, demanding to know why the monies owed to East Florida as part of its royal subsidy were never forthcoming. All he obtained in response was a reprimand from Someruelos, warning him not to jump the chain of command again. Aid was being readied on Cuba, Someruelos said. Estrada would just have to wait.[27]

Even Florida's temperamental climate seemed determined to afflict Estrada with misfortunes. In mid-October, a late-season hurricane struck the coast, wrecking ships and causing considerable damage at St. Augustine. The governor set about organizing a relief effort, assisted by donations from the merchants at Fernandina.[28]

Then, in November, Lopez forwarded copies of the Foster-Monroe correspondence. It confirmed Estrada in his belief that the Madison administration intended to take East Florida by force. Almost at the same time, Onís wrote from Philadelphia to report on the president's annual address to Congress. Madison, he said, had reiterated the secretary of state's statements about a claim to East Florida, underscoring it as an official government policy. A month later, on December 30, Estrada heard that Commodore Hugh Campbell had relocated from Charleston, South Carolina, to St. Marys. There were already four gunboats stationed on the St. Marys River, and Campbell had arrived on a brigantine that off-loaded eighteen 18-pound cannons, 500 cartouches of gunpowder, and ball for muskets.[29]

General Mathews Meets a Crisis

After the commotions of 1811, the year 1812 opened along the Georgia-Florida border on a scene of deceptive calm. All the attention of the American government was turned to other concerns. In the domestic arena, Congress began debates on admitting Louisiana into the Union as a new state. Responding quickly, Americans at Baton Rouge, West Florida, petitioned vociferously to be excluded from the arrangement. They wanted instead to pursue statehood by attaching themselves to the Mississippi Territory. In foreign affairs, the government occupied itself with national grievances against England. The president was already preparing the nation for the onset of war, something he expected to come in the spring. "The prospect of the death of George III still keeps up a hope of avoiding war," Thomas Jefferson suggested in a letter, to which Madison replied, "All that we see from G[reat] B[ritain] indicates an adherence to her mad policy towards the U.S." Disputes about the Spanish Floridas had disappeared from everyone's agenda. "I hear no more said on the subject," Foster told the British government in January. The governing council of the Spanish Regency, distracted by another major offensive against Napoleon in Spain and by disturbing reports of separatist and independence movements in the colonies, seemed relieved to have escaped confrontation with the United States.[1]

In Georgia, too, attention was focused on other events. In the midst of news about comets and earthquakes, about the discovery of an ancient elephant skeleton, about itch cures and miracle powders, readers of the *Georgia Journal* and the *Georgia Argus* were following the deliberations of Congress and the progress of war in Europe. Affairs in West Florida continued to arouse minor interest. Portions of the congressional record pertaining to the annexation of Baton Rouge had finally leaked to the press, and the *Journal* was publishing Governor Vicente Folch's letters, in which he had offered to cede Spanish West Florida to the United States. There was no mention of East Florida, however.[2]

George Mathews's affairs were in the doldrums. He still lacked the recruits he needed to risk a decisive move against St. Augustine. Practically no one in East Florida had signed on with him. "So far was Mathews from succeeding in alluring the inhabitants," George J. F. Clarke later recalled, "that he had said if five Floridians, or even three, would join him, he could then go on." The Spaniards watched and waited for dangers that seemed to have evaporated. As late as March 16, 1812, Governor Estrada reported to his superiors that "everything appeared tranquil." Just two days later, he was opposing an invasion.[3]

For Juan José de Estrada, the year 1812 would be a test of loyalty and endurance. For the people of northeast Florida and Camden County, Georgia, it would be a year that plunged them from peace and prosperity into chaos and alarums. For General George Mathews, it would be the last year of his life. It would also be the year in which he snatched victory from the jaws of defeat, only to find a greater defeat awaiting him.

The implications of the Foster-Monroe correspondence were all too clear to Governor Estrada. Perusing the published version of the letters, he came to the conclusion that the United States would follow its previous course of action in West Florida and back up its claim to East Florida with a show of force. Counteracting an American threat was easier said then done, however. The troop strength of the Third Infantry Battalion of Cuba, stationed in St. Augustine, consisted of four companies of grenadiers, each company with approximately forty men plus the officers, and an artillery company to operate the guns of the Castillo and various redoubts. In the district between the St. Marys and St. Johns Rivers, Estrada could muster two companies of militia. For each of these, he had appointed three officers, two sergeants, and four corporals, with command over sixty men in the first company and fifty-two in the second. Amelia Island provided a third company. In addition, there were four companies in St. Augustine—those for the Españoles, or Spanish; the Mahoneses, or Minorcans; the other white residents; and the free blacks—amounting to perhaps 240 men at arms. All told, then, Estrada commanded about 600 regular troops and citizen-soldiers, weighted heavily toward untrained men in the militias, who made up three-fifths of the total. This force, ultimately protected by the defenses of St. Augustine, was sufficient to hold off a border raid or a minor fracas with Georgia. An organized attack by American regulars, should one materialize, was another matter.[4]

Hopes for reinforcements also remained bleak. In Cuba, Don Sebastián Kindelán y O'Regan, an experienced and tenacious veteran of the Spanish frontiers, was preparing to bring additional men and supplies. In other respects, Estrada had little reason for optimism. The Regency Council, in response to the threats menacing East and West Florida, had issued instructions to the governors of the border colonies. Far from adopting a bellicose posture, the council declared that Spain could not risk military confrontation with the United States. It cautioned governors not to provoke a conflict. Instead, they should employ a strategy of diplomatic overtures and prevarications in order to buy time. The United States, noted the council, operated under a weak federal system of government, constrained by its Constitution, and divided up into political factions. By "vigilance, firmness, and policy," the governors could drain American resolve and give anti-Madison blocs in Congress a chance to frustrate the president's plans regarding the Floridas. In the meantime, the Regency would confer with the British government to formulate counterstrokes against the American menace.[5]

As an analysis of American politics, these instructions were an astute piece of reasoning. As a guarantee of succor, they were useless. Loosely translated, they told Estrada that Spain could provide no help, that he was on his own, and that he was expected to hold off the forces of the United States for as long as possible while evading direct hostilities. If he failed, everyone would know where to place the blame.

In any case, Lieutenant Colonel Estrada was no diplomat. He knew of only one way to discourage an American attack and that was by organizing East Florida's limited military resources along the best possible lines of resistance. In this, he listened closely to the advice and recommendations of William Craig. The Irish planter remained skeptical that the United States would invade. Yet even without the threat of invasion, the border area remained an easy target for raiders from Georgia. The Georgians, he told Estrada, were the real danger and the one that most worried the planting interests in the colony.

"In the state of Georgia there are a number of Individuals who entertain a rancorous hatred for this Government," noted Craig. "[They] have heretofore expressed their determination of breaking into the settlements with the avowed object of plunder at the first favorable opportunity." Planters on the west side of the St. Johns River, anxious about potential hostilities with Georgia, were fortifying their houses with enclosures to keep their slaves from being carried off. Given these circumstances, Craig recommended several courses of action "calculated to guard against the threatened Evil." The rural militias, he said, were "totally incompetent to any prompt or sudden movement." If only ten men from Georgia crossed the border, they could seize slaves and horses and be gone again before the militia assembled to pursue them. Only a third of the men in the militia had horses fit for service, and even these men could not organize themselves quickly enough to chase down and capture intruders. Hence, with the governor's permission, Craig wanted to establish a squad of dragoons, or picket of observation, consisting of twenty or thirty men, each with a dependable mount. They would muster and train every month and stand ready to answer an alarm at an hour's notice. This troop could rapidly pursue small raiding parties and report on the movements of a larger force. Once they commenced patrols, robbers and "banditti" in Georgia might think twice before trying to infiltrate the province.

Craig's second recommendation was to augment the guard for the public ferry station at the Cowford by reinforcing the nearby outpost of Fort San Nicolás. The ferry was the most vulnerable spot in the northern district and one that any group of invaders would strive to secure. If they gained control of the ferry, they would have much of the province at their mercy. "Forty armed men might be crossed over and, after plundering the Inhabitants, again re-cross the River. . . . By destroying the flat[boat], not a Horse could be got over to pursue after them. . . . One white man should always attend the flat and should never approach the opposite Bank nigher than Gun shot untill [sic] well assured who the persons were that wanted to cross over, and on no account cross any person at night." At the first hint of an invasion, Craig said, the guards at the ferry must move all the boats to the south bank of the river and secure or destroy them, thus denying enemies an easy means of advance.[6]

In effect, then, Craig was advising Estrada to follow a strategy similar to the one that had been employed during the troubles of 1794 and 1795. Spanish forces should make their stand at the St. Johns River rather than at the border with Georgia. If the dragoons could not oppose a superior force, they could at least delay it and gather intelligence on its intentions.

Estrada adopted all of these measures, and a month later, on February 16, he received word that the picket of observation had formed. Twenty-six men volunteered their services. Craig appointed Reuben Hogans, a sublieutenant in the Second Militia Company of the St. Johns District, as their commander. Hogans was known for his skill as a rider and for his familiarity with the roads and bridle paths.[7]

These minor adjustments in colonial defenses comprised almost all of Estrada's preparations in lieu of reinforcements from Cuba. He directed the rest of his efforts toward refurbishing the fortifications around St. Augustine and to gathering as much information as possible on American activities along the border. At the beginning of February, Justo Lopez reported from Fernandina that the American Congress was issuing a call for 25,000 men at arms, to be held in readiness at the northern and southern frontiers of the Republic in case of war with England. A large number of men who seemed to be volunteers and mercenaries were gathering on the Georgia border, and the American navy had fifteen gunboats patrolling the St. Marys River. "The gunboats maintain such vigilance," he told Estrada, "that no vessel can enter or leave the port [of Fernandina] without them being aware of it."[8]

Not far away, Mathews was striving with equal diligence to raise a fighting force capable of attacking St. Augustine. In late January, he asked Secretary of State Monroe for a company of artillery and one of infantry. He was disheartened at the news that Sebastián Kindelán y O'Regan was slated to take over as the new governor of East Florida. Mathews was well acquainted with Kindelán. He had negotiated with him in the aftermath of the 1795 rebellion to restore peace on the Florida-Georgia border. The incoming governor was not the man Mathews wanted to confront on the field of battle. "He is a gentleman of handsome talents and military experience," said Mathews. Kindelán would come with troops and supplies and would probably have the wherewithal to repair and strengthen the Castillo de San Marcos that guarded the capital, "which will render the fort difficult to be taken."[9]

Meanwhile, the ranks of the Patriots remained thin, so Mathews visited Governor Mitchell in Georgia to enlist support. Mitchell expressed immediate interest in Mathews's mission and ordered Major General

John Floyd of the state militia to hold militia troops in readiness along the border. Naval preparations were also under way. Commodore Hugh Campbell had added three more gunboats to his forces on the St. Marys River and was requesting seaworthy ships to patrol the coast. Midshipmen were in short supply, he warned his superiors, and a few of the marines were so deplorably dressed and equipped that he hesitated to send them on duty. On February 28, Mathews paid a visit on Campbell to make a formal request for aid in any action against East Florida. The secretary of the navy had not given Campbell specific instructions in this matter, so he carefully reviewed Mathews's commission and his other papers. Not entirely sure of his ground, he nonetheless promised to help in an assault on St. Augustine.[10]

By early March 1812, more than a year after first implementing his plans to overthrow Spanish authority in East Florida, General George Mathews had at last managed to attach 125 men to the Patriot cause. Most of this group consisted of volunteers out of Georgia—"waggoners and carters," Augustus J. Foster later scoffed—with a small command staff of Spanish subjects, of whom McIntosh and Lodowick Ashley were the principals.[11]

The first target of the Patriots would be St. Augustine, and Mathews knew it was not a target to be trifled with. Although Estrada reportedly had only a hundred soldiers fit for duty there, the town's defense lines, artillery redoubts, and great stone fort posed ample challenges to any assault. With this in mind, sometime in the first week of March, around Thursday the fifth or Friday the sixth, the general called a council of war at Major Jacint Laval's quarters. Dr. James Hall was among those he summoned. Ever since his expulsion from East Florida in 1810 on charges of conspiring against the government, Hall had been living in Colerain, at the plantation of his close friend James Seagrove, and hence knew from hearsay and indirect participation a great deal about Mathews's intrigues. Major Laval was also present at the meeting, and, though the record is unclear, Colonel Isaacs and Captains Woodruff, Massias, and Ridgeway were probably also in attendance. Lieutenant Colonel Smith was, at this time, away from Point Peter.

Mathews told his fellow officers about his plans for arming John Houston McIntosh and the Patriots and taking St. Augustine. He took down a map of the town from a shelf and spread it out for Hall's examination, indicating a sector at the northwest corner of the streets and blocks where it seemed possible to outflank the defense works (see fig. 3). "Almost the first question General Mathews asked me," Hall recalled,

> was whether it was a correct map of St. Augustine, and after looking over it some time I told him it was. He then asked me if I knew whether the marsh coming up toward the Spanish burying ground and next to the St. Sebastian River was hard ground. I told him it was. He then asked me if I could Pilot a detachment of armed men through there in a dark night, into the Spanish burying ground, and from thence by the Tan Yard into the main street by the Government House in St. Augustine. I told him I could do so on the darkest night. Major Laval then said, "General, if you will give me the orders, I will take St. Augustine in a very short time." "No," says the General, "I cannot do that, but we *will* have it in a very short time."[12]

After dining with Mathews, Hall stayed up late conversing with Daniel Appling and Elias Stallings, two of the camp's lieutenants, and received more information. These two officers would be providing McIntosh and the Patriots with additional men for their attack. They could not do this as officers in the U.S. Army, they said, for the army had no orders to initiate hostilities against Spanish territory. Instead, "they and seventy-five men, well armed, were to desert the service of the United States and to be piloted to the [mouth of the] St. Johns River, and from thence up the [river] to the head of Pablo Creek, where they were to land and join McIntosh about seven miles from St. Augustine—after which I was to Pilot them to St. Augustine and take possession of the city. They were then to be pardoned and restored to their former service and rank."[13]

Down to the last, then, Mathews intended to abide by the spirit, rather than the letter, of his instructions. His commission gave him no authority to use regular troops to overthrow Governor Estrada. But the Patriots needed fighting men, and he therefore intended to "borrow" soldiers from the army. The next morning, as Hall was leaving camp, Mathews told him to wait at Colerain and to expect a summons in about ten days.[14]

Although Hall did not realize it, he had witnessed the first scene in a breach between Mathews and Major Laval that would destroy the entire strategy for capturing St. Augustine and would also wreak havoc with the chain of command at Point Peter. The major was increasingly distressed about Mathews's secretive activities. Ordinarily, the task of cooperating with Mathews or assisting his mission would have fallen on Lieutenant Colonel Smith. In March, though, with Smith away on business, Laval had command of the cantonment.

During the previous months, in the cramped confines of their shared cottage, Laval had become reluctantly and unhappily privy to much of Mathews's scheming and plotting. He did not like what he heard. The two men had drastically different codes of personal honor. Mathews, fiercely patriotic, held the values he had acquired as a self-made frontiersman, an officer in the Continental Army, and the governor of an expanding state. He had no qualms about seizing East Florida by force, nor did he shrink from using devious methods to achieve his goal. It was all in a day's work for the good of his country.

Laval, on the other hand, a fellow veteran of 1776, exhibited little sympathy for Mathews's ambitions. The general's intrigues, far from being noble, struck the major as dubious and mercenary. Personal prejudice also affected relations between the two men. Laval disliked Jews and often gave vent to anti-Semitic remarks, some of them aimed at his own junior officer, Captain Abraham Massias, or at Mathews's aide, Colonel Ralph Isaacs. These men, in return, loathed the major and sided against him in all things pertaining to Mathews's plans.[15]

The makings of a full-blown showdown between Laval and Mathews started quite innocuously on Tuesday, March 10, when Mathews made an off-hand request for munitions. "Major," said Mathews as he was leaving their quarters, "there is a bag of buck shot upon my mantel piece. I wish it made into cartridges." Then he added, "I expect we will have a [scrap] soon." Laval looked up questioningly but nodded his assent.[16]

Later that same day, a spy in the employ of McIntosh and Mathews sent a worrisome note, warning them to expedite their plans: "I conceive myself imperiously bound by the feelings of a Gentleman, the ties of friendship, and by gratitude, to advise you, not to delay even *for one day* the accomplishment of your object."[17]

Troubled by the note, Mathews redoubled his efforts to rush a force down to St. Augustine during the next week. The Spanish were usually least vigilant on Sundays, a day given to rest or revelry, so Mathews scheduled the Patriot attack to start between 1 and 2 A.M. on the morning of Monday, March 16. Under cover of darkness, his recruits would surprise the sentries and soldiers on guard at the town's defense works.[18]

This narrow timetable gave Mathews only five days to finalize his plans. Early on Wednesday, March 11, he therefore wrote to Commodore Campbell to secure arms. "I have to request you to furnish fifty muskets and bayonet, fifty pistols, and an equal number of swords," he said, "for the whole of which, I will, by my receipt, make myself accountable. You will also please to permit Mr. McIntosh at this time to select out of the swords and pistols, such, and as many as he may deem expedient."[19]

He then went back to see Major Laval. According to the major, Mathews told him to put a ball in the cartridges with the buck shot. "I then asked [Mathews] who would account for these balls? Were they to be used for the garrison, or elsewhere? Never mind, answered the General; if they go out of your hands, a receipt will be given you, and that is all you want. I promised to have them done."[20]

Mathews's additional request sparked Laval's curiosity, and the major began to make inquiries about who Mathews was arming and why. When he discovered that Mathews was equipping the Patriots and not regular troops, Laval immediately countermanded the order. The first of many confrontations with Mathews soon took place.

Laval's action astonished Mathews. He marched back to Point Peter, taking along General Floyd as a witness. They caught up with Laval in the quarters of Captain Massias. There, the three officers—Mathews, Floyd, and Massias—argued heatedly with their recalcitrant comrade. Unwilling to release any powder or shot, Laval could barely contain himself when Mathews blurted out his next request. "Major," said the general, "will you order a detachment of 140 men from your command to cross the St. Marys?" Laval, hearing Mathews ask for more than half of his contingent, replied with a single, furious word: "No!"

The general glared at him. Stiffly he reminded Laval of the chain of command. As the officer currently in charge at Point Peter, the major was under orders from his superiors to render Mathews assistance and to occupy, hold, and defend East Florida, as it was offered by the local authorities.

Laval, however, was beginning to put things together—Mathews's refusal to march American troops openly against St. Augustine, his assurance that the capital would nonetheless soon be in American hands, his evasiveness about use of the shot and powder, and finally this request, for Laval to turn over his men to an independent command. Facing down his three fellow officers, he stoutly refused to aid them in a sneak attack on the Spanish, "having no instruction," he said, "that extended to this measure."[21]

Now it was Mathews's turn to become angry, and he ranted against the major's effrontery and defiance. The quarrel grew so ugly that Laval bellowed at Mathews to leave the cantonment of Point Peter and never come back. Mathews could hardly believe it. He stalked off the base in a sullen temper and went to report on Laval's behavior to his friends Seagrove and Clark in St. Marys. There, later in the afternoon, he was discussing the situation with John Houston McIntosh and Commodore Campbell when he caught sight of Laval walking up the street.[22]

Heedless of making a public display, Mathews descended on the major in a fury, mouthing threats and imprecations, blaming Laval in advance for the losses he would suffer if he attempted to take St. Augustine without sufficient force, and "violently exclaiming about his power *to force [Laval] to march*." Faced with such an outburst, Laval backed down and agreed to send a detachment of fifty soldiers—but only fifty—to lend support to the Patriots.[23]

This compromise seemed to placate Mathews. The truce between the two men did not last long, however. Upon returning to Point Peter, Laval discovered the rest of the general's plan. Lieutenants Appling and Stallings were assigned to head the detachment sent to St. Augustine, and they intended to go not as officers and soldiers of the U.S. Army but as deserters, out of uniform, and with no official insignia.

At this news, Laval became so incensed that no further remonstrance or bullying from Mathews would move him. He recanted his promise of aid and took steps to ensure that no one left Point Peter. His soldiers were not going to abandon their posts and join what amounted to a paramilitary force while he commanded the camp.[24]

Late that night, yet another quarrel broke out. Ralph Isaacs and Lieutenant Appling appeared in Laval's quarters bearing a letter from Mathews. The men found Laval in a state of great agitation, fully dressed in his neat blue-and-white uniform and wearing his sword. His agitation only increased when he read what Mathews had to say. The Patriots, the constituted local authority of East Florida, would soon be in possession of Rose's Bluff, on the Spanish side of the St. Marys River, Mathews wrote. They wished to surrender this territory to the United States. Mathews, as authorized in his commission, was therefore ordering Laval to send a detachment of fifty troops to Rose's Bluff and secure it. He expected Laval to comply at ten o'clock the next morning.

After scanning the letter, Laval asked Isaacs if Rose's Bluff was a military post. It was, said Isaacs. It was a base for the Patriots. Laval took a moment to reflect before answering. "I will not march any detachment from Point Peter. If ever I order a force into East Florida, it will be my entire command, and then only after giving the contractor timely notice, so he can furnish provisions."

Isaacs then pressed him. Was he refusing to allow his men to cross the river, either as volunteers or as U.S. soldiers? Yes, replied Laval. Would he put that decision in writing? No, said Laval, not until he had time to compose his thoughts and to consider matters. As Isaacs continued to needle him, Laval grew excited and began to gesticulate. "There's no need, sir, to work yourself into a passion," commented Isaacs. "I am not angry," returned the major, "I'll consider writing to General Mathews later." With that, Isaacs and Appling left, saying they would return in the morning for an answer.[25]

The unseemly debacle between Mathews and Laval spiraled further out of control the next day, Thursday, March 12, as the deadline for an attack continued to near. By this time, Mathews's mercurial temper was fully aroused against the major. He decided to lodge charges against Laval and, if necessary, remove him from command. Indeed, over the next few days, Mathews exhibited a streak of ruthlessness that shocked those around him. At his request, Captain Massias and Lieutenants Appling and Stallings drew up an indictment against Laval, charging him with conduct unbecoming an officer and neglect of duty. In particular, he was charged with showing contempt and disrespect toward General Floyd, Captain Massias, and General Mathews. Thirteen witnesses signed the indictment.[26]

Laval, meanwhile, had doubled the sentries at Point Peter to prevent his junior officers from absenting themselves and joining the Patriots. Soon he had fifty soldiers, or a quarter of his command, standing guard on the others. Then he confined Appling and Stallings to their quarters. Discipline at the cantonment was rapidly breaking down.[27]

When Dr. Hall returned to Point Peter that Thursday, he found everyone's nerves on edge. At Isaacs's bidding, he had come from Colerain late Wednesday night, bringing a change of clothes and expecting to guide the Patriots into St. Augustine. Instead, he "found General Mathews and Major Laval in a high dispute, so much so that I was afraid there would be some fighting going on." A short time later, Hall encountered Mathews in St. Marys. The general told him to stick close, and "notwithstanding the obstructions Major Laval is throwing in my way, you shall be walking in St. Augustine's streets in 10 days."[28]

In the midst of all this uproar, the Patriots themselves were busily preparing to take the field. John Houston McIntosh rose early on March 12, probably before sunrise, dashed off a letter to Congressman George Troup, and then bid farewell to Eliza and the children. "Before you can receive this," he told Troup,

the Province of East Florida will have undergone a Revolution and probably be in the quiet possession of the officers of the government of the United States. Our Plan is all arranged to take the Fort of St. Augustine and the governor on Monday night next [March 16] by surprise and in half an hour I set off to head a few chosen Friends to execute this commission. The thing has been for some months in a gestation between General Mathews and myself, but I am afraid never would have been accomplished had not the General been governed by the Spirit of his Instructions and the declared wishes of his Country. My Horses are at the Door and my Wife and Children are all around me in tears. Adieu, My Dear Sir, and let me assure you that my last breath would declare that I have ever valued the rights and Privileges of a Citizen of the United States as the greatest blessing on Earth and that I would rather leave my Children in the enjoyment of them than of the mines of Peru.[29]

Confident of an easy success, McIntosh, Lodowick Ashley, and George Cook departed St. Marys and crossed into East Florida to take up their respective commands at Rose's Bluff (see fig. 2). Their chosen site was a modest table of land on the far bank of Bells River, just below the point where it forked from the St. Marys River. For the time being, this makeshift camp of sixty to seventy men was the headquarters of the Patriots of East Florida. Only eight or nine men at the camp were actual residents of Spanish East Florida, the rest being recruits out of Georgia.

At Ashley's house, just west of Rose's Bluff, the Patriot leadership composed a manifesto, voicing the grievances that vindicated their break with the Spanish Crown and urging the people of East Florida to join their cause. They promised lands to those who would become adherents and threatened banishment and confiscation of property against those who would not. Mathews also attended the meeting, warning that if plans against St. Augustine went amiss, they would have to capture and hold other parts of the province.

The next day, Friday, March 13, McIntosh read the Patriot manifesto to the men at Rose's Bluff. Shortly afterward, he was appointed as a commissioner for the rebel government, and Lodowick Ashley became military commander.[30]

General Mathews waited impatiently all Friday to hear from Major Laval. On Saturday, March 14, around 8 A.M., having received no communication, he sent the major another message, asking three questions: Would Laval use his forces to occupy territory ceded by the constituted local authorities of East Florida? Would he occupy the province if it were threatened by a foreign power? And would he comply with his solemn promise, given before McIntosh and Campbell in St. Marys, to send fifty soldiers to assist the Patriot cause? Later in the day, Mathews followed up with another note, stating that the Patriots possessed Rose's Bluff and that Laval should secure the position as he had promised.[31]

By nightfall, the general still had no answer. With his anger mounting, he wrote a long letter to Secretary of State Monroe, transmitting the charges drawn up against Laval and asking Monroe to relieve Laval of command.

> Major Laval positively refuses to support me with the troops under his command. He is so confident in his own abilities and military knowledge that it is not possible to make him believe he can do wrong, and for my part I have no confidence in him, and think his conduct here since he had the command has been a compound of error and folly. And even had his conduct as an officer been correct, his being a Frenchman was an objection to his being in command in the vicinity of East Florida. From this you will perceive the necessity of his being superceded in his command if anything is to be [done] for the good of our country here and the safety of Florida.

Mathews contrasted Laval's intransigence with the freely given assistance he had received from Commodore Campbell and the junior officers at Point Peter. "In fact," he said, "many of the officers have offered to resign and act as volunteers." Had it not been for Laval, East Florida would already be independent of Spain. "I have pursued the intent and meaning of my instructions with as sound a discretion as my judgment was capable of. I have the approbation fully of my conscience, that beneficial effects will result to our country from my pursuing the path of my duty [that] my judgment indicated."

"The time has arriv'd when *something must be done*," Mathews concluded, "and if ever you expect the Floridas, send on immediately the companies of Artillery and Infantry I requested in my former letter. Recall Major Laval, and if the president has confidence in me, leave *no discretion* in the officer commanding in complying with my requests and orders. . . . I wish also that 250 muskets with bayonets and cartridge boxes, and 250 horsemen swords may be sent on as speedily as possible."[32]

Even as Mathews wrote this letter, the Spanish forces at Fernandina were slowly awakening to their peril. On March 13, word had come that John Houston McIntosh was removing all his slaves across the border into Georgia. Then, on March 14, Charles Clarke, the brother of the surveyor general, traveled to St. Marys on business and rushed back to Amelia Island bursting with news about men gathering under arms to invade East Florida.[33]

Mathews also sensed that events were reaching a denouement. Shortly after completing his note to Monroe, he finally received Laval's response to his requests. The major remained obdurate—he would not allow troops to enlist with the Patriots. He would comply with his instructions from the secretary of war, he said, and occupy any part of the Floridas east of the Perdido River and south of Georgia and the Mississippi Territory, provided an agreement had been reached with the constituted local authorities to surrender the places in question. However, troops from Point Peter would not assist in the taking of those places. As for occupying Florida to challenge a foreign power, he had no specific orders on the matter. Under no circumstances would he allow fifty men, or any other number, to act as volunteers for Mathews.[34]

These words were a bitter setback. To make matters worse, Commodore Campbell also rejected a request for aid. Earlier in the day, Mathews had asked the Commodore to send a gunboat to the mouth of the St. Johns River and another one up the river to the ferry station at the Cowford. These two boats were needed to drive off Spanish patrols and allow the Patriots free passage along the waterway on their advance to St. Augustine. Campbell balked at the idea. He was still somewhat shaken by the violent exchange of words he had witnessed between Mathews and Laval in the public streets of St. Marys a few days before, and he knew that Laval was refusing to cooperate with the general. Under these circumstances, he said, he could not send navy gunboats so far into Spanish territory.[35]

With these two refusals, Mathews's hopes of capturing St. Augustine collapsed. The capital was beyond his reach, and he knew it. He could not risk a small, untrained force and a year's worth of preparations on an assault requiring disciplined troops. But he could no longer retrace his steps. With his Patriots assembled inside East Florida and the streets of St. Marys ringing with gossip, he had to act. He was losing the momentum of the moment and would soon relinquish the element of surprise so crucial to success. And so the wily old general played his last trick. If he could not seize the capital of East Florida and its formidable fort, then he would change his target. The Patriots would attack the undefended town of Fernandina.

Fig. 1. *A new map of part of the United States of North America containing the Carolinas and Georgia,* by John Cary, 1811. Cary's map shows Spanish East and West Florida as they existed on the eve of the War of 1812. The United States had already occupied the Baton Rouge District in West Florida. The boundaries of Georgia as depicted here were out of date. Georgia, in 1811, ended at the Chattahoochee River, the area to the west being the Mississippi Territory. Courtesy of the Florida Historical Map Collection, P. K. Yonge Library of Florida History.

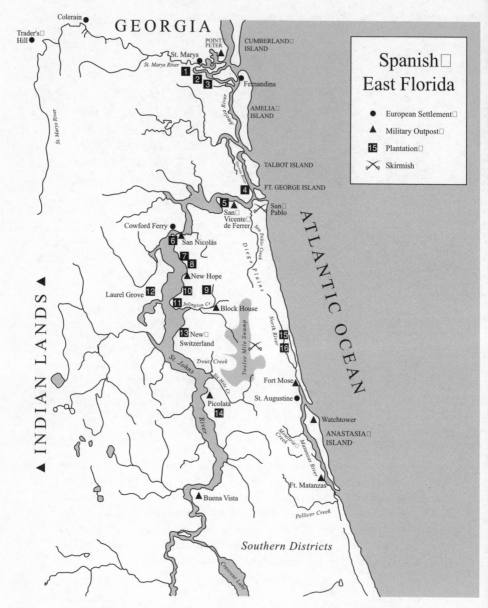

Fig. 2. A portion of Spanish East Florida, with the border towns of Georgia. Graphics by Office of Academic Technologies, University of Florida. (1) Lodowick Ashley/Rose's Bluff; (2) Eleazer Waterman/Waterman's Bluff; (3) John Lowe's plantation; (4) William Fitzpatrick/Cedar Point; (5) Atkinson family's Shipyard and Precher plantations; (6) William Craig's plantation; (7) Farquhar Bethune/New Ross; (8) Francisco Roman Sánchez/San José; (9) Gunby and Follis sawmill; (10) Prudence Plummer's plantation; (11) Anna Kingsley/Hartley/Mandarin area; (12) Zephaniah Kingsley/Laurel Grove; (13) Francis Philip Fatio Jr./New Switzerland; (14) Edward Wanton/Chancery; (15) Maestre plantation; (16) Cosifacio plantation.

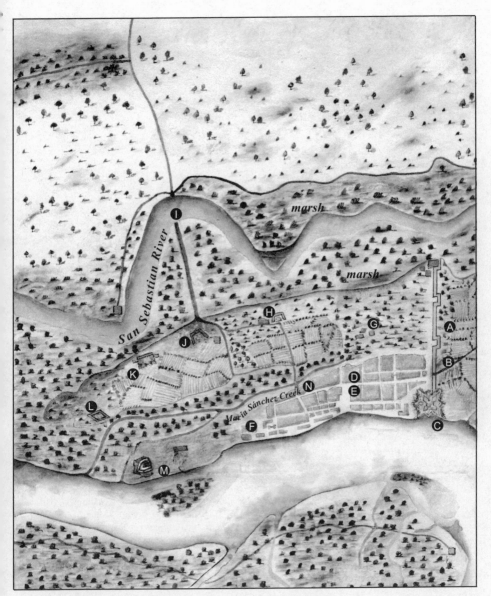

Fig. 3. The Plan of the Bay of San Agustin de la Florida (detail). This map is probably similar to the one that George Mathews used to plan his attack. He intended his force to go down the San Sebastian River, around the Cubo Line, and into town through the area labeled "G" to seize the governor's house at "D." Courtesy of the Jay I. Kislak Foundation. (A) Cubo Line; (B) town gate; (C) Castillo de San Marcos; (D) governor's house; (E) parish church; (F) barracks; (G) old redoubt (abandoned?); (H) redoubt (Primera Fería); (I) Solana's Ferry Station; (J) redoubt (Paso de Solana); (K) redoubt (Segunda Fería); (L) redoubt; (M) redoubt; (N) bridge across María Sánchez Creek.

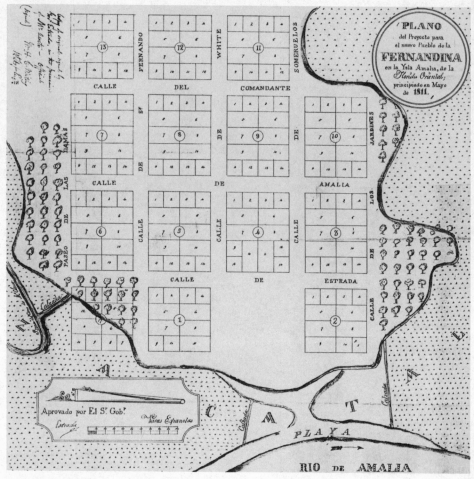

Fig. 4. Plano del Proyecto para el Nuevo Pueblo de la Fernandina, by George J. F. Clarke, 1811. Map Division, National Archives.

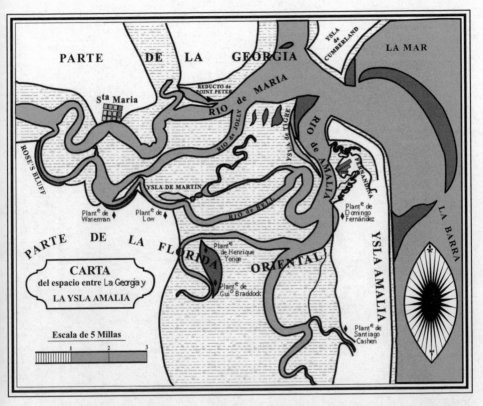

Fig. 5. Carta del espacio entre La Georgia y la Ysla Amalia, by George J. F. Clarke, 1811, Section 47, showing the relative locations of Fernandina, St. Marys, Point Peter, Lowe's plantation, and Waterman's plantation. East Florida Papers, Library of Congress. Graphics by Office of Academic Technologies, University of Florida.

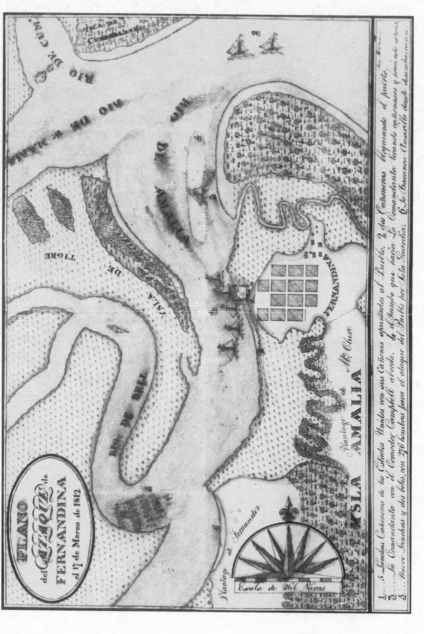

Fig. 6. Plano del ataque de Fernandina en la Ysla Amelia, by George J. F. Clarke, 1812, Legajo 1789, Papeles de Cuba. The gunboats are depicted in their final positions, March 17, 1812. The Patriots are shown in oared transports on Bells River. Courtesy of the Archivo General de Indias, Seville.

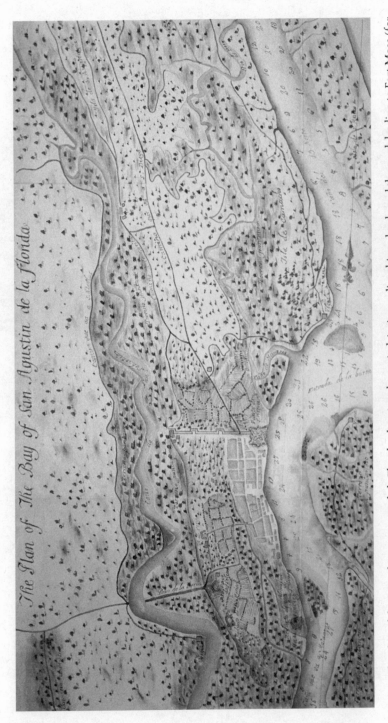

Fig. 7. The Plan of the Bay of San Agustin de la Florida, showing the capital, its immediate hinterlands, and the creek leading to Fort Mose (*far right*). Courtesy of the Jay I. Kislak Foundation.

Fig. 8. The Castillo de San Marcos, southwest bastion. Photograph by the author.

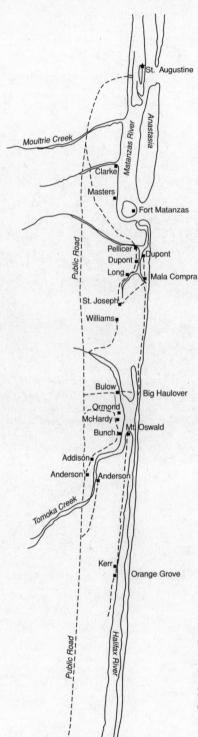

Fig. 9. The roads and plantations south of
St. Augustine and around Fort Matanzas.
Redrawn from a map in the Claim of the
Estate of Samuel Williams, No. 76,042, RG
217/347, National Archives. Graphics by
Office of Academic Technologies.

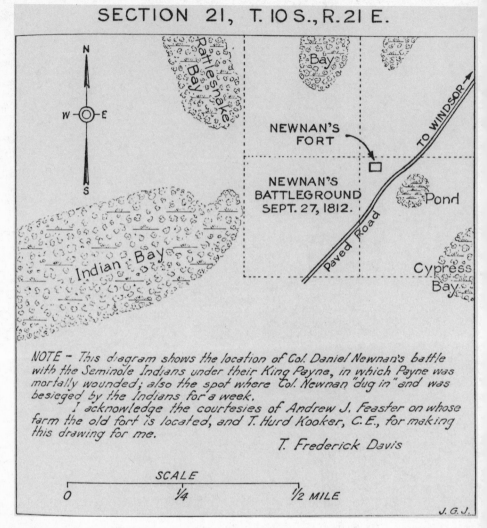

SECTION 21, T. 10 S., R. 21 E.

N
W — E
S

Rattlesnake Bay

Bay

NEWNAN'S FORT

TO WINDSOR

NEWNAN'S BATTLEGROUND SEPT. 27, 1812.

Indian Bay

Paved Road

Pond

Cypress Bay

NOTE — This diagram shows the location of Col. Daniel Newnan's battle with the Seminole Indians under their King Payne, in which Payne was mortally wounded; also the spot where Col. Newnan "dug in" and was besieged by the Indians for a week.
    I acknowledge the courtesies of Andrew J. Feaster on whose farm the old fort is located, and T. Hurd Kooker, C.E., for making this drawing for me.
                                    T. Frederick Davis

SCALE
0   1/4   1/2 MILE

J. G. J.

Fig. 10. Newnan's battlefield. Courtesy of the *Florida Historical Quarterly* and Florida Historical Society.

7

The Fall of Fernandina

Twenty-four-year-old Pedro Pons first caught sight of the Patriot flag as he was piloting his sloop through the maze of braided waterways that meandered off the St. Marys River six miles west of Amelia Island. His vessel was homeward bound, loaded with flour and provisions for the Pons bakery in Fernandina and had just entered a loop in the channel of Bells River, hard by the plantation of John Lowe, when a flicker of movement on shore attracted Pons's attention. There, fluttering on a pole in a field of knee-high corn shoots, was an odd-looking banner. It was white, he recalled, and "on said White Flag was a Latin inscription, *Agilis populis, Lex suprema*, with a human form."[1]

This was one of three different descriptions of the Patriot flag as seen and recorded by eyewitnesses. According to one story, the flag was fashioned by George Mathews's secretary, Ralph Isaacs, and bore the image of a soldier at the charge with fixed bayonet. Originally the motto, taken from Cicero, read *Salus populi, Lex suprema* (a corruption of *salus publica, suprema lex est*, the good of the people is the supreme law). However, when certain wags in the border area commented that revolution and war were hardly conducive to anyone's "good," the motto was changed to *Vox populi, Lex suprema* (the voice of the people, the supreme law). Most settlers who wrote accounts of the Patriot War cited this banner as the one that the Patriots unfurled. Yet another statement about the flag came from John Abernathy, a midshipman on board American gunboat No. 165. His commanding officer, Captain Robert Cutchins, set him the task of producing a standard for the Patriots, and he sewed one together from the scraps of cloth he had on hand. "Its device," he said, "was a man presenting a musket—there was no motto."[2]

No authentic Patriot flag has survived to the present to tell us which description is correct. In all likelihood, there were several versions of the flag. One thing is certain, though. In March 1812, the Patriots (and their flag) came to Spanish East Florida. The people of East Florida were afforded many additional opportunities to see the invading forces firsthand. During the next eighteen months, companies of Patriots would rampage all over the province, from the St. Marys River to the Halifax and Indian Rivers, gathering supplies, raiding plantations, and penning up the settlers behind the trenches and redoubts of St. Augustine. And the first people to witness this bitter future were the residents of Fernandina.

The commercial enclave of Fernandina was bustling with its usual activity in March 1812, its harbor full of ships from Europe and the United States, its streets ringing with the raucous laughter of sailors, the high-pitched calls of the hawkers, and the echoing noise of hammers and saws as carpenters and slaves raised new wharves, warehouses, and domiciles. The 600 or so inhabitants were still shifting and realigning their homes and yard lots in accordance with the newly prescribed regulations for the arrangement of streets and blocks. From the bluff of their town site, elevated about fifteen feet above the Amelia River, they had a panoramic vista of the low-lying islands, waterways, and mainland to the west. The cotton fields were newly planted, the corn stalks just a month along, the orange groves still ripe with winter fruit, the season wet and promising abundant rain.

Fernandina was the commercial and social apex of the landed gentry of Amelia Island. It was a roughly U-shaped settlement, located on the western, or landward, side of the island, with its open end abutting the Amelia River. The plaza, or parade ground, occupied the interior of the town's U, and the residential lots formed the letter. Its principal streets were named for local and national Spanish figures. Calle de Estrada ran along the west side of the plaza, and the other main streets—Amalia, Comandante, San Fernando (after the patron saint of the king), White, and Someruelos (after the former governor and the captain general)—formed a small grid of about a dozen blocks. At the south end, just before the land descended steeply into marsh, was the Calle de Los Jardines (Avenue of the Gardens) and on the northern side was the Paseo de las Damas (Ladies' Walk). All Spanish towns of consequence boasted a paseo—a kind of boulevard for strolling—but Las Damas bore a more licentious reputation as a street with brothels. Another unseemly characteristic of the town could be found on virtually any street—scurrying rats from off the nearby ships (see fig. 4).[3]

The most prominent residences and places of business clustered immediately around the plaza and the waterfront. Elsewhere, rich and poor
lived as neighbors. There were a few blocks owned almost entirely by individual families and a few that formed enclaves of free people of color,
but for the most part the social classes were far less segmented than the
layout suggested. Cabins and large, elegant wooden homes, eateries, inns,
and stores stood everywhere in groups.

Don Justo Lopez, the military commandant, lived at the south end of
the plaza, facing the Calle de Los Jardines, in a house adjacent to George
Clarke's cotton warehouse and to the grounds of the town's unfinished
church. Around the corner, on the Calle de Estrada, Antonio Martínez ran
an eatery and Domingo Estacholy, one of the Minorcans in the province,
had a house and store. On the other side of Estrada was the inn of Francisco de Salas, then the merchant houses of Forbes and Company and of
Archibald and George Atkinson, another inn, the Pons brothers' bakery
and store, and properties belonging to Samuel Harrison, George Clarke,
and William Lawrence, all prominent traders or planters. The residences
of James Cashen, planter, and Henry Yonge, attorney and merchant, faced
the parish grounds from the north side of the plaza. Farther north were
wharfs for a variety of shipping firms. From the Amelia River, the large
buildings and houses on the plaza presented a facade of prosperity and
newfound wealth.

The other blocks were similarly divided into a mixture of residences
and commercial enterprises. Don Felipe Solana, son of a prominent landowner and cattle baron, lived just a few lots east of the plaza. In a central
block, Charles Clarke lived next to his free black consort, Anna Wiggins,
and across from Flora Clarke, the black consort of his brother. In surrounding blocks could be found the homes of Pedro Peso di Burgo, a
Minorcan; Farquhar Bethune, an English merchant; and Franics Philip
Fatio, another scion of the planting community, as well as those of Felipa
the Witch and Felicia the Laundress, free women of color. Along the
northern perimeter of Fernandina ran Egan's Creek, and here, apart from
the town, George J. F. Clarke, the surveyor general, had a house, a horse-
powered sawmill, extensive grounds to store lumber, and a flota of lighters to transport it.[4]

About half a mile north of town, the broad current of the St. Marys
River emptied into the Atlantic Ocean, and the mouth of this river sepa-
rated the northern tip of Amelia Island in Spanish East Florida from the

southern tip of Cumberland Island in Georgia (see fig. 5). Immediately inside the mouth of the St. Marys, two north-south waterways formed the Amelia River and Cumberland Sound. The Amelia River served as Fernandina's harbor, capacious enough for schooner, sloop, or frigate. On any given day, dozens of ships anchored in the protected waters southwest of the town. A bewildering labyrinth of rivers and streams parceled up the surrounding landscape into something resembling a minor Everglades, a jigsaw puzzle of islands, marshes, shallows, and shoals. West of Fernandina, the low contours of Tiger Island divided Bells River and the Jolly River. Farther south, the Amelia River joined the hooked loop of Lanceford Creek to form a peninsula off the mainland. Then it passed through a constricted channel appropriately called the Narrows and flowed into the Nassau River down at Talbot Island. The Amelia, Narrows, and Nassau formed a long inland water route, running behind East Florida's barrier islands, that connected the St. Marys and St. Johns Rivers.[5]

Wealth abounded at Fernandina and Amelia. Traders reaped enormous profits during the years of the American Embargo Act (1807–9). War—or at least war between England and France—was working out very much in favor of the local merchant classes. At the height of the embargo in 1809, Fernandina exported close to a million pounds of cotton to England (about 10 percent of English imports at the time) and more than half a million pounds of rice. Only a small proportion came directly from planters in East Florida, for cotton and rice were also transshipped through the port. The local lumber business was booming. Mills in the area were driven by a variety of methods, water power, animal power, and steam. Some 2 million linear feet of sawed timber were shipped in 1810 and 1811. Merchants so dreaded an outbreak of peace that they had petitioned Governor Estrada to alter the customs schedule for the town. Unless Estrada lowered the duties and converted Fernandina to a free port, they said, the end of the wartime economy would quickly see the town "return to its old sad state, years passing by without seeing the arrival of a single ship."[6]

While planters and lumbermen could count on a ready market for their goods in European markets, it was another trade—the African slave trade—that powered much of the town's wealth. Profits from slave auctions lay at the root of nearly every major fortune on Amelia Island. After the United States and England banned the slave trade from their possessions in 1808, Spanish East Florida became a major base of operations. John Fraser, Zephaniah Kingsley, Fernando de la Maza Arredondo, the elder, and the firm of Hibberson and Yonge accumulated vast wealth through it. Arredondo, in his second major slaving expedition to the African coast in 1811, acquired 343 slaves and sold them at a total profit of 21,848 pesos—about four times the annual salary of the governor and ten times what a settler could make, in total net worth, on a year's harvest of oranges and citrus. It was this potential for riches that quashed all qualms among the affluent about the trade and its human cost.[7]

*   *   *

Even as people in Fernandina attended to daily routines, all hell was breaking loose just a few miles away in Georgia. The rift between Mathews and Laval at Point Peter had widened into a chasm, one that was destroying military discipline at the cantonment at Point Peter and breeding mutinous talk. Laval no longer trusted Captains Massias and Woodruff and the tensions among the officers were communicating themselves to the rank and file. The major felt compelled to stand guard duty at Point Peter and remained on watch throughout Sunday, March 15, to make sure none of his men deserted to the Patriots.[8]

When rumors of this stir reached Fernandina, they were not taken seriously. "We had repeated information that an attack, aided by the naval and military forces of the United States, was intended on us," George Clarke later told a friend, "but you know how often such reports have blown over unregarded." The first piece of definite news arrived on Saturday, March 14. Two settlers, Samuel Russell and Hugh Stellings, who resided along the St. Marys River near Reed's Bluff, sent word that troops were coming across from Georgia and gathering at Lodowick Ashley's house, which stood between their estates and Fernandina. Besides that, John Houston McIntosh was transferring his slaves to Camden County, Georgia, because, the writers said, "there was likely to be a Rupture between this country and the U.S." Ill at ease at this news, Lieutenant Justo Lopez sent for his brother-in-law, Don Felipe Solana.[9]

The Solanas were a powerful and influential family in East Florida. Felipe's father, old Don Manuel, had fought at the Battle of Pensacola, Spain's most significant victory during the American Revolution. Like all the Solanas, Felipe was a horse lover and an excellent rider, accustomed to spending the entire day in the saddle. He ran the northern portion of his family's cattle-raising concerns, supporting his wife, Catalina, and their four boys by supplying fresh meat to Fernandina and its complement of foreign sailors. In 1812, he had some 200 head of cattle on pasture along Bells River, a few miles west of Fernandina, tended by a slave and a free man of color. On Saturday, when Lopez summoned him, Felipe was busily supervising construction of his new house in town and had just finished putting up the frame.

The commandant greeted him with somber news. McIntosh, he said, was up to something in St. Marys. Someone had to warn Governor Estrada that the Americans might be advancing into the province. Felipe immediately volunteered to carry messages south. Well acquainted with the route to the capital, he only needed a mount. His own black mare and his two other horses were stabled at Lowe's plantation, across the Amelia River, handy to the cattle ranges. So he borrowed a horse from George Clarke, accepted Lopez's loan of a bridle and saddle, and rode off, vowing to cover the full fifty-five miles to St. Augustine by nightfall. He had no way of knowing, as he galloped away, that a year and a half would pass before he saw Fernandina again.[10]

Only a few hours later, Charles Clark brought word that men were arming themselves at St. Marys. Then, at 9 P.M. Saturday came a message that a large contingent of Americans, with John Houston McIntosh in their midst, was encamped at Rose's Bluff in Spanish territory. Anxiety spread across Fernandina, and a fretful citizenry spent the rest of the night patrolling the town, weapons at the ready.[11]

On Sunday, March 15, the Patriots advanced to Lowe's plantation, located on the south bank of Bells River six miles west of Fernandina (see figs. 2 and 5). John Lowe, a long-time resident of East Florida, had one of the last landholdings between Rose's Bluff and the town. He had sent his son, Bartley, over to the bluff to investigate what was going on there and had written to Lopez, promising to send word. Now he found himself trapped in the middle of an insurrection.[12]

The Patriots immediately commandeered his homestead, which suited their needs to perfection. There were two houses, some eighty head of stock cattle (besides Felipe Solana's 200 head that ranged nearby), and sixty or so hogs. The coops and pens were full of poultry, and the stable contained both Lowe's and Solana's horses. Only the fields were disappointing, for they were newly planted in corn and potatoes and the crops were many months short of harvest (see fig. 5).[13]

Throughout the day, more recruits trickled in to this camp, checking in with the marshals before spreading out into the countryside. They took over Eleazar Waterman's lands, immediately west of Lowe's, and flushed other rural settlers from their homes, telling them to report to the rebel leadership. For the first time, people in East Florida heard the conditions the Patriots were offering: They could join the cause and enjoy protection of their property or they could resist, in which case they had to leave the province within three days, forfeiting all their lands and possessions.

Some local men, seeing the turn things were taking, picked the Patriots as likely winners and readily signed on. Others, afraid of losing their homes, agreed to join under compulsion. A few, though, wanted no part of insurrection and became camp followers, bundled along as prisoners, until their minds might change. Over and over again, in different words, residents made the same observation: "There was no such thing as neutrality, you had to join the invaders or leave the country." By the end of the day, the Patriot force, willing and unwilling, had nearly doubled in size, to about 150 men.[14]

William McCullough was among those pressed into service out of fear but with a latent sympathy for the Patriot cause. "I was with them by force and under threats, having no choice," he said many years later, "but I admit I thought at that time the American government would be better than the Spanish."[15]

Samuel Russell, on the other hand, recalled being taken captive. "I was taken prisoner by the Patriots before they went to Fernandina, and was carried with them—that is to say, they took my father and I went with him. I was then a boy. My father took me with him to bring my horse back. I was there when they took Fernandina."[16]

If anyone doubted the Patriots' sincerity regarding confiscation of property, they had only to observe the fortunes of John Lowe. The Patriots were short on all manner of supplies and made up the deficit at the planter's expense. They fed their horses on the young stalks of corn growing in his fields and stocked their camp messes by butchering his cattle, hogs, chickens, and tame pigeons. The smoke from their campfires could be seen for miles. When Lowe rebuked them for their treatment, they laughed cheerily, telling him "he might as well hold his tongue, and still his complaints, for they should take just what they pleased." Late in the day they seized upon several Spanish scouts who had ventured into the area to spy on them. The easy capture of these men put the camp in an even better mood. McIntosh, who was drafting a call for Fernandina's capitulation, decided to employ them as emissaries to Justo Lopez.[17]

The American gunboats also went into action that day, and it was their maneuvers that most alarmed residents at Fernandina. Two boats took station at the mouth of the Amelia River to impede passage to and from the sea. Seeing these signs of blockade, Justo Lopez decided to send a protest to the officials at St. Marys. Hastily composing a letter in Spanish, he gave it to George Atkinson, telling him to deliver it to the town magistrates, translate the contents into English, and then wait for an answer. The Atkinsons—Andrew, the head of the family, and George and Archibald, his sons—were confidants of Lopez's and had his complete trust. His message was short and to the point. "Having learned, with certainty, that a number of citizens of the United States have entered our province," he told his Georgia counterparts, "I hope you will have the goodness to inform me if the government of the United States have any part in or knowledge of said proceeding, or permit it that her citizens should be the instruments of a like nature contrary to all the treaties of amity existing between [us]."[18]

Awaiting a reply, Lopez summoned and consulted with the captains of Fernandina's militia and began to place the town in a state of defense. He had only nine regular soldiers at the post, so the task of repelling an attack fell on the shoulders of the inhabitants. At his request, James Cashen, captain of the Third Militia Company, and Joseph Hibberson, also of that company, armed the white residents, and George Clarke took command of the free black and *moreno* militia. The small wooden fort constructed to defend the town had long ago fallen into such a state of disrepair that it was useless. Its only artillery, two 6-pounders, lay half buried in the sand. Making the best of what they had, members of the militia unearthed these guns, cleaned them, and primed them with powder. Shop owners provided some lagrage shot, and townsfolk scavenged for scrap iron, nails, and other bits of metal to load into the muzzles.[19]

The only other defenses were natural. To the north and south of town, marshes prevented a direct overland assault. To the east and west, the town had no protection at all, and Lopez detailed work crews to begin digging trenches and raising barricades.[20]

In St. Marys, the magistrates refused to answer any of George Atkinson's queries about American transgressions into Spanish territory. Amused at his consternation, they politely bowed him out of their office, insisting that he seek out General Mathews, Major Laval, or Commodore Campbell. He left them in disgust and decided to tackle Hugh Campbell.[21]

He had just entered Campbell's lodgings and was still introducing himself when General Mathews and Ralph Isaacs unexpectedly burst into the apartment. They had come from the camp of the Patriots, they said, "where they had about two hundred fine fellows under arms." Campbell, surprised to hear them speak so freely in front of an emissary from East Florida, tried to interrupt them. Far from calming down, Mathews flew into a tirade. The sight of Atkinson seemed to mortify him, possibly because the Atkinsons had once expressed sympathy for his cause and were now working against him. In any case, he delivered a message intended to intimidate both them and Lieutenant Lopez. The Patriots were going to descend Bells River and force the surrender of Fernandina, he announced. They would have the assistance of five heavily armed American gunboats, and if the people of the town resisted, then "the gunboats would knock it down about their Ears."[22]

Campbell later confessed to being dumbstruck by this statement. Mathews had told him that the gunboats were chiefly needed "to prevent interferences from the crews of British vessels" that were anchored in Fernandina's harbor. Nothing had ever been said about firing on the town. But Mathews continued to bluster. Doubting that the inhabitants of Fernandina would put up a fight, he did not intend to give them the chance to think it over. He threw more hot words at Atkinson, until the planter finally excused himself and hurried back to Fernandina.[23]

Evening was by this time descending, and the harbor lamps of a dozen ships at anchor twinkled on the Amelia River as Justo Lopez listened to Atkinson's news. He knew now that some sort of assault was coming. If it included the gunboats, he might have no option but surrender. Even so, he could not leave the town completely unprotected. He issued orders to construct a breastwork across the western face of the plaza. By torchlight, men threw open the doors of George Clarke's cotton warehouse, and seventy or so members of the militia, assisted by slaves, began to wrestle out heavy bales of cotton. They arranged them into a rampart, three or four bales deep, facing the river to seal off the town square. Inside, on a wooden firing step, they mounted one of the 6-pounders they had resurrected earlier in the day.[24]

Other men worked through the night at the eastern end of the town, digging two trenches and raising another breastwork across the neck of land fronting McClure's Field, in case a party of Patriots landed and attempted to attack from the rear. Then, around 8 or 9 P.M., the Spanish sentries who had been taken prisoner by the Patriots arrived, bringing an ultimatum from John Houston McIntosh.[25] Lopez and his officers gathered by candlelight at his house to read it, the bilingual officials translating the words into Spanish for Lopez's benefit:

> The determination of the United States to take possession of our province by conquest have caused us to agree, who have interested ourselves in the advantages which we actually enjoy, to place it under their protection. Therefore we have already secured all the country between the St. Johns and St. Marys, and, had it not been for an unexpected circumstance, we would have had possession of St. Augustine and the fort on tomorrow night; so that you see how far I am engaged in this business, and that I cannot now retrocede.

> Be assured, sir, that in whatever light my present conduct may make me appear, that I yet have, and hope to possess always, the feelings of a gentleman and a man or honor; and permit me to say to you, that the attention which I have received from yourself and from my respectable friends, the old and young Arredondos, will always give you claims upon my services.

> Two gun boats, which is all we have required, will enter St. Johns today; and we are encamped, increasing like a snow ball; and we have sufficient forces to conquer all the province; we intend laying siege to Amelia Island, or, more properly, to invite you to unite with us in our glorious cause. And I assure you, that if our proposition is admitted by you without objections, none of our soldiers shall place their feet upon it; but otherwise, if you do not admit to it, no one can answer for the consequences.

Toward the end of the letter, McIntosh included a statement intended for the ears of any British captains with vessels in the harbor. As long as the town surrendered peacefully, he said, Fernandina would remain open to British trade during the next twelve months. Once Lopez surrendered, two gunboats would be stationed off the town "to preserve good order, and to prevent any difficulties, which is my greatest wish."[26]

The cordial remarks that McIntosh extended to Lopez and to the Arredondos probably concealed a hidden threat: he knew these men had conferred with George Mathews in 1810, and he was giving them a last chance to choose their loyalties. Otherwise, the letter brought Lopez only a modicum of cold comfort as he sifted through McIntosh's various statements. The forces across the water could not possibly have secured the entire northern district of East Florida, as the letter indicated. A plan to attack St. Augustine had also apparently failed and would buy Governor Estrada time to prepare. Having placed pickets at all the approaches to the town and having inspected the lines, Lopez sat up late writing out his dispatches to the governor. He put the Patriots' strength at 250 men, including fifty-nine Spanish subjects.[27]

In St. Marys, General Mathews was also up until the wee hours of the morning. He sought out Dr. Hall and told him "to cross over to Lowe's plantation . . . and tell General McIntosh and others of the Patriots to be ready at 10 o'clock the next day to go down Bells River with all the forces they had collected." Captain Woodruff of the riflemen handed the doctor a hunting musket. "You will know how to use it," he said. "It is well loaded with eighteen buckshot." Hall clambered into a boat and vanished across the river.[28]

On Monday, March 16, dawn broke over Fernandina to reveal an apparent act of sabotage. Lieutenant Lopez rose early, dressed, clutched his great coat around him, and went out among the long, westward-reaching shadows darkening the plaza. Walking past George Clarke's cotton warehouse, he saluted the sentries at the jerry-built breastwork, greeted Henry Yonge, another early riser, and gave orders to hoist the Spanish colors. Then he glanced at the 6-pound cannon mounted inside the cotton bales and stopped short, astonished.

Someone had spiked the gun, driving a long iron nail into the touch hole. Instantly, Lopez summoned the sergeant of the regular troops, *las tropas veteranas*, and demanded an explanation. Amid looks of dismay and suspicion, the sergeant replied that he had spiked the cannon himself.

Lopez and Yonge were incredulous. They ordered the militia to assemble. As men came stumbling to their stations, white and black alike, shuffling off the morning chill, Lopez exhibited the incapacitated gun. He was placing his sergeant under arrest when Domingo Estacholy stepped forward. It was his understanding, he said, that Lopez wanted the gun spiked, and he had ordered the sergeant to do it.

The commandant now found all eyes turned his way and had to think back to his instructions. His orders, he told Estacholy, were to place nails near the gun, as a precaution in case they had to spike it, and that was all. An abashed Estacholy responded that he had misunderstood. Exasperated,

Lopez told his men to remove the useless gun and to mount their sole remaining 6-pounder in its place. It was not a propitious beginning to the day. Later, when weapons began to disappear, Lopez again suspected that the Patriots had agents at work inside the town.[29]

The commandant read out the terms of McIntosh's ultimatum to the townspeople and summoned his militia officers to a council of war. James Cashen, Joseph Hibberson, and Andrew Atkinson attended him, representing the town militia. George Clarke spoke as captain for the men of color and Philip Yonge and José de la Maza Arredondo as other commanders. With the exception of Arredondo, the men were all of English, Irish, or Scottish descent and were closely tied to British commercial interests. Cashen was the second-richest man on the island and the local judge magistrate, as well as captain of Fernandina's militia. Joseph Hibberson and Henry and Philip Yonge were partners in commerce and figured prominently in trade with London, Portsmouth, and Liverpool. As for George J. F. Clarke, his position as surveyor general and sawmill owner made him known to everyone. More than anyone else, he urged Lopez to ignore the ultimatum and defend the town. His stance owed something to family background. George and his brother Charles were sons of an English family that had remained in St. Augustine after the general evacuation of English residents in 1784 at the close of the American Revolution. Their older brother, James, was serving as an officer in the Hibernian Regiment in Spain. Besides ties to England and Spain, the Clarkes also had affiliations with the local free black community of East Florida. Both George and Charles were raising families with free women of color. George had met his future consort when he was an apprentice at the Panton, Leslie Indian Trade Company and she was a company slave. He had bought and freed her. All the Clarke children were mulatto boys and girls. If the laws promulgated against free blacks in Georgia were introduced to Florida, his entire family might be disenfranchised, or worse.[30]

Now, standing before the junta, Clarke told Lopez he could count on fifty able-bodied whites and a like number of men of color to take up arms and should seek additional support from the sailors investing the harbor. With that force, and the loan of some artillery off British ships, they could beat back any bunch of "rag-a-muffins from the fag end of Georgia." The other militia officers concurred. Bolstered by this resolve, Lopez agreed to fight, and Captain Cashen and Lieutenant Andrew Atkinson addressed the militia on his behalf. The determination of the commanders, they said, was to defend the town to the last extreme.[31]

Even as the war council broke up, two partisans from the Patriot camp, George Cook and Seymour Pickett, landed a skiff near the plaza and came under guard to see Lopez. They brought two more letters, the first written by John Houston McIntosh and addressed to José de la Maza Arredondo, and the other, also in McIntosh's hand but signed by Lodowick Ashley, addressed to the commandant. Lopez listened intently as the letters were translated to him. They were nearly identical in content—another appeal for surrender. The rebels gave Lopez one hour in which to answer.

"The patriots of the district situated between the rivers St. Johns and St. Marys invite you to unite with them in their patriotic undertaking, or they summon you to surrender the town of Fernandina, and they will grant you the following conditions." Five stipulations or guarantees were then made. (1) The town garrison must march out and surrender its arms and receive its parole. (2) The Patriots would respect and protect all property. (3) Fernandina would be ceded, within twenty-four hours, to the government of the United States; however, its right to accept British commerce would continue for one year. (4) Rights to cut timber in the area would remain the same as under the Spanish government. (5) The town had to appoint commissioners and send them at once to Lowe's plantation to negotiate terms.

These conditions were only a slight elaboration on those offered the previous day. Before closing, though, McIntosh and Ashley had one final statement for Lieutenant Lopez: "We are informed, sir, that you have armed the Negroes on the island against us. We hope it may not be true. For if we find it to be so, you will recollect that we solemnly declare to give no quarter in the town of Fernandina. Finally, we supplicate you to reflect well upon this subject, that you may not bring upon yourselves, by fruitless opposition, those excesses of which yourselves, more than we, will be the authors. The United States gunboats will cooperate for the purpose of preventing [any] British vessels from acting hostilely against us."[32]

Asked for his response, Lopez refused to give one. He would send envoys to Lowe's when it suited him, he told Cook and Pickett, and then dismissed the two men from town.

This second ultimatum caused another debate among those gathered around Lopez. The commandant paid less attention to the terms and more to the final paragraphs threatening punitive reprisals if he employed black militia or sought aid from the British ships in the harbor. His officers, however, still counseled resistance. They decided to find out if McIntosh really had the backing he claimed. Joseph Hibberson and José de la Maza Arredondo offered to visit Major Laval at Point Peter and discover what the Americans intended to do about the impending attack on Fernandina. After that, they said, they would seek out Mathews, if possible, and also confront McIntosh and Ashley. George J. F. Clarke and George Atkinson decided to interview Commodore Campbell.[33]

It was 10 A.M. The townspeople remained in good spirits, apprehensive but somewhat encouraged by the fact that the Patriots had so far done nothing more than issue threats. Over the course of the morning, sailors arrived to reinforce the militia, two British captains donated barrels of gunpowder, and the defenders managed to collect fifty muskets, some pistols and swords, and about nine cannons. Then news spread that Lopez was dismissing the men of color who wished to serve under arms. The Patriot threat had shot home. Despite his need for soldiers, he would not provoke Ashley or the Georgians by mustering black troops. When the black militiamen heard his order to disarm, some looked up in disbelief. Others threw down their weapons in disgust and left the plaza.[34]

Meanwhile, Lopez's envoys proceeded with their respective missions. Clarke and Atkinson caught up with Commodore Campbell around 3 P.M. aboard gunboat No. 164 at the mouth of the Amelia River. The commodore, uneasy and embarrassed, evaded their inquiries about the intentions of the gunboats. Though he tried to mask his feelings, he was much perturbed about the direction things were taking. Just that morning he had quarreled with Mathews about his handling of the proposed uprising. "General," he had said, "the public way in which the Patriots are to be assisted by our gunboats will be cause for England to join her ally, Spain, in a declaration of war on the United States." Mathews was characteristically cavalier in his reply. "If that happens, it will serve a good purpose. We need a war with England. But don't worry about using the gunboats. I'll hold myself accountable for your acts."[35]

Bound by his pledge of support to Mathews, Campbell equivocated with Clarke and Atkinson. He was awaiting instructions, he said, and could make no statement. He finally got rid of them by promising to contact Lopez later in the day.[36]

José de la Maza Arredondo and Joseph Hibberson spent much of Monday in transit. Learning that Mathews was at Point Peter, they decided to go there first, to see him and to meet with Major Laval. Upon arriving at the cantonment, a captain escorted them before the general. Mathews was closemouthed and cagey with his visitors. When they offered him a letter from Lopez, addressed to the commander of the American forces, he declined it, saying such was not his title. He was a commissioner for the U.S. government, empowered to accept possession of East Florida if it should be offered. If they wanted to speak with him in that capacity, he would be glad to answer their questions.[37]

During this discussion, Major Laval walked in on the men. He refused to talk in front of Mathews and invited Hibberson and Arredondo to his quarters instead. The major was tired and haggard. For almost three days, he had deprived himself of rest, keeping guard over his junior officers, who seemed more and more ready to rebel against him. On top of this, he did not know how to respond to the emerging attack on Fernandina. He knew the action was illegal, but if he stood by and did nothing to assist it, he could be court-martialed for dereliction of duty. All of this came out in his meeting with the envoys. "He informed us," they reported, "that the conduct of General Mathews had placed him in the most extraordinary and disagreeable situation; that he was compelled to become a sentinel himself in his own camp; that [Mathews] had attempted to seduce his troops to leave him, but that we might rest tranquil on that point, because his troops would not move one step without him."[38]

Laval was candid, giving his opinion that "the conduct of General Mathews could never be approved by a great nation like the one he had the honor of serving." Then he composed a letter for Lopez. "You desire to know of me, sir, if the United States are to be considered as principals or auxiliaries? I have the greatest satisfaction in informing you that the United States are neither principals nor auxiliaries, and that I am not authorized to make any attack upon East Florida; and I have taken the firm resolution of not marching the troops of the United States, having no instructions to that effect."[39]

Arredondo and Hibberson subsequently returned to Mathews and found him with Ralph Isaacs and General Floyd. He left no doubts as to his mission. He was appointed, he said, to receive East Florida from the local authorities and to oppose any move by the British to take possession of it. And who were these local authorities with whom he was negotiating? asked Arredondo and Hibberson. McIntosh and Ashley, replied Mathews, and he brought forth a treaty already concluded with them. From this, Ralph Isaacs read out several clauses regarding the delivery of the province to the United States. Then Mathews mentioned British designs on East Florida. Referring to rumors from the previous year, he said the English intended to land black troops from Jamaica and that he would stop them by force.[40]

The two envoys listened impatiently to these excuses and justifications. "Before we departed," they told Lopez, "we assured General Mathews that *this was truly an American invasion*, that the greater part of the people armed against us were American citizens brought to our province by the offer which he had made to them . . . but that if he would withdraw his support from them for one week, we would obligate ourselves in your name that Amelia Island would surrender to him, if before the expiration of that time, we had not driven the Insurgents to the other side of the St. Marys River."[41]

Mathews made no reply to this, and they left him, deciding, as the day waned, to take their craft up the Jolly River and go to the Patriot camp at Lowe's plantation. They had seen two vessels near the bar of the St. Marys River and suspected that one of them was a newly arrived English warship. They therefore resolved to speak with the Patriots and delay any plans they had for an attack, in hopes of obtaining additional aid for the defense of Fernandina.[42]

It was ten o'clock at night—twelve hours since their departure from Fernandina—when they reached the rebel camp. Here another hostile interview occurred. Arredondo delivered a letter from Lopez to Colonel Ashley, in the presence of George Cook and John Houston McIntosh. But, he added contemptuously, the commandant would not enter into any treaty with them or deliver up the island to them. Accusations and threats were soon flying back and forth. Seeking only to unsettle the rebels in their schemes, the envoys struck a deal to return to the camp at 10 A.M. the next day for another meeting with General Mathews.[43]

It was nearing midnight when the two weary men returned to Fernandina. Lopez had heard nothing from Commodore Campbell. Somewhat encouraged by the news that Laval refused to support the Patriots, he assigned Philip Yonge and George Atkinson to see General Mathews the following morning at Lowe's.

At Point Peter, events once again continued into the midnight hours. No one in the camp ever seemed to sleep. After meeting with Clarke and Atkinson, Major Laval went in search of Dr. Hall and sounded him out on the subject of Mathews's treaty with the Patriot leaders. Did the doctor know John Houston McIntosh, Lodowick Ashley, and George Cook? Laval asked. Hall replied that he did. According to the doctor, the following conversation then took place: "[Laval] then asked me if I considered these men to be the constituted authorities of East Florida. I told him no. Who then do you consider to be the proper constituted authorities of East Florida? I told him that I considered the Spanish Governor and his council the lawful authorities. Major Laval then says to me: Hall, General Mathews says that McIntosh, Ashley, and Cook are the constituted authorities, but I take them to be three constituted d——d Rascals, and ought to be hung, by God!"[44]

A few hours later, just after the evening meal, Laval was strolling across the parade ground at Point Peter when Captain Massias accosted him. Their confrontation, the stormiest of the week, exploded in pent-up resentments:

"Stop!" [Massias] shouted at the major, "I want to see you. You've acted contrary to the wishes of our government. All the officers disapprove of your arbitrary conduct. Why don't you leave the post?"

"Captain Massias," replied the major, "report to your quarters and hold yourself for further orders."

"You bastard! You damn Frenchman!" shouted Massias. "If you leave this camp for fifteen minutes, I'll march the troops to East Florida and use the military stores and ammunition to . . ."

"You are under arrest!" cried Laval.[45]

Having placed Massias in custody, Laval retired momentarily to his own quarters and, still quaking with anger, composed charges against the captain. There was a knock at the door and a naval officer, Winslow Foster, came in with a request from Commodore Campbell for some arms. Laval signed the chit, then told Foster to relay a message to Campbell. Tell him, said Laval, "this is a damn rascally business, and get your neck out of the halter as soon as possible." Buckling on his sword and taking a pistol in each hand, Laval went out to his self-imposed sentry duty "to watch my men from being swindled away."[46]

Around midnight, there was yet another commotion at the base, and Laval learned that Lieutenant Colonel Thomas Adam Smith had returned. The stiff and hard-nosed military officer found his well-ordered camp in a state of utter confusion verging on mutiny. Three officers were under arrest, and there were charges and countercharges leveled against nearly all of them.[47]

When called to account, an exhausted Laval offered only the briefest explanations, surrendered command, and went back to his cottage. He sat at his desk writing until two o'clock in the morning, composing a lengthy report to the secretary of war that recounted all the events of the previous five days. He needed to come to Washington, he said. It was imperative that he communicate the true state of affairs on the border.

It is also very important you should apprise the President of the danger the United States are in, of being involved in war with Spain, if the agent, General Mathews, is suffered to proceed. He has broken the bounds of prudence. The Americans are taking possession of East Florida by force, through his advice. . . . They expect to cover themselves with the names of Patriots, there being 8 or 10 of them mixed with the force. They are about 60 or 70 deluded militia. They take possession of places where there is nobody to oppose, and declare it independent, and send manifestos. General Mathews sees them—encourages them. How he will get out of it I know not; the whole must fall upon the government.[48]

Laval was now extremely worried. He had read and reread his instructions and could find nothing in them that justified acquiescing to Mathews's demands. Lieutenant Colonel Smith had immediately backed his decision about preventing desertions to the Patriots; however, in all other respects, his superior officer was clearly of the same mind as Massias, Woodruff, and the others. "Should you find I have acted wrong," Laval wrote the secretary of war, "I request you will inform the President of my desire to have a court of inquiry held over me immediately." His account trailed off into incoherence. Mathews had finally prevailed upon Commodore Campbell to order gunboats into Spanish waters, he said. "The terror has been in Amelia all this week." Then he repeated his request for an interview, saying he had documents to put before the secretary that he could not trust to the post. The next morning, much as he feared, Smith

placed him under technical arrest, pending an investigation into his conduct.[49]

On Tuesday morning, March 17, at 10 A.M., Philip Yonge and George
Atkinson left Fernandina by boat, bound for Bells River and another
meeting with General Mathews. Before they departed, word came from
Commodore Campbell. His gunboats were called upon "to aid in support
of a large proportion of your countrymen in arms, who have thought
proper to declare themselves independent . . . yet flatter myself it will be
accomplished without the effusion of human blood."[50]

With this notification, the gunboats went into action. As the oarsmen
in Yonge and Atkinson's boat rowed them across the Amelia River, they
saw a small flotilla sailing south. One gunboat dogged the wake of their
craft until reaching the outlet for Bells River. Four others stationed themselves in midstream immediately opposite Fernandina. Each was a single-
mast vessel, with sails rigged fore and aft, carrying a crew complement of
about fifty men per ship, including a corporal's guard of six. Every boat
was equipped with a 32-pounder mounted on a section of deck that could
be swiveled to point the gun, and among them they also had an assort-
ment of other cannons, including one long-18, and some 12- and 18-
pound carronades. The 32-pounders and the Long Tom alone were formidable weapons, capable of smashing apart the thick, well-fitted timbers of
a warship. Against a town of frame structures like Fernandina, they would
wreck devastation in minutes, reducing houses and stores to a shambles of
splintered wood. As for the breastwork, composed of cotton bales and
standing at point-blank range, the defenders would be lucky to survive
even the first salvo (see fig. 6).[51]

The opposing armaments of the Spanish shore battery could offer little
to counter this threat. Lopez had between nine and sixteen pieces of
small-caliber artillery, some of it off of nearby ships. He could mount a
fearsome barrage against any water transports the Patriots might have,
but the gunboats outclassed him.[52]

Two more gunboats were still blockading the mouth of the Amelia
River, and an eighth flying the commodore's pennant, patrolled up and
down the waters off Amelia Island. With this sobering sight at their rear,
Yonge and Atkinson proceeded into the winding channel of Bells River to
see what awaited them at Lowe's.[53]

John Houston McIntosh and William Ashley, Lodowick's brother from
St. Marys, met them as they disembarked. It was probably the first time

William had come to East Florida since 1795, when he had fled the province as a rebel. He and McIntosh blindfolded their visitors and escorted them to Lowe's house. Lodowick Ashley, now a colonel in the Patriot army, and George Cook, a major, were already waiting for them there. All the men were on edge, and the mood was harsh. Mathews had not arrived, and Yonge and Atkinson refused to negotiate with the others, saying they would wait one hour for the general. During that time, the Patriot leaders urged them to surrender and threatened to march at once on Fernandina.[54]

Toward the end of the hour, General Mathews came in. He had orders, he said, to receive East Florida from the local authorities of the country, "and considering the Patriots as such, he had received it from them." As far as he was concerned, everything between Rose's Bluff and Lowe's plantation was already American territory. Retreating from his stance of the previous day, he said the gunboats had no orders to attack Amelia Island, only to assist the Patriots. He also repeated the charge that the British were planning to land black troops from Jamaica in the colony.[55]

Yonge and Atkinson contested all these points. Lopez, they said, was ready to surrender to the U.S. Navy, which represented a superior force. He would not surrender to the Patriots. "This is an affair between yourselves," said Mathews indifferently, "because the United States gunboats will not fire a gun, nor will they interfere with you, unless some British vessel should aid you, and in that case they have orders to fire upon you." He paused momentarily before adding, "and I am informed that you have been supplied with arms and ammunition by some [English] vessels that are now in port."[56]

"We have a right," countered Yonge, "to ask of the British, who are in our port as allies, their assistance."

"They had *no* right to interfere in this business," huffed Mathews, "and if they did, as I have understood they intend doing, the gunboats have orders to fire upon you."

You Americans are the aggressors, came the rebuttal, "by the entrance of [your] gunboats at this critical time into our waters of Amelia, evidently with the intention of deterring our town with their threats!"

"You may think what you please," Mathews responded, "because this is an affair of my government." He was now merely toying with the two men. It was clear they had no intention of treating with him, and he no longer cared. When they called attention to all the men from Georgia who were taking part in this so-called Spanish rebellion, he replied that the participants were outside his knowledge and, in any case, beyond his command. "You ought to appeal to the authorities of the State of Georgia," he said.[57]

These words concluded the interview. As Yonge and Atkinson returned to their boat, Lodowick Ashley came forward and handed them a letter. It was, he told them, the last offer of clemency they would receive.

It has been the voice of humanity, and our desire to avoid the shedding of blood, which has delayed our march. I see, with regret, that your conduct has been equivocal and evasive, and, therefore, I inform you that the negotiation is at an end; and I charge you on pain of death to return to the island, and inform the inhabitants that I will this day make my landing upon it; and I will not fire a single gun, or commit any disorder, if they do not fire upon me. But, in the event they do, we will show no quarter, and we will proceed to confiscate the properties of all those who should do so . . . but if they surrender, I obligate myself, in the most solemn manner, to comply with my first proposals.[58]

By the time the two men returned to Fernandina, five gunboats were arrayed in front of the town, within a pistol shot of the plaza, and had their cables sprung so that they were converted into floating gun platforms, unaffected by wind or tide (see fig. 6).[59]

The atmosphere in town, which had been resolute when they left, was now glum. The presence of the gunboats was causing murmurs of panic to spread among the groups of militia and townsfolk gathered in the plaza. From the shore, people had a clear view of the cannons. They were charged and ready, the men at quarters, the tampions out, and the gunners standing with lighted matches near at hand. At least some of the guns were loaded with canister, or grapeshot, to cut down the defenders behind the breastwork.[60]

Aboard the boats the mood was also tense. Commodore Campbell, still hesitant about the role he was playing, was sending contradictory orders to his squadron. Early in the day, he had summoned his commanders to repair aboard his vessel, where he told them to approach the battery at Fernandina "as near as possible without incurring the danger of going aground." They were to assist the Patriots and cover them until the Spanish surrendered.[61]

Shortly afterward, as the boats first approached the town, Lopez sent James Cashen to demand an explanation for their hostile maneuvers. The commanders of the boats said nothing. Then, two hours into the morning vigil, Campbell fired a signal gun and ran out a series of flags, instructing the boats to leave station and return to the harbor mouth. He was losing his nerve. He could not open fire on a defenseless town.

But some of the gunboat captains took no heed. Winslow Foster, in command of gunboat No. 62, a Virginia-made craft with a 32-pounder and two 12-pound carronades, refused to acknowledge the commodore's signals. He called across to John Grayson, commanding the next boat over, No. 164, saying, "You can go back, but No. 62 is staying." After a few moments of delay, Grayson and another commander raised sail and headed for Campbell. The commodore then made additional, almost frantic signals to withdraw, but Foster and the remaining gunboat commanders continued to ignore him. Finally, he sent down a skiff. Do not communicate with the shore, came the order, and "in *no event* fire upon the town."[62]

Lopez, too, was having second thoughts about his position. On his orders, soldiers hauled down the Spanish colors, and a messenger was rowed across to the gunboats, offering to surrender Fernandina to the U.S. Navy. This overture was refused, and shortly afterward Lopez again raised the Spanish flag.

Around 2 P.M., after the gunboats had been at their stations for nearly four hours, Commodore Campbell made another series of gun-and-flag signals from his vessel. These, it soon became apparent, were intended for the Patriots. Their force at Lowe's was just visible to observers with spyglasses at Fernandina. As the report of the last gun died away, lookouts saw them begin to climb aboard seven or eight flatboats. Soon, with their banners flying, they came sculling downstream under a press of oars, helped along by the ebb tide, their vessels crowded with thirty or so men per boat and darting along Bells River in spurts and splashes like giant waterbugs (see fig. 6).[63]

At their approach, the defenders in town grew agitated. Several persons called from the shore to the nearest gunboat. "Keep off," they cried, "or remain neutral until we decide the contest with the Patriots!"

Others along the breastwork cheered this proposal. But their cheers were silenced by the reply that echoed back across the water. "If you fire on them, we will fire upon you."[64]

With the westward sun gleaming full in his face, Justo Lopez stood on the front porch of his house, watching the boats. He had less than 100 men under arms, packed into an indefensible position, and he faced an attack of more than 200 American seamen with artillery, as well as an assault from the Patriots with another 250 to 300 men. It galled him to concede to rebels and rabble. Yet, outnumbered and outgunned, he had no other recourse. Around him, arguments began to break out. "Some few, actuated by desperation, still called for a battle, while a large majority clamored to our Commandant for a surrender. The land was irretrievably lost, and humanity called aloud to save what stood upon it." American observers noted that the crowd, after their earlier shouts of defiance, gave increasing signs of fright as the gunboats and the Patriots closed quarters.[65]

Finally, people appealed to Lopez, saying he should decide what to do. It was just nearing four o'clock in the afternoon. The Spanish officer pondered for a moment and then said, "We must surrender. Resistance would be unavailing." Looking about him, he asked, "Who will take the flag of surrender?" George Clarke immediately offered to do it. Under a white flag of truce, he had himself rowed out into the Amelia River to speak with the Patriots. "Upon coming up with them, he told them that he was prepared to surrender the city and take down the Spanish flag." A tremendous huzzah went up from the men crowded aboard the flatboats. Then, on a signal from Clarke, Lopez struck the Spanish flag, acknowledging capitulation. More cheers rang out from the Patriots. Quickly they rowed across the river to the foot of a bluff on the lands of Domingo Fernández, about a mile south of town, where they waded ashore. From there, "they began their march by a circuitous route"—going around the marsh— "and at about five o'clock of the same evening they entered the City and took possession of it."[66]

On the plaza, there was a brief and formal ceremony to deliver the town. With the Patriots and the town militia standing in ranks, Lopez stepped forward, tears in his eyes, and unbuckled his sword and handed it to Lodowick Ashley. Ashley immediately strapped the weapon around his waist. The Patriots ran their own colors up the flagstaff, the gunboats withdrew to the middle of the Amelia River, and twilight descended over a stunned populace. The Patriots were masters of the second largest town in Spanish East Florida, and they had captured it without firing a shot.[67]

Reactions

News of Fernandina's surrender spread far and wide in the weeks immediately following the capitulation. The inhabitants themselves had little time for reflection. On Wednesday, March 18, Lieutenant Colonel Smith threw his full support behind the Patriots and sent Lieutenant Appling with a detachment of fifty riflemen to secure the town. This was merely an advance guard. To occupy East Florida, Smith would have to empty Point Peter of men. He was determined to proceed with caution, however, until the national government confirmed its intentions regarding the province. "Having doubts about the propriety of exceeding my instructions," he informed Secretary of War Eustis, "I will not attack any Post until further ordered." Quickly and succinctly he summarized the needs of his contingent. His field pieces were unfit for service; he had neither quartermaster nor surgeon; and he wanted new rifles, 200 muskets, and a supply of bayonets to equip his men. "The Troops are shabby beyond anything I have witnessed," he added, "not having received any clothing for the present year."[1]

As the Americans took station on Amelia Island, George Mathews prepared to carry out the next phase in his plans: to cede East Florida, bit by bit, to the United States. The general spent much of the eighteenth in the house of Justo Lopez, conferring with John Houston McIntosh about the terms of surrender that Lopez and other town residents had signed. Then, at four o'clock in the afternoon, both men appeared in the plaza to begin the ceremony that would officially deliver northeastern Florida into American possession. Smith's troops were drawn up in ranks around the open square, so that the plaza looked like a military parade ground. Despite their worn-out uniforms, his soldiers made a gallant showing. On one side stood Captain Woodruff and the riflemen, very neat in bottle green uniforms with black facings, their caps decorated with green plumes and their cap plates and buttons polished to display the "RR" of their corps. Across from them stood Captain Massias before the infantry. They were less consistent in appearance, some wearing the older 1810-style uniforms of blue and white, the jacket breasts closed by an elaborate herringbone pattern of hooks and eyes, others wearing the more recently issued single-breasted coatees. Captain Williams of the marines was also there, with his men lined up, all in blue jackets, white pants, and bicorne hats, closely resembling the costume of their colleagues in the navy. An array of Patriots completed the formation, watching with pride as McIntosh made the offer of cession and General Mathews accepted it. To conclude the formalities, the troops lowered the Patriot colors (which had flown for a mere twenty-four hours), raised the Stars and Stripes, and fired off a rifle salute. Amelia Island and its environs had become American territory.[2]

Behind the ranks of their conquerors, Fernandina's townspeople watched the proceedings with sullen faces. "The British party who were accumulating fortunes, having monopolized all the trade, can scarcely contain themselves on the Cession," General Floyd reported to Senator William Crawford. "They encouraged resistance to the last, and are yet very sulky." George J. F. Clarke, a partisan of this so-called British party, expressed the emotions of many when he told the brother of St. Augustine's priest: "Amelia, alas my friend! Is no longer ours. . . . the Stars and Stripes now flies triumphant over our feelings, and publishes their disgrace."[3]

In contrast to the downcast mood of the residents, the Patriots were ebullient, and McIntosh and the other leaders had to keep close watch on their men to make sure they observed decorum and discipline. Fernandina offered rich pickings to would-be looters, with goods and silver worth some $200,000 and a harbor full of valuable ships. Despite this, the transition to American rule passed without incident. There was no seizure of property, as there had been at Lowe's. The restraint of the tired and hungry men was all the more admirable, according to General Floyd, because many were "in want of dinner and without a single coin in their pockets." Even so, "there was not the least irregularity or Excess committed, not to the taking of a chicken."[4]

Justo Lopez, out of uniform and under house arrest, looked with disbelief upon the rough-and-tumble band of rebels and frontiersmen who had defeated him. Already, he had composed two brief messages to Governor

Estrada, sadly announcing the fall of his post. Despite his own misfortunes, he discounted the Patriots' chances of taking St. Augustine: "All these people, sir, have no organization whatsoever, and can only succeed in their enterprise by surprise." At best, he thought, McIntosh might attract 500 supporters, assuming he could recruit more settlers to his cause. Of the 250 or so men who had marched into Fernandina on Tuesday, only 180 waited for the changing of the flags. The rest, dispersing into small squads, had scattered southward, taking various routes toward the outposts on the St. Johns River, where they intended to regroup. Some, as they left, had boasted that other influential Spanish subjects would soon switch sides and join them, and some said that William Craig, Estrada's key magistrate at the Cowford, was already a partisan.[5]

In the wake of this exodus, the task of securing Fernandina and organizing an occupation force for the rest of the province fell to Smith. He proved far better suited to the job than either Campbell or Laval. At age thirty, Smith was a vibrant young career officer married to the interests of Georgia. His brother-in-law, Peter Early, was one of Georgia's representatives in Congress, and his close-knit circle of friends included Senator Crawford, Congressman Troup, and General Floyd. Like so many others in the southern military, he had a personal grudge against the Spaniards. His brother had been a captive for nearly three years in a Spanish prison. Although full of zeal, Smith was well aware of the limitations on his authority and refused point blank to mount offensive strikes against Spanish-held positions. "I will not attack any Post until further ordered," he told the secretary of war, "[but] as I consider the order imperative as to occupying and defending places peaceably surrendered, I shall do it to the last extremity." Thus, from the outset, Smith found himself in a position dreaded by all military leaders: authorized to defend but not to attack. In those early hours of his assignment, he little suspected how onerous and thankless his duty in East Florida would soon become.[6]

It took Smith several days to advance his full force of about 200 men into East Florida. He was short on officers, as Major Laval and Captain Ridgeway were still facing charges stemming from the confrontation over Mathews's directives. He therefore set aside charges against Captain Massias and returned him to active duty. The lieutenant colonel's next dilemma was to find quarters sufficient to house his troops, for Fernandina could not accommodate so many men. His soldiers took over the makeshift Spanish redoubt, emptied Clarke's cotton warehouse and converted it into a barracks, and pitched dozens of tents in the plaza. Then, too, he had to worry about conveying his men deeper into the province. Scouting parties foraged through nearby plantations, hunting for flat-boats and other river craft that could serve as troop transports. At the Saw Pit, they seized the *Elizabeth*, a boat belonging to James and Mary Smith, and pressed four slaves to row it. On Talbot Island, at the plantation of Louis and Spicer Christopher, they confiscated the *Lord Nelson*, an enor-mous canoelike *periagua* made out of cypress that was capable of carrying forty to fifty bales of cotton and required a crew of eight oarsmen. Offic-ers also discovered the Christophers' fine stock of thoroughbred horses—a rarity among the Indian ponies and frontier breeds of Florida—and helped themselves to an Arabian and several English mares.[7]

Settlers loyal to the Spanish cause at Fernandina could do little to op-pose these forced requisitions. No one was allowed to leave town. Justo Lopez and his men were on local parole, and American sentries kept watch on all the residents. Nor could they expect any sympathy from General Mathews. The success of his plans had turned him giddy with triumph. "From one of the Most Grave, silent, and prudent men I ever Knew," com-mented Commodore Campbell, "he is now more gay and unreserved than any Man upon the Station." With all of the obstacles and cares of past days behind him, Mathews had turned his considerable energies to practi-cal matters, setting up a police force for Fernandina, appointing his own officials for the customhouse and civil authority, and writing excitedly to Secretary of State Monroe. The Patriots were still increasing in number and confident of taking St. Augustine, he said. Commodore Campbell dis-patched the fourteen-gun brig *Vixen* under Master Commandant Chris-topher Gadsden to explore St. Augustine's harbor entrance. Mathews re-minded Monroe of his request for infantry and artillery companies and suggested that an engineer experienced in siege work should be sent south. "Make my respects to the President," he concluded, "and inform him that I hope to complete my mission as to meet his unqualified appro-bation."[8]

Not everyone shared Mathews's confidence about an easy American victory. In the harbor, ship captains were "puzzled and perplexed" by the sudden change in flags. William Adgate and Robert Thompson, aboard the *Good Friends*, wrote to the vessel's owner, Stephen Girard of Philadelphia, saying President Madison might disapprove of everything that had taken place in East Florida once he learned how it was accomplished. "How far the government will sanction this business God Knows," observed Thompson, "as it seems to be done underhanded."[9]

The flagrant use of American armed force also nagged at the minds and consciences of Floyd and Campbell. George Mathews, Floyd told Senator Crawford, had broken all the bounds of honorable conduct when he menaced Fernandina with men and cannons. No one believed the president would approve such actions. "Every Officer feels little in his own esteem in this hidden policy—all the sin of direct invasion Rests on the shoulders of the Government or its agents, and too, against a weak defenseless, unoffending Neighbor." Better an outright attack, Floyd argued, than this flimsy mask of internal rebellion, which would deceive no one. And resistance at St. Augustine was not negligible. Properly reinforced, that stronghold could defy the Patriots indefinitely. Yet Georgia might profit from the conflict. Should the Seminoles assist the Spanish, he said, "it will afford a pretext for [us] to penetrate their Country and Break up a Negroe Town, an important Evil growing under their Patronage; the Number of these Negroes from the lowest calculation Exceeds 500."[10]

In St. Marys, Commodore Campbell remained ill at ease over his role in the proceedings. Racked with doubts about his authority to use coercive force against Fernandina, he called back all his written instructions regarding deployment of the gunboats and kept them to himself. Then he appealed to the secretary of the navy. Mathews was placing him in a most "unpleasant and unofficer-like situation," he complained. Was he or was he not supposed to be cooperating with the general? He believed his use of the gunboats had ultimately prevented bloodshed at Fernandina. But he required instructions on his future course. In particular, he desired to know if he should enforce a blockade of the harbor at St. Augustine.[11]

As for Major Laval, his letters to his superiors were filled with nothing but condemnation and venom. Pending an investigation into his conduct, he was living quietly and off duty at St. Marys, where he continued to nurse an implacable hatred for Mathews and his "confidential Jew, Col. Isaacs." "Is it possible," he asked Secretary of War Eustis, "that the government cannot be better furnished with officers [than with] Jews, rogues, traitors, and conspirators? Good God! What age is this? What Prospect has an officer, who would die at his post Sooner than seeing his honour and that of his flag tarnished?" Indeed, there were many other people waiting to see if the Madison administration would condone Mathews's brazen coup d'état.[12]

Although Lieutenant Colonel Smith moved quickly to establish a military cordon around Fernandina, he was not quick enough to stop a few individuals from escaping or sending off pleas for help. Just before the Patriot attack, Charles Clarke visited the cattle ranges of Felipe Solana. Pointing to the smoke from the Patriot campfires, he warned two ranch hands—a slave named Manuel and a free black named Long John—to clear out of the area. The men disappeared into Indian territory, spending the next seven months there and bringing word of the invasion to the Seminoles. Slaves and free blacks from the lumber camps on the St. Marys River, as well as fifteen slaves from nearby plantations, also fled south, heading for St. Augustine.[13]

In the last moments before surrender, Justo Lopez and Joseph Hibberson had also been busy, arranging to smuggle dispatches to Governor Estrada and to the Spanish and British consulates. Having made copies of their correspondence with Laval, Campbell, Mathews, and the Patriots, they handed these to contacts on board ships that were preparing to weigh anchor. Within a few days, when the Amelia River was no longer under blockade, these ships slipped free of port, taking word of the surrender and the circumstances surrounding it to Washington, Philadelphia, Havana, and the Bahamas.[14]

The Patriots in the meantime marched onward to the St. Johns River. They traveled quickly, meeting little resistance and leaving only a few men to secure their lines. Their main force headed for their next key objectives: the ferry station at the Cowford, Fort San Nicolás, and the plantation of William Craig.

William Craig's tribulations thus began early on the morning of March 16 when he awoke to find a strange sloop anchored in the St. Johns River opposite Fort San Nicolás. He crossed over the river and, upon boarding the vessel, discovered that it belonged to McIntosh. The hold was crammed to capacity with supplies of flour, beef, and other provisions. Asked about their business, the captain and three black crewmen claimed they were sailing to McIntosh's Ortega estate, a few miles farther on, to deliver the goods to the overseer, George Morrison, and pick up a return cargo of cotton. This did not ring true to Craig, and he detained them and impounded the boat, moving it across the stream to the south bank near the fort. Then he returned to his plantation to await developments.[15]

In the evening, he received word from people fleeing Fernandina that American troops had crossed the St. Marys River and that a party of seventy or eighty horsemen were already headed for the St. Johns River. At midnight, Philip Dewees, who was also coming south from Amelia Island, crossed at the ferry station and brought Craig confirmation of an American attack. All this made for a busy night. Craig sent word to residents living along the St. Johns that they should remove all boats to the south or east banks of the river. By the next morning—March 17, the day Fernandina fell—he was in communication with militia officers William Lawrence and Nathaniel Hall, telling them to muster their units and come at once to join him at Fort San Nicolás. Lieutenant Reuben Hogans headed across the river with the picket of observation to reconnoiter the road to Colerain and St. Marys. Then, thinking of the large watercraft that were moored at Laurel Grove, Zephaniah Kingsley's plantation on the western banks of the St. Johns, Craig made arrangements to have these boats secured as well so that they could not be commandeered by enemy forces as transports. "Should [the enemy] arrive," Craig notified Estrada, "no means of crossing will be left them except rafts which will give time to the Militia to collect, when I hope to be able to check them for some time, and probably entirely prevent them crossing."[16]

Even as Craig struggled to organize a defense, Hogans reported in, saying that 200 rebels were marching due south from Fernandina on the mainland, hoping they could find a way across the St. Johns River to reach the vicinity of Pablo Creek, whence they could proceed to St. Augustine. Nathaniel Hall had stationed his men at the Horse Crossing, sixteen miles east of the Cowford, in hopes of intercepting the enemy.[17]

Down in St. Augustine, Governor Estrada already knew much about the problems along the border. Felipe Solana had delivered Lopez's early dispatches and had added his own observations about conditions in the province. Seeking more information, Estrada sent Fernando de la Maza Arredondo, the younger, galloping north by horse with a party of cavalry. Traveling by way of the King's Road, Arredondo arrived first at Levin Gunby's house and sawmill, hard by the Sweetwater branch of Julington Creek, a little above Davis Creek and about halfway between the city and the Cowford. Gunby disclaimed any knowledge of trouble, but a *moreno* slave of Zephaniah Kingsley's, who was also at the house, informed Arredondo that the province was invaded. Continuing north, Arredondo's party arrived at Craig's plantation late in the evening of March 17, and here a tense discussion of affairs took place.[18]

Craig and Hogans were both present at the plantation house and did not seem pleased to see Arredondo. When Arredondo told them that Estrada was trying to raise an auxiliary force of Seminoles to repulse the invaders, Craig immediately protested the policy. "For God's sake," he added at the end of the report he was preparing for the governor, "do not send any of them this way, as the Inhabitants seem to dread them very much, and with good reason."[19]

Hogans then urged Arredondo to return at once to St. Augustine, before some of the disaffected settlers on the south side of the river came to seize him. The youth ignored the advice. It was too dangerous, he said, to return to the capital in the dark. He was full of questions, too. His father and older brother were at Fernandina, perhaps already prisoners. He wanted to know the whereabouts of the militia and inquired about McIntosh's boat, which was still anchored at Fort San Nicolás. The next morning, he pressed Craig upon this matter. It would be convenient, he said, for him to take charge of the sloop and return with it to St. Augustine. Craig refused to allow it and again told Arredondo that he should go back south at once, before an enemy force surprised them. With many reservations, Arredondo finally sent a few scouts across the St. Johns River and then departed to take Craig's letters to Estrada.[20]

In St. Augustine, bad news seemed to be coming in from all sides. Governor Estrada viewed the reports of Arredondo and Craig with increasing consternation. Forewarned by Justo Lopez about the impending threat to Fernandina, the governor had sent Francisco Solana, a soldier with the Cuban infantry, into the Alachua territory to warn Chief Payne of the Seminoles that an American invasion was under way. Now, as he met with Arredondo, he learned that even this preemptive measure had failed. Word came back from Solana saying he could get no farther west than Fort Picolata. The flatboat at the fort was unaccountably missing, and he had no way to cross his horse over the St. Johns River. Instead, he had hired an Indian to go to Payne by canoe and on foot—but that would delay the transmission of the governor's messages. Solana was waiting at Picolata until a reply came back from the Seminoles.[21]

With only his regular troops and the town militia at his disposal, Estrada ruled out an attack on the rebels, "preferring the defensive to the offensive," he explained, "that I might not risk all." He wrote urgently to Captain General Someruelos at Havana, stressing his need for reinforcements, and gave his dispatches to Antonio Mier, captain of a small, armed schooner, telling him to sail at once for Cuba. As he made clear in his reports, there were too few men to defend the region around St. Augustine, and his artillery company was woefully short of experienced gunners, leaving him no choice but to employ untrained and untried militia as gun crews. He mustered his regular and volunteer forces and sent word to the commanders at the Castillo and the battery on the Matanzas River to inventory their munitions and supplies. Then he decided to deal with the rebel leaders.[22]

The betrayal of men like McIntosh, Cook, and Ashley was extremely disconcerting to Estrada and those around him. Arredondo expressed additional doubts about the true loyalties of William Craig and the settlers along the St. Johns River. He feared it was all too likely that they would strike a deal with the rebels. Estrada, however, was in no mood to anticipate further treacheries. All his anger was reserved for John Houston McIntosh. He wrote at once to Craig, praising him for his zealous and prompt efforts to secure the riverboats and asking him to discover who was loyal and who was a rebel, "so that I will know whom to trust." "As for Mr. McIntosh and Mr. Cook," he continued, "I declare them from now on as men deserving the severest punishment . . . and authorize you to do all possible harm to them, in their persons and in their property." Craig should muster a force at once to seize McIntosh's Ortega plantation and send another expedition to his place on Fort George Island. Take everything, Estrada ordered, the baled cotton, the livestock, everything except the houses. Keep the sloop safe, and send its captain and crew as prisoners to St. Augustine. If nothing else, Estrada thought, this confiscation of property might frighten would-be rebels into reflecting on the penalties for treason. But St. Augustine still had to repel those traitors already in arms.[23]

Four hundred miles to the north, in Milledgeville, Georgia, news of an attack on East Florida caught another governor completely by surprise. David Mitchell, the keen-minded and patriotic Scotsman who headed Georgia's government, was stupefied. Hitherto, he had received only perfunctory reports from General Mathews about a possible rebellion in Florida. He suspected American troops would assist, but no one had bothered to give him the details. "It is to me a matter not only of great surprise, but of real regret that the United States should so manage their affairs, that in so important a transaction as the occupancy of a province belonging to a friendly power, their agents and officers should be left without such positive instructions," Mitchell wrote angrily to Major General Floyd. At the very least, he said, Georgians required time to prepare. Depending on the success or failure of the Patriots, their whole frontier might be opened to retaliations from the Spanish, the British, or the Indians, and he was almost powerless to respond. He would, of course, issue an immediate call to arms, but it was already too late to send men from central Georgia to aid Mathews or the regulars in their drive on St. Augustine—they would never arrive in time to be of use. On top of that, Mitchell had no means to pay the men or any constitutional authority to attack foreign territory with state militia. In a huff, he told General Floyd to send word at once if the Spaniards repulsed the Patriots. The border must at all costs be protected. The only good news, he said, was that Benjamin Hawkins, as Indian agent, had passed a message about the troubles to the Creeks, and they in turn vowed to intercede with the Seminoles and keep them out of any war.[24]

Word from East Florida spread rapidly to Washington as well, where reports about General Mathews's activities reached the ears of President Madison and Secretary of State Monroe at the worst of all possible moments. In recent months, the two men had given little thought to Mathews and his plots and stratagems. All the administration's attention had been focused on preparing for war with England. Congress was awash in bills to strengthen American armed forces, to build frigates for the nonexistent navy, to raise or borrow money for a war effort, and to impose a new trade embargo. President Madison was urging Congress to pass a declaration of war against Britain before the end of its current session.[25]

As if war fever was not enough cause for excitement in Washington, 1812 was also an election year, and both the Federalists and Democratic Republicans were hunting for issues with which to smear their opponents. Newspaper editors—espousing their sympathies to one or the other of the parties—carried on debates about the necessity of war and published the latest political scandals. Among the most prominent of the latter, meriting pages of attention in the broadsheets, was the furor over the so-called Henry letters.

What started as a minor attempt to tarnish the reputations of Federalist office seekers erupted into major scandal as Washingtonians absorbed the details of President Madison's latest political gaffe. The center of attention was James Henry, an Irishman in the pay of Governor James Craig of Canada, who had turned informer. In 1808 and 1809, Henry had been working as a British secret agent in New England. Part of his mission was to court the goodwill of Federalist politicians, especially those who opposed war with England because of the harm it would do to trade. England might want to look upon these men, Henry hinted to his superiors, as potential friends and collaborators.

Early in 1812, hard up for cash, Henry approached the Madison administration and offered to sell his confidential and potentially embarrassing files on New England Federalists to the government. It was exactly the kind of electioneering ammunition that the president's followers most desired. Hoping to expose secret English schemes and taint northern Federalists with allegations of treason, the administration agreed to buy Henry's letters for $50,000. On March 9, President Madison released copies to Congress. He accused the British government of employing a spy in the northern states to promote dissension and disloyalty inside the Republic, with active assistance from misguided Federalists.

The threatened exposé caused a blanching of faces among many of Madison's enemies in Congress. But their apprehensions soon turned to outrage. The Henry letters proved largely innocuous, containing little more than routine intelligence reports. When word leaked out that the administration had purchased the letters for an exorbitant price (in fact, the entire annual budget of the Secret Service), Federalists went on the attack. The president, they said, had allowed himself to be hoodwinked and robbed of public monies by a clever confidence trickster.[26]

Newspapers from both political camps reveled in the details of the Henry letters, introducing them to their readers as either a dastardly example of English espionage or as a cheap campaign trick to hurt Federalists at the polls. The scandal—which had little to sustain public interest—was short-lived. However, just when the furor was at its height, newspapers around the country discovered that the United States had its own secret agent at work in Spanish East Florida and that this agent, far from merely gathering intelligence, was engaged in overthrowing the local government.

On March 23, the *Charleston Courier*, a paper with Federalist sympathies, ran a short account of the surrender of Fernandina. The *Georgia Argus* followed suit with a brief report on March 25. Two days later, the *Courier* published a lengthier firsthand description of events, and by March 28 its editor was openly blasting the government for its support of

George Mathews. "At the moment when [Spain] is struggling for her existence, we are despoiling her of her colonies," he commented. "These outrages have taken place, too, at the very moment when our own government are [sic] crying out against the conduct of Great Britain for an alleged outrage of similar kind." Soon broadsheets from Georgia to Massachusetts began to pay attention to East Florida. The *National Intelligencer* and the *Niles Register*, strong supporters of the president, ridiculed the idea that the administration had orchestrated an attack on Spanish possessions. The editor of the *Georgia Argus*, busily publishing the Henry letters as evidence for British malignity, ducked the question of government involvement and instead endorsed a military occupation of East Florida, which, in his opinion, was long overdue. "If the government recognizes the transactions in that quarter," he said, "it might be advisable for them to reinforce the Patriots as early as convenient, that they may be enabled to reduce [St. Augustine] before the approach of the sickly season." In contrast, the *New York Evening Post* ran two long eyewitness accounts of the attack on Fernandina, one saying "the Americans have usurped our Island" and the other berating the "friendly" intervention of Campbell's gunboats: "We then plainly discovered their friendly intentions, to hold the guns to our breasts whilst a banditti plundered us." The *Post's* editor expressed amazement at American actions. The seizure of Fernandina, he noted, "must be considered the act of the troops, and an outrageous act of depredation, or, if countenanced by the government, an act of open war on a nation with whom we are at peace. We wait for some sort of explanation." Papers in Massachusetts and Connecticut made similar comments, to the effect that General Mathews's actions were a blemish on the national honor.[27]

Accompanying this debate in the press were official protests from the Spanish and British consuls. By April 2, Augustus Foster possessed all the facts about Fernandina's capitulation, as forwarded to him by Joseph Hibberson, and Don Luis de Onís had a similar cache from Justo Lopez. Armed with this evidence, Onís wrote to Secretary of State Monroe from Philadelphia, and Foster confronted him directly.

The president, in the meantime, caught off-guard by the revelations regarding East Florida, distanced himself from events. "Mathews has been playing a strange comedy in the face of common sense, as well as of his instructions," he wrote peevishly to Thomas Jefferson. "His extravagances place us in the most distressing dilemma."[28]

Seeking some way to defuse diplomatic protests, Madison and Monroe called a hasty conference with southern leaders. Congressman George Troup, looking back to the case of Baton Rouge, suggested bold denial: Conceal Mathews's role and finger McIntosh as the culprit behind the rebellion. Then all the arguments used to justify the occupation of Baton Rouge could be applied again for Amelia Island.[29]

The administration quickly rejected this idea. There was too much evidence tying Mathews to the Patriots. Word was already leaking to the press that a squad of navy gunboats had assisted in the attack and had pointed their cannons at Fernandina, threatening to fire. After a few days' consideration, Madison and Monroe came to the same conclusion. Mathews was delivering East Florida into their power, but he was doing it at too high a cost. "At present they could not vindicate his conduct," concluded Monroe.[30]

On April 4, as the only means of resolving the president's "most distressing dilemma," Monroe drafted an official repudiation of George Mathews. Any connection between the general and the government had to be completely severed. Monroe's tone was regretful but firm.

> I am sorry to have to state that the measures which you appear to have adopted for obtaining possession of Amelia Island and other parts of East Florida, are not authorized by the law of the United States, or the instructions found on it, under which you have acted . . . a forceful wresting of the province from Spain was never contemplated, but only an occupation until a settlement could be reached by future amicable negotiation with Spain. The president has the utmost confidence in your integrity and zeal for the welfare of your country, and to that zeal he imputes the error into which you have fallen. . . . You will therefore consider your powers as revoked on the receipt of this letter.[31]

Armed with this disavowal, the secretary of state prepared to confront foreign diplomats. Despite the tense situation, he declined to meet with Luis de Onís. Instead, on April 10 he spoke with Foster and assured him that the president had never authorized an attack on Spanish East Florida. The United States, he said, would take steps to return the occupied areas to Spanish control.[32]

These assurances masked the government's true intentions and marked the beginning of a vacillating policy on East Florida that largely depended on other matters—especially the waxing and waning of American fortunes in war with Great Britain. Plans to declare war against England were steadily progressing, and the fate of East Florida became enmeshed in other considerations about national defense. Initial hesitancy to pursue armed conquest soon passed. The president, aside from his one outburst to Jefferson, gave no indication that he was alarmed about the situation. In the immediate embarrassment of the moment, he issued orders to withdraw American forces. Within a week, however, rethinking what he stood to gain, he reversed his decision. Incoming reports continued to emphasize Patriot successes, saying the rebels were encamped before St. Augustine and that regular troops were joining them there. In truth, the administration's displeasure over an attack on East Florida rested on its timing and in the unfortunate publicity it received, not on the results. Monroe freely admitted there was "much cleverness" in General Mathews's espionage and that something might yet be salvaged from it, at least with respect to Fernandina and Amelia Island.[33]

To prolong a military occupation, however, the government needed someone to take Mathews's place, a more reliable and openly acknowledged representative who could assume supervision of affairs in East Florida. Ideally, it had to be someone close to the scene who could call up military support and who had a vested interest in subduing the Spaniards. Thinking hard on this question, Monroe focused on an obvious and somewhat ironic choice. With the president's approval, he decided to put Governor Mitchell of Georgia in charge of affairs in East Florida. On April 10, as Mitchell was angrily working to counter the threats and dangers that a war in East Florida posed to his state, Monroe wrote to him, saying the president wished to appoint him as a U.S. commissioner to negotiate with the Spanish authorities. That same day, the president ordered Lieutenant Colonel Smith to hold his position and await further instructions.[34]

In his letter to the governor, Monroe set forth guidelines for a parley with the Spaniards. Mitchell should reassure them that the United States would withdraw its troops and "restore back to the Spanish authorities Amelia Island." At the same time, he should keep alive the possibility of a peaceful cession of the province and should delay as long as possible the actual removal of Smith's contingent. The government had an obligation to shield the Patriots from Spanish retribution, and Mitchell could use this issue to draw out negotiations by insisting on a "most explicit and satisfactory assurance" of amnesty for the rebels as a precondition for an

American evacuation. This would afford the president and Congress the necessary time to consider their next move with respect to East Florida. In later instructions, Monroe again pledged government protection for the Patriots.[35]

When Mathews's secretary, Colonel Ralph Isaacs, arrived in Washington a few weeks later bearing messages from East Florida, Monroe broke the news about General Mathews's dismissal. Isaacs was understandably irate at the callous treatment of the general, his friend and employer, and raised objections. Monroe could not be moved. The government was "never so much embarrass'd, in any business since [he] had been official in it," he said. Yet in spite of the difficulties, it was essential that East Florida remain in American hands. If Isaacs still wished a role in the mission, he should visit Governor Mitchell on behalf of the administration and convey Monroe's instructions. Impending events—namely, the likelihood of war with England—rendered "the restoration of the Province utterly impracticable," Monroe said. "Governor Mitchell will understand this, won't he?"[36]

"He is not dull of comprehension, Sir," Isaacs replied. Reluctantly, he agreed to act as Monroe's emissary to the Georgia governor. Monroe then assured Isaacs that the government was "concerting measures to keep the province and save . . . the Patriots." It might even be possible, he added, to reinstate General Mathews.[37]

This vague assurance was the only thought given to the effect of disgrace and disavowal on the government's agent. A month would pass before the general even learned of his fall from favor. "Poor old Mathews," observed Senator William Crawford, his long-time friend, "I am fearful he will die of mortification and resentment."[38]

The Patriots, of course, knew nothing of these transactions or that their activities had become the topic of discussion in dozens of newspapers. They were busy with their own arrangements. Around March 20 or 21, John Houston McIntosh, Lodowick Ashley, and a large party of Patriots reached the juncture of the King's Road and the St. Johns River, managed to secure boats for a crossing of the Cowford, and immediately captured Fort San Nicolás. They made prisoners of the garrison, three Spanish soldiers, none of whom offered to make trouble against such a large opposing force. A separate detachment of rebels had already seized the Spanish supply depot of San Vicente de Ferrer, located some distance east on St. Johns Bluff.

Force of arms now favored the insurgents. From Fernandina, Mathews was passing the word that new volunteers could apply for up to 500 acres of land as a reward for their services instead of the previous fifty. This incentive, coupled with the threats of banishment and loss of property against those who opposed the Patriots, helped swell the rebel ranks to between 400 and 600 men. Faced by this multitude, William Craig, Reuben Hogans, and other settlers along the St. Johns River dropped any pretense of resistance. Making the best of matters, Craig absolved himself of his Spanish loyalties and surrendered McIntosh's sloop full of supplies. In return, McIntosh appointed him as a military commander and promised him a position in the rebel government. Every adult male in the north of the province was now either an adherent of the Patriots or a captive.[39]

At Fort San Nicolás, McIntosh divided the men under arms into two companies, with Ashley retained as commander over the first and Craig placed in charge of the second. The tiny core of leadership widened to include other men out of Georgia and northern Florida. Daniel Delany, a prominent East Florida planter, was appointed as McIntosh's co-commissioner in the rebel government. James and William Dell, brothers who owned properties to the north of the St. Johns River, assumed command of small contingents. Somewhere in the ranks were two Georgians, Buckner Harris, a general in the Georgia militia, and Captain William Cone, the son of a Revolutionary War hero. Both were destined to become local folk heroes.[40]

Craig's first unpleasant task as a rebel was to inform John Houston McIntosh that the Spaniards intended to arrest him and to confiscate his property. This news unsettled the planter. Apparently, he had convinced himself that the Spanish authorities—like so many settlers—would see the futility of opposition and embrace an American takeover. Craig gave him a more sobering assessment. If the Patriots failed to subdue St. Augustine, history would come full circle, and McIntosh would face the same fate that overtook his grandfather in 1740 and his cousin in 1794—imprisonment, ruin, or worse.

In any case, the rebels had no time for hesitancy or doubt. The weather was rainy and chilly, their supplies were limited, and they would not see the comforts of a town again until they entered St. Augustine itself. Leaving only a small garrison at Fort San Nicolás, they split into their newly designated companies and got under way once more. McIntosh and Craig, with their men, went by boat up the St. Johns to Fort Picolata. Ashley and his company marched south along the King's Road, heading toward the Follis and Gunby Mill on the Sweetwater branch of Julington Creek as fast as poorly clad feet and hungry bellies would allow (see fig. 2).

News of their coming passed on ahead of them. At the homesteads and plantations along the middle stretches of the St. Johns, settlers and slaves heard of an invasion that seemed too incredible to believe. Tony Primus, a twenty-year-old free black, first learned about the Patriots around March 21 at the house of James Plummer in what later became known as Mandarin. Plummer and his two neighbors, Henry and William Hartley, all local planters, cautioned Primus that a large band of rebels and Americans had crossed the Cowford. They "advised me to flee to St. Augustine," he recalled later, "that perhaps if they caught me they would sell me for a slave." At the time, Primus was working with thirteen other free men of color at one of George J. F. Clarke's logging camps, a crude settlement of palmetto huts in the swamps of Julington Creek. They had been cutting timber in this location for two and a half months and had more than 22,000 linear feet of hewn red cedar piled up on the banks of the creek ready for rafting to the St. Johns. Primus was well known in the area, for he had a small farm nearby on the Gilbert plantation, where his mother and sister lived. He did not immediately heed the counsel to flee.[41]

The following day, two other planters came out to the logging camp and again warned the workers that an armed party was on its way south. William Garvin, Clarke's partner in the lumber trade and the camp overseer, scoffed at their words and told Primus that "they only wanted to run me off from my work." At his insistence, the loggers resumed their labor. Then, the next day, they began to hear gunfire coming from the direction of the King's Road, about six miles distant. With this confirmation of trouble, all the men hurriedly abandoned their camp and headed into St. Augustine as quickly as they could. They reached the city gates around eleven o'clock at night on March 23. Having reported in, Primus and the others immediately took up arms to serve in the free black militia.[42]

That same day, the Patriots who had departed from the Cowford by boat arrived at Fort Picolata, thirty miles south of Julington and twenty-one miles west of St. Augustine (see fig. 2). They quickly chased off the small Spanish garrison occupying the post and took possession of it. The fort consisted of a two-story masonry tower, about six yards square at the base, finished off in its upper story with frame construction and situated inside a wooden palisade. On the side along the river, the palisade had been reworked into a double stockade filled with rubble built to protect the tower from storm erosion. Seizure of this key point allowed the Patriots to cut communications between St. Augustine and the nearest towns of the Seminoles in the Alachua country and gave them complete control over the boat traffic of the middle St. Johns River. On March 24, knowing he must reestablish communications with Ashley's men, McIntosh detailed an advance scout to press eastward toward the capital. They rode off on good mounts while the rest of the Patriots tramped along behind, following a narrow forest bridle path thickly matted under heaps of stringy yellow pollen and decaying leaves shed from the overhanging live oaks.[43]

Late that same evening, the scouts, still far ahead of the main body, reined in their horses on the marshy western banks of the San Sebastian River and got their first glimpse of St. Augustine. This time they found the Spaniards were ready for them. The boats were withdrawn to the east side of the river, the redoubts on that side and the bridge across María Sánchez Creek were defended, and a mounted picket of dragoons, barely discernible in the gray twilight, shadowed their movements from the other side of the glistening waters. The rebels headed north, using a path that ran along a low ridge paralleling the San Sebastian, until they found a crossing point at a northern ford. Then they came south again to inspect the town's defenses. Unfamiliar with the terrain, they ventured too close, and gun crews at the Castillo opened fire on them. A squad of Spanish horsemen suddenly burst out of ambush and captured one of their number, a man named Abner Broadway, who had served as a courier for McIntosh and Ashley at Fernandina and had carried the Patriot flag as the rebels' standard-bearer. Quick as lightning, the Spaniards whisked him away into St. Augustine and clapped him into a cell in the Castillo. The other Patriots escaped, fleeing back to the north to await the arrival of their main force.[44]

At the Gates of St. Augustine

On March 25, some 200 Patriots emerged from the woods on the western fringes of St. Augustine and paused to regroup. Tattered and tired, and glad to be within sight of the town, they little realized how greatly the nature of their enterprise was changing. So far, they had vanquished and conquered with ease, and their leaders were predicting another effortless victory. McIntosh assured his contacts in Washington, "The Patriot Army will meet with no formidable opposition except the Indians . . . [and] should they yield to the solicitations of the Spanish Party their tribe must meet destruction." There was no way for him to anticipate the other factors that would interfere with his plans—the vacillations in government policy, the Spaniards' resolve to resist, and the coming of war with England. All these things still lay weeks or months in the future. From rooks and knights on the chessboard of East Florida, the Patriots would soon find themselves relegated to mere pawns, caught in a growing conflict that would have neither leader nor direction.[1]

For some among them, such as McIntosh and Craig, St. Augustine was a familiar and unremarkable sight. To the settlers from the border regions, though, and the Georgians from Colerain and St. Marys, the capital's fortifications provided sobering evidence of how far they had come into a foreign territory. During their transit south from Amelia Island, the province of Spanish East Florida had hardly seemed Spanish. In most respects, it closely resembled southern Georgia, a land of pine barrens, marshes, cotton and rice plantations, and frontier outposts. Here, though, was something distinctly alien. No turn of the imagination could transform San Agustín de la Florida Oriental into an American town. The squat and sprawling *vecindario*, with its fortress and redoubts, resembled something out of medieval romance. It was well sited for defense, situated on a narrow sliver of peninsula formed by the confluence of the San Sebastian River, on the town's western perimeter, and the wide brackish bay of the Matanzas River, which formed its harbor. The river and bay system provided St. Augustine with a kind of natural moat, which the Spaniards had further augmented by military works (see fig. 7).[2]

The town's western face presented a view of widely spaced groves, fenced yards, and modest outlying houses. This was only the straggling edge of the town's core. Hundreds of shops, warehouses, and residences were neatly arranged around the plaza and along the harbor front. The shabbiest were little more than clapboard shacks; the stateliest were fine stone houses, smoothly plastered, two stories tall, with balconies, loggias, and front entrances dominated by a massive door, or *portón*. In their midst stood larger public buildings—the governor's house and the parish church on the plaza and the soldiers' barracks at the south end of town. Gardens and citrus groves occupied many intervening lots, the groves so numerous that sailors claimed they could smell the gardenia-like scent of the orange blossoms two miles out at sea.

St. Augustine's principal fortification was the Castillo de San Marcos, a massive stone fort located along the Matanzas River at the town's northeast corner (see fig. 8). Artillery fire from its gun deck could protect both the harbor and the surrounding countryside to the distance of a mile in all directions. In 1812, the Castillo was more than a hundred years old, a square, compact edifice of coquina stone, two stories tall, arranged around a central court. Its ramparts were thirty-six feet high and fifteen feet thick, and it had a protruding bastion at each of its corners, along with dozens of artillery embrasures cut through its parapet. Thirty-four pieces of artillery, including a mortar, ten 24-caliber cannons, and eight 16-pounders, made up its large armaments. A deep dry moat surrounded the core structure and the sole entrance, a sally port facing south, could be sealed off by lowering a portcullis and raising two drawbridges that connected the fort to its ravelin and glacis.[3]

Any enemy fleet hoping to capture the harbor had to endure gunfire from the Castillo while negotiating a treacherous inward passage, first over a shallow bar that never had more than ten feet of clearance and usually less than eight, then down the eastern shore of Anastasia Island, a barrier island that practically concealed the town and fort from view. Lookouts stationed at a watchtower at the north end of Anastasia Island could monitor enemy movements. As any attacking ships finally began to round the island, they had to tack into the Matanzas River directly in front of the fort's guns.[4]

A land expedition attacking the Castillo had to contend with equally unfavorable circumstances, for the approach required an advance up the glacis surrounding the fort. This glacis dropped off into a sunken expanse, or covered way, just before the moat and ramparts. Defenders could stand in this area and shoot at attackers without exposing themselves to return fire, while more men fired down from behind the parapet.

To reach either the fort or the town also meant winning through the northern defenses. The first line, the Hornwork, had once been a major barrier but had crumbled from disuse and lack of repair until it was merely a broken and largely indefensible embankment, secured only by covering fire from the Castillo's artillery. The real barrier was the Cubo Line, a nine-foot-high log-and-earth defensive wall that stretched from the Castillo to the San Sebastian River and demarcated the northern limits of St. Augustine (see fig. 7). The Cubo Line had three artillery redoubts and contained the town's main gate. To make the line more formidable, the Spaniards had fronted it with a forty-foot-wide dry moat, hedged in Spanish bayonet, the local variety of yucca plant that sprouted sharp, spearlike leaves. A drawbridge spanned the moat at the gate and was flanked, for further protection, by two sentry stations that supported the heavy gate doors.[5]

The southern end of St. Augustine, while not so strongly encased in fortifications, was doubly protected by water, cut off from the mainland by the flow of both the San Sebastian River and María Sánchez Creek where they emptied into the bay. Here, marshes, redoubts, ditches, more hedges of Spanish bayonet, and the surrounding agricultural fields impeded attack.[6]

Hence, it was the long western side of the town facing the Patriots that actually posed the greatest chance for vulnerability. At first glance, mounting an attack across the San Sebastian River seemed like a poor option, the classic "forlorn hope." The banks of the river were marshy and soft (Spanish maps called them "impassable"), and this pseudoground made it difficult to launch boats into the stream or to effect a landing once across. The eastern side of the river was guarded by a widely spaced string of redoubts left over from the British occupancy of St. Augustine in the 1770s and maintained by the Spaniards (see fig. 3). One redoubt terminated the Cubo Line. The next one south commanded the fields adjacent to the cemetery and powder house. Another (designated Primera Fería or Puente) barred the way to the bridge crossing María Sánchez Creek, and two others (Paso de Solana and Segunda Fería) defended a wide causeway through the marsh (leading to a ferry station) and a narrow meander in the San Sebastian River (called the southern ford). Soldiers and cannons stationed at these redoubts could pour a deadly fire of musketry and canister shot into any force that attempted to win its way across the water and through the marshes.[7]

As General Mathews had been aware, however, the western redoubts were not as impervious as they seemed. They should have been reinforced by a second defense work, the Rosario Line, to protect the western boundary of St. Augustine as the Cubo Line protected the northern one. The Rosario Line, though, was virtually nonexistent, at most a hedge of Spanish bayonet, so that behind the redoubts, the way into town lay wide open, and the defenders, if forced back from their first string of defenses, would have few places to reorganize and make a stand. They could slow an enemy advance by defending the bridge at María Sánchez Creek, yet a strong attacking force would simply outflank them and burst into St. Augustine at the northwest extremity of town—the same route Mathews had planned to use for his surprise attack.

Indeed, Governor Estrada was gravely concerned about the threat the town faced from the west, for he could not garrison all the redoubts and was making the best of scant resources to keep a battalion gun and what soldiers he could spare at just two, the Puente and the Paso de Solana (see fig. 3). He intended to hold his core troops in reserve, inside the town and fort, and to place only enough men at the redoubts to discourage an enemy crossing. Detachments of soldiers (each composed of ten men under a sergeant and corporal) received instructions to keep on the move between Puente and Solana. "The greatest care of these patrols ought to be directed toward the river," Estrada instructed,

> observing if noise is heard, people, barks, lighters or anything suspicious is seen, that indicates that the enemy intend to ford it. In which case, the two patrols of each redoubt should reunite and proceed to arrange themselves in due order . . . and all should fire continually upon those that intend to ford it, who may be afloat on barks or lighters, and the troops of the redoubts [should do] the same, using at

the proper time the gun of battalion which each post should direct, whose shots delivered with effect can prevent the arrival of the enemy to the margin of our part.[8]

Should the attackers manage to land on the eastern bank, Estrada expected his troops to pull back and repel them. Or, if faced with overwhelming force, they could retreat into town—the outskirts of which were barely 400 yards behind them—withdrawing by way of the María Sánchez Creek bridge and bringing the field artillery with them as part of the rear guard. Then the battle would be fought in St. Augustine itself, block by block, with the artillery used to clear streets of attackers, as the regulars, militia, and townspeople took refuge inside the Castillo. It was an old strategy. Ever since the seventeenth century, Spanish military officers, faced with superior force, had withdrawn into the fort and had held the province by defending its key stronghold. Two previous attacks on the town had been foiled by this maneuver. Neither James Moore, in his attack of 1702, nor James Oglethorpe, in 1740, had managed to capture the Castillo, and against its stone face all their efforts to occupy St. Augustine had come to nothing, though wreaking great havoc.[9]

Now it was the Patriots' turn to see if they could defeat the town and its fort. As the rebels spied out the land, they discovered their counterparts standing ready, men with guns in their hands and men training telescopes on them, infantry and artillery officers, soldiers in the white uniforms with red facings and trim of the Third Infantry Battalion of Cuba, volunteers from the militias, all taking up positions with their respective units. From across the San Sebastian River came the sounds of the townspeople shouting to each other in Spanish, Catalán, and English; the lowing of cattle being herded into corrals; drum beats and bugle calls; and the jangling and squealing of chains and axles as cannons were wheeled into position.

The Spaniards were also keeping watch. Lookouts on Anastasia Island focused their spyglasses on the sea and bar. Fourteen miles south of town, an outlying garrison under Lieutenant Blas Crespo defended the stone battery of Fort Matanzas, a modest artillery emplacement designed to stop hostile ships from rounding the southern tip of Anastasia Island and gaining the Matanzas River by means of a shallow inlet (see figs. 2 and 9). The fort consisted of a broad, flat-topped rectangular tower, set on a gun deck, which itself surmounted a low shelf of scarp work. The lower story of the tower was looped for musketry on the west side and had a window on the east to give a view of the sea. Erosion and leakage had taken their toll on the fort, which dated from 1742, but its location on a small island about one and a half miles north of the river's Barra Chica, or little bar, gave it plenty of natural protection. Crespo's job was to make sure no enemy craft slipped by his fort to fire upon St. Augustine. Only small vessels, such as gunboats or schooners, could clear the Barra Chica, and Fort Matanzas was adequately armed with two 8-pounders to deter such vessels. Estrada sent down word to keep an eye not only on the inlet but also on the roads leading into the southern plantation district and to report enemy movements. To speed replies to St. Augustine and lessen the need for couriers, Crespo assigned a sentry to operate a signal station (probably a semaphore tower) situated halfway between Fort Matanzas and the capital.[10]

Inside St. Augustine, too, lookouts at various vantage points were observing the Patriots. Three tall structures projected above the peaks and ridges of the town's cypress-shingled roof tops—the stone watchtower on the northeast corner of the Castillo, the graceful belfry of the parish church on the central plaza, and the tower of the governor's house. All at once, the bells of the church and the watchtower began to peal and guns from the fort spouted off warning shots, as the Spaniards passed the *alerto*, telling town and countryside that the enemy was within sight.

The Patriots, though, were not ready to attack. Instead, McIntosh led his men north, around the far reaches of the San Sebastian River, and encamped them at Daniel Hurlburt's plantation at a place called Araquay. Nearby, and also soon in their possession, was the old ruin of Fort Mose, two miles from town and the only shelter in the vicinity that an invader could reinforce and invest (see fig. 2). Everything else fell within range of the Castillo's guns. From this headquarters, on March 26, McIntosh issued an ultimatum to Estrada: surrender St. Augustine or the Patriots would besiege and take it. "The people of East Florida," he said, "having long suffered under the tyranny of an arbitrary government and being threatened that a body of merciless savages would be thrown into their country have unanimously, with the exception of St. Augustine, declared themselves an independent people." If Estrada cooperated, McIntosh promised he would gain the same terms given at Fernandina, full security of life, liberty, and property; payment of debts; freedom of religion; and "the beneficial consequences that must result from an annexation to the United

States." The Patriots also demanded the immediate release of Abner Broadway. Estrada could signal his willingness to parley, McIntosh indicated, by firing the guns at the Castillo at three-minute intervals, and the rebel leadership would then arrange to meet with Estrada's representatives at noon the next day at Solana's Ferry on the San Sebastian River (probably the ferry station at the end of the causeway but possibly the southern ford). The first signature on this ultimatum was Lodowick Ashley's, followed by William Craig's, George Cook's, Reuben Hogans's, James Smith's, John Houston McIntosh's, and Daniel Delany's.[11]

Estrada opened and read these demands before a Junta de Guerra of his officers. He was somewhat comforted to receive a confirmation of the rebel leadership and concluded that the Patriots, though numerous, were not as formidable as rumors had made out. Several hundred men, armed with nothing but muskets, could not seriously menace the town. "They shewed [sic] themselves first on one side, then on another," he noted in his reports, "pretending they had a large force."[12]

All in all, Estrada calculated that 106 men had turned traitor and that the rest of the Patriots were Georgians. Many families from the middle and lower St. Johns River were implicated, notably the Hollingsworths, Deweeses, Maxeys, Dells, Braddocks, Armstrongs, Williams, Harts, Hendrickses, Loftins, Turners, Tuckers, and Sumeralls. A few other names drew his attention, that of Zephaniah Kingsley, the slave trader; Levin Gunby and Abraham (Arbino) Follis, owners of the colony's largest sawmill; Francisco Roman Sánchez, son of a leading Spanish family; Nathaniel Hall, the militia captain who had supposedly tried to turn the rebels back at the Horse Landing; and Spicer Christopher Jr. and Louis Christopher, heirs to an estate on Talbot Island.[13]

Many of these settlers would later claim they were compelled to join McIntosh in order to protect their families and property. In any case, even at this early date there were conflicting loyalties among the Patriots. The Georgians, naturally enough, looked to their own ranks for leadership and soon would be following men like Major General John McIntosh, Colonel Daniel Newnan, General Buckner Harris, and Captain William Cone. The Spanish subjects included a hard core of Florida settlers with genuine grudges against the Crown—William Braddock and William Dell, for example, who had been taken to task for mistreatment of slaves, and Lodowick Ashley and Timothy Hollingsworth, whose families had suffered in the 1795 rebellion. Then there were the Johnny-come-latelies—Kingsley,

Craig, and others—who pledged their loyalties to the stronger side. As might be expected, the Patriots also attracted grasping men, full of private resentments, who took advantage of war to engage in slave hunting and banditry. William (Llewellyn) Williams and William Fitzpatrick gained notoriety in this respect. Young bloods, too, found a role for themselves, boy-men in their twenties, caught up in the excitement of events. Francisco Roman Sánchez was prominent among the latter, just turned twenty, headstrong, and apparently unworried about the consequences of treason. As the rebellion ceased to be a lark and became a life-and-death affair, the seeming unity among the Patriots would begin to fracture.

With the rebel demands before him, Estrada outlined to his war council the extent of their peril. American reinforcements were already on the way, he said, and St. Augustine was hardly as impregnable as it tried to appear. The capture of Fernandina had deprived him of at least 150 militiamen, who were now either prisoners or rebels. Only about half of the regulars in the Third Infantry Battalion were truly fit for duty, and the Castillo was short on artillery crews. Normally, the town's regular troop strength would have been augmented by the addition of the urban militia, but mustering of the militia was proceeding slowly, since many settlers lived in the surrounding countryside. So far, of approximately 230 men on the rolls, only 42 had actually reported for duty. The shortage of men was so serious that Estrada had released twenty-seven convicts to help defend the town. All in all, he had fewer than 300 men to repel an attack, and many were exhausted from standing guard duty, since he did not have enough men to divide his force into watches.[14]

A siege would pose additional problems. St. Augustine needed to stockpile food for all the men under arms, as well as for the inhabitants and slaves in town and for refugees from the countryside. Besides this, the rebels had severed contact with the Indians and, if the Americans blockaded the harbor, St. Augustine could easily lose contact with Cuba.

But Estrada was not going to treat with McIntosh and his associates. "It was our judgment," he said, "that no answer should be given to men unworthy of the name Spaniard and unfit to live in the same land where Spaniards walked."[15]

Instead, on March 27, Estrada presented himself in the plaza of St. Augustine and addressed the people. With the governor's house and church as his backdrop, standing beneath the red and gold banner of Spain, he told them they must stiffen their determination to resist. A group of settlers, he said, conspiring against the mother country that had adopted them as sons was determined to commit treason and to this end had issued a series of empty threats against loyal subjects. "But we should regard what they say with the greatest contempt. . . . In fulfillment of our sacred duty, we stand ready and prepared with weapons in hand to defeat them." Then he recalled to everyone's mind the saga of Oglethorpe's siege of St. Augustine in 1740. Not so long ago, he told them, in this very province, the English "besieged us for the space of a month and a half by land and by sea— and yet we forced them to lift the siege and retreat." Now they would repeat this brilliant success of their forebears and match the valiant resistance that Spaniards in the home country had recently made against Napoleon's troops at Zaragoza and Gerona. Having concluded his proclamation, Estrada reiterated his standing orders, that no one should cooperate with the rebels and that settlers still living in the countryside should be told to repair to town, where they would be safe and could help in the defense. By the end of the day, the lines were drawn. The Patriots would not withdraw; St. Augustine would not capitulate.[16]

When no reply came from the capital, McIntosh, William Craig, and Daniel Delany, desiring the advice of General Mathews, temporarily departed the camp at Fort Mose and retraced their steps northward. Seeking him first at the Cowford, they discovered he had not yet left Fernandina. Bad weather had fouled American plans to advance, and the general was still with Lieutenant Colonel Smith, collecting transports and waiting for the winds and whitecaps on the rivers to abate. McIntosh, when he reached Amelia Island, was in a mood as nasty as the weather. Estrada had called his bluff. For the first time he appeared nervous and nettled, openly berating Mathews and saying the general had deceived him into believing St. Augustine would yield without a fight. Despite this tiff, the three Patriots completed their business with Mathews, apprising him of their progress and presenting him with a revised cession of territory that delivered all of East Florida into the power of the United States "to the gates of St. Augustine."[17]

As the time arrived to return to camp, McIntosh and Delany found themselves stranded by the same contrary winds hindering Smith's contingent. They had to beach their river craft at Maxey's Creek and continued their journey overland by walking to Delany's plantation and then to the Cowford. From Delany's, they sent a courier south to Fort Mose, reporting, "The late province of East Florida is ceded in due form. . . . The

Troops of the United States embarked and came part way with us and will advance as quick as possible."[18]

The gusting winds and rain did not abate, however, and Lieutenant Colonel Smith had to suspend the advance of the bulk of his troops, first to April 2, then to April 3. Only the brig *Vixen*, ordered to sea by Commodore Campbell, braved the storm and headed south, under instructions to sound the bar and channel of St. Augustine's harbor. Three gunboats were to follow the brig when weather permitted.[19]

Through all of this, Mathews remained serenely confident. On April 4, when the weather finely cleared, he embarked in the boats with Smith's troops. Standing on the wharf at Fernandina, he raised his hat to onlookers. "I go to St. Augustine," he proclaimed, "and from there our victorious men move on Mobile and Pensacola. But we will not stop. On to Venezuela, to rout the autocratic Spaniards and plant the flag of freedom over all of South America!"[20]

It was one of his last moments of victory. Even as Mathews gave this speech, James Monroe was hard at work in Washington, writing out the letter that rescinded the general's powers.

Smith and the rest of the troops followed close behind the advance party, crammed into a flotilla of flatboats normally used for carrying lumber and cattle. The lieutenant colonel emptied Fernandina of troops, taking all the infantry and riflemen and leaving only Captain Williams of the marines behind with a small garrison of men. The river voyage south was anything but comfortable. Despite Smith's urgent requests for new issues of clothing, many of his soldiers had to make do with old patched uniforms worn thin by long use. Chill rain, an unwelcome introduction to Florida, pelted them as their transports negotiated the shoal-choked Narrows and the Nassau River and finally entered into the broad stream of the St. Johns River. Many in the contingent would see sickness before they saw action.

On April 7, after a brief stop at the Cowford, Smith stepped ashore at Fort Picolata, where he found General Mathews waiting for him. Smith dispatched a detachment of men by boat to establish a supply depot at Six Mile Creek. Then the regulars entered the hammocks and pine barrens and marched east to find the Patriots.[21]

As Smith advanced his men, the Spanish forces and the loyal inhabitants continued to watch the rebels from the security of St. Augustine. Estrada was in constant communication with Blas Crespo at Fort

Matanzas, wanting to know what the Patriots were doing to the south of town. With a good strategic location, Crespo felt confident about deterring an attack on his battery but was fearful for the safety of his advance pickets and for the isolated semaphore station.[22]

On March 30, three local planters, Francisco Pellicer, John Addison, and Robert McHardy, reported to Crespo to tell him that Patriot scouting parties, slipping into the southern district by night, were beginning to harass their families. They had already detained Pellicer by force, interrogating him about Estrada's troop strength. The rebels seemed especially interested in procuring livestock. Crespo recommended that the men abandon their homes and go to St. Augustine—something they refused to do—and then, after conferring with Estrada by courier, he decided to round up some of the area's long-horned cattle and transfer them to Anastasia Island, beyond the reach of the rebels. A supply of fresh beef for the capital would be crucial to resisting siege. By April 7, he had 150 animals corralled along the west bank of the Matanzas River, just to the south of the fort and across from Little Bar Island.[23]

From a safe distance, Patriot scouts kept watch on this roundup. When Crespo's corral contained some 390 head of good beef cattle, the scouts suddenly saw the flaw in the Spanish plan. The Spaniards had no large flatboats nearby to move the cattle safely across the Matanzas River and into pastures on Anastasia Island.[24]

On the evening of April 9, a party of thirty to forty Patriots on horseback rushed the cattle corral. From atop his tower, Crespo grasped their intentions and ordered his artillery crew to fire off the 8-pounders in a vain attempt to disperse them. The rebels ignored the shots. With whoops and hollers, they swept in, captured a Spanish sentry, and then galloped madly for the penned herd. Within minutes they had thrown down a section of the corral and were stampeding the frightened cattle to the north. Amid shouts of anger from the Spaniards standing atop Fort Matanzas, they managed to get away with almost every beast, wiping out a week's worth of work and denying St. Augustine several weeks' supply of food. To add insult to injury, they also demolished the signal station.[25]

Even as Crespo and Estrada absorbed the impact of this raid, new threats appeared from the sea. Lookouts at the Castillo and on Anastasia Island sighted a brig flying the Stars and Stripes tacking back and forth outside the bar. It was the *Vixen*, taking soundings of the channel entrances. After a day or so, it disappeared south, and Crespo soon reported that it was sounding the Barra Chica inlet near his battery. Gunboats No. 62 and No. 63 joined the brig, and each day, for the next week, sailors aboard the boats and in the *Vixen's* cutter busied themselves with charting the north and south entrances into the Matanzas River.[26]

In the midst of these alarms, Smith's contingent of infantry and riflemen marched into sight from the west. On April 11, he set up camp at Fort Mose, a little in advance of the Patriots and nearer to St. Augustine. The next day, around 10:30 A.M., the Patriot colors dipped from sight, and at 4 P.M. the Spaniards saw the American flag flying above the old fort.[27]

The arrival of American ships and troops was a severe blow to Spanish morale. There was still no sign of aid from Cuba. On the tenth, Antonio Mier's schooner had entered the harbor, unmolested by the *Vixen*, bringing news from Havana that the captain general intended to help. But the only cargo in Mier's hold was forty sacks of rice. In fact, Captain General Someruelos was distracted with his own alarms. Throughout early 1812, planters in Cuba worried over rumors of a slave conspiracy to attack sugar works. On March 15, panic spread through the city of Havana at the news that an uprising had begun, led by José Antonio Aponte. For the rest of the month and into April, Someruelos was in the midst of arresting, trying, and executing the leaders of the revolt. He was also about to turn over the reins of his authority to his replacement, Juan Apodaca. Under these circumstances, he had little time to spare for the troubles in East Florida.[28]

Estrada, meanwhile, was determined to challenge the latest intrusions into Spanish territory. Some show of force was essential to maintain morale. In the darkness of April 13, a Spanish launch, mounting a 6-pounder in its bow, left its harbor station just off the Castillo and sailed up the North River toward the creek that led to Fort Mose. The crew anchored three-fourths of a mile from the enemy encampment. Just as dawn was breaking and as Smith's contingent mustered to the bugle call of reveille, the launch opened fire on his troops. Four successive shots ripped over the heads of the Americans. One cannon ball kicked up a shower of sand and half buried a drummer boy without doing him any harm. In response, the men from Point Peter stood to arms and raised the Stars and Stripes. As soon as the colors went up, the launch ceased its attack. After a few moments, it put about and left. To get at the Patriots, Estrada now had to fight his way past the U.S. Army, and he was not yet willing to commit himself to such a battle.[29]

Lieutenant Colonel Smith, however, fully comprehended the message

Estrada had sent him. "I think the situation a bad one for defense," he noted, "and will take a new one in a day or two." Shortly after this, the Patriots sent another deputation to the Spanish lines with an offer to negotiate. They were turned away without a hearing.[30]

Despite confrontations between opposing sides, Mathews's filibuster had so far been a bloodless one. This changed as rebels began to invest the plantations south of the capital. The first casualty in the Patriot War was a young slave named Jim, who was killed at the Pellicer plantation, six miles south of Fort Matanzas, around the time of the Patriot cattle raid. At this time, the rebels were making forays into the southern district, prompted in part by a need for sustenance and military intelligence and in part by a desire to explore the rich estates (see fig. 9). It was relatively easy for them to evade Spanish patrols. The chief attraction at Pellicer's was a consignment of Jamaican rum that had been salvaged some months earlier off a wrecked brig at the Haulover, thirty miles south of the capital. Francisco Pellicer Sr. had acted as the salvage agent. He had deposited seventy-five puncheons in St. Augustine and had kept another seventy-five as his fee, storing them under a lean-to shelter at Dupont's Old Field, a few miles from his own holdings. Once discovered, word of the rum spread rapidly in the Patriot encampment and enticed not only rebels but also some of Smith's soldiers to come south in search of the main supply.[31]

The quest for the rum led to many incidents. On one occasion, Captain John Miller, having come across the stash at the lean-to, treated his men to a night of revelry, boasting to the soldiers at camp the following day that they "had a great spree and drunken frolic at Pellicer's on his Rum, & amused themselves by shooting Balls through the heads of the puncheons." At another time, drunkenness almost cost several Patriots their lives. Fifteen-year-old James Pellicer, in company with a mulatto slave, stumbled across the men while they were passed out from inebriation. The slave suggested butchering them all with an ax and using their horses to escape, but the teenager balked at the prospect of such a massacre and insisted on leaving.[32]

Access to the rum was facilitated by the absence of the Pellicer family. The two eldest Pellicer sons went away to serve in St. Augustine's militia. The rest of the family moved to an encampment at Fort Matanzas and later lived for about a month in a kind of shanty camp on the south beach of Anastasia Island, making only occasional visits to their homestead.[33]

They did not leave their homestead completely deserted, however. Jim, a slave of the Arredondo family who had been hired out to work for the Pellicers, remained behind, as did another slave, Pompey, whose wife and children lived at a neighboring plantation. During the day, the two men watched for intruders from the main complex, a cluster of buildings consisting of residence, corn and cotton houses, sheds, and a kitchen. During the more dangerous hours of darkness, Jim slept in the kitchen building, armed with a musket.[34]

Sometime between April 9 and 14, a party of twenty-five rebels made a night raid on the Pellicer property to confiscate supplies before paying a visit to the rum. Their leader, James Dell of north Florida, was a fairly recent recruit to the Patriot cause, having joined at the Cowford, along with his brother, William, and his extended kin, the Maxeys and the Deweeses. Dell was fast establishing himself as one of the Patriots' principal subalterns in the southern district. He and some of the other men in the party had taken part in the April 9 cattle raid and had also been the group that detained and questioned Francisco Pellicer. On this particular night, their group included another captive, twenty-year-old Matthew Long, a neighbor of the Pellicers, whom they had coerced into serving as a guide.

Leery of a possible ambush, the men reached the plantation at midnight. They were just making their way up the steps of the main house when a crack of light appeared at the kitchen door. The rebels turned to see a young man, clearly a slave, walk out of the building armed with a gun. Their reaction was predictable. According to Long, "the boy Jim came down from the kitchen with a gun in his hand, and the light shining from the kitchen door, which was open, he was seen by Dill [sic], who sprang from the steps, and ordered the negro to stand. But, as he attempted to move, Dill [sic] shot and killed him dead." The ball passed clean through Jim's body and chipped the brickwork of the kitchen chimney. Rushing over to the body, another man in the party removed the gun from the corpse.[35]

The shooting of Jim attracted almost no attention at the time. The rebels, in fact, visited the stores of rum and proceeded to tap the puncheons and draw off the liquor into bottles and jugs. "They used the rum freely, and wasted a good deal of it," Long recalled. Only Dell, a teetotaler, refrained. The following day, when Blas Crespo heard about the raid, he sent one of his men to investigate, then submitted a perfunctory report to Estrada, mentioning the slave's death amid other news. The Arredondos, Jim's masters, were among the few who kept the incident in mind. Holding the Pellicers culpable for leaving the slave at the plantation, they sued for compensation and received $400—the amount of money, according to the precepts of slavery, that Jim's life was worth. Within a few weeks, there would be more bloodshed, and the next deaths would touch both the Patriots and Spaniards closely.[36]

In the meantime, affairs took another unexpected turn, as help for the Spaniards suddenly materialized in the form of a British sloop of war. On April 15, watchmen looked seaward to discover the H.M.S. *Colibri* off the harbor mouth. The sloop's commander, Captain Thomas Thomson, was an acquaintance of Governor Estrada's. Having heard news of Fernandina's fall while in the Bahamas, Thomson had set sail immediately to offer his services and protection.

The arrival of the *Colibri* proved an unpleasant surprise for the crew of the *Vixen*. According to a newspaper account, the British sloop spent much of April 17 attempting to get the weather gauge over the more lightly armed brig. "Both vessels had all hands to quarters, matches lighted, etc. But after maneuvering in this way for about a half hour they parted without either vessel hailing the other." Had the ships fired into each other, the War of 1812 would probably have started in April instead of in June. Thomson was soon ashore, promising to stand patrol over the channel for as long as he could and to take Estrada's dispatches away with him when he left.[37]

The *Vixen* soon afterward departed the area. Captain Gadsden had already completed his mission and merely wanted to make his report to Commodore Campbell at St. Marys and sail to Charleston, South Carolina, for a badly needed refit of the *Vixen*'s main mast, top mast, and rigging. His information about the harbor entrance was disheartening, much as Campbell had expected. General Mathews, forever importuning the commodore with requests, wanted the navy to take a more active role in ejecting Estrada from St. Augustine by moving gunboats into the Matanzas River or by establishing a blockade. If nothing else, he expected Campbell to parade some gunboats before the town and the Castillo (to "droop the spirits of the Spaniards") or else sail them up the North River to assist Smith. None of these ideas, Campbell confided to the secretary of the navy, seemed practical. Although the gunboats could enter St. Augustine's outer channel, staying outside the range of the Castillo's guns, the bottom was too sandy to hold an anchor, and an easterly gale would wreck the boats on Anastasia Island. A blockade meant keeping ships on station at both the north and south ends of the island, which would also prove difficult in bad weather. Seizing Anastasia Island was a third option. However, a landing of troops required more ships and men than Campbell had under his command.[38]

As for trying to send gunboats to the camp at Fort Mose, it would be suicide. To cross the harbor and reach the North River, the gunboats would have to weather a raking fire from the Castillo, then point-blank fire, and then a further artillery barrage as they headed toward the American encampment. Assuming they survived (which was unlikely), the boats would be useless except as floating gun platforms, for they would never get out of the river again. And yet, Campbell had to admit, as long as the Spaniards had free access to the sea, St. Augustine could hold out against a besieging force for a very long time.[39]

With the Spanish forces confined to town and Estrada on the defensive, one would have expected Thomas Adam Smith's spirits to be somewhat higher than those of his adversaries. Shortly after arriving at Fort Mose, he had received the welcome news of his promotion to the rank of colonel. Yet he, too, had many misgivings about his situation. Judging from a letter written by Zephaniah Kingsley on April 1, no one had anticipated a sustained resistance from the Spaniards. "[I] expect daily to be sent for to assist at the siege," Kingsley wrote to an associate, "and perhaps storming the town of St. Augustin [sic] before which the Revolutionary Army is now lying, and only waiting . . . some small reinforcement to proceed against by storm as we are without cannon. I wish you could assist us by sending on some soldiers and military characters who wish to be shot at. We will pay them in lands such as might produce sugar, etc., and perhaps Coffee." His closing sentence was distinctly lacking in levity, however. "God knows what will be the end of this. We must now either conquer or fall like soldiers, perhaps both."[40]

Colonel Smith fully grasped the gravity of the situation, and expounded on it, again and again, in letters to his superiors. Where the rebels saw victory in one grand action, he saw only problems. Conditions at Fort Mose did not meet his approbation. He had no cavalry to keep surveillance on enemy movements and, as Kingsley had noted, no artillery to shell the fort. His supply depot at Six Mile Creek was fourteen miles distant, and he lacked even a wagon and team to cart supplies to camp. On their first trip from the depot, his men had been obliged to carry everything through pine barrens on horseback or on their own shoulders.

The provisions themselves were desperately thin, ensnared in the same bedeviling contract system that would plague the U.S. Army throughout the War of 1812. To feed his men, Smith had to rely on private contractors, and the procedures for paying a contractor in Georgia and transporting the supplies into Florida were hopelessly muddled. Guns and powder were about the only things he had in adequate supply, for he had armed his men with new weapons before leaving the border, primarily with the .70-caliber smoothbore musket and the .40-caliber rifle that were standard issue. The first, a muzzle-loaded flintlock, had an effective range of a hundred yards, the second a range of about 300 yards. These replaced the antiquated guns the men had carried at Point Peter. In other respects, the men were miserably equipped, something Smith considered a disgrace. Every morning he had to wake to the sight of soldiers standing picket duty in bare feet, and his earliest requisitions included demands for shirts and shoes. Food rations were short, the stock of coffee and sugar already gone, and the medical kit empty. For shelter, the men lived in tents or makeshift huts thatched with palmetto. By April 19, still awaiting a restock of foodstuffs, Smith ran out of flour, and he sent Lodowick Ashley north to talk with the contractor at St. Marys in hopes of spurring him to action. Smith told his superiors that if the Spaniards attacked, he would have to abandon his munitions in the field because he lacked a rapid means of removing them.[41]

As the trips for rum indicated, discipline was also a problem. The Patriots—over whom Smith had only marginal control—spent much of their time away from camp, scouting or hunting or foraging, and the regular soldiers began to resent the come-and-go freedom of their sometimes-allies. Initially, hopes of action kept morale high, but as a wet winter turned into an equally wet spring, men began to sicken or started to grumble, and some left camp to wander the countryside in search of food or amusement.

A shortage of capable officers added to Smith's difficulties. He was furious with Captain Ridgeway, who was (deservedly, in Smith's opinion) arraigned on charges of perjury, cowardice, "and many other crimes that degrade the officer and the gentlemen." For want of an alternative, Smith had to put Ridgeway in charge at Point Peter but planned to transfer him to some other command. Lieutenant Stallings, in whom Smith had greater trust, was stationed at Fernandina with instructions to come south at once if he received orders from Washington. More than anything else,

Smith wanted confirmation from President Madison or Secretary of War Eustis that he was engaged in a legitimate campaign and that more help would be coming.[42]

By any measure the colonel faced an arduous assignment in East Florida. With 109 regulars, he was supposed to capture a fort garrisoned by 180 Spanish infantry and a growing number of militia. Still, even he was infected, to some extent, with hopes for glory. He spoke excitedly about the prospects of battle to Captain Williams, his military commandant at Fernandina. "We meet with innumerable difficulties in getting our provisions on, but trust in a week or two arrangements will be made to obviate every difficulty of that kind. My little Detachment is in high spirits and anxious to storm the Town. I hope and trust I shall have orders that will warrant it soon. The inevitable fate of many women and children that will be unavoidably sacrificed in a combat in the night gives me more pain than any other consideration."[43]

The Patriots were also facing difficulties. The surge in recruitment that had swelled their ranks to 400 men in March was dissipating almost as quickly as it arose. As mid-April approached, with no sign of action and no indication that St. Augustine would surrender, volunteers melted from the ranks. The early predictions of General John Floyd, voiced to Senator Crawford just after the taking of Fernandina, seemed to be coming true. "If they meet with unconquerable resistance," he said, "every volunteer will go his own way." Rebel settlers from East Florida deserted camp to check on their families and plantations. Other Patriots, denied the lands and rewards they had been promised as a condition of service, took to looting deserted homesteads.[44]

With men and supplies both falling short, the rebels were beginning to chide and harass those settlers who had not yet committed themselves to the rebellion or who were daring to espouse the Spanish cause. Again and again, rebel emissaries delivered the same ultimatum: Pledge support to the Patriots or quit the province with the loss of all property.

Zephaniah Kingsley, who owned vast estates along the St. Johns River, and Robert McHardy, a wealthy planter from the district south of Fort Matanzas, provide examples of the different choices settlers made. Kingsley was among the first to be confronted by Patriot recruiters. A party of Georgians arrested him one night at his house at Laurel Grove, on the west bank of the St. Johns River, just as he was finishing dinner (see fig. 2). They took him by boat to William Craig's plantation near the

Cowford, arriving around 2 A.M. There, Mathews, McIntosh, Craig, and the Georgia lumber merchant Archibald Clark demanded to know his loyalties. According to Kingsley's own later deposition, he quickly made it clear that he did not favor an American takeover of East Florida, for the United States would outlaw the African slave trade on which his fortune was based. The rebel leaders applied more pressure. What about your estates of Laurel Grove and Drayton Island, they asked, and the five-acre holding at Mandarin that belongs to your wife, Ana Madgigine Jai Kingsley? You will lose everything unless you pledge support. In that case, Kingsley responded, he preferred to be considered a prisoner of war. Otherwise, Estrada would brand him as a traitor.

His captors considered this request but rejected it as an unwelcome precedent. No, they finally told the planter, he must either sign up or they would banish him from the territory and seize his plantations. Faced with this choice, the slaver did not hesitate: "I, of course, signed their act of Independence and afterward went down to the Ferry to see their Army, which seemed to consist of about 250 men mostly mounted and from frontier counties of Georgia." All around the Cowford the Patriots had posted placards admonishing settlers not to oppose their revolution.

Having made his choice, Kingsley returned to Laurel Grove the next day and began to fortify some of his buildings. Within a week, he received a summons to the camp before St. Augustine, where his change in allegiance was put to the test.[45]

Robert McHardy, in contrast, defied a summons to appear at the Patriot camp and spent the early days of the war hiding out from the rebels in the southern district while he relayed intelligence to Blas Crespo and helped to organize a defense. McHardy's abode was in a cluster of plantations called the Tomoka Settlement, which also included the estates of John Addison and John Bunch. These properties lay about halfway between the lands of the Clarkes, Pellicers, and Longs to the north and the estates of two widows, Mrs. Samuel Williams and Mrs. Frances Kerr, farther south (see fig. 9).[46]

In an effort to punish McHardy for his defiance, a group of Patriots ransacked his plantation, knocked down his fences, and sent their horses to graze in his cornfields. They were unable, however, to corner the man himself. Mrs. Williams found them engaged in a manhunt for the planter when she visited the Tomoka Settlement toward the middle of April. She was herself trying to locate McHardy, to get his advice and assistance, for she was a widow with young children and lived some fifty-five miles south of St. Augustine, at a place on the Halifax River called the Orange Grove—far away from most sources of help or protection. Her overseer, William Williams, a kinsman of her late husband, had run off to join the Patriots, leaving her to manage the plantation by herself. Now, as she came north by horse along the coast road, she was suddenly reunited with her former overseer, encountering him with a band of rebels at the Bunch plantation, adjacent to McHardy's.[47]

The rebels immediately accosted her. "They were loud and boisterous in their conduct," she remembered, "inquired for Mr. McHardy, and swore they would have his life. The party consisted of ten in all—and upon their caps they wore a paper label on which was written the word 'Patriot' in large letters."[48]

Frightened at the men's behavior, Mrs. Williams nonetheless upbraided her former overseer. "[I] asked him if he were not ashamed of his conduct, and why it was he was declaring vengeance against one of the inhabitants without provocation. He said he had received provocation enough, and would take Mr. McHardy's life whenever an opportunity for doing so presented itself."[49]

In spite of a lengthy search, the group turned up no sign of McHardy and eventually departed. The planter continued to escape detection for several months. Far from being chastened or dismayed by rebel threats, he worked as a scout for Governor Estrada and freely visited the southern plantations, offering settlers his aid. He went frequently to Mrs. Williams's estate at Orange Grove, and when she decided to move her household to St. Augustine, he escorted her, her four children, her stepdaughter, and seven house slaves on the journey. It was not until July 12 that a party of Patriots finally caught up with him. They took him as a captive to camp, amid many threats, but he fared better than other partisans of the Spanish cause. After a month in confinement, he was released and returned home.[50]

These early sorties into the Tomoka Settlement were soon followed by others. The Bunch plantation became a regular haunt for the rebels and proved an ideal base of operations. It was virtually deserted, for Bunch's slaves had fled the area and Bunch himself was an old man, crippled by rheumatism, who lived in St. Augustine with his wife. The plantation was also easy to defend. Bunch cultivated cotton on reclaimed marshland, and a low morass of swamp bordered one side of his property. Only the road gave viable access to his main compound, and the Patriots kept a watch on it. They dragged the machinery and gins out of his cotton house and used it as a barracks and lookout. James Dell eventually established his men at Bunch's and acted in almost complete independence from McIntosh, Ashley, and the main body of Patriots at Fort Mose.[51]

Notwithstanding their efforts to enlist more members, the number of Patriots at Fort Mose dropped to between 90 and 100 men in April, most of them taking their inspiration not from their appointed leaders but from General Mathews, who still spent much of his time in their midst. Since no courier from Washington had yet arrived, the general remained oblivious to the cancellation of his powers and wrote happily to James Monroe and to the president on April 16, counseling them about suitable candidates for a territorial government of Florida. He suggested rewarding John Houston McIntosh or General John Floyd with the governorship and asked that his old friend James Seagrove be considered as surveyor general and that his faithful secretary, Ralph Isaacs, be appointed as attorney general. Perhaps aware from newspaper accounts and from talk among his colleagues that his actions in East Florida and his methods of recruitment were being questioned, he defended his actions: "I have not in any instance committed the honor of Government or my own reputation, by any act. Nor have I pursued any clandestine means to accomplish the objects of my mission with any subject of E. Florida. The applications were made to me to know on what terms the government would receive them, to which I gave such replys [sic] as were justified by my instructions, & in every instance I confer'd with men whose rank in society was respectable."[52]

As word of events in East Florida spread far and wide, other prominent Georgians came south to see what was going on. On April 17, Major General John McIntosh of the Georgia militia rode into camp. He was eager to see his younger cousin, John Houston McIntosh, and to witness a Patriot and American victory against the Dons. The old warhorse had not forgotten the humiliations he had suffered at Spanish hands in 1794 and 1795, when his own attempt at rebellion had gone sour and he had been forced out of the province.

His arrival brought forth cheers and acclamations from the many Georgians who had enlisted in the Patriot cause. Not only was General McIntosh well known for his service during the American Revolution (particularly for his defense of Sunbury, Georgia, against a superior British force), but he was also a confidant of Governor Mitchell and thus a man of influence. The men coupled his name to Mathews's as an honored veteran of 1776, and his presence in camp soon began to eclipse the prestige of local leaders. Some recruits even begged him to take over command of the rebellion. "Their little army," said General McIntosh, "were determined in a body to Elect me their Commander in Chief, which they did unanimously, requesting my acceptance or they would abandon the course they had so warmly espoused." This sudden elevation of the general to supreme command did not sit well with several Floridians. According to one witness, Lodowick Ashley, George Cook, and Reuben Hogans were so offended by the decision, which impinged upon their authority, that they retired from the siege in disgust.[53]

General McIntosh, for his part, while flattered by the adulation, was not altogether pleased with affairs at Fort Mose. On April 26, having reviewed the rebel ranks, he informed Smith that the Patriots would never make much of a fighting force, even as auxiliaries. He was surprised, too, that the *Colibri* was openly defending St. Augustine and that the American government had done nothing to rush reinforcements to Smith's command.[54]

The general seems to have had little contact with his cousin, John Houston McIntosh, who was busily hatching a scheme of his own. With the approval of Ashley, Craig, Daniel Delany, George Cook, and other Patriot leaders, he dispatched an elderly woman to the Spanish lines with a confidential message for Juan Blas Entralgo, one of the Spanish officers. Addressing Entralgo as "a Gentleman who may have influence with the Governor," he urged a surrender of the capital and, in a separate letter intended for Estrada, offered $5,000 for "speedily inducing a union of St. Augustine in this noble and glorious cause." McIntosh concluded this attempt at bribery with "assurances that our friends will be recommended to and noticed by the government of the United States."[55]

Once again, the rebel leader had miscalculated. Governor Estrada was not about to sell his honor. Indeed, his sentiments were very different. On April 22, Captain Thomas of the *Colibri* announced that he had to report to his superiors and offered to deliver Estrada's dispatches to the British governor at New Providence in the Bahamas and to the captain general at Havana. In a lengthy report, Estrada set forth all the major incidents of the conflict and vowed: "Rest assured, Señor Captain General, that this place is in a state to make a vigorous resistance and that in the event of the enemy possessing himself of it, that it will be only of its ruins, under which I shall be found buried."[56]

All this while, the consequences of decisions in Washington were slowly making themselves felt in the South. Shortly after the arrival of General McIntosh at Fort Mose, George Mathews became concerned about rumors that the Seminoles might enter the hostilities. At the end of April, he left the Patriot camp and traveled to Fort Picolata to hold a conference with representatives from the principal chiefs, Payne and Bowlegs. He hoped to negotiate a treaty that would convince the Seminoles to remain neutral.

During Mathews's absence, word finally arrived that the U.S. government had repudiated every aspect of his work in East Florida and had taken away his powers. The shock of this news turned the entire Patriot endeavor topsy-turvy. Commodore Campbell, alone among the American military commanders, expressed elation. When he found out on April 25 that he no longer had to comply with orders from Mathews, he pronounced himself "the happiest of mortals." Men loyal to the Spanish cause also rejoiced. On April 24, José de la Maza Arredondo, writing from Fernandina, informed Estrada that President Madison was revoking Mathews's commission: "This," he said, "will be a decisive blow for the rebels." On April 30, the *Savannah Republican* ran the text of the disavowal. By May, everyone in East Florida had learned about it—everyone, that is, except the general himself.[57]

The dismissal of Mathews stunned the Patriots. He was still away from camp on his odyssey to the Seminoles and could not be reached—and no one wanted the job of breaking the news to him. "This thing is kept a profound secret here," General McIntosh said in a private letter to Governor Mitchell. "God only knows what will be the consequences with the unfortunate characters involved in this transaction—I think the government can never abandon them to inevitable ruin, after being in some degree invited to this revolution."[58]

Smith, too, was thrown into a quandary. In amazement, he realized that his government had stranded him almost a hundred miles inside foreign territory, his lines of supply and retreat held by small, scattered garrisons and gunboats. Now, it seemed, there would be no reinforcements, and he could see the Spaniards strengthening their defense works. After several uneasy days, he learned with some relief on May 4 that Governor Mitchell of Georgia was going to assume command over the situation and had already ordered Campbell to safeguard the passages of the St. Johns River. Soon Mitchell sent direct confirmation to Smith, saying that he was sending aides to St. Augustine to advise Smith and parley with the Spaniards.[59]

At this moment of dashed hopes and confusion, the Patriot leaders proved surprisingly resilient. They, after all, had the most reason to panic. Instead, John Houston McIntosh called an emergency meeting of the commanders. On May 2, William Craig, acting as chairman of the constituted authorities of East Florida, sent out calls for 500 new recruits to make up a volunteer militia called the Second East Florida Infantry Regiment. His proclamation highlighted, for the first time, some shifts in the rebel leadership. Craig and John Houston McIntosh took charge of organizing the new regiment and appointed Zephaniah Kingsley to assist them, in his first open action on the Patriots' behalf. They also accepted the services of General Buckner Harris of the Georgia militia. Indeed, since they expected to gain most of their recruits from Georgia and had designated Lodowick Ashley's house on the St. Marys River as a muster station, the help of General Harris was sorely needed. He was well known on the Georgia frontier, and from this point onward, his influence among the Patriots increased.

Terms for enlistment were generous. Volunteers had to remain in service until St. Augustine fell—but a colonel in the new regiment would receive 3,000 acres of land, a lieutenant colonel 2,500 acres, and so on down the ranks, with 500 acres for ordinary soldiers (a fairly generous bounty, comparable to the $124 and 320 acres being offered to men who enlisted as soldiers in the American army in 1812). Other rebel declarations boded ill for the inhabitants of Florida. The Patriots intended to pay their troops with monies collected on captured and confiscated property. There would no longer be any reluctance to capitalize on the spoils of war.[60]

McIntosh also penned a general appeal to the southern newspapers, espousing the Patriot cause and pleading with Americans to throw their support behind the revolution. Nervous about the possible collapse of his rebel force, he marshaled his considerable talents as a propagandist to decry the version of events circulated by Spanish loyalists and sympathizers. "We have been called insurgents and Banditti but we feel conscious of having deserved, and are assured of possessing the esteem of good and honest men," he wrote. The government was wrong to disavow General

Mathews. The act of Congress, under which Mathews had proceeded, clearly left open the possibility of assisting a rebel government in Florida, the Foster-Monroe correspondence provided ample justification for it, and the Patriots had succeeded largely on their own efforts, not by American force of arms. Indeed, claimed McIntosh, they had solicited help from the U.S. Navy at Fernandina only to prevent English ships from firing upon their ranks. But if the United States now abandoned them, "to whom shall we appeal but to God above." Without help, they were at the mercy of Spanish retribution, and that all too clearly meant a dungeon.[61]

The tides of war were shifting in East Florida. For nearly two months, the Patriots had been on the attack, while the Spaniards attempted to stave off defeat by publicizing their plight in diplomatic channels and in the American press. Now the Patriots were resorting to propaganda—and Estrada was readying his forces to strike back.

Governor of Florida vs.
Governor of Georgia

At the beginning of May 1812, American involvement in East Florida seemed to have reached the point of extinction. The Madison administration had discarded George Mathews and had almost discarded his enterprise. Yet after the initial embarrassment of public exposure, several voices, raised in chorus, were urging the administration to stand fast. General John McIntosh, Governor Mitchell, Senator Crawford, and others asked about the fate of the Patriots. They believed the nation owed protection to men who had taken up arms, rightly or wrongly, with American encouragement. To withdraw support and expose them to Spanish retaliation would be a blot on American honor.[1]

National interests also argued against evacuating East Florida. There was no longer any doubt that the United States intended to declare war on England, and with war preparations already under way, it seemed unwise to leave East Florida in Spanish hands. In Georgia, people feared a combined English and Spanish campaign against their state. It was for this reason, in part, that the administration turned for help to David Brydie Mitchell. Further deployment of the U.S. Army in East Florida required congressional backing. In the meantime, it was essential to find a reason for holding fast to American-occupied territory south of the St. Marys River. This tricky task fell, by default, to the governor of Georgia.[2]

Governor Mitchell harbored no doubts about the threat East Florida posed to his state. His reactions to the invasion were mixed. To some extent, he regarded it as a political blunder, precipitated by George Mathews's overly ardent sense of patriotism. Nothing in the Florida campaign made sense to him. Prior to March, the Spaniards, if not exactly allies, had at least exhibited docile neutrality in their dealings with the United

States. Now they had good reasons to treat Americans as enemies. Throwing Smith's contingent into the fray and then banning it from acting on the offensive also seemed folly. Intelligence reports confirmed that Cuba was sending a relief force, several hundred men strong, to St. Augustine. What was the point, Mitchell wanted to know, of keeping Smith idle until the Spaniards received more soldiers and launched a counterattack? Writing to Secretary of War Eustis on April 20, he had nothing but criticism for this policy: "You must be sensible how extremely vulnerable the frontier of Georgia is on the St. Marys. What must be our situation if St. Augustine shall be reinforced? The manner in which this business has been conducted has placed Georgia in a very dangerous and critical situation."[3]

Hence, when Mitchell learned of his appointment as U.S. commissioner, he vowed to take quick action. The Florida problem, as he saw it, was one of practicalities. To comply with his official instructions, he had to secure Smith's line of retreat, maintain control of the border, and find some means of settling things between the Spaniards and the rebels. This would demonstrate American goodwill and an earnest desire to restore peace. Beyond this, he hoped to identify some pretext or grievance that could justify keeping troops in the colony. The real dilemma Mitchell faced was not Spanish operations in Florida but the dreaded menace of British intervention. During the American Revolution, the British had struck hard at the South, blockading ports, luring slaves to defect, and arming Indian tribes to raid or terrorize settlements. They had even made contingency plans to sponsor a slave revolt. As war with England loomed again, it was crucial to keep British forces away from the frontiers of Georgia.[4]

The state of uproar Mitchell found at the border, when he arrived there after a hurried journey through Milledgeville and Savannah, only stiffened his resolve to take a firm stance regarding an American military presence in East Florida. "The province may be justly said to be in a complete state of civil war, anarchy, and confusion," he told Secretary of State Monroe. On Amelia Island, factions loyal to the Spaniards were vying for power against rebels supporting the Patriots. Pro-Spanish residents had begun shipping cargos of food to St. Augustine for the relief of the siege, and, even worse, the governor at St. Augustine was sending back caches of weapons to help arm his party on the island. Several Patriots, catching Mitchell's ear, claimed the loyalists were conspiring with their slaves to massacre rebel sympathizers. Mitchell discounted the rumor yet noted with anger that "the negroes in the province have become insolent, and have recently committed some violent outrages upon the property and persons of some of the inhabitants."[5]

Military operations did not meet with his approval, either. "I found the progress of the revolution stopped before St. Augustine, the patriots being unable alone to attack that formidable post, and the American troops not permitted to act on the offensive." There were terrible conflicts in orders. Commodore Campbell had received instructions to withdraw his gunboats from the St. Johns River. Captain Williams was being told to pull his marines off Amelia Island. If they obeyed, Mitchell said, Smith's men would be cut off. He had therefore suspended the orders and had sent word to Smith to hold his position and await reinforcements.[6]

Amid these problems, Mitchell quickly perceived what was required in Florida and apprised Monroe of his plan of action. He would open communications with Estrada, he said, making no mention of American intentions toward the province, while awaiting the president's official decision on whether to retreat. He also requested authority to occupy the province if the British decided to aid Spanish forces—a power previously vested in Mathews. Thus, assuring Monroe he had matters well in hand, Mitchell dispatched his aide, Colonel Cuthbert, to rendezvous with Smith's forces at Fort Mose and to sound out Estrada on a parley.[7]

Mitchell's allusion to civil war was no exaggeration. Local jurisdiction in East Florida was all but collapsing under the competing sovereignties of the Spaniards, the Patriots, and the U.S. Army. No place better exhibited the "anarchy and confusion" that Mitchell witnessed than the town of Fernandina. Ever since its capitulation, the inhabitants had been in a state of foment, refusing to reconcile themselves to the Patriot victory. On April 4, Lodowick Ashley, exercising his authority as a rebel military commander, responded to continuing anti-Patriot agitation by warning residents against further acts of defiance. He circulated copies of a harshly worded proclamation, threatening to punish any person collaborating with Spanish officials. The text bore the distinctively inflammatory rhetoric of John Houston McIntosh: "Whereas some evilly disposed persons are inciting disaffection, aiding and abetting resistance to the cause of freedom by correspondence with men in St. Augustine, and are by vile and infamous deeds arming the barbaric Negro, they shall be guilty of high treason and on conviction, suffer death." When the notice appeared on a posting board in Fernandina's town plaza, loyalists showed their contempt for it by tearing it down.[8]

The nullification of General Mathews's powers made a bad situation worse. In early May, Justo Lopez donned his Spanish uniform, broke house arrest, and went out among the townspeople. Attempting to resume his authority, he shut down the Patriot-operated customhouse and announced that he intended to raise the Spanish flag. On May 13, pro-Spanish residents met in a junta and drafted a public statement, affirming their loyalties to Spain. "Having understood that a Petition or Representation has been made by certain persons styling themselves Inhabitants of Amelia to his Excellency Govr. Mitchell, stating this district as being in a defenseless state, and requesting the continuance of American troops for the protection thereof—Resolved unanimously, That said Petition or Representation is not the sense of the Loyal Inhabitants of this district." The rebellion in East Florida, they said, was the work of a minority. Five-sixths of the men besieging St. Augustine were Americans, not subjects of the province. Under these circumstances, the residents rejected American sovereignty and appointed José de la Maza Arredondo, Joseph Hibberson, and James Cashen to serve as a committee of public safety for the defense of Amelia Island against the rebels. Copies of the resolution, written in both English and Spanish and bearing ninety signatures, were sent to Mitchell, Estrada, and the American press. The Arredondo family had already expended some $14,000 in support of Estrada's war effort.[9]

In Fernandina's harbor, merchants and ship captains were also reasserting their independence and moving to break out of port. On May 15, the captain of the Spanish ship *Fernando*, tired of having his vessel penned up as a supposed prize of war, told his crew to raise sail. As his ship entered the channel of the Amelia River, it was intercepted by Lieutenant John Hulburd in gunboat No. 168. Hulburd had been transferred to the area in April to help reinforce the naval contingent there, and he now ordered the *Fernando* to put about and return to the harbor. The *Fernando* refused to acknowledge. Closing upon the Spanish ship, Hulburd's gunboat fired off two shots, damaging the *Fernando*'s quarter sail and forcing it to heave to. Seeing this, the captain of a British ship, the 18-gun H.M.S. *Sappho*, immediately interceded and threatened to pound Hulburd's gunboat into matchsticks unless he desisted from his attack. Overmatched, the American lieutenant had to withdraw, and the *Fernando*, with the *Sappho* escorting it, escaped Fernandina and proceeded to sea. Other merchantmen followed suit. The firm of Hibberson and Yonge dispatched a thousand bushels of corn to Governor Estrada aboard their sloop the *Speedy*, and an English warship chased off American gunboats that tried to detain the vessels of George and Andrew Atkinson.[10]

These signs of resistance took the Patriots by surprise. William Craig and D.S.H. Miller, in an effort to sway local opinion, issued an appeal that was more conciliatory in tone than Ashley's proclamation of April and noticeably lacking in threats. The Patriots, they announced, pledged themselves to an absolute protection of all property rights and would justly compensate anyone who suffered losses. Contrary to what the Spaniards might say, the Patriot government would respect the rights of the Indians and free blacks in East Florida, would confirm loyalists in their lands, and asked nothing more than their allegiance and a repudiation of the "nefarious projects" of the Dons, who wanted to exterminate freedom and independence. They posted the appeal around Amelia Island and distributed it to the southern press.[11]

This power struggle between the Patriots and the loyalists—or the Patriots and the Anglo-Spaniards, as they came to be called—created daily dilemmas for Captain John Williams, the sensitive, forty-seven-year-old Virginian who headed the marine detachment in Fernandina and served as the town's military commandant. Like other officers, Williams was unhappy with the restrictions imposed on his freedom of action. "I wish someone could find the reason why U.S. troops are being kept in this province without the liberty of firing a gun unless we are fired upon," he told his superiors. The true source of his headaches, though, was his untenable position in the town. Both the Patriots and the loyalists insisted on exercising civil jurisdiction there. Unwilling to relinquish authority to either side, Williams placed Fernandina under martial law and did his best to protect American interests while shielding residents from personal reprisals or property confiscations. Unfortunately, this evenhanded treatment was winning him few friends among his supposed allies, the rebels. Local Patriots pestered him with grievances and accused him of coddling his country's enemies. When this heckling had no effect, they besmirched his name with gossip and sent complaints to Colonel Smith, saying Williams socialized too freely with the loyalists, voiced opinions in private that the United States would cease its occupation, and indulged in local hospitality to the point of becoming "lordly drunk." "I have never been placed in such a disagreeable situation in my life," lamented the marine, as he stolidly endured the stings of these slanders upon his honor.[12]

These personal attacks against Williams apparently raised doubts in the mind of Colonel Smith, doubts that increased when he heard disturbing rumors of a loyalist plot to retake Amelia Island. In a temper, he lashed out at Williams, saying he had his hands full with the siege and could not afford trouble at the border. Thinking over the situation, he sent Captain Massias north with orders to arrest the most outspoken defenders of the Spanish cause. Williams, however, refused to permit the arrests, and soon he and Massias were also exchanging heated words. It took intervention on the part of Governor Mitchell to set matters once more on an even keel.[13]

While these matters played themselves out on Amelia Island, Colonel Cuthbert reached St. Augustine to talk with Governor Estrada. The two men met on May 4, and the encounter did not go well. Estrada received Cuthbert with ill grace and waved aside his effusive protestations of respect and his polite offers to negotiate. As the Spaniard subsequently stated in writing to Governor Mitchell, everyone had seen the official disavowal of General Mathews in the *Gazette of the United States*. The United States had admitted it was in the wrong, and Estrada had no intention of treating for peace until American troops left Spanish soil. "Spain has procured to herself the reputation of scrupulously adhering to good faith in the fulfillment of her engagements," he said, "and cannot believe that she has given reason for the insulting treatment which this province of East Florida under my care has suffered."[14]

Cuthbert, after spending several futile days in town without making headway, finally agreed to carry Estrada's messages to Mitchell and then to return with an answer. He asked Estrada to maintain a truce until talks resumed, but the governor would give no assurances. Indeed, Estrada had no interest in a truce. For the first time since the fall of Fernandina, he thought he had the upper hand on his opponents. He had conceived of a way to attack the rebels without engaging American forces and was eager to try it. Instead of focusing on the enemy camp before St. Augustine, he decided to launch a sortie against a group of rebels who had invested the San Pablo Creek settlements, near the mouth of the St. Johns River. Ever since mid-April, a party of Patriots had frequented this area, raiding the plantation of Don Bartolome de Castro y Ferrer, which was located along the southern stretch of the creek, and taking shelter with the Dewees family, who lived on lands close to where the St. Johns emptied into the sea. San Pablo was well behind the American lines, some thirty-four miles north of St. Augustine, but lay open to a Spanish assault if Estrada could introduce an armed ship into the St. Johns River. Aiming to discomfit the unsuspecting rebels—who regarded themselves as beyond his reach— Estrada decided to risk it. He issued letters of marque to Captain Pedro de Cala, in command of a private sloop, the *María*, which was armed with two two-caliber guns and a supply of muskets and swords. De Cala was instructed to sail north along the coast with a contingent of men, enter the St. Johns River, capture or kill any Patriots who were posted at the Dewees's plantation, and otherwise "pillage and commit hostilities against the Rebels."[15]

Don Felipe Solana volunteered to lead the expedition. He already had a score to settle with the Patriots, for he had not seen his family in Fernandina since the day, six weeks past, when he had galloped from the town on a borrowed horse, carrying news of the rebel attack. Joining him in command was Don Francisco de Entralgo, a twenty-four-year-old resident of St. Augustine who was serving as an auxiliary in the Third Infantry Battalion of Cuba. Altogether, the detachment totaled fourteen men, including Juan Leonardi and Jaime Martinelli, sons of prominent Minorcan families, and Juan Bautista Witten and Benjamin Wiggins, officers in the free black militia who brought along three additional men from their company. Boarding the sloop, they sailed to the St. Johns River, encountered no American gunboat, and on the night of May 7 made a sudden assault on the house of Philip Dewees, just east of the creek mouth on the south bank (see fig. 2). Here they trapped three Patriots: Sergeant James Gardner (sometimes given as Garnett), William Dell (the brother of James Dell and a relative by marriage to the Dewees family), and a third man (never identified). Storming the house in the predawn darkness, the Spaniards fired salvo after salvo into its timbers and windows. Dell was the first to fall, killed during the opening volley. From within the house, his two companions blazed back at the Spaniards with their shotguns. There was an explosion of buckshot, and Felipe Solana, at the front of the attack, collapsed to the ground, his chest peppered by bloodstains. A moment later, Francisco de Entralgo stumbled, taking a ball through the abdomen that penetrated his bowels. Seeing the Spaniards reach the porch, Gardner, who was wounded, fled from the house and disappeared into the darkness. Entralgo, in spite of his wound, seized upon the remaining Patriot and made him a prisoner. Then the furious attackers tried to torch the building, setting it alight three times but giving up when the flames would not catch. As dawn broke, they rounded up any booty within easy reach, took eighteen slaves as captives, and broke into and pillaged the nearby warehouse of Catherine Baker, removing what provisions they could.[16]

Catherine Taylor, Philip Dewees's niece, later recalled the scene as she found it when she came to investigate the commotion: "that she came to Pablo . . . and saw Mr. Dell dead there, that the Spaniards were just about leaving the place." Standing to one side was a group of slave women, previously captured by the Patriots and now taken by the Spaniards. They were later identified as Madrissay, a woman about forty-five years old; her daughters, Betty, Venus, and Delia; her son, Cupid; and another woman, Mary, age thirty-five. Venus, holding her infant and keeping her two young children close, told Taylor they were being taken to St. Augustine and "that all the Negroes were gone and that she was going." As the Spaniards retreated to their ship, Taylor sent another slave girl to St. Iago plantation, about eight miles away, to find someone to bury William Dell, and then ministered to the Dewees family, who were huddled inside their house in terror.[17] Back in St. Augustine, Estrada listened with satisfaction to the report of his men and then compensated the raiding party by giving them the captured slaves and dividing up the other spoils.[18]

Coming three days after Colonel Cuthbert's overture of peace to Estrada, the fight at San Pablo caused great bitterness on both sides. James Dell never forgot the killing of his brother. In the months to come, while others deserted the Patriot cause, he continued to lead forays and ultimately joined in the punitive raids against the Indian territory of Alachua.

For the Spaniards, the raid also exacted a grim price. Jaime Martinelli came away from the attack with only a few minor wounds. Felipe Solana, on the other hand, was more grievously injured, and although he survived the shotgun blast to his chest, he remained an invalid for the rest of his life. "A double part of the booty would not compensate even for the expense of his cure," recalled Francisco Marin, another participant. Felipe's father, Manuel Solana, one of the proudest and fiercest old men in East Florida, was outraged at his son's injury. He held John Houston McIntosh personally responsible, not only for crippling his son but for all the other misfortunes that the rebellion was inflicting on the colony. In a confrontation that would later pass into folk history, he issued a challenge to the rebel planter, insisting on the satisfaction of a duel and adding that he would "fight him by day or night, on foot or on horseback, with any weapon." McIntosh mocked the challenge. "Was he a private man and Don Manuel Solana (whom he did not even know) a decent character, he would meet him by day, with any weapon but a knife or stiletto," he told friends. But in truth, he was an official of the Patriot government and therefore above Solana's station. If he dueled with anyone, he said, it would have to be the governor.[19]

With the Martinelli and Solana families now holding personal grudges against the Patriots, it was the fate of Francisco de Entralgo that most aroused general anger in St. Augustine. Entralgo was a dead man as soon as the ball entered his bowels, but he did not die right away. Don Pablo Maestre, the garrison surgeon, attended him on May 9 and wrote a meticulous description of the wound: "the ball entered through the right side of the lateral oblique muscle of the abdomen, piercing part of the intestine, colon, and rectum, as well as the spleen, before becoming lodged in muscle tissue." Infection and gangrene set in almost at once. For two days Entralgo writhed in torment on a cot in the barracks hospital. His right leg went numb, his complexion turned to a yellow-green, and he vomited and fainted between bouts of hiccups. Maestre could do nothing to save his patient, who finally weakened into coma and death. The passing of the "good and intrepid Spaniard" Entralgo was a crushing blow to his mother, Catalina de los Hijuelos. Francisco was her only son and her principal means of support since the death of her husband. Estrada, and later Governor Kindelán, pressed the Regency government to award her a widow's pension, even though Entralgo's death in a fight with rebels did not strictly qualify for compensation. However, the unusual circumstances of the Patriot War apparently convinced officials in Cádiz to grant an exception. They assigned her the pension about a year later.[20]

If there was any flickering hope for a reconciliation of differences in East Florida following the raid of May 7, it vanished a few days later. Encouraged by the attack on San Pablo, and perhaps angered at its cost, Estrada decided to strike directly at the besiegers. He was losing patience with inactivity. Even a minor Spanish victory would boost the morale of his men and would reach the ears of the Seminoles, whose help was desperately needed. His audience with Colonel Cuthbert had convinced him that Governor Mitchell was using negotiation as a tactic to stall for time. There was no sign at all that Smith's occupation force intended to withdraw. Rather, it seemed likely that they were waiting for reinforcements.

Estrada was not far wrong in his conjectures. Like Mathews before him, Mitchell had been left in limbo by ambiguous instructions from Washington. He suspected the administration was going to renew its efforts to acquire East Florida and did not want to close the door on this possibility. Therefore, as he explained to Monroe in a letter, he was indeed playing for time. In his first overture to Estrada, he had offered nothing more than an affirmation that the United States wanted peace. Now, with the rebuff to Colonel Cuthbert, he decided to set some preconditions for withdrawing American troops. The United States, he stipulated, expected Spain to pardon the Patriots and to abjure taking any reprisals against them. Such a demand was likely to enrage Estrada, Mitchell told Monroe, and would cause another postponement in removing Smith's forces. "I trust the President will not send any preemptory order to recall the troops," he confided later, "but that he will let us gain a little time and probably some circumstances may arise out of our present situation that will bring us relief."[21]

As far as Estrada was concerned, however, the time for parleys was long past. Before Mitchell's new proposal could reach him, he was putting his men in the field again. On May 12, the Spanish line opened fire on Smith's pickets, to drive them away from town so that they could not see what was being prepared. Then Estrada assembled a force to drive the invaders away from Fort Mose.[22]

Smith had no inkling of what was under way until early on the morning of May 16, when he looked out from camp and saw a small flotilla of ships sailing up the North River. In the lead was a topmast schooner flying a British flag and armed with two 24-pound cannons and some smaller-caliber guns. Four armed launches packed with Spanish soldiers followed in the schooner's wake.

Surprised, he immediately deployed his men to repel an attack. The Patriot and American encampment at Fort Mose was, at this time, divided into three sections. The advance position was at the old fort itself, a ruin situated on a narrow spit of land that jutted toward the North River. Smith had strengthened the place with a wooden stockade and a crude blockhouse. The main American camp was located several hundred yards farther north, and the Patriot camp was farther back still.

With little time to think and with neither artillery nor ships to counter the Spaniards, Smith opted for a *ruse de guerre* to lure them ashore into an ambush. He evacuated his main camp and put a small party of troops at Fort Mose in the advance position. They were only there for show, however, and had instructions to fall back as soon as the schooner brought its artillery to bear. This feigned retreat would conceal a trap. A squad of fifteen men would remain behind and hide inside the fort. Their orders were to wait for the Spanish troops to come within range and then fire into their ranks before they could gain the shore. The rest of the rank and file could then rush back and press the attack to its finish.[23]

Even as he made these preparations, the schooner anchored off the mouth of the creek leading from the North River to Fort Mose. A Spanish flag broke forth from the schooner's mast to join the British colors streaming from the masthead. At 11 A.M., the gun crews on the vessel discharged their 24-pounders, and the launches, under cover of this barrage, began to wend their way up the creek.

At Fort Mose, Smith's men commenced their ruse, pantomiming a panicky retreat while those in the ambuscade crouched down behind the stockade walls. They had to endure a fierce bombardment. The twenty-second shot fired from the schooner punched a hole through one side of Fort Mose's palisade and then passed through the fort's compound and exited through the back wall. Canister shot rattled like hail against the palisade's timbers. Undaunted, the men in the ambush maintained their position, listening and waiting as the launches drew closer and closer to shore. They had orders to fire when the boats were sixty yards away.[24]

Things went wrong at the last minute. The shouts and jeers from the Spanish troops and an abrupt halt to the schooner's artillery fire seemed to be the harbinger for a landing. The sergeant in charge of the ambush, eager to strike at the enemy, leaped up from his place of concealment and loosed off a shot. But he had miscalculated. The launches were still 400 yards away. Acting on the sergeant's signal, more men fired on the boats, though the range was hopeless for both musket and rifle. Seeing resistance from the shore, the crews in the launches suspended their advance, and a few minutes later the schooner resumed its bombardment. With shot falling all around them, the party in ambush had no choice but to withdraw to the main camp, scurrying through a rain of kicked-up sand. Then the gun crews on the schooner redirected their artillery, aiming for the camp itself, using the American flag and its staff to gauge the distance.

With Smith's men repulsed and pinned down, the Spanish landing parties beached their craft, raced into the fort, and set fire to the blockhouse and the standing portions of the stockade.

The schooner continued to shell Smith's camp for five hours. Although the bombardment was unnerving, it did little damage, for his men had retreated out of range. There were no injuries, Smith reported later, aside from some tents pierced by balls. Finally, around 4 P.M., having reunited with the launches, the schooner ceased its attack and sailed back to St. Augustine.[25]

This assault infuriated Smith. "The indignity of which I would most complain is the insult offered the American flag," he wrote angrily in his report to Mitchell. In truth, he was growing sick of sitting in front of St. Augustine. To the adjutant general, he later spoke more openly of his anger: "Nothing but the knowledge which I possess of the President's having disavowed the acts of the late Commissioner [Mathews] prevented my laying the Town in ashes after the affair of Moosa."[26]

Convinced that Fort Mose was indefensible, Smith relocated his camp a mile and a half farther north, taking the Patriots with him. "Our situation is extremely critical," he told Mitchell, "should the Spaniards be reinforced and this late success embolden them to venture another attack."[27]

If the army was to advance, Smith needed supplies, men, wagons, and artillery. If they were to retreat, then Mitchell must at all costs keep Fernandina secure. "The time has arrived when I trust your Excellency is fully empowered to render us that assistance of which we stand in so much need."[28]

Governor Mitchell was equally outraged about the attack. Noting that he still considered himself to be engaged in a parley with Governor Estrada, he told Monroe, "I believe it to be a gross insult to the honor and integrity of our government." However, the incident provided the pretext he needed to escalate American involvement in East Florida "in consequence of the Spaniard preferring the application of force to remove the American troops . . . to the more tedious operation of having it done by negotiation in a peaceful manner." In May and June, he used his authority to reinforce the regulars, justifying his actions by citing the necessity of maintaining a defensive posture and protecting American lives: "I will not suffer any sacrifice of that detachment either as to health or the enemy." To prevent Spanish gunboats from resuming a barrage on Smith's camp, he dispatched two bronze 6-pounders from Point Peter along with a hundred rounds of munitions to serve as a shore artillery. He also promised to send Georgia militia units to Smith's aid. An evacuation of East Florida seemed unlikely, he told the colonel. American troops were expected to maintain their occupation until the Spanish Crown granted amnesty to the Patriots. The Point Peter contingent should therefore hold its position and act as a buffer between the Spaniards and the Patriots, in fulfillment of an American pledge of protection. There were three gunboats securing the lines of communication via the St. Johns River.[29]

Georgians fully approved of Mitchell's actions. The editor of the *Augusta Chronicle* called for the total obliteration of Spanish power in East Florida. It was only a matter of time, he noted, before England tried to exploit the situation. Allow the British to enter the peninsula and the United States could bid adieu to the entire Mississippi Territory. Restoring the province to Spain was also ludicrous. The Spanish would acquiesce to every English demand and make George III the true sovereign there. To surrender Florida, he concluded, "would be injurious to the United States and fatal to the lower part of Georgia." The *Georgia Argus* took a similar stance. On June 17, one day before the U.S. Congress declared war on England, it promoted "the immediate occupancy of East Florida by the U. States as essential to the interests of the country and the safety of the southern frontiers."[30]

Ordinary citizens echoed these sentiments and rallied to the Patriot cause. Militia enrollments underscored their fervor. In Savannah, a hundred recruits with the Republican Blues and Savannah Volunteer Guards signed up for two months' service in East Florida. Crowds cheered them as they embarked ship for Fernandina. At Dublin, Colonel Daniel Newnan was busy mustering an even larger force. Residents of Milledgeville hosted a gala at the state capitol to honor troops from central Georgia who were heading south. By mid-June, some 500 members of various Georgia militia units were crossing the Georgia-Florida border.[31]

Smith was only too anxious for the arrival of these reinforcements. Realizing he had to hold his position, he ordered his troops to dig entrenchments around his camp. He also sent Buckner Harris north to bring back any men Governor Mitchell could provide. The Spanish made no further advance against him, yet the situation of his contingent was increasingly filled with risk. Smith's temper began to fray under the constraints placed on his command. Colonel Isaacs arrived to see him on June 5 and confirmed Mitchell's revised instructions. If the Spanish attacked again, Smith was "to commence a system of annoyance by doing them all the harm you can." It was a command the colonel welcomed—but how was he to accomplish it? As he pointed out with barely repressed anger, his lack of logistical and tactical support precluded almost any action he wished to take.

> With a weak detachment, but badly provided, laying before one of the strongest fortified places on the Continent, containing a garrison five times our numbers, what can be expected of me? We cannot always calculate upon the present disposition of the Spaniards. Our own tardiness must inspirit them. For the want of Cavalry we remain ignorant of their movements and are unable to cut off their parties. Upon any alarm the Infantry are forced to perform forced marches for the protection of the depot near the St. Johns River, my force not permitting me to leave the guard necessary for its protection.[32]

After nearly two months in East Florida, Smith seemed to be waging war on his own. There had been plenty of promises given him on his way to St. Augustine, he observed sarcastically. Now that he was in front of it, all support from the national government had vanished. No one was disbursing funds to cover his expenses, and he had purchased the last shipment of supplies on his own credit. To remain in the field, he required $1,200 a month for food, clothes, and arms. "Is it intended I shall remain here and permit myself to be insulted with impunity?" he railed. "If so, I must insist upon being relieved of the command."[33] To his friend Colonel Alexander Macomb, he simply confided: "I could tell you enough on this subject to make you damn the profession of arms as things are conducted in this misguided country."[34]

On June 11, however, Smith saw more of his hopes dashed to the ground. There was a flurry of activity at St. Augustine, gunfire from the fort, and a fanfare of signals. Studying the distant harbor with a telescope, he could make out sails in the channel and in the Matanzas River. One ship, two, three—a squadron. After months of delay, the captain general of Cuba had finally acted on his promise. St. Augustine was reinforced.

The arrival of Sebastián Kindelán y O'Regan in St. Augustine brought the last major player into the struggle for Spanish East Florida. Estrada at once surrendered the office of governor and returned to his responsibilities as commander of the infantry. He did so with some sense of pride, having preserved the capital, struck at the rebels, and halted the American advance.

The new governor wasted no time in disembarking his men, two companies of *moreno* soldiers and one company of *pardos* of the Cuban Disciplined Black Militia who had volunteered for service in Florida. With the addition of these 270 recruits, the total troop strength in St. Augustine rose to between 800 and 900 men. Kindelán, though, confided to Estrada that he had little confidence in the fighting qualities of the recent arrivals. "There is not one among them that does not shut his eyes when he fires his rifle," he remarked. He was also displeased to learn that some of Estrada's Cuban infantry had deserted—with at least one man going over to the enemy. Over the next few days, he reviewed the garrison, including the local black militia, whom he regarded favorably as men with military experience, and saw to the unloading of supplies: 150 barrels of flour, 130 *fanegas* of corn, and 5,000 pesos for the depleted coffers of the Real Hacienda.[35]

Perhaps no governor had taken office in East Florida at a less propitious time—the colony occupied by a foreign power, a rebel force at the gates, and the empire itself in a poor position to defend its possessions. Yet the situation was not unknown to Kindelán. Born in Ceuta of Irish descent, Kindelán was the son of a brigadier in the Real Ejército and had commenced his training for a military career in 1768 at the age of five. As an adult, fighting against the English, he had risen rapidly in the ranks, a protégé of the powerful Las Casas, and had been sent to East Florida in 1794 at the head of three companies of soldiers to help Governor Quesada quench the fires of revolt. Since then, he had served as captain general of Santo Domingo and governor of Santiago de Cuba. Indeed, his extensive military experience and his previous role as head of an expedition to Florida had convinced his superiors he was the natural choice for the job. Now a brigadier general and knight of the Order of St. James, Kindelán had seen rebellion, had taken the field with and against Americans, and had even crossed wits and words with George Mathews.[36]

Shortly after his arrival, he debriefed Estrada concerning recent events. Antonio de las Reyes, an infantry soldier, had deserted to the American camp, and it was assumed he had given the enemy a full résumé of St. Augustine's state of defense. Estrada blamed himself. He had sent Reyes to the Pellicer plantation with orders to retrieve some of the rum that was stored there. It had been a poor decision. Rebels frequented Pellicer's as one of their favorite haunts, and Reyes apparently took the opportunity to change sides.[37]

Kindelán, however, was more concerned with the besiegers at Fort Mose than with one deserter. In an odd way, he was in much the same position as his adversary, Colonel Smith. He had been sent to take charge over a situation for which he had no clear-cut orders. Neither the Spanish Regency nor the captain general at Cuba wanted war with the United States. Indeed, Captain General Juan Apodaca, having recently arrived in Havana to replace the marquis de Someruelos, was doing his best to encourage American trade with Cuba. Deeming it best to parley with the invaders, Kindelán dispatched couriers to Smith and Mitchell, informing them of his arrival and demanding to know why American troops where still on Spanish soil.

Smith responded by sending Captain Joseph Woodruff of the riflemen and Lieutenant George Haig of the dragoons to meet with Kindelán. Their embassy encountered even more difficulties than Colonel Cuthbert's, for they immediately made two mistakes. First, they informed Kindelán that Governor Mitchell, not their commanding officer, was authorized to negotiate for the United States. Then they denounced Estrada for the attack of May 16. Kindelán was curt in his response. He may have regretted Estrada's decision to engage American troops, yet he had every intention of upholding and defending Spanish honor. Foreign soldiers were in his country without justification, he told the envoys. If Colonel Smith had no powers to negotiate, then only one thing was required of him: to withdraw his troops at once beyond the St. Johns River and cease his support of a "banditti" of rebels.[38]

This demand infuriated Smith when he heard it. He was the injured party, he fumed, for he had been attacked without provocation. Writing back to Kindelán, he said he had no orders to abandon the Patriots nor any to leave his position. If the Spanish wished to avoid a conflict, they would be wise to stay inside the town.[39]

Kindelán, equally irate, brushed off this threat. "I do not admit and never will admit to be dictated to for my troops," he responded. "In the future abstain from sending any further communication here, for the bearer will be sent back without a hearing."[40]

Negotiations with Governor Mitchell over the next several weeks were soon mired in similar recriminations. Why was it, Kindelán asked, that

American troops still held Spanish territory, in contravention of assurances that they had no hostile intentions and would withdraw? His king and government, he told Mitchell, could no longer tolerate a foreign presence on their soil. Spaniards had no wish for a confrontation with the United States, but the American troops must leave East Florida in eleven days. After that, bloodshed and international opinion would decide the contest.[41]

Like Smith, Mitchell reacted angrily to an ultimatum. Writing back to Kindelán, he reiterated his conditions respecting amnesty for the Patriots and issued new demands. The Spaniards must apologize for their unwarranted attack of May 16 and explain to his satisfaction why they had fired on the American flag. Estrada had exhibited bad faith, Mitchell said, by initiating hostilities in the middle of negotiations. If the Spaniards repeated the error of menacing Smith's troops, they would discover that American forbearance was at an end.[42]

Kindelán would not be drawn off the main issue. He had no intention of apologizing for efforts to defend the province, he told his counterpart. The Spaniards had a right to engage a rebel force holding their capital hostage. They intended no attack upon American troops, and if Americans came under fire, it was a regrettable mistake. However, the troops themselves bore some responsibility if they protected and mixed among the rebels. In any case, he observed, the forces of the United States no longer had any reason for occupying Spanish territory, and he could not negotiate terms for peace until Smith's troops had left.[43]

Mitchell responded by hammering home more objections to Spanish actions. It could not be denied, he asserted, that Spanish soldiers had fired on the American flag in a deliberate action. They had done so after the United States had made a public disavowal of George Mathews. The attack on Smith manifested Spain's hostility not against the Patriots but rather against the United States. Moreover, Mitchell noted, Kindelán had brought several hundred black soldiers into East Florida. That was an additional provocation. The United States, said Mitchell, would never tolerate an army of black troops on its southern border.

Despite being stung by these barbs and accusations, Kindelán broke off further communications. His aide Benigo García eventually responded to Governor Mitchell's statements regarding black troops by publishing an answer in the American press. He pointed out that Spain expected all its subjects, black or white, to serve under arms in time of need. Furthermore, he said, the governor's protests about black soldiers were like those of a burglar who, having stolen into someone's house with a pistol, objects that he is met with a blunderbuss.[44]

In any case, Kindelán had no authority to grant amnesty to rebels and therefore no way to comply with Mitchell's conditions. He referred the question to Luis de Onís, who in turn set in motion the ponderous machinery of international diplomacy. From Philadelphia, Onís wrote to the Regency, advising that perhaps, given the circumstances, it would be best to allow the rebels of East Florida to return peaceably to their properties if, in return, President Madison would reciprocate by removing American soldiers from the colony.[45]

Kindelán busied himself with other arrangements. It was clear to him that Smith's men would not leave the province voluntarily and would have to be ejected. The Spaniards held the superior force in men and munitions. Yet they could expect no further help from Cuba, while the United States had thousands of troops in reserve. So, like Estrada before him, Kindelán considered approaching the Seminoles. The panic of an Indian war might drive the Patriots from the field and cut essential American supply lines. Smith would be left without a means of provisioning his men. Confronted by a quick-moving enemy who could strike at weak points between Amelia Island and St. Augustine, he would have to pull back and consolidate his scattered detachments.

There was a second military option open to Kindelán. Though he had doubts about the free men of color who accompanied him from Cuba as volunteer soldiers, he was impressed with the behavior of St. Augustine's own free black militia. They were accomplished guerrilla fighters well acquainted with the countryside, and their leaders had fought in the 1795 rebellion and in the local Indian wars of 1800–1803. Indeed, he himself could recall their exploits from 1795. Their recent actions, too, during the raid on the Dewees's house at San Pablo denoted valor and cunning in the field. Kindelán therefore decided to employ them again. To create disarray in the American lines, he put together a force of a hundred men, composed partly from the black militia and partly from his infantry, and sent them across the San Sebastian River in the dark of night, June 20. Their orders were to reconnoiter the area around Fort Picolata and then raid up and down the St. Johns River, causing as much havoc as they could and securing more food for the town.[46]

Smith found out about the expedition the next day. "The Dons are out," he told a friend, and they would find a hot welcome. He sent 160 men, Patriots and regulars, rushing westward to intercept them.[47]

The two detachments played a game of duck and run against each other for several days without coming to blows. Then, on June 24, the 100-man force of the Savannah Blues, having just come south from Amelia Island, landed at Fort Picolata. The advent of these men inhibited the Spanish troops and militia from risking an attack on the fort. Discouraged to find it strongly garrisoned, they confined themselves to foraging for provisions and livestock. By July 2, most of them were back in St. Augustine. However, they had accomplished their task. They had forced Smith to disperse his men and run them about the countryside, and they had brought back ninety-five head of cattle.[48]

Smith's expedition was also soon back at camp, along with the men of the Savannah Blues, who joined them on the march east. At the beginning of July, then, the American, rebel, and Spanish forces found themselves in a desperately familiar situation: Smith had just over 400 men sitting outside St. Augustine, some of them falling ill with dysentery and other ailments as the summer progressed. Kindelán had twice that number, about 800 men fit for duty, but he was bottled up inside the town. The Americans could not attack St. Augustine with so few men, while the Spaniards were hesitant to risk a major confrontation in the field. The two sides had reached a stalemate.[49]

While Kindelán, Smith, and Mitchell matched wits against one another, the attention of the American nation was turned elsewhere. On June 18, momentous news swept through the drawing rooms and parlors of Washington. At the president's bidding and over the objections of the Federalist opposition, the Twelfth Congress had declared war on Great Britain. The old enemy was once again the new enemy, and Americans who had grown up too late to witness their country's war for independence looked forward to fighting the adversary that their forebears had vanquished.

The War of 1812 proved to be one of the great ironies in American military history. Even as Congress acted, conciliatory words were coming from Europe. For two years the British government had dragged its feet about appeasing the United States and repealing policies that had instigated and encouraged attacks on American shipping. Warned for more than six months that the American republic was bracing for war, the British had finally resolved upon peace. They decided to discontinue search and seizure of American merchantmen. The aggravation it was causing was not worth the tactical value, especially as the tide of war in Europe finally seemed to be swinging against Napoleon Bonaparte. But their decision came too late. Americans had reached a determination to fight England, "whose almost every act," said one popular petition, "since the establishment of our Independence, has evinced the malignity of her heart towards us."[50]

Georgians, much in favor of war, received the news enthusiastically. "The present crisis," Governor Mitchell said, "is one in which the state of Georgia has not only an equal, but a greater interest, in proportion to her wealth and census, than any other state in the Union." He and Commodore Campbell acted swiftly against British shipping trapped in the St. Marys River. American gunboats swept down upon English vessels, capturing seven brigs and schooners and impounding them, to wild acclaim and public approbation from the Georgia press.[51]

The outbreak of war also galvanized calls to conquer the Spanish Floridas and secure the southern frontiers. "Is it better that our government should take St. Augustine, Pensacola, and Mobile while they are weakly garrisoned and not able to make formidable resistance or wait until they fall into the hands of the British and are strongly garrisoned?" asked the editor of the Georgia Journal. "Would not East Florida be the resort, and St. Augustine the safe refuge, of your runaway slaves and free booters? When the safety of a territory imperiously demands the adoption of a strong measure, it is not time to quibble about its justice. The necessity of the case will completely justify the act."[52]

A gathering of citizens in Savannah wholeheartedly agreed. "The safety of our southern frontier," they concluded, "greatly depends on an absolute dominion by the United States over the province, to be held subject to ulterior negotiation." A deputation in Milledgeville went even further: Declare war on England, punish France for its privateer raids on American shipping, and deprive Spain of the Floridas, they urged. Americans wanted no part of the bloodshed in Europe, but if it was forced upon them, they should show no quarter.[53]

Such appeals played into the existing stratagems of Governor Mitchell and encouraged him to strengthen the American hold on East Florida and defy Spanish threats. The Patriots might have initiated the crisis in East Florida, but Georgians had a chance to finish it. He had 500 men headed for the province, and his call to arms in June raised another 1,200 ready for service.[54]

Among other things, he was intent on ending the troublesome presence of armed blacks in the colony before it led to further difficulties inside Georgia. "It is also a fact," he told Secretary of State Monroe, "that most of our negroes on the Sea Board are restless and make many attempts to get off to St. Augustine, and many have succeeded, which . . . renders it necessary to have constant guards and patrols."[55]

The one thing lacking in all these war plans was a clear directive from Washington. Mitchell, felled by fever in midsummer, was forced to convalesce at Milledgeville, often dictating letters and edicts from bed and unable to actively supervise the course of affairs in East Florida. He waited anxiously for news from the president or from Monroe. Friends told him that after the debacle of Mathews's repudiation and the drift in national policy, the president had at last steeled himself to use military force against the Spanish provinces and had asked Congress for explicit authorization to seize both West and East Florida. The House and Senate were meeting behind closed doors to vote on approval of a military occupation and to allocate $100,000 to carry the campaign forward.

In all this commotion, there was one Georgian who was understandably too sick at heart to greet the declaration of war against England with his usual ebullience. While others prayed for martial glory and eternal fame, George Mathews was sadly reflecting on the collapse of all his ambitions. The news of his repudiation had finally reached him on May 9, just after he had signed a treaty of nonaggression with Payne and Bowlegs of the Seminoles. Ralph Isaacs, back in East Florida after his trip to Washington, had great difficulty in calming the general, who was, he recalled, "in a most unhappy frame of mind," threatening to protest his dismissal and to embarrass the Madison administration by publishing all the secret instructions that former secretary of state Robert Smith had given him. Senator Crawford, anticipating such a reaction, had forwarded a message to Mathews saying he could expect the governorship of East Florida as a reward for his services. Gradually, the old campaigner suppressed his combustible temper and, with cold formality, acknowledged Monroe's suspension of his services. "I have no doubt I could justify my conduct to an impartial court," he wrote to the secretary of state, "but I think it highly improper at the present crisis to do any act that would lessen or injure the president in the opinion of his fellow citizens."[56]

Even so, the disgrace bit deeply into Mathews's soul, and he continued to brood on it while serving among the Patriots as a mere private citizen. When he found out that Mitchell had been appointed to replace him and that the administration still harbored plans for keeping East Florida, he could no longer contain himself. To be humiliated was bad enough, but to suffer such treatment so that others could grab his laurels—even a fervent appeal to his patriotism could not silence him on this account. Again, Senator Crawford wrote and explained the ugly scandal and diplomatic furor that had necessitated his dismissal from government service. It meant nothing to Mathews. Late in the summer, he announced that he was going to Washington to confront the president and cabinet, and he would "be damn'd if he did not blow them all up." Crawford wrote to Monroe, warning him to expect some "harshness of expression" when the general arrived.[57]

Mathews never made it, however. Loyal Ralph Isaacs accompanied him north, enduring an arduous journey in terrible August heat. As with so many journeys in the past, the exertion overtaxed Mathews, and he was stricken with fever. This time he did not recover. On August 30, his seventy-third birthday, General George Mathews expired at Augusta, Georgia, worn out by his tribulations. In death, he did manage to win back some of the respect denied him in life. "Whatever political errors he may have fallen into, in the course of a long public life, let them rest in oblivion," said Governor Mitchell. The Augusta newspapers agreed. "Though his heart was stung by some recent transactions, yet never was his patriotism more conspicuous."[58]

As with everything else related to East Florida, Congress's decision about American intervention did not follow an expected course. On June 19, the day after the declaration of war against England, Congressman George Troup introduced a resolution in the House of Representatives affirming American rights to East and West Florida and authorizing a military occupation of both provinces. Other Democratic Republicans reworked the bill into a simple and straightforward proposition: to empower the president "to take possession of a tract of country lying south of the Mississippi Territory, and of the State of Georgia." From retirement in Virginia, Thomas Jefferson, perhaps mindful of previous duplicity at the

Capitol, followed the proceedings with anxiety. The soldiers of his local militia, he said, did not need Congress to make up their minds about confronting Britain or Spain. "The only inquiry they make," he said, "is whether they are to go to Canada or Florida." Yet all things seemed to favor the administration. The House passed the bill by a vote of seventy to forty-eight.[59]

On June 26, the bill moved forward to the Senate. According to its provisions, the president was authorized to hold any or all of the Floridas, East and West, and to use the military and naval forces in the South at his discretion, replete with an appropriation of $100,000 to cover expenses. American claims to the provinces would be reviewed and adjudicated during future negotiations with Spain.

Federalists and disaffected Democratic Republicans in the Senate immediately began to cause trouble. John Randolph insisted on making the contents of the bill and the attendant floor debates part of the public record, something he knew the bill's supporters would never allow. This request held up the proceedings for several days. A number of amendments also generated arguments, including one by William Crawford that empowered the president to establish temporary governments in Canada in case the American military captured territory there. Despite strong opposition, initial balloting suggested the bill would pass by a narrow margin of sixteen to fourteen. In the final tally, however, just as victory seemed assured, the Senate dealt President Madison a crushing defeat. The vote was sixteen to fourteen—but for a rejection of the bill.

Several factors contributed to the bill's defeat. Federalists in the Senate were still bitterly resentful about the declaration of war against England, which they had strenuously opposed. Some of them thought that the war had been rammed down their throats and that their objections and calls for public debate had been ignored. Now they were being asked to acquiesce in a war with Spain. Determined to reassert themselves against their hawkish colleagues, they used the Florida bill to make known their dissent. Newspaper accounts of affairs in East Florida helped them to underscore their objections. The *New York Evening Post* and other northern papers had published the various communiqués between Justo Lopez and his representatives, on the one hand, and Commodore Hugh Campbell, General Mathews, and the Patriots, on the other—including the note in which Lopez had asked if the United States was declaring war on Spain. These letters clearly implicated Mathews and Campbell as men who took a direct role in the attack on Fernandina and showed so much evidence for American threats and intimidations against the residents of Amelia Island that it was impossible to maintain a pretense that the Spaniards had been the aggressors. Personal animosities also played a role in the balloting. Samuel Smith, voting against the bill, avenged himself for Madison's dismissal of his brother, Robert, from the post of secretary of state. William Branch Giles of Virginia, never reliable as a Madison supporter, apparently withheld his support simply because Madison had never offered him a cabinet post.[60]

Six Federalist votes and ten Democratic Republican defections consigned the measure to oblivion. Senators Giles, of Virginia, Michael Leib, of Pennsylvania, and John Pope, of Kentucky, by voting with the Federalists, were instrumental in tipping the balance against the administration. There would be no federal money or troops for deployment in the Floridas. When the news reached Milledgeville, the *Georgia Argus* vilified those who opposed the bill as puppets of Great Britain. The editor had nothing but admiration for the Patriots: "This looks like men determined to be free, and in all their laudable exertions we must heartily wish them success." The *Georgia Express*, of Athens, encouraged Georgians to volunteer on an individual basis to fight against the Spaniards. "It is essential to the *real* Independence of America, that both East and West Florida become an integral part of the United States," the editor claimed. Other newspapers also expressed surprise at the Senate vote. "So long as Augustine, Pensacola, and Mobile are occupied by the enemy or their allies," predicted the editor of the *Georgia Journal*, "so long is the tranquility of our Southern frontier jeopardized." "This extraordinary circumstance considering the time, and our situation in that country, may truly be considered a national misfortune," said the *Augusta Chronicle*.

Neither public sentiment nor public policy, however, was the true arbiter of events in East Florida. The conflict in the province had by now developed a momentum of its own. Far from coming to an end, it was about to enter its most violent stage.[61]

11

Life in the Occupied Land

By the midsummer of 1812, as William Hull's campaign against the British at Fort Malden commenced in Canada, rebellion and espionage in East Florida were also rapidly taking on all the trappings of war. Three months into the military occupation, settlers who chose to remain in the countryside lived in a kind of no-man's-land, never sure when rebels or soldiers might show up at their homesteads to make demands. In a few areas—like those between the North and Guana Rivers north of the capital or those along the coastal river systems south of Fort Matanzas—the full impact of the invasion had not yet affected rural life, and residents braved the perils of marauders as they tried to save crops, livestock, and houses.

The American sphere of influence in East Florida remained extensive but weak. Colonel Smith's forces garrisoned a string of outposts stretching from Amelia Island to St. Augustine (see fig. 2). At the border itself, Fernandina continued to be a center of unrest. With England and the United States at war, Captain Williams kept up a keen surveillance on all residents of English, Scottish, and Irish ancestry, whose activities were more suspect than ever. Meanwhile, on the St. Johns River, Smith had strengthened his supply lines by establishing a new base at the Hollingsworth plantation on Goodby's Creek. This post, which he renamed Camp New Hope, lay nestled in the midst of several sizable estates—those of Farquhar Bethune, Francisco Roman Sánchez, and Prudence Plummer—and served as a stopover point for men and supplies coming south from the Georgia border. The camp was protected by natural barriers of water, marsh, and swamp and consisted of the plantation buildings, a barracks, a hospital, and a quartermaster's depot. Buckner Harris ran the depot, furnishing it with livestock and other supplies confiscated from the surrounding landholdings.

At the same time, Smith reinforced his hold on the Julington and Mandarin area, assigning Lieutenant Stallings the task of constructing a blockhouse there. It was situated at the confluence of Julington and Davis Creeks, not far from the Follis and Gunby lumber mill. Sometimes referred to as Camp or Fort Stallings, the Davis Creek blockhouse provided a fallback position between Fort Mose, the advance position, and Camp New Hope, the anchor for American forces, and was essential for supplying and provisioning the front lines. With the establishment of Camp New Hope and the blockhouse, the eastern shores of the St. Johns River became a regular haunt for American patrols and foraging parties.[1]

The Spanish realm of influence, by contrast, had shrunk to St. Augustine and its immediate defenses. With the landing of Kindelán's troops and supplies, the town was far better protected and provisioned. Even so, sorties from the capital could not restore Spanish suzerainty over the hinterland, and increasingly, the territory outside St. Augustine became the domain of roving bands of men who treated the settlers and their property as they saw fit.

What had begun as a campaign of swift American advances was turning into one of stagnation, inactivity, and boredom, without even the excitement of a skirmish or an exchange of fire to alleviate dull routine. For the men in Colonel Smith's detachment, May and June brought all the usual miseries of camp life in Florida—sweltering heat, drenching cloudbursts of rain, mosquitoes, stinging gnats, and infestations of chiggers that could turn men's legs or waists into a rash of oozing red welts. Even worse was the shortage of comforts like coffee, tobacco, and whiskey. His men quenched their thirst with brackish and tepid creek water and paid for it with bouts of dysentery, the sick list growing longer by the day. With nothing to occupy their time except drill and sentry duty, regulars and Patriots alike began to idle and malinger. Some found amusement in searching nearby plantations for hunting and fishing equipment, liquor, clothing, and comestibles. As the summer progressed, theft of property became a way of life.

Smith's military tactics were partially to blame for this. With no field artillery and virtually no naval support, the colonel had only one viable means of forcing St. Augustine to surrender, and that was by starving out the defenders. Besides this, his own contingent was desperately short of food ("for the last ten days almost in a state of starvation," he said in mid-May), and so he tacitly condoned the rustling of cattle, the principal activity of his Patriot volunteers, who became his provisioning agents. Competition for fresh beef engendered a kind of "range war" in East Florida. Whenever possible, the rebels stocked Smith's corrals with cattle, and when it was too difficult to drive the beasts, they destroyed them. This at least had the effect of denying them to the enemy. Members of St. Augustine's black militia, foraging for cattle near the capital, soon realized they would have to go farther afield. The roadways and woods around the capital were littered with the rotting carcasses of livestock, discarded, as one man recalled, "to the Buzzards, Dogs, and Wolves."[2]

The discovery that the province's cattle—one of its richest resources—were being deliberately and maliciously slaughtered came as hard news to a people who prided themselves as ranchers. A quarter century later, when people began to testify about their wartime experiences, they left a collective memory of depredations, of which the "battle for cattle" was among the most vivid. James Pellicer remembered seeing American soldiers torture and kill beasts that had been cornered near the Matanzas River. "They shot the cattle for mere sport or cut them down with their bayonets," he stated. "One of them, Cruise, showed his broken sword and boasted he had shivered it in an attack upon an old Bull. The carcasses of slaughtered cattle were strewed upon the shore for miles." Other settlers saw soldiers use the animals for target practice, testing the accuracy of their rifles by picking them off. At the American camp, boredom and the surfeit of beef on the hoof prompted men into frenzies of killing. "Every man was his own quartermaster and killed as he thought fit," said Francisco Roman Sánchez, an adherent of the Patriots who was much involved in cattle rustling. "[I] saw a man kill three beeves before he found one to his liking, and then did not use thirty pounds of the flesh. The cattle were wantonly destroyed, not one out of ten eaten. They were often shot down and left upon the ground."[3]

By some estimates, as many as 10,000 head of cattle were either stolen away or killed and left to decompose in East Florida during the thirteen months between April 1812 and May 1813. The Solana family lost their entire inventory, about 1,000 head of breeding stock and another 400 beef cattle, pastured at Buena Vista, as well as 200 head on Bells River west of Amelia Island. When Charles Clarke and Felipe Solana reconnoitered the St. Marys River area after the Patriot War trying to recover portions of Felipe's scattered herds, they "found no cattle, not even a track of one." Bernardino Sánchez lost 550 head from his pastures on Diego Plains, north of St. Augustine, and troops ran off 600 animals from the herd of the Christopher family of Talbot Island. Witnesses in later compensation suits were very specific about where and when cattle were stolen or destroyed. They knew the owners because of the brand marks. Manuel Solana's brand, for example, was an O with a horizontal bar through it, and each animal had a swallow fork cut in one ear and either an "underbit" or "under fishhook" in the other. His son, Felipe, used a brand of two overlapping S's. Bernardino Sánchez's cattle were marked by the brand BS, with a crop and a slit in the ears, and Spicer Christopher's cattle could be distinguished by the brand SC and by swallow fork and smooth crops in the ears.[4]

Theft of livestock, however, was only the first in a litany of robberies and abuses that soon came to characterize the occupation. From the Spanish attack on May 16 until the beginnings of raids by the Seminoles in late July, there was little military work to occupy the hundreds of regular soldiers, militiamen, and Patriot volunteers stationed around East Florida. The Patriots, in particular, were eager to glean a practical return for their months of service. Some tried to make good on General Mathews's promises of land by becoming squatters and establishing their own small farms. Others simply became looters, at times in the service of the regulars and in other cases for their own sakes. McIntosh and Ashley had established a precedent at Fernandina by declaring that abandoned plantations, and those of loyalists, were fair game as spoils of war. Indeed, in the absence of other rewards, the right to loot was about all they could offer their adherents. In the deserted plantations north of St. Augustine, rebels broke into houses to haul away furniture, crockery, and cooking utensils. They smashed down the doors of barns and corn houses to retrieve corn. They carried off cotton, which they burned in the campfires to ward off summer mosquitoes. They searched for muskets, guns, casting nets, and other useful items. They raided beehives for honey and poultry coops for chickens, broke up fences to make firewood, and, on hot days, harvested watermelons to slake their thirst.[5]

Attempts to curb these excesses occurred only at the beginning of the war and met with little success. On one occasion, when a man was brought into camp for stealing slaves, the Patriot leadership threatened to execute him. In another case, Major General McIntosh put a man on bread and water for eight days for pillaging a plantation. These punishments, however, applied only to men who robbed a friendly plantation. The outpost at

Davis Creek was itself a monument to property confiscation. To build the floors and walls of the barracks and blockhouse, Lieutenant Stallings's men emptied the lumberyard at the Follis and Gunby sawmill of its timber and then tore down sections of the buildings to obtain beams and planks. There were corrals for rustled livestock at both the blockhouse and Camp New Hope, and Patriot press-gangs drafted local residents into service tending the herds.[6]

Although cooperation with the Patriots supposedly brought exemption from confiscations, few residents found this to be true. A case in point was Henry Hartley, a young planter, "new settled," as his neighbors said, who kept a modest ten-acre farm in Mandarin. Hartley lived there with his mother and his wife and two children, next door to the holdings of his half-brother, eighteen-year-old James Plummer. He reaped between 120 and 150 bushels of corn, planted some potatoes and vegetables, and kept forty head of cattle and some hogs. The Hartley and Plummer homesteads were only a few miles from the mouth of Julington Creek and eight miles from the Davis Creek blockhouse. Soldiers and foraging parties passed by all the time. "U.S. troops made Hartley's a stepping place as they went back and forth," recalled John Moses Bowden, another resident of the area.[7]

When Patriot recruiters first showed up at Hartley's house, he declined to join them, hoping, like so many others, that they would leave him to his own devices. Soon after, however, a party of men out of Georgia arrested him and brought him to Camp New Hope. There he was given the same ultimatum presented to every other resident. "The Patriots told Hartley he must join them or they would take all his property." Confused and fearful, he replied that his wife was ill and needed him at home. His captors agreed to reprieve him on a kind of parole at the cost of his horse and saddle.

After several more harassing visits, Hartley finally agreed to assist the rebels. He spent four months with them, not in arms but taking care of the cattle in the corrals at Davis Creek. Whenever he could manage it, he went back to his farm. He soon learned, though, that his pledge of support was not going to indemnify him against looting. Soldiers carried off his cattle and hogs. Finding it impossible to maintain his family, he took them away to Fernandina. His farm was in ruins by the end of the war.[8]

Abner Williams, a willing and prominent adherent of the Patriots, suffered similar losses at the hands of his rebel friends and American allies.

Williams's plantation straddled Julington Creek, directly on the route between the St. Johns River and the blockhouse. He had "a dwelling house, a
cotton house, and about twelve negro houses"; planted twenty-five acres
of corn; and, with the labor of some thirty-five slaves, produced about
4,000 pounds of cotton. The Patriots set up camp on his plantation, sending corn to the blockhouse and living off his cattle. Later in the summer,
when the tide of war turned against the rebels, both the free black militia
and the Seminoles raided Williams's plantation, and he thus found himself victimized by friend and foe alike.[9]

Among the first settlers to lose their livelihoods from the war were the
poorer, small-scale farmers who planted immediately north of St. Augustine and supported their families on the garden crops they could harvest
and sell at the town market. Most of these settlers were from the
Minorcan community, a group of immigrants out of the Balearic Islands,
Greece, Italy, and Corsica, who had come to East Florida during its period
of British rule (1763–83) to work as indentured servants on Dr. Andrew
Turnbull's New Smyrna indigo plantation. Though many rose to affluence and influence under the Spanish, others remained people of fairly
humble and modest means, living in clapboard shacks with palmetto
thatch roofs and farming between four and six acres of land. Their homesteads, situated between the Cubo Line and Fort Mose, obscured the lines
of fire from the Castillo's artillery and were always at risk in times of
conflict, for they were the first places the governor would sacrifice to im-
prove his defenses.

In March, these families fled into St. Augustine at the initial appearance of the Patriots. From the ramparts of the fort, they watched Spanish
soldiers set fire to their homes so that enemy scouts and sharpshooters
could not use them for cover. The fall from peasant farming back into
abject poverty took a mere twenty-four hours. Such was the case for
Francis Triay, Andres Lopez, Juan Andreas, and Juan Ponce, all of whom
joined the urban militia and fed their wives and children off government
rations during the war. Andreas took a job as a pilot on a Spanish gun
launch. Ponce, despite his losses, helped to support both his family and
that of his son-in-law, Andres Pacetti—a kindness, Pacetti later recalled,
he could never adequately repay. Wealthier Minorcans, like Juan Seguí,
who owned several dozen acres of land to the north of town, also had to
flee into St. Augustine. Once there, Governor Estrada refused to let them
depart and put them into the militia companies. "So soon as Seguí came to

town," his neighbor Francis Triay remembered, "a musket was placed in his hands and he was detained like the rest in defense of the city." Meanwhile, in the undefended countryside, agriculture collapsed. At night, hungry American soldiers went out to grub through fields for potatoes, turnips, cabbages, corn, beans, peas, and onions, until whatever they left vanished into the weeds.[10]

In contrast to this early destruction, settlers living farther north, in a long string of farms and plantations between the North and Guana Rivers, were not immediately exposed to raiding. The North River presented a barrier that was difficult for rebel or American forces to cross, and it was guarded by Spanish gunboats. In April, though, foraging parties began to show up in the lands between St. Augustine and Diego Plains. Just after Easter Sunday, March 29, a party of rebels captured the family of Philip Weedman, a surgeon Governor Estrada had detained in St. Augustine to help with militia duties. They also made a prisoner of Weedman's father-in-law, Antonio Hinsman, and converted Hinsman's house into a repository for ill-gotten gains, filling it with all the booty they recovered from other homesteads. Hinsman and the Weedman family were packed off to Camp New Hope, where they remained under close confinement for the duration of the war.[11]

Much of the comings and goings in this area were witnessed by two young boys, eleven-year-old Paul Maestre and his sixteen-year-old brother, Antonio, who lived with their widowed mother at "the Neck," a narrow spot between the North and Guana Rivers, not too distant from Pablo Creek and immediately adjacent to the lands of the Cosifacio family. The boys' older brothers, thirty-three-year-old Juan and twenty-two-year-old Pedro, had both taken up arms with the Spanish and were serving in St. Augustine's militia, sometimes under the command of Captain Pedro Cosifacio, their neighbor, and sometimes with Don Francisco Miranda. Their duty gave them the chance to make forays outside of town, and they would use these opportunities to come by boat to visit their mother and siblings. All in all, the four Maestre boys saw much of what was happening in the countryside and remembered it all their lives.

Because of their youth, both Paul and Antonio Maestre were able to travel about the settlements in relative freedom, without fear of coming to harm. Three or four times a week they rode or walked to the Cosifacio plantation to visit with the overseer, John Moill. The Cosifacios had all gone into St. Augustine, taking their slaves with them, and had left Moill and one elderly slave behind to watch over the estate. Their plantation encompassed 110 acres of cultivated fields, stretching for three-fourths of a mile between the rivers and worked by thirty-five field hands. Besides the usual crops of corn, peas, sweet and Irish potatoes, and vegetables, the Cosifacios also kept hogs, poultry, and cattle; drew honey from about two dozen beehives; and had a small manufactory for producing castor oil. At the time of the war, they still had between twenty and thirty bushels of their 1811 corn crop stored on the cob in the corn house. Pedro Cosifacio, with duties as a militia captain, had rushed to town at the first sounding of the *alerto*, so quickly that he had left his reading books open upon a table. The rest of his household had soon followed, taking little with them.

Antonio Maestre, on one of his regular visits to the Cosifacios, was the first in his family to hear of the Patriots. He went to see John Moill and came running home to tell his mother and older brothers that soldiers were invading the colony. It was about two weeks later, around April 10, that his younger brother, Paul, got a glimpse of American troops. Going over to Cosifacio's, Paul found Moill in the middle of an altercation. A party of soldiers was trying to take some furniture from the house, and Moill had interposed, blocking their way. "They threatened to tie him up and whip him," Paul recalled, "and he quit the place and came to our house and they then set fire to the Barn or Corn House and burned it. Before the fire, the troops took out a good deal of corn and carried it to the dwelling house and afterwards carried it away."[12]

A few days later, Paul was out on Diego Plains, trying to round up some of his family's cattle, when he was stopped by a group of Patriots under Captain William Fitzpatrick, a planter who lived at Cedar Point on the Nassau River. They offered to let him go if he would give up his horse, but the eleven-year-old rather boldly refused. "No, I will go wherever my horse goes," he told them.[13]

At the Patriot camp, his captors brought him before General John McIntosh. The old Revolutionary War veteran was greatly amused by his young sprig of a prisoner. "I promised under oath that I would not take up arms against them," Paul recalled later in life,

and then they let me go. . . . General McIntosh at that time told me to let him know if any of his people took our property and he would see us righted—and he told me at the same time that the property of those who fled from their homes and joined the Spaniards would be used and destroyed, but those who remained peacefully in their homes would not be disturbed and if their property was taken that they should have it restored if they complained to him. After that I frequently went to the encampment and made complaints of having property taken from us by the Patriots, and it was restored. . . . Their rule was to burn and destroy every person's property who quit their places and came to St. Augustine to take arms against them. That was often told by the Patriots and by the commanding officers of the parties who went about to plunder and destroy.[14]

Despite McIntosh's assurances, the plantations where the Maestres lived did not escape pillage. Antonio Maestre remembered seeing American troops and rebels on the Cosifacio lands five or six times. Paul was present at his mother's house one day when two soldiers arrived and stole a cast net for fishing. "Do you want a string of beads? said one soldier [looking at the weighted net]. His companion replied he did not, and immediately the other seized the net and said, I do, and carried it off." Ultimately, when the Maestres left home to live in town, raiders picked their plantation clean of sixty head of cattle, eight horses, and thirty-five hogs, as well as provisions, tools, and a corn mill.[15]

Occasionally, Spanish sorties managed to recover stolen property. The two older Maestre boys were part of a detachment of militia that discovered a stash of looted goods inside the ruined plantation house of Antonio Hinsman. "There were a party of about sixty of us who went up in three barges to the place, about nine miles up the North River . . . which the enemy used as a depot for property they had plundered from the country," said Juan. "I had charge of one of the barges. We found there a large quantity of corn, some pots of honey, hides, saddles and bridles, and among the rest we found the two caldron kettles belonging to Cosifacio's [castor oil operation]." Everything in the house was transported back to St. Augustine and sold at auction.[16]

Mrs. Maestre was only one among several widows or female heads of household who ran large estates in East Florida, sometimes with the help of young sons and sometimes through overseers and slaves. Unlike the male planters, who were pressed into military service by either Estrada or the Patriots, the women were able to remain on their properties. By midsummer, though, the province was becoming a hazardous place even for widows. In the southern district, Mrs. Samuel Williams gave up trying to manage her plantation of Orange Grove on the Halifax River and came into St. Augustine with seven slaves and her four children and stepdaughter, "in consequence of the annoyances she received from the Patriots United States highwaymen." With her came two other widows, Mrs. Ormond, a distant neighbor, and Mrs. Kerr, her near neighbor and "a fearless old woman." They rented lodgings in town for about $2 per day. Other women remained in their homes until the outbreak of Indian hostilities, when the disruptions became too much for them. Prudence Plummer, the widow of a British lieutenant colonel who had fought in the American Revolution, refused to leave her home, situated only a few miles from Camp New Hope, until conditions forced her out. "Widows and single women received no more protection from the invader than did the male inhabitants of the Province," Francisco Roman Sánchez later recalled. Plummer "was loyal and used harsh language occasionally to the Americans." Sánchez could not recall her "selling even a chicken" to them. In mid-September, on the advice of her neighbor and son-in-law, Dr. Hall, who warned her that the war was going badly for Colonel Smith and might get very bloody, she finally departed for Fernandina. In her absence, her estate was repeatedly rifled, sometimes by American soldiers and Georgia militia, sometimes by passing parties of Seminole warriors. Around the same time, in a more mysterious case, an unknown party of men burned Rebecca Richards out of her plantation near the Cowford. William Munroe, the master's mate on gunboat No. 149, was often on patrol duty along the St. Johns River in that area and would stop at Richards's plantation to obtain fresh poultry and to check up on the widow, whom he described as "a pretty good planter, and a thriving and industrious woman." Eight days after one such visit, he returned to find the two-story house and other buildings burned down, the citrus grove hacked into stumps by axe, and the place abandoned. Richards also spent the rest of the war living in Fernandina.[17]

Those who fled to Fernandina ended up at the center of some of the worst cases of pillage. Far behind the lines, with no chance of aid from Spanish forces, the town seethed with resentments, as Patriots attempted to enforce their authority and loyalists continually sought means of confounding them. Although Captain John Williams endeavored to shield inhabitants from cases of private vengeance, George J. F. Clarke had to flee the town to save his life. As possibly the most loyal man in the colony, Clarke had been marked for special attention by the rebels. Everything linked him to the preservation of Spanish rule in East Florida—his English Catholic upbringing, his free black consort and mulatto children, and his booming lumber trade at Amelia Island. Moreover, he was known to be an agitator against the Americans. It was Clarke who had confronted Dr. Hall in 1810 over an attempted invasion, Clarke who had urged Justo Lopez to defy the Patriots. Almost as soon as Fernandina fell, he began to receive death threats. Within two weeks, he had to leave the town in the dark of night to seek refuge in St. Marys, Georgia, where he had friends to protect him. Over the course of the summer, rebels looted his plantation on the Matanzas River and burned his stockpile of cut cedar at Julington Creek. In Fernandina itself, they robbed his cotton warehouse, ransacked his house and sawmill at Egan's Creek, and seized or destroyed his flatboats and lighters.[18]

Other known loyalists were also targeted. Felipe Solana earned the undying hatred of the Patriots for leading the attack at San Pablo that killed William Dell. "If Solana had returned [to Fernandina] they would have been glad to see him," recalled Francisco Roman Sánchez, "to make him a present of a bullet." Instead, someone took revenge on his partially built house. Sometime in early May, the structure simply disappeared. The two-story frame was torn down and removed, and some 8,000 cypress shingles and 2,000 clapboards, stored in the yard, were carried off.[19]

Things became even worse for the loyalists when Colonel Smith transferred Captain Williams to Fort Mose and appointed Captain Fiedler Ridgeway as the new commandant in Fernandina. It proved a bad mistake. Ridgeway had a long record of drunkenness and court-martial and was already in Smith's bad graces because of it. He was also an early and avowed partisan of General Mathews and the Patriots and a man ready to rule with an iron fist. Under his command, "the inhabitants of Fernandina were considered prisoners of war and remained so." On July 3, in preparation for celebrating the anniversary of the Declaration of Independence, Ridgeway ordered a sweep of the town. Fearful that agitators might seize the day's revelries—and attendant inebriation—to stage a revolt, he ordered a search of every house and confiscated all firearms and other potential weapons. Some outspoken loyalists, like George J. F. Clarke's brother, Charles, were arrested and thrown into prison. From the jail, Clarke remembered watching the wives of American soldiers tearing clapboards off his brother's warehouse to use as firewood. Other residents were confined in the stocks or were manacled.[20]

The Pons brothers, Francisco and Pedro, also invited retribution for trying to run relief supplies into St. Augustine, the equivalent of aiding and abetting the enemy. Their sloop was tied up at Yonge's wharf, loaded with twenty-two barrels of wheat flour, a barrel of coffee, a firkin of butter, sixteen bushels of corn, two casks of rice, a barrel of lard, and boxes of candles and soap. One night, before it could sail, a party of men boarded the vessel, cut it loose in full view of the American sentries, and then sailed it across the Amelia River to Tiger Island, where they set it ablaze. A few days later, Captain Ridgeway issued orders to demolish the Pons's house and bakery on the southeast corner of the plaza, saying it blocked his lines of fire. At the same time, he ordered the destruction of the warehouse of James Cashen, another prominent loyalist.[21]

Beyond the limits of Amelia Island, the loyalists living between the St. Marys and Nassau Rivers were also subject to reprisals. This was especially true for establishments at Lanceford Creek and O'Neill's Creek, where there were several prosperous plantations, all belonging to pro-Spanish families. In that vicinity, the Patriots took to bivouacking on the lands of Robert Andrew, turning his plantation into a point of rendezvous. They evicted Eber and William O'Neill from their homesteads because they were "violently for the Spanish" and the rebels "owed them a spite."[22]

The outcry against Ridgeway soon prompted Smith to remove him. Indeed, having no confidence in the officer, he had intended the appointment "to be of short duration." In August, he substituted Captain Abraham Massias into the command and recalled Ridgeway to Fort Mose. Despite the change, anger over the American occupation continued to smolder on Amelia Island. Massias was regarded as a hard but just man by some and as little better than Ridgeway by others. The task of governing Fernandina suited him, however, for campaigning in Florida had broken his health, and he was no longer able to remain active on the front lines. He showed no sympathy towards the Spanish loyalists, yet he did reinstitute many Spanish laws and regulations in order to maintain order and to clamp down on the smuggling trade. Caught between Patriot and loyalist aspirants, Fernandina waged its own minor war of espionage and counterespionage. "Keep an eye on young [José] Arredondo," Smith cautioned Massias, "and if you have the slightest pretext you will have him confined. He is a foolish, hot-headed youth and may induce persons of his own description to acts of hostility."[23]

The fate of East Florida's approximately 2,000 slaves during all these disruptions remains difficult to assess. Among the largest slave owners at the time were John Fraser (375 slaves), John Houston McIntosh (approximately 200 slaves), Spicer Christopher Jr. (117 slaves), John Forbes (119 slaves), Zephaniah Kingsley (approximately 100 slaves), the family of Francisco Xavier Sánchez (approximately 100 slaves), and the Harrison, Atkinson, Fatio, and Arredondo families, who also relied on a labor pool of between 50 and 100 enslaved people. In addition, there were at least a dozen families who owned between 30 and 40 slaves, another dozen with between 20 and 30 slaves, and many households with a dozen field hands or a few domestic servants or attendants. At most of the large plantations, slaves and their families remained behind when their masters retreated into St. Augustine or Fernandina. Planters seeking compensation for war damages from the U.S. government in the 1830s did everything they could to prove that these slaves had been killed or seized by the Patriots and the American troops. In fact, many ran away, and others were taken by Indian raiding parties and became part of the black maroon population that would see battle once again in the First and Second Seminole Wars. In their initial raids of July 1812, Bowlegs's war parties seized some 80 people from the slave quarters of various plantations, including at least 13 men and women from the Fatio plantation and, according to some accounts, 41 people from the Kingsley estate at Laurel Grove.

It might seem that the chaos of war would provide a perfect cover for slaves to rise up in an insurrection. However, the only hint of an uprising involved free men of color among the militia companies from Cuba. According to one newspaper story—unsubstantiated by other sources—these volunteers threatened to kill Governor Kindelán if he surrendered to the Americans. Among the slaves, the better option seemed to be flight. Sampson, a thirty-five-year-old field hand, ran away from his master, Gaspar Papy, and surrendered to the American troops at Fort Picolata. Sam, one of Manuel Solana's slaves who helped to arrange purchases of cattle from the Seminoles, also disappeared, probably into the Indian territory he knew so well. Nancy, a woman in her thirties, fled from the plantation of John Lofton, taking her seven children with her, and lived for a time among the Seminoles. She was recaptured after the war. For others, the Indian territory was only one stopping point in a longer route to escape. "Many of the fugitives did not remain with the Indians," said one witness after the war. "They went down to the capes and passed over to the Bahamas." Two slaves from the Bethune plantation, a husband (Roger) and wife (Phoebe), apparently followed this route and went to Cape Florida. Others headed westward and came under the influence of British agents operating along the Apalachicola River, on the border of East and West Florida, where the British were trying to arm the Creeks for strikes against the American South. Eventually, a large maroon community took over a British fort there and in the years following the War of 1812 maintained a fierce independence. In 1816, American troops finally attacked and destroyed this fort. Robin, a slave trained as a carpenter who escaped from the Plummer plantation during the Patriot War, was apparently among the hundreds of casualties of the 1816 battle. Other men and women tried to escape, only to die in their bid for freedom. Eight people drowned at sea while fleeing Amelia Island by boat, and a young woman and her two-year-old child perished from exposure while trying to leave the San Pablo area in the winter of 1812–13.[24]

Most slave families seem to have survived the war by hiding out in whatever natural refuges they could find, frequenting their quarters and plantations during the daytime and then retreating into the security of the woods or to the beach at night. This was true for the slaves of Mrs. Williams and Mrs. Kerr on the Halifax River, for those at the Bunch plantation at Tomoka, for the thirty-five people left behind at the Richards's plantation on Pottsburgh Creek, and for others all across the province. Few received any aid from their masters, although Mrs. Williams did try to send shipments of food to the slaves she had left behind at Orange Grove, dispatching about twenty-five boatloads of provisions. It became increasingly difficult, however, to hire oarsmen and teamsters to make the trip. For the most part, the slaves at Orange Grove fended for themselves, fishing in the Halifax River, hunting for pelicans and wild game, and eating heart of palmetto, often used by the Minorcans and the Seminoles as a "starving times" food. Fifteen families, most of them with children under the age of ten and totaling about sixty-seven people in all, survived in this manner as refugees on the southern perimeter of the war zone. At times, slave families also took in their masters' younger children as wards. Both Daniel Vaughn and Ephraim Harrison, youths of Amelia Island, recalled hiding with slaves during the war.[25]

Under these circumstances, it was impossible to completely evade the danger of capture or death. Slave hunters exploited the war to turn a profit. Sometime over the summer, soldiers stole away a woman named

Betsy from the Peso di Burgo family because she was noted in the province as an excellent French cook, and the officers wanted her to prepare their meals. Cook and Jim were listed among seven slaves taken from the Spicer Christopher plantation on Talbot Island, their fates unknown. One of the worst travesties of the war befell Carlos Hill, a former slave who had purchased his freedom and was living in 1812 on a small homestead with his wife, Maria, a free woman of color, and their young children. William Williams came to the house at the head of a party of rebels and seized Hill and his family. They let Hill go but carried off his wife and children into Georgia. Hill tried to locate his family after the war, but he never saw them again. These kidnappings grew bolder as time went on. By 1813, slave hunters out of Georgia were operating in East Florida. At times parties of up to sixty men attacked plantations and terrorized slave quarters.[26]

Slaves also took an active part in the war, frequently acting as spies and passing along information to the Seminoles or the Spaniards. News traveled from slave quarter to slave quarter faster than by any other means. Slaves acted as couriers, as well, and at times became casualties. Isaac, the personal attendant of Colonel Daniel Newnan, Georgia's adjutant general and leader of the Georgia Volunteers, was fatally wounded during a shootout with the Seminoles. A young mulatto slave, identified only as Daniel Delany's manservant and courier, died in a Spanish ambush two miles outside the perimeter defenses of St. Augustine at the abandoned farm of Peter Capo. Black soldiers, sent out from town to entrap Patriot patrols, arrived at the farm in the night and concealed themselves in the ruins of a hut. Hearing a horse approach, they sprang from hiding and opened fire. Instead of a rebel scout, the hail of bullets struck down Delany's slave, who was coming to the Spanish lines with a message. "The Black Troops buried him by the side of Capo's fence." According to one account, before burying the boy, they cut off his ears to take back to St. Augustine as trophies.[27]

Throughout the summer, then, the quiet and orderly maintenance of the siege masked the true battle being waged in the province, a battle to uproot settlers, force them into rebel service, seize property, or exact retribution. All across the province, homesteads and plantations met with similar fates. Eleazer Waterman's plantation on the junction of the St. Marys and Bells Rivers had as many as a hundred men at a time quartered on the premises, living off the planter's provisions and livestock. They drove off 220 head of cattle, took twenty-five horses, requisitioned his boat and slaves to employ in a ferry service, and confiscated guns, munitions, blankets, and tools. Sometime during the course of the war, groups on one or the other side burned his sawmill and his hewn timber. In Diego Plains, Ramon and Nicolás Sánchez lost 460 head of cattle; a pair of oxen; sixteen horses, including mares and colts; thirty-nine hogs; and a boat. In addition, their beehives and plantation buildings were destroyed. Not far away, at the plantation of Bartolome Castro y Ferrer, rebels carted away 4,350 pounds of ginned cotton worth nearly $1,000; took the livestock and provisions; robbed the house of its furnishings, silverware, and bedding; and then burned the buildings.

Matthew Long, a young man loyal to Spanish interests, spoke years later about the traumatic effects of such destruction. Testifying in a claims suit, he dismissed the idea that money alone could compensate his family for the afflictions they had suffered. The Patriots had taken him prisoner during their early sortie to the Pellicer plantation. After his release, he discovered that his mother, father, and brothers had been evicted from their plantation and were struggling to survive in a camp they had built on Little Bar Island in the Matanzas River. Joining them there, Long watched his father slowly weaken and die from a mixture of exposure, deprivation, and grief. "The Invader came, drove him from his house, pillaged his property, devastated his farm, burnt his houses, imprisoned his sons, and, literally heart broken he died at the close of 1812," Long told Robert Raymond Reid, the presiding judge in his family's claims case. "But neither your Petitioner nor his suffering kindred seek from the United States compensation for a father's death, or for a life of poverty and blasted prospects. They have it not in their Treasury!"[28]

War Even to the Knife

The refusal of the U.S. Senate to support further action in East Florida had little impact on affairs below the border. Governor Mitchell, aghast at the Senate's decision, declared that removal of American forces was unacceptable. If Congress would allocate no aid, he told Secretary of State Monroe, Georgians would have to deal with the situation on their own. The Spaniards "have armed every able bodied Negro within their powers," he wrote, "and they have also received from the Havana reinforcements of nearly two Companies of black troops. It is my decided opinion that if they are allowed to remain in the Province, our Southern Country will be in a State of insurrection." Convinced that the Madison administration would eventually endorse a full-scale military assault on St. Augustine, Mitchell observed that he had "carefully avoided making any proposition for withdrawing the troops, under the fullest conviction that such a step was not intended." Instead, he sent whatever militia detachments he could spare marching south to reinforce Colonel Smith. On July 4, one of the patriotic toasts given at an Independence Day celebration in Milledgeville was to "Smith before St. Augustine" and defeat of the Spaniards. Citizens of Greene County petitioned President Madison to take immediate possession of East Florida before England used the area "to annoy our Southern coasting trade [and] to stir up against us the merciless and unrelenting Savages. . . . And, from a history of the revolutionary war, have we not much to fear from her seductive overtures to our black population, exciting them to abandon their owners and perhaps rise up in rebellion against them."[1]

Thus, in the South, the immediate impact of war with England was to strengthen the American hold on East Florida in order to defend a vulnerable frontier. Even as news circulated of American victories at sea, followed by William Hull's retreat from the invasion of Canada and further disasters in the Niagara campaigns, Georgians harkened to events along their own border and wondered what would come next.

Throughout June, July, and August, the three contending powers in East Florida—American, Patriot, and Spanish—each developed a strategy for victory over their adversaries. Often, they based their plans on erroneous intelligence. Colonel Smith, for example, repeatedly and mistakenly predicted that the Spaniards would take the field against his smaller force, a notion purveyed to his detachment by a deserter from the Spanish ranks named Antonio de los Reyes. Governor Kindelán, from various reports, miscalculated Smith's strength at close to 1,000 men and thus declined to offer battle even while Smith braced for it. In the end, the Spaniards, who probably had enough men to rout Smith, opted to wait, while Smith, intent on making an attack, could never assemble sufficient men and munitions to challenge St. Augustine's defenses. He spent much of the hot summer months further consolidating his forces, accruing reinforcements, and collecting ordinance, unable to comprehend why things had come to a standstill. "The Spaniards have not altered their conduct since the arrival of the one hundred black troops," he noted with some impatience, "and it is difficult to determine whether they or the Patriots are the most inactive."[2]

Summer was, in fact, a poor season for conducting a military campaign in Florida—hot, humid, prone to rain, and generally debilitating to soldiers in the field. At Fort Mose, July's weather alternated between stifling heat and drenching downpours. When the wind died, clouds of tormenting mosquitoes hovered around the horses, tents, and shelters. Sickness riddled Smith's detachment, as man after man collapsed with heat prostration, dysentery, or typhus, until sometimes a third of the contingent was unfit for duty. Captain Fiedler Ridgeway complained of an aggravating wound in his right leg that would not heal in the moist climate. Smith himself was beleaguered with a lingering fever. Lacking a staff physician, he summoned Dr. James Hall from Amelia Island to attend to the more serious or festering cases of disease.[3]

Boredom and inactivity afflicted the men as much as the climate. They congregated in small groups to hear the latest news from the gazettes, or held shooting contests, or reread the scant mail from home. Some deserted, while others sneaked from camp to raid nearby fields for vegetables, pumpkins, potatoes, melons, and corn. A few were more ambitious. John Walker of Captain Ridgeway's company was caught and punished for robbing a Spanish woman of $500 in gold and for rifling one of the Atkinson estates of its silver plate, table linen, and clothing. To put a halt to drunkenness, Smith eventually sent a detachment of marines down to Pellicer's plantation, telling them to destroy the stock of rum there. "In truth I am truly tired of this Damned Province," he told a friend at one point, "and would not remain (if it rested with me) one month longer in my present situation for a fee simple to the whole of it."[4]

William Kinnear, a young medical orderly, voiced the feelings of many comrades when he bemoaned his fate to his family in Virginia. East Florida, he said, was "but a fit receptacle for savages and wild beasts, the scenery of the country exhibiting nothing except desert—pine barrens and vast regions of untrackless swamps." He spent much of his time tending to men hospitalized in camp, in an atmosphere "pregnant with sickness and death," having sometimes as many as thirty-three charges on his hands and losing several to a contagion of typhus fever.[5]

Militia volunteers soon grew as disenchanted as the regulars with the dreary duty of maintaining the siege. The Savannah Blues, their term of service expired, demanded transports to return home, where they might do some good taking arms against the English, who now seemed a bigger threat than the Dons. Colonel Daniel Newnan, commanding the Georgia Volunteers, had to arrest fifteen soldiers, an ensign, and three sergeants when they tried to desert. His stout, hard-fighting men would march barefoot for miles, but they grumbled bitterly over empty stomachs, and Newnan, like Smith, was hardly able to squeeze three-days' rations out of the provisioning agents. "The desertions and the shameful defalcations in the contractor's department has [sic] perplexed me considerably," he wrote Smith from his encampment on the St. Johns River. "Had it not been for our own efforts, we would have been left without anything to eat."[6]

The inefficiency of the supply lines and the crass indifference of the War Department to his detachment's predicaments troubled Smith deeply. Despite this, American forces did manage to entrench themselves in several new outposts. Smith still hoped, with support from Georgia, to break out of stalemate and initiate action. Colonel Newnan had some 250 Georgia militiamen stationed along the river between Camp New Hope and the Davis Creek blockhouse. They were collecting horses, munitions, and supplies while Smith pondered his next move—an attack on St. Augustine or an expedition into Indian territory. Several pieces of artillery and, more important, some large mortars were also being sent to him from Georgia. With these, he could mount an assault against the Castillo and its fortifications.[7]

The Patriots, in the meantime, employed the summer to reorganize themselves. President Madison's failure to deliver on promises of assistance dashed the hopes of many. They seemed to be losing their bid for recognition as the legitimate government of East Florida. To rectify this, on July 10 John Houston McIntosh convened a constitutional convention made up of fifteen delegates and officially established the territory of East Florida. In a document of 4,000 words, the delegates set forth the grievances that justified their break with Spain and outlined the powers and responsibilities of an executive, legislative, and judicial authority. "It might have been expected," they stated in the preamble, "that a people who neither Idolized their priest nor could think it an honour to lick the dust from the feet of their oppressors . . . would have been the first in the Spanish Territories to have declared themselves Free and Independent." They had resorted to arms, however, only after mature deliberation and against a government that "could no longer afford protection without which allegiance cannot be claimed." Following various state constitutions as their model, they placed limits on executive power, gave the vote to all free white males who had reached twenty-one years of age, and placed some additional restrictions, mostly related to property ownership, on who could hold public office. They also reiterated their desire for annexation to the United States. On Saturday, July 25, in a general plebiscite of their membership, the Patriots chose McIntosh as the new "Director of East Florida" and elected fifteen other men to seats in the legislative council. Lodowick Ashley, William Craig, and Buckner Harris were among the new representatives. The government held its first session at the house of Zephaniah Kingsley at Laurel Grove on July 26.[8]

Buoyed by his appointment as director, McIntosh sent a lengthy appeal to James Monroe, begging the United States to intercede in East Florida as it had done in Baton Rouge in 1810. It was essential, he said, for President Madison to pledge full support to the Patriot cause, not only for the protection of men who had taken up arms at American instigation but also for the greater good of the Republic. Echoing the sentiments of Mitchell, McIntosh characterized Spanish East Florida as a direct threat to the safety of the South:

Our slaves are excited to rebel, and we have an army of negroes, raked up in this Country, and brought from Cuba, to contend with. Let us ask if we are abandoned, what will be the situation of the southern states, with this body of men in the neighborhood? St. Augustine, the whole province, will be the refuge of fugitive slaves, and from thence emissaries can and no doubt will be detached, to bring about a revolt of the black population in the States. A nation that can stir up the savages around your western frontiers will hesitate but little to introduce the horrors of St. Domingo into your southern country. . . . Upon the principals [sic] of justice and humanity we call upon the protection of the United States. With it, we become free and happy. Without it, we must become wanderers upon the face of the Earth, or tenants of loathsome dungeons, the sport of cruel and inexorable tyrants. . . . A great Many of us have been accustomed to the sweets of affluence, and most of us to the enjoyment of plenty. We in common with other citizens would willingly have sacrificed all we have, had it been in defense of the U. States, but to be beggared and branded as traitors is wretchedness indeed to men who thought they were acting as some of their forefathers in 1776.[9]

As he waited and prayed for an encouraging answer, McIntosh inaugurated plans to annoy the forces at St. Augustine. Three and a half months of American occupation had served to prove only one thing: the capital would never fall as long as the defenders had access to the sea. The recent arrival of relief from Cuba and the continued flow of supplies from sympathizers at Amelia Island constituted a major flaw in the American plan to force surrender. With this in mind, McIntosh applied to the commanders of American privateers and corsairs that were preparing to descend on English commercial shipping, seeking captains who would harass East Florida. The route to the ocean had to be shut, once and for all, and then it would be possible to starve the townspeople out of their stronghold. If he could not muster an army against the Spanish, then he would hire a navy.

Governor Kindelán, meanwhile, was laying plans of his own. News reached him daily that Smith might soon have the capabilities to attack the capital. Realizing he had to hinder American operations, the governor was relieved to hear that the Seminoles of Alligator town and Alachua were preparing to take the field on the Spanish side. The Indians expected weapons, powder, and gifts, and they would keep any spoils of war that fell to their warriors. Under these conditions, however, they agreed to strike the Americans and the rebels. Kindelán offered to pay $10 for every Patriot scalp and $1,000 for that of John Houston McIntosh.[10]

The principal bands negotiating with Kindelán were those of Payne and Bowlegs, whose domains stretched along the "great Allatchua Savannah" described by the naturalists John and William Bartram. This area was a three-day march into the interior and had for decades lapsed beyond direct Spanish control, though it had once fostered Franciscan missions. During the years of the American Revolution, the Seminoles of Alachua, under Cowkeeper, had allied themselves firmly with British interests but had gradually come to regard the Spaniards as allies. By 1812, their lands in north-central Florida were rich and prosperous, supporting their various endeavors in the pelt trade, horse and cattle breeding, agriculture, and hunting. Payne, who had succeeded Cowkeeper in 1784, owned a great European-style plantation house, with 20 slaves, 400 horses, and 1,500 head of cattle. Bowlegs, his younger half-brother whose main village was just a few miles farther south, was also a powerful and influential chief who sold 1,000 head of cattle annually. As leaders of a numerous and thriving people, they did not take to the warpath wantonly or gratuitously. Like the Creeks, Payne and Bowlegs were divided on the issue of choosing sides in war between whites. Payne counseled his people to eschew the conflict, while Bowlegs, angry at the disruption in the deerskin trade and pessimistic about keeping American settlers out of Indian territory, advocated combat.[11]

During May and April, both the Spaniards and the rebels had sent emissaries to the chiefs. Estrada reminded Payne of Spanish friendship and warned that the Georgians coming into the country would eventually challenge him in order to eradicate the runaway slaves and maroons who found shelter with his people and to seize land and drive off cattle and horses. General Mathews, aware of the threat the Seminoles posed, had tried to counter Spanish overtures and to dissuade the Seminoles from hostilities. In his first meeting with them, he advised an assembly of chiefs to remain neutral. When Bowlegs offered to join the Americans in a joint attack upon the Spaniards, Mathews rebuffed him, saying, "It was a quarrel among white people and he did not want their assistance." His words were also intended for the maroons who stood nearby, listening to the conference. The general balked at the very idea of allying the Patriots with former slaves.[12]

In early June, Mathews had organized a second "talk" at the Forbes trading post near Fort Picolata, where he repeated his message before a gathering of twenty-seven chiefs. The Patriots wanted no quarrel with the Seminoles, Mathews told the assembled leaders, but they would punish the Indians severely for interference. "Set you down at home and mind your business, and I will be your friend," he reportedly told Payne. McIntosh also addressed the council. "You suspect us, you are wrong," he said. "Sit down and take care of your women and children. . . . You have large stocks of cattle, when we want beef, we will send to you . . . and we shall have something to pay you for them." Some of the chiefs and warriors took offense at these words, which sounded patronizing and which sidestepped the issue of what would happen in Indian territory under an American government. They were better off with the Spanish king, some chiefs told Payne, for in thirty years the Spaniards had never molested them. The Americans had promised them peace in Georgia and then had taken their lands. It would be the same here. Yet Payne continued to defer.[13]

This disagreement among the Seminoles was not reflected among the slaves and maroons living in their midst. Their status among the Indians contrasted markedly with their former life among whites. For the most part, the Seminoles gave them greater liberty—for tribal economy did not rely heavily on slave labor—and left them unsupervised at their tasks of cow punching and planting. They had their own settlements, where they could rent lands and raise their families secure from the auction block. During times of war, they took up arms side by side with the warriors. In times of peace, their knowledge of Spanish, English, and other languages, as well as their skills in blacksmithing and carpentry, gained them positions as interpreters and artisans. The prospect of being returned to slavery in the American South or of seeing slave hunters and land jobbers invade Alachua filled them with dread and anger.[14]

In the end, several factors forced the issue for the Seminoles and overrode Payne's policy of neutrality. Word leaked back to the tribes that the Patriot leaders were already carving up portions of Florida's interior into land grants "and that five hundred acres of land is promised to each volunteer, and in proportion to each officer, who will assist in burning and laying waste the Indian villages." A slave returning from the American camp told the chiefs about a conversation he had engaged in with an officer. "When are you going home?" the officer asked him. "I will see you again soon for I will soon be eating beef in the Seminole village." These indications of intended treachery deepened existing distrust. The interruption in the hide trade also weighed in as something that angered the Indian towns. Without access to an exchange system, the Seminoles were deprived of an important channel for obtaining both luxury goods and basic munitions. However, the decisive tip of the balance occurred during a final "talk" held at Payne's Alachua settlement in July. Aware that Governor Kindelán was seeking envoys to take his messages to Payne, Mathews and McIntosh decided to preempt him. In order to facilitate a meeting with the Seminoles, they kidnapped a slave, Tony Proctor, who was the most adept interpreter of Muskogee and Mikasuki in East Florida. Born in Jamaica around 1743, Proctor had lived through the American Revolution as the manservant of a British officer, apparently arriving in Florida while it was under British rule. Subsequently, he became a slave of the Panton, Leslie Indian Trade Company, where he absorbed knowledge about the culture and language of the Seminoles, Miccosukees, and Creeks. By 1812, he was famous in local circles for his skill as a translator.[15]

The Patriots' efforts to exploit Proctor proved a grievous mistake. At the meeting, speaking before the chiefs, he pretended to translate Mathews's offers and promises, while surreptitiously warning the Seminoles "that violence would come upon them and that everything he was relating to them was a falsehood."[16]

"These fine talks are to amuse and deceive you," he is reputed to have said. "They are going to take your country beyond the St. Johns, the old people will be put to sweep the yards of the white people, the young men to work for them, and the young females to spin and weave for them. This I have heard and this I tell you." Mathews, seeing his embassy go awry and not understanding the cause, flew into one of his tantrums, telling Payne "he intended to drive him from his land" unless he kept to the road of peace, while McIntosh vowed to make Bowlegs his servant.[17]

Proctor, however, was not finished with his sabotage. On the return trip to Fort Mose, he slipped away from the rebels, taking with him Manuel Rendon, a soldier of the Third Infantry Battalion of Cuba who had been captured. The two returned to the Seminoles, held an impromptu conference, and communicated all of Kindelán's plans and requests: the governor would arm them, would reward them with gifts as soon as he could obtain them from Cuba, and (according to some accounts) offered payment for the scalps of rebel leaders. Their mission completed, the two men headed into St. Augustine, where a grateful Kindelán, astounded at Proctor's loyalty and resourcefulness, raised 350 pesos to purchase the slave's freedom and commended him, besides, to the captain general.[18]

Even after the stormy interview with Mathews, Payne continued to urge his people to stay out of a conflict. His braves, however, stirred up by Bowlegs's equally ardent calls for war, refused to listen. The old chief finally capitulated. "Go and fight," he said, "and if you are able to drive the white people, go and do it."[19]

Final arrangements with the Seminoles were secretly coordinated through another Spanish agent, Edward Wanton, a former trader with Forbes and Company, who lived on a plantation south of Fort Picolata. Wanton apprised Kindelán that American forces were weak. Smith had only a hundred men at Fort Mose, having taken a detachment with him on a trip to the Georgia border, and the garrison at Fort Picolata consisted of no more than twenty-eight men. Payne's and Bowlegs's warriors could therefore cross the St. Johns River below Fort Picolata, running little risk of detection, and rendezvous with Spanish forces at Solana's Ferry, just outside St. Augustine's defenses. Sometime around July 20, said Wanton, "by the Grace of God, you can expect relief from 600 Indian warriors, more or less, who will present themselves and treat with Your Excellency before commencing their hostilities." To reassure the governor of their fidelity, Payne and Bowlegs sent eight of their black vassals to serve under arms in St. Augustine, acting, they said, as their surrogates.[20]

On July 26, after consulting with Kindelán, Bowlegs and his braves launched a sudden onslaught on positions in the rear of Colonel Smith's lines. One war party killed a white settler and five slaves and captured thirty-two others on the north side of the St. Johns River. The next day, the Seminoles struck within a few miles of Fort Mose, shooting down and scalping two more men. Just as Kindelán hoped, these raids threw Smith's forces into disarray. Hearing about the attacks at Point Peter, Smith immediately sent couriers galloping north to find Governor Mitchell. He urged a counterstrike against the Seminole villages, for which he would need 200 additional men. Mitchell received the message promptly and promised to send help, but afflicted with a "bilious fever," he was unable to manage the arrangements and for many weeks lay in bed at Milledge-ville, incapacitated and barely able to lift a pen.[21]

The impact of the raids confounded Smith. Though the casualties were low, the grisly nature of the deaths prompted a mass defection by the Patriots. Hurrying from Point Peter back to Fort Mose, Smith came across one disconsolate group of rebels at Camp New Hope. "They appear to have lost sight of the first grand object, the conquest of the province," he commented, "and from the rapid decrease of their numbers, having dwindled to nothing, it is doubtful whether the 'Patriotic Army' will ever revive again."[22]

The colonel had no time to worry about them. The retreat of the rebels left him with only 103 men to hold position before St. Augustine. In a single week, the Seminoles killed eight or nine people, burned all the holdings in the vicinity of Fort Picolata, and carried away some eighty slaves into the Alachua territory. "They have, I am informed, several hundred fugitive slaves from the Carolinas and Georgia at present in their towns," Smith told Major General Thomas Pinckney, "and unless they are checked soon they will be so strengthened by desertions from Georgia and Florida that it will be found troublesome to reduce them."[23]

Meanwhile, Bowlegs's braves, anointed in war paint and well mounted on Florida-bred steeds that gave them the advantage of mobility, continued their depredations. They attacked Kingsley's Laurel Grove plantation, burning all the buildings except the main house, which was protected by a stockade. They also ambushed Smith's couriers, caught off-guard as they passed through the countryside bearing dispatches. In early August, a raiding party jumped two Patriots—James Hollingsworth and Daniel Pritchard—when they halted to water their horses on the road between Fort Picolata and Fort Mose. The braves scalped and tomahawked the men, leaving their mutilated bodies on display as a warning. On August 12, another courier, Maxwell, departed the Davis Creek blockhouse. As he drew near Fort Mose, an ambuscade of blacks and Indians grabbed him, tortured and killed him, and then left his naked body in the middle of the bridle path where it could be easily discovered. "From the appearance of the body," Smith wrote angrily to Governor Mitchell, "he had been flogged, his nose, one ear, and privates cut off. He had three shot wounds in his body and his scalp was taken."[24]

The Spaniards renewed hostilities as well. On July 20, St. Augustine's free black militia unit, supplied with eight days of rations, headed toward Julington Creek with orders to ransack the area. Specifically, they were to surprise a party of rebels at the plantation of Fernando Quinby, wreck any pieces of artillery being off-loaded for the blockhouse, and seize horses and cattle. The terms of service stipulated that they would be remunerated for any livestock, supplies, and equipment they captured, though slaves and munitions would be the property of the Crown. On August 9, they returned to town, bringing ninety-three head of cattle driven away from the corrals at the Davis Creek blockhouse.[25]

Even ordinary settlers took part in the campaign. In a ploy that was common among the Spanish guerrillas fighting against the French in Spain, a group of Minorcan women lured several of Smith's men into a trap. They appeared along the banks of the North River and beckoned to a party of five soldiers, pleading with them to escort them to town for fear of the Indians. When the men came down the river in an open boat, a party of militia sprang from concealment and shot them down. All five men were killed—one by drowning as he tried to escape—and three of the bodies were scalped. By the end of August, Smith had lost ten men without inflicting a single counterblow.[26]

Besides attacking the Americans, the Seminoles loosed a series of raids against the Patriots, setting fire to their plantations and ravaging their farms. In some cases, they made no distinction between friend and foe. The Fatio family, for example, who had a large plantation called New Switzerland three miles south of Julington Creek, was caught in the middle of the raiding. On August 13, Dublin, one of the Fatio slaves, rushed up the steps of the main house and warned Francis Philip Fatio that a band of warriors was coming to burn them out. Although the family members were loyalists, Fatio had been inducted under compulsion into the Patriot army and had also allowed the Georgia Volunteers to bivouac on his property. As the war party approached, the family fled, taking along Dublin, Scipio, and another slave and making their escape by skiff on the St. Johns River. They took refuge with Zephaniah Kingsley at Laurel Grove, who sent back a party of Patriots to chase the Seminoles off. In spite of this, the Seminoles captured thirteen slaves and burned a portion of the plantation, including some of the slave cabins, before retreating to the west side of the St. Johns. A few days later, they ambushed and slaughtered a group of Patriots who rather foolishly ventured into Fatio's fields to pick watermelons.[27]

"The Indians continue to commit depredations in my rear almost every day," Smith wrote to a colleague. "They have burnt and destroyed improvements on a number of plantations and carried off a great number of slaves. The inhabitants are all removing to the Islands, many of them having been reduced in a few hours from affluence to beggary." Others, unable to reach the islands, were fleeing into Georgia. It was Colonel Daniel Newnan and Captain Tomlinson Fort who saved the situation. The two officers, with a joint contingent of nearly 300 militiamen, set up patrols and garrisons around Camp New Hope, around the Davis Creek blockhouse, and along the river to intercept the raiding parties.[28]

The Seminoles' horrifying tactics infuriated the regulars and militiamen, and they damned the Spanish as dirty and dishonorable fighters for allying themselves with "savages." "They are certainly the most cowardly as well as the most cruel of the human family," raged Smith of the Dons. The damage was done, however, and the losses and the danger to his supplies lines forced him to consider retreat. "Unless the Indians are checked soon," he informed John Houston McIntosh, "I shall be compelled to fall back to the St. Marys, where I can obtain supplies without difficulty." A few days later, he wrote to Newnan, saying, "I expect in a short time to be compelled to retire to some healthy position on the St. Johns, until I am sufficiently reinforced to maintain such position near St. Augustine." He admonished Lieutenant Stallings at Davis Creek to keep all of his men close to the blockhouse, quartered inside at night with the doors barred, and to watch the nearby swamps, which flanked the northern end of the fort, in case the Seminoles launched an assault on the outpost from that direction.[29]

Even as war parties assailed the Americans, Bowlegs risked several raids farther north along the Georgia border. The killing of a young man at Trader's Hill drew immediate cries for help from frightened frontier families. Shortly afterward, on August 18, warriors appeared on the south side of the St. Marys River, across from the town of Temple, where they attacked an encampment of slaves held by Abner and William Williams. After taking captives, they "fired across the river at the family of Mr. [William] Ashley, wounded one of his Negroes, and another shot struck the house very near Mrs. Ashley," reported General Floyd. "Mr. Ashley returned the fire, and wounded one of the Indians in the leg, who for revenge killed and scalped a mulatto boy (one of the number of Negroes which they had surprised) alleging that he had white blood in him." The Seminoles retreated but reappeared at Trader's Hill, where they "attacked three Negroes . . . killed one and carried off another."[30]

Unable to catch and punish the marauding warriors, soldiers and rebels vented their wrath against Edward Wanton, Kindelán's go-between with the Indians. In August, they swept down on Wanton at his plantation of Chancery, where he lived "in ease and plenty," and seized him before he could flee. The soft-spoken planter, "a great scholar [who] spent much of his time in reading and writing," was hauled away to Fort Picolata in chains. Angry Patriots ran riot on his estate, breaking up his furniture and library, burning his house, hacking down citrus trees, and confiscating slaves. They blamed Wanton directly for the macabre deaths of their couriers and despised him besides as someone who had been a Tory during the American Revolution and as a man who was raising a family with a woman of color, Margaret Gray, a former slave from South Carolina. For the next eight months, Wanton lived as a captive at Camp New Hope, shackled hand and foot and sometimes put on display in the stocks. "He was treated with great severity and was in a most loathsome and wretched condition," friends later recalled. "The marks of irons were upon his limbs and he was reduced to a shadow." Even after Wanton was released, the Patriots continued to persecute him. They burned him out of a second homestead in 1813 and a third one sometime later. Long afterward, settlers remembered him as a man who was "loyal to the King and among those who suffered most from the incursion."[31]

To repulse the Seminoles, Smith requested help from the various units of the Georgia militia already encamped in East Florida. Besides some 250 men with Colonel Newnan, stationed temporarily at the Fatio plantation, there were 125 with Captain Tomlinson Fort at Kingsley's plantation and 40 more with Captain William Cone at the Cowford. It was a considerable force, although some of the men were nearing the expiration of their terms of recruitment and others were falling sick. Still, from among them, Smith hoped to dispatch an expedition into the interior, with orders to burn out the Alachua villages and thus quell the Seminoles' ability to send out war parties. His own detachment, with ninety men on the sick list, was in no condition to support the militia, especially as he now had to send armed escorts with his supply wagons to protect them from attack. He could not even find spare guns and powder to assist in arming

Newnan's men. "I have not a musket, cartridge, flint, or haversack to furnish them," Smith complained.[32]

Colonel Newnan was undaunted by these problems. He had come to fight, he told Smith, and would carry through anything required. Sickness had already struck down thirty-seven of his men, he said, and Captain Cone had only ten men healthy enough for a long trek, but he was ready to retaliate. "If I thought the scoundrels I command would not desert, and would extend their service," he noted, "I would prefer joining your detachment, but almost all of them will go home the moment their time expires, which will be in about four weeks. . . . Under all these discouraging conditions I am still determined to march . . . and am of opinion that with one hundred brave men the whole of the Indians may be driven." He regretted that he could not advance until he had assembled packhorses and found guides who knew the territory; however, Zephaniah Kingsley was doing his best to provision him with all these things.[33]

Around September 5, the Seminoles resumed their strikes, this time targeting Fort Picolata. Taking its small detachment of a corporal and five men by surprise, a party of twenty-six warriors set fire to the storehouses and razed the nearby structures. The soldiers returned fire from the cover of the tower and killed one of the warriors. Soon afterward, another group of thirty Seminoles came from Alachua and encamped near the fort. "This information has given me considerable uneasiness," admitted Smith. He asked Colonel Newnan and Lieutenant Stallings to find out if the garrison was still in possession of Fort Picolata. By all indications, the Seminoles were becoming bolder, and he wondered if their tactics were leading to a concerted assault. Then, on September 9, within a few miles of Fort Mose, a war party ambushed Benjamin Armstrong, a Patriot employed in the driving and tending of cattle. They shot and scalped him, leaving his body on display along the road that passed through Twelve Mile Swamp. With reports that additional bands of Indians were on the move along both sides of the St. Johns River, everything seemed suddenly ominous, and the American position more vulnerable then ever. Captain Ridgeway, who had lost two members of his company to the attacks, wrote his brother, "Our Supplies as to Hospital Supplies and provision are bad. We are now become sickly. Our aim is at Fort St. Augustine. Five times the force we have will not be able to take it by storm. . . . We must hem them in and starve them out but even our present force will not do that, for the Spanish have the Indians to Sculp [sic] us when they can find us."[34]

The only good news Smith received was from Captain Fort, who came to Fort Mose and notified him that the blockhouse had received a new shipment of supplies. If Smith could provide wagons, Lieutenant Stallings was ready to transfer everything to the front lines. Smith was glad to hear it. Now perhaps he could evacuate some of the sick as well. With Newnan making ready to march on the Seminole towns, Smith vowed to hold his ground before St. Augustine, whatever the cost. Another week or two might gain him the upper hand. And should the Spaniards overwhelm him, "I console myself," he said, "with the belief that if we should be sacrificed, it will promote the national good as the government will then no longer hesitate about taking immediate possession of the province." Around September 11, having conferred with Captain Williams of the marines, Smith organized a wagon convoy to bring back the desperately needed supplies from the blockhouse. The convoy would require a heavy escort, he said, to protect it on the outward and return journey. But the return journey would be the most dangerous. After all, who would attack empty wagons going west?[35]

During all this time, the main body of Spanish troops remained inside St. Augustine. Although the Spaniards outnumbered their American adversaries by two to one, Kindelán, like Smith, faced grave obstacles in mounting an offensive. Even with his 900 or so men, he was hard-pressed to maintain an adequate guard on St. Augustine's sprawling defenses. The size of his force was deceptive, for most of his men belonged to militia units and could not be trusted to carry through an assault against Smith's well-trained infantry, marines, and riflemen. With 400 additional veteran troops, Kindelán told the captain general, he could push the Americans back. But there were no more troops available, and he was reluctant to risk the infantry of the Third Battalion in an open-field engagement against the entrenched position of Smith's main force. A defeat would break the town's morale and force him to surrender, while a victory would almost certainly prompt the Madison administration to launch a massive and overwhelming attack against East Florida. Hence, Kindelán confined himself to feints, occasionally throwing open the town gates and parading his men to alarm the Americans. His true objective was to wear Smith down through dogged resistance and by harassing him with raids and ambushes. The war with England, he thought, might come to his rescue and force the American government to seek a truce and a compromise in East Florida.[36]

Inside the capital, however, the long months of the siege were taking their toll. St. Augustine was certainly no stranger to the hardships of siege. In 1702, the entire population had been forced to flee into the cramped and crowded confines of the newly finished Castillo to escape Colonel James Moore's attack. They remained inside for weeks waiting for relief. In 1740, during James Oglethorpe's siege, residents had endured a fierce artillery barrage. This time, although the siege was already the longest in their history, they were at least in control of the town and could even escape for brief periods into the countryside if they were careful. Yet difficulties were beginning to mount. With all the soldiers, residents, and refugees, St. Augustine's population had doubled from 2,000 to nearly 4,000.[37] Kindelán was extremely worried. Even with the forays for cattle and the supplies of flour, corn, rice, and codfish from Amelia Island and Cuba, the warehouses were emptying rapidly of food, candles, medical supplies, and spare clothing. At the end of July, the town's provisions amounted to 293 barrels of flour, 28 barrels of rice, 28 barrels of pork, and 20 barrels of salt beef. To fully stock St. Augustine for six months, said Manuel Lopez, keeper of the public stores, they would need 795 barrels of flour, 200 of rice, about 788 bushels of corn, and more than 1,000 *quintales* of fresh meat, quite apart from such items as lard, sugar, coffee, salt, cheese, vegetables, and liquor. Knowing that the captain general in Cuba would ridicule such a request, Kindelán submitted one that was more modest, nonetheless asking for 600 barrels of flour, 100 of rice, 1,000 *fanegas* of corn, 100 barrels of salt pork, and 400 of salt beef. Meanwhile, he placed the town on short rations. The soldiers were living on half a pint of corn per day. Some of the poorer Minorcans and free men of color had to support their families, and sometimes the families of others, on government allocations of sixteen ounces of bread a day, received in exchange for militia service. Others lived on the thin hauls of mullet, catfish, and oysters they collected when not on duty. The Company of Free Morenos of Havana complained of their wretchedness. They spent all of their time, they said, trying to buy or beg shoes or finagling deals to get bits of clothing to cover themselves. Meanwhile, people with hard coin were bribing the bakers to get extra bread, paying as much as a doubloon for a loaf that ordinarily cost twelve cents.[38]

Given this desperate situation, Kindelán had little compunction about unleashing the savagery of an Indian war upon his foes. War by ambush was problematic, however. Admittedly, the Seminoles' hit-and-run tactics disrupted American operations, but they came at a heavy cost, for the braves spent ammunition liberally, and their attacks achieved only transitory successes. As Kindelán explained to the captain general at Havana:

> If these people remain constant, they can do great damage. But with the capture of a negro, horse, or any other prize, they abandon the campaign in order to secure things in their Towns, and in this way their successes are momentary. I have tried to place them at points where they can intercept the supplies of the [American] camp, but ineffectually, because they are reduced to pillaging without remaining one day in the same place. They are boastful of their exploits and services, and in this respect, insatiable in their petitions. One of them consumes more in supplies and munitions than three of us.[39]

So, as the water in the Castillo's main well ran sour and the free black militia's cattle raids brought back fewer and fewer animals, Kindelán sat tight behind his defenses, each week asking for an enumeration of the remaining stores and bundling up his reports and *expedientes* for shipment to Cuba. With Spanish gun launches in control of the Matanzas and North Rivers, the Castillo protecting the channel, and the frigate *Pizarro* on guard at the bar, he knew, at least, that he could keep the sea lanes open. As long as he controlled the sea, the town could survive—and then the privateers came.[40]

To counter the terror of Indian attacks, John Houston McIntosh had arranged a terror campaign of his own. In the first days of August, two armed American corsairs reached the coast of St. Augustine, hired to intercept and molest all Spanish shipping in the area. The smallest of the vessels, the *Hornet* of Norfolk, was a schooner with a 12-caliber gun and a crew of sixty. Accompanying it was the more intimidating *Nonesuch*, a larger schooner out of Baltimore, listed as being under the command of a Captain Levely and fitted out with ten 12-caliber cannons and two 8-pounders. More than a hundred armed men, mostly Americans but also some Spanish, Portuguese, and French, worked the schooner's rigging and swarmed its crowded deck. Their plan of operation was simple. They would cruise off the coast of East Florida between St. Augustine and the Halifax River, chase down any ships that tried to enter or leave the inlets at Anastasia Island, and strip them of everything movable. Since the United States was not officially at war with Spain, the privateers could not claim their captures as legitimate prizes in an admiralty court. Their instructions from the Patriots were clear: to rob and intimidate Spanish passengers and crew and to shut down communication between St. Augustine and the outside world. A contest was now under way to see whose supply lines collapsed first—Smith's or Kindelán's.[41]

On August 4, the privateers opened their campaign by ambushing the small Spanish schooner *Los Dos Hermanos*, two days out from St. Augustine. The ship was bound for Cuba to obtain supplies and was sailing in ballast. Its most valuable cargo consisted of Kindelán's dispatches to the captain general at Havana and to the British governor in the Bahamas. Besides the captain, crew, and pilot, the schooner carried thirty-nine passengers, including Don José Zubirarreta, St. Augustine's elderly *escribano*, or notary public, who had fallen ill in March and, with little hope for recovery, was returning to Havana with his family. Just off Mosquitos and Cape Canaveral, the lookout on the *Dos Hermanos* shouted down to deck that two vessels were approaching on an intercept course. One displayed the flag of France, the other flew the colors of both France and England. People debated whether they were seeing two French ships or a French ship with an English prize. At two-thirty in the afternoon they got their answer. The suspicious-looking vessels, acting in unison, closed in on both sides of the Spanish schooner and forced it to heave to. The *Hornet* and the *Nonesuch* had sprung their trap.

A boarding party of armed men from the *Nonesuch* took charge of the *Dos Hermanos* and quickly fell to looting. They broke open every container in sight, rummaged through the luggage, searched the passengers, confiscated all the provisions, and stole 4,000 pesos in money and silver. To make sure the ship turned back, they also seized the log, the charts, the instruments of navigation, and all the government dispatches. As soon as the sailors from the *Nonesuch* departed, men from the *Hornet* took their place. Again and again, parties from the ships came and went, hooting and jeering at their mortified and humiliated victims. "As soon as the first retired, the other advanced," recalled Juan Tirac, the pilot on the *Dos Hermanos*, "and the two acted in consort, although having the appearance of enemies, repeating the looting and mistreatments all day long."

Having detained the schooner for nearly twenty-four hours, the privateers made sail and disappeared. On August 6, four days after its departure, the *Dos Hermanos* limped back into St. Augustine's harbor. A traumatized owner went ashore to give his report to Kindelán, and eighteen-year-old Casimiro Zubirarreta carried back the body of his father, who had collapsed and died under the stress of the ordeal. Angry and bitter over his father's death, Casimiro told everyone that the Patriots were responsible. "[I] specifically recognized by face three of them that were on the small corsair," he said. "They were inhabitants of the St. Johns River, one 'Burch,' and another called 'Jayme,' and the third a trader from the town of St. Marys."[42]

The news stunned Kindelán. Here in one terrible blow his minor victory in forging an alliance with the Seminoles had been countered and dashed. He had never anticipated attack from the sea. And he realized, too, that the enemy would soon be translating and reading his dispatches, in which he described all too clearly his need for food and other provisions.

The very day the *Dos Hermanos* arrived back at port, the *Nonesuch* struck again. On August 6, the privateer overhauled the *Eugenia*, another small Spanish schooner, as it returned to St. Augustine from a trip to Havana. With the helpless vessel wallowing under his cannons, Captain Levely shouted at his men to lower the boats. Methodically they transferred the vessel's cargo into the privateer's hold: a *pipa* of rum, two barrels of sugar, two sacks of coffee, a supply of flour, textiles, candles, dry goods, and all the crew's provisions, valued altogether at 600 pesos. Then they released Captain Mier, chiding him to go about his business.

With the wind and current against him, Mier abandoned his trip to St. Augustine and set sail instead for St. Marys in Georgia. There, the *Eugenia* spent seven days before setting forth once more for East Florida. But the *Nonesuch* was lying in wait. On August 15, the Patriot privateer appeared again and resumed the chase. This time the *Eugenia*, fleeing southward, proved too swift and gained the channel before the *Nonesuch* could overtake it. Undiscouraged, Captain Levely swept down upon the Spanish commercial frigate *Pizarro* as it was lying at anchor off the harbor mouth and proceeded to loot the ship. Its captain, ashore with Kindelán, saw the *Eugenia* come in and rushed back to take charge of his vessel. He arrived too late. The *Nonesuch* had wreaked havoc and departed.[43]

The cumulative effect of the *Nonesuch*'s exploits was catastrophic. Three ships had been pillaged within two weeks. Admittedly, the pitiful cargo of the *Eugenia* was a mockery of Kindelán's urgent requests for supplies. Yet even this pittance had been denied him. Instructions from the captain general joined his own dispatches in enemy hands. Worst of all, Kindelán knew for certain that his port was under blockade and his shipping bottled up.

And more bad news was coming. Before learning of the *Eugenia's* ordeal, Kindelán had sent forth yet another ship. The *Barbarita* was a small vessel, sometimes described as a gunboat, purchased for government service by John Russell, a local East Florida planter. On August 11, under the command of Don Miguel Acosta, it had sailed for New Providence, in the Bahamas, and Havana, Cuba, trying to complete the journey that had originally been assigned to the *Dos Hermanos*. Two days out on its southward journey, the *Barbarita* met the *Nonesuch* and the *Hornet*, "the same," Captain Acosta would later report, "that so cruelly robbed the family of the Escribano."

To begin with, Captain Levely treated Acosta with civility, saying his crew and passengers would be allowed to retain their personal luggage but not any money or silver. As soon as Acosta transferred himself to the *Nonesuch*, however, the privateers initiated their usual regimen of looting, "the boats passing back and forth all night taking sailors to pillage."

Their robberies complete, the privateers were preparing to depart when a British officer on board the *Barbarita* called attention to himself. Captain Forrest of the H.M.S. *Russell* demanded to see Levely. Acosta could not believe what happened next. Forrest "had in his charge an English registry to be delivered to the Customs House at [New] Providence, and when he presented himself aboard the corsair, he declared to the captain that the *Barbarita* was an English schooner called the *Perseverance*, that he was in command, and he displayed the English papers, adding a thousand other lies!"

If Forrest had hoped to intimidate the Americans by a bit of British flag-waving, his plans completely miscarried. As soon as he made his declaration, Captain Levely seized the *Barbarita* as a hostile British vessel and a prize of war. This time, the crew and ship were not released. Instead, Levely put a prize crew on board, with instructions to sail the *Barbarita* to Charleston, South Carolina, and submit a claim to the Admiralty against the ship, its entire contents, and all of the slaves who were accompanying the passengers.

A miserable Miguel Acosta wrote to Governor Kindelán from Charleston on August 23 relating the disaster. The American authorities were well disposed to treat the *Barbarita* as a Spanish ship, he said, but he could not authenticate her registry because the privateers had taken all of his papers and licenses. For weeks, Carlos Mulvey, the Spanish consul at the port, quarreled with American authorities about the incident. They finally restored the ship to Acosta and permitted the passengers and slaves to leave.[44]

Assessing the damage, Kindelán was not optimistic. He had been congratulating himself on the success of the Seminole raids. Now, he realized, the intervention of the Seminoles might have come too late. The townspeople were beginning to lose heart. No one could set foot outside the city. When his supplies ran out, he would have to plead for terms, and such an eventuality was fast approaching. His stock of flour had dwindled by another hundred barrels, and he had only enough cattle to provide fresh meat for two weeks. Even if he could find more, the pasture on Anastasia Island, where the cattle were kept for safety, was beginning to wear thin, and, with no one able to go to their fields to bring in their crops, he had no fodder or hay to feed the herds. News from the American lines further depressed him. If Georgia continued to supply Smith with militia, Kindelán noted in a report, the American commander would soon be able to move against Anastasia Island. St. Augustine was unprotected on the side facing the bay. Attack from that direction would be fatal.[45]

Even his writing supplies were running out, and he drafted his report to the captain general in watery ink using old passport applications, censuses, and treasury forms for paper. Expressing disbelief at the wretched state to which Spain had fallen in the world, Kindelán compared his successful defense of East Florida during the rebellion of 1795 with the defeat that now loomed over him. How different things had been in 1795. Then, he told Apodaca, Don Luis de las Casas had provided him with three companies of experienced troops to combat rebels who had no resources, whereas the Patriots were fully supported with U.S. troops and state militia. Then, against a smaller rebellion, a whole battalion had garrisoned St. Augustine, with artillery, dragoons, four companies of white militia, another of *pardos*, another of *morenos*, and three of cavalry. Now he had only 508 volunteers, 180 soldiers in the Third Infantry Battalion of Cuba, 20 artillerymen, 13 dragoons, and 90 *moreno* militia. "Then, not only were men paid punctually, but besides that the Viceroy of Mexico, the Conde de Revillagigedo, sent 50,000 pesos for extraordinary expenses, and now, for four years, no one has received their pay. Then there was an abundance of all manner of comestibles, and now every day the supplies shrink away. Since the 15th of [July] we have scarcely received one barrel of flour, one grain of rice or corn, or an ounce of lard or dried beef. It is urgent," Kindelán pleaded, "that we be reinforced with 480 veteran soldiers, whose presence might finally restore order! There is no longer any doubt that all of the [enemy] forces are directed toward completely severing the routes by which we might receive relief."[46]

Hoping the urgency of his words would steel the captain general to make a staunch defense of East Florida, he searched for some means of delivering his dispatch. With the privateers still on patrol, he decided to try sending a courier south along the inland waterways. Summoning Jaime Martinelli of the urban militia, he asked him to travel by canoe toward Cape Canaveral. Once there, he was to signal any British ship that might be near the coast. If no ship appeared, he was to paddle the canoe all the way to the Florida Keys and find some means of contacting Havana. It was a ludicrous tactic, an act of desperation. But Kindelán was becoming desperate.[47]

Only days after Martinelli's departure, the governor learned of the capture of the *Barbarita*. "This event is without doubt a mortal blow for this Plaza," he wrote in yet another missive to Apodaca, "for it has deprived us of those supplies we anticipated from [New] Providence, and Your Excellency knows that it will not be easy to furnish many of the articles I have requested, above all for the indispensable gifts needed for the Indians."

By September 7, St. Augustine's situation was critical, and Kindelán felt the same imminent foreboding that was assailing the thoughts of Colonel Smith. To feed the thousands of people in town, he had thirty-five barrels of flour, eight and a half barrels of rice, eighteen barrels of dried beef, and twenty-four barrels of pork. He could calculate the town's resources in days rather than weeks. His pessimistic mood found bitter expression in an outburst of rage. To try to retain the Floridas, he told the captain general,

> Permit me to say, Your Excellency, that *it is an illusion*, which must compromise our arms and each of the misfortunate officials picked to govern here. What a cruel position! Destined to be victims of our impotency, at the end of their careers, in the last third of their lives, brought by a fatality that has no remedy, and by a single blow, to the loss of any reputation which, by their prior meritorious conduct,

they had earned. . . . All or the greater part of this Province is in
rebellion. Amelia Island, the St. Marys River, the St. Johns River are
in the possession of the troops of the United States. The Treasury
hasn't a *real* nor any credit. The port is blockaded. The Battalion of
Cuba is totally without clothes, the Pickets and *Morenos* who came as
reinforcements lack adequate garb for the hard winters that they
have here. In the stores and public warehouses there is no kind of
supply.[48]

And so, like Smith, Kindelán came to the last throw of the dice. Once
more, he had sent a detachment of the free black militia, augmented by
Indian allies and maroons, patrolling outside the town. His hope was that
they could bring back food, yet he had heard nothing from them since
their departure. They had left St. Augustine by means of the western redoubts, crossed the San Sebastian River, and were said to be heading
north, to an area where they had previously sprung ambushes—to Twelve
Mile Swamp.

The local free black militia had already been the salvation of St. Augustine on more than one occasion. During the long hot months of July and
August, they ventured forth four times to capture cattle and restock the
town's corrals. The risks they took were terrifying. Apprehension by the
enemy might mean anything—summary execution or the slave auction
block. Yet they never declined action. Tony Primus, a free-born lumber
cutter and farmer, recalled participating in one cattle hunt near Julington
Creek. "They furnished us with horses and provisioned us, four dollars a
head for all cattle we could bring to Town—a party of us (all colored
people for no whites would go) went out. We got some twenty or thirty
head on this expedition. We were intercepted and fired upon by the Patriots but escaped."[49]

Although the men of color comprised a small militia unit of no more
than fifty, they had the advantage of well-trained and experienced leaders.
Their unit had originated under the auspices of a former slave turned professional soldier—Jorge Biassou—who had arrived in St. Augustine with
his family and retinue in the 1790s. Biassou had fought his way to command in the bloody slave uprising that started the Haitian Revolution on
Saint Domingue, and had subsequently taken up arms for the Spanish.
Deemed too dangerous to reside in Cuba, where his reputation as a blood-
thirsty rebel slave was viewed with horror, he had been sent away to East

Florida. Proud and colorful, he soon attracted a broad following from among the town's free people of color, a cohesive community bound together by ties of kinship and intermarriage. Although Biassou was long dead by 1812, his kin and protégés still commanded the free black militia. Among the officers were Jorge Jacabo, his brother-in-law; Juan Bautista (Prince) Witten, who had escaped from slavery in South Carolina; and Benjamín Seguí, a native of Santo Domingo. Like other settlers, these men had been compelled to retreat from their landholdings and had taken refuge in St. Augustine when the Patriots came into the country. All had seen prior military service during the troubles of 1795 and in various skirmishes with the Indians. They were, in fact, closer to "professional" soldiers than most militia officers, ready to employ the bloody tactics of guerrillas when necessary, and they countered Patriot threats with a "no quarter" policy of their own. On one occasion, at least, Governor Kindelán had found it necessary to caution them against being "excessively sanguinary." Lieutenant Witten was especially active against the Patriots, spying on their positions, taking part in the raid at San Pablo, and leading the cattle drives. He took command of the militia shortly after abandoning his homestead (a small house of sawed lumber on about ten acres of land at Sweet Water) and reporting in to St. Augustine. Known as a ferocious war leader with no love for the rebels, he was even less inclined to forgive them after they burned his house. Governor Kindelán, well aware of the value of his black officers, had promoted all of them for their exemplary bravery, a move that encouraged further recruitment.[50]

On September 11, Lieutenant Witten was once again in command of a field detachment, this time composed of twenty-five of his militiamen, thirty-two blacks from the ranks of the Seminoles' auxiliaries, and six Seminole braves. Well informed about American movements, this group was hunting the convoy that was headed from Fort Mose to the blockhouse at Davis Creek—and late that night they found it.

Since his removal as commandant of Fernandina, marine captain John Williams had reconciled his differences with Colonel Smith, and the two men had even become friends. Williams was shocked when he first entered Smith's camp before St. Augustine. His marines, fresh from Fernandina, marched into the camp wearing trim blue jackets and white pantaloons, with the brass on their uniforms gleaming and polished and their plumed caps well manicured. Smith's infantry and riflemen, by contrast, were emaciated and ragged from their months of sentry and garrison duty. Although eager for action, Williams was not entirely happy with duty in East Florida. He had requested reassignment to the American fleet, where he thought his men would be of far greater use in the war against England, but the request for transfer had been rejected. Smith might have smiled sympathetically, for he, too, had sought transfer on several occasions, without result. Like it or not, his contingent was committed to Florida.

During the worst days of the Indian raids, Williams lost three marines killed in ambushes, besides another man lost through desertion to the Spanish. In the absence of supplies and other relief, morale at Fort Mose was at an all-time low. Something had to be done at once to rectify the situation and raise the men's spirits. It was natural, then, for Smith to put the affable and reliable marine in charge of the supply train he was about to dispatch to the blockhouse. He hoped to see them back in a few days, bringing all the recently arrived goods and munitions. Knowing the convoy would require a sizable escort, Smith assembled a force of nineteen privates, with Captain Fort and a young corporal as Williams's junior officers, and delegated a party of Patriot volunteers to handle the two wagons, the pack animals, and the mule teams. In the early afternoon of September 11, with the empty wagons creaking and groaning across the rutted and uneven track of the King's Road, the party set forth on the twenty-mile trek that would take them to Davis Creek. They had completed about ten miles of the journey, and the sun was sinking low to their left, when they reached the twisting and mucky trail leading westward through Twelve Mile Swamp (see fig. 2). This was the area where a Seminole raiding party had lately mutilated the body of the rebel Benjamin Armstrong, and some of the men must have glanced around with apprehension each time the road dipped down and passed through morasses of gloomy cypresses and motionless pools. Undeterred, for they had made the transit of this swamp many times, they tramped onward, picking their way back to the high ground, their lamps and torches doused so that the descending darkness would shield them from watchful eyes.

But it was already too late. Just a little way ahead, among the dense palmettos and scattered hammocks that encroached upon the trail, Witten's men were waiting, all of them painted and dressed like Indians and concealed in ambush.

As the moon rose around 8 P.M. to cast a dusky light on the file of men and wagons, whoops and war hollers broke out on all sides, and the men under Witten's command fell upon the rear of the American detachment. Tongues of musket fire—from perhaps sixty guns at a range of twenty paces—lit up the scrub. The first volley ripped into the Americans and their horses, wounding six men. There was a pause as the attackers reloaded, and Captain Williams glanced around to locate the enemy and form up his marines for a charge. Then a second volley exploded and Williams fell. In panic, soldiers refused to heed orders and began to fall back, dropping down into the safety of a nearby thicket on the edge of the swamp. From behind trees, they fired out into the darkness, trying to hit unseen foes and provide cover for their comrades as they, too, plunged into cover. It was pandemonium. Two more musket balls slammed into Williams as he lay on the ground where he had fallen. Rushing to his side, Captain Fort lifted him up and helped him to limp from the line of fire. They reached the edge of the swamp, where Fort called out to the men to regroup. Even as he shouted his orders, a musket ball knocked down the corporal next to him and then ricocheted into his knee. He collapsed, struggled back to his feet, grabbed up the gun of the fallen corporal and fired it, and continued to rally the men. Several marines wrestled Captain Williams into their ranks, hearing more shots thud into his body as they did so. Behind them, eerily lit by the moonlight, terrifying painted figures emerged out of the shadows. Several of them leaped upon the fallen corporal, scalping him in full view of his comrades.

For a moment it looked like the Americans would break. Then Fort reasserted command, and Williams shouted orders from where he lay. With yells and war cries all around them, the marines, riflemen, and militia fired twenty-four rounds into the gray trees, picking what targets they could and using up the entire contents of their cartridge kits. They saw figures dashing around the empty wagons in fury. Suddenly, from the high ground above came an organized charge down into the swamp as Witten and his black soldiers bore in upon them. Tomahawks and bayonets glinted and clashed in the darkness. But the defenders, with no powder left, fought off their attackers hand to hand and forced them to give ground and withdraw.

For two more hours, Witten's men and their Indian and maroon auxiliaries prowled around their quarry, firing into them but also counting their casualties. Five warriors and two members of the black militia had been wounded. Unable to get at the enemy and running out of ammunition, Witten ordered his men to burn one of the wagons and then hauled away his injured in the other.

In the confusion of the fight, a few of Captain Williams's men had escaped the trap, grabbed their horses, and ridden hard for the Davis Creek blockhouse to summon help. Lieutenant Stallings immediately dispatched a relief force. As dawn came, they found the convoy from Fort Mose still stranded in the middle of the swamp. They constructed stretchers for Williams and the other wounded and provided escort to Davis Creek.[51]

In St. Augustine, the success of the ambush brought forth praise and rejoicing. From the captured correspondence, translated into Spanish the very same night, Kindelán learned that Smith was as hard-pressed for supplies as he was and depleted in ranks by sickness as well. He wrote at once to the captain general, lavishing praise on Witten's detachment for their resourcefulness and courage.[52]

Smith, meanwhile, met the news with consternation. Of the twenty-two soldiers he had sent out, one was dead, and eight others, including Williams and Fort, were wounded. Williams had been hit eight times, suffering a broken arm, a ball in the groin, a punctured stomach, three wounds to his right hand, another in his shoulder, and one to his left leg. Sent to Camp New Hope with scant chance for recovery, he died seventeen days later on September 29. In a rare display of sympathy for an American officer, the people of Fernandina mourned his death, writing to Georgia newspapers to acknowledge his decency and "gentlemanly conduct" when he was commander of their town.[53]

The ambush in the swamp finished Smith. With no supplies and with a contingent too weak to disperse on more expeditions, he sent an express rider to Colonel Newnan, telling him to leave off all preparations for a march on the Seminole towns in Alachua and come at once in support. "Without your aid I shall not be able to secure our baggage and save the sick," he said, "fifteen or twenty of which are unable to march."[54]

At 10 A.M. on September 14, the American commander raised camp, burned his huts and shelters, and began a retreat. From St. Augustine, the besieged looked on in joy, guns firing, bells pealing. That evening, Smith's battered detachment, five and a half months after first entering the province, reached the shelter of the Davis Creek blockhouse. They had been outwitted and outmaneuvered. The siege of St. Augustine was over.[55]

13

The Price of Victory

In the aftermath of the skirmish in Twelve Mile Swamp, Spanish and American forces lapsed into inactivity, and a lull fell over Florida. Beyond the borders, the attack brought southern affairs surging once more to the forefront of national attention. The *National Intelligencer* regaled its readers with a vivid description of the battle between the wagon convoy and the free men of color, while the *Federal Republican and Commercial Gazette* mourned the death of Captain John Williams from his injuries. In Georgia, angry citizens pressed Governor Mitchell to repay blood with blood. "Every exertion is making by Governour Kinderland [*sic*] to excite disaffection among our slaves," wrote the editor of the *Georgia Journal*. "It is high time the eyes of the people were opened to their situation. Under existing circumstances, the reduction of St. Augustine, as we have before repeatedly stated, is essential to our safety." American breasts were "swelling with indignation against that banditti at St. Augustine," raged the editor of the *Savannah Republican*, and "burning with indignation of the nefarious conduct of the Spanish authority in employing savages of different shades," observed Major General John Floyd. President Madison and James Monroe, although preoccupied with the war in Canada, were compelled to refocus their attention on the South. They had largely ignored the growing plight of American soldiers in East Florida. Now they began to assemble federal troops and militia in the Carolinas and Georgia and pledged themselves to a forcible seizure of the peninsula. In St. Augustine, a worried Kindelán read the reports of Onís and other consuls and sent plaintive appeals to his superiors, warning that he had achieved merely a reprieve, not a victory. If the actions of his militia provoked a further invasion of American troops, he was lost.[1]

The inhabitants of St. Augustine, after their initial rejoicing and celebration, also found they had little cause for exuberance. The lifting of the siege did not alter their immediate dilemma. A desolate waste of burned-out farms, ransacked plantations, and overrun fields surrounded them on all sides. During the five months the invaders had lived off the land, they had stripped the countryside bare. The only cattle in evidence were those the Spaniards had previously collected. There would be no harvest. The cornfields, potato patches, and vegetable gardens were uprooted, choked with weeds, or trampled and consumed by foraging horses and deer. To the west, on the St. Johns River, Patriot campfires had run wild, setting the grasslands and pine forests ablaze. Slaves hid from masters or refused to go back to work.

Colonel Smith, in the meantime, was trying to revitalize his sickly contingent into a fighting force. Taking stock of his wounded and ill, he at first hoped to keep 120 men in the field. A head count quickly proved, however, that only 70 of the infantry, riflemen, and dragoons were fit for duty. The ranks of the Georgia Volunteers exhibited similar depletion, with as many as 105 men on the sick list at one time. For two weeks, Smith remained at the Davis Creek blockhouse, then pulled the bulk of his contingent all the way back to Camp New Hope. The disheveled state of the men roused his compassion and also his anger. "What in the name of God can our rulers be about," he demanded of General John Floyd, "that they have not before this time ordered a force to join me, sufficient to enable me to maintain my position before St. Augustine?" His message to Governor Mitchell was much the same: "The period has at length arrived when it is absolutely necessary to order a respectable reinforcement to aid me in the reduction of St. Augustine and the destruction of the Indian settlements, or that we should withdraw. The latter would be to me the most painful moment of my life."[2]

If nothing else, his sojourn in East Florida had taught Smith the limitations of war by proxy. The militia was of no use, he told Mitchell. Most men enlisted for two months, and by the time they reached Florida they had only four or five weeks left to serve. Unless their term of service could be extended, they were a handicap more than a help, a force that he had to provision but could not effectively exploit. Though he acknowledged Colonel Newnan's and Captain Fort's bravery and valor in protecting his flank, yet he yearned for trained soldiers capable of a sustained offensive.[3]

The disloyalty of the Patriots also tasked him. They had deserted him in droves at the first sign of Indian attack, leaving his troops to fend for themselves. Angry at the rebels' lack of gratitude for American protection, Smith told Captain Massias, stationed at Fernandina, to ignore them and "in no instance to acknowledge them as a Public body, but afford all the aid in your power to deserving individuals."[4]

The loose-knit cooperation between the rebels and the army was, in fact, disintegrating. Members of the regulars and the Georgia Volunteers grew increasingly contemptuous of the Patriots. Writing from the Fatio plantation of New Switzerland on September 2, just two weeks before Smith's retreat, one recruit with the Volunteers complained,

> We are now under orders to march into the Indian nation, which is about three days march, and the only thing which delays our expedition is the want of *a few pack horses and guides.* We apprehend considerable difficulty in obtaining them, for we have never received any assistance from the inhabitants of this country, and if the whole world were drained to the last dregs, there could never be found such another collection as the constituted authorities of this province, I mean the Patriots—although we protect their lives and property, they would willingly receive every soldier's knapsack in the detachment for a quart of milk.[5]

Even some Patriots expressed disgust with the state of affairs. "I am almost ready to set fire to my house," said one, "and go off by the light to some other country."[6]

Determined to preserve American honor and regain lost ground, Smith petitioned Governor Mitchell with plans for an elaborate campaign against St. Augustine. He would need 300 additional men, he said, to join the 270 regulars and militia he could currently equip. With this force, he proposed to construct and garrison several new blockhouses at Six Mile Creek, Twelve Mile Swamp, and Solana's Ferry and to reinforce or reoccupy Fort Picolata, the Davis Creek blockhouse, and Fort Mose. This ring of fortifications would sever Spanish communications with the Seminoles and strangle St. Augustine of resources, preparatory to bringing in mortars and siege artillery. "It will then be an easy matter to destroy the Town," said Smith, "and see what effect *that* will produce." As bloody and ambitious as it sounded, the plan never materialized into anything more than an outline on paper.[7]

In truth, the only campaign Smith was capable of launching was one of retribution against the Seminoles, and even here he was plagued by doubt.

Colonel Daniel Newnan was certainly game for a fight. Hotheaded and eager for action, he was as outraged as Smith by the ambuscades of the "merciless" red foe. The Georgia Volunteers, though, were of a different mind. They had already done their share, they thought, in rescuing Smith's contingent, and besides, they were comfortably dossed down on the grounds of the New Switzerland plantation, with only a week left to their enlistment. Prior to the Seminole raids, the vast estate, with its mansion house, wharves, smithy, coopers sheds, gin, cotton house, stable, and granary, had offered welcome shelter to Newnan's troops. They had stopped there numerous times during their patrol duty along the east banks of the St. Johns River. Francis Philip Fatio Jr., head of the household since the death of his father in 1811, had at first welcomed the visits, hoping the presence of a large body of militia would keep the plantation secure from harm. Protection came at a cost, however, for over the course of the summer, the Volunteers took to the habit of confiscating whatever they needed. One of Fatio's large boats was dispatched to Six Mile Creek to serve as a supply boat, and Newnan's officers appropriated a herd of English and Bermuda sheep, which provided them with a supply of mutton for their dinners. When the family fled from the Seminoles in August, they left all their possessions behind, and the contents of the house and library soon began to disappear. A large bell, stolen from the yard, eventually turned up in the public market of St. Marys. Although the Seminoles had partially burned the plantation, the main house was still standing in mid-September, and Newnan was using it as a convenient headquarters. During a search of the house, some of his men discovered evidence that Fatio's father had once served with the British army. The discovery apparently aroused anti-English sentiments, for a short time later, according to one account, soldiers "broke open the family vault, and took out the body of Francis P. Fatio, Sr., and left his bones scattered about, which were afterward gathered together by his friends and again interred."[8]

Though Newnan exhorted his recruits to extend their enlistments, praising them for their bravery or upbraiding them for their stubbornness, his appeals and chastisements failed to elicit a response. Only a quarter of the contingent was willing to march on the Alachua towns, eighty miles into the hostile interior. Colonel Smith, hearing this, concluded the endeavor would be foolhardy and observed that Newnan, while amply supplied with audacity, "certainly does not use his thinking faculties much." Mitchell also questioned sending a small detachment on such a mission. "I fear there is a want of willingness somewhere," he said, "which is more the cause of the delays than the want of pack horses."[9]

In the end, the promise of land succeeded where other appeals had failed. Displaying the survey equipment he had at hand, Newnan told his men the expedition into Alachua could serve two purposes: to drive the hostile Indians from their strongholds between Payne's Town and Cuscowilla and to investigate the value of the vicinity for homesteaders (with the assumption that these would include his men). With this offer before them, most of the Volunteers agreed to sign up for an additional two months. One recruit not only reenlisted but wrote home to friends, saying they should try to reach Newnan's camp before he marched, for "such another opportunity will never present itself for young men to advance their fortunes in so short a time."[10]

By September 24, Newnan had a force of 117 soldiers ready to depart, including twenty-three men provided by Smith, nine Patriots under the command of Captain William Cone, and Newnan's own slave and manservant, Isaac. Cone's men were going along to act as guides. Supplies and transport remained a problem. A sweep of nearby plantations turned up only a dozen horses to carry baggage, and provisions were short. Each man had four days' rations, enough to reach the Alachua territory but not to return. Newnan reassured them, saying they would replenish their supplies from the herds and corn houses of the Indians. In the early afternoon, the detachment crossed the St. Johns River at Fort Picolata and commenced the first American offensive of the war. A rainy Florida autumn was now upon them, the long sixteen-hour days of summer dwindling to about twelve hours of daylight, the weather wet and changeable, and the temperatures ranging from the seventies or eighties in the heat of the day to the forties and fifties at night.

For three days, Newnan's column advanced westward without incident, passing through pine barrens where visibility was good and the march fairly easy. Captain Humphries, upset with Newnan over some remarks about his courage, stayed at the front of the column among his riflemen. Newnan held the center with Fort's militia under the command of Lieutenant Abram B. Fannin. Lieutenant John H. Broadnax of Captain Thomas Coleman's company and Captain William Cone, with his Patriot volunteers, provided the rear guard. At night, the three companies camped in a triangle around their baggage and horses. The men slept fully clothed, with musket or rifles at their side, ready to jump up in case of ambush.

On Sunday, September 27, when they were approximately eight miles from the nearest Seminole villages, Newnan called his officers to a council and reviewed plans for the attack. Around 10 A.M., the column again got under way and arrived almost at once before a large expanse of cypress swamp directly in the line of advance. Just as suddenly, the scouts came running back, saying that a party of sixty or seventy Seminoles was emerging from the swamp to meet them. By prearranged plan, Captain Humphries and the riflemen deployed to the right, moving to outflank the enemy, while the other two companies pressed forward (see fig. 10).

Although the Seminoles typically exploited terrain to ensnare their foes, using swamps as moats and hammocks as redoubts to slow and then repulse an attack, on this occasion they, with Payne in their midst, apparently encountered Newnan by accident. They were not painted for battle, had their packs on their backs, and were carrying their muskets unloaded. Newnan's men caught sight of the eighty-year-old Payne, very splendid on a white horse, directing his braves to fall back and ready their arms. The Georgians and Patriots did not wait but charged the warriors, hurrahing and firing as they came. In confusion, the Seminoles gave ground, taking refuge in the swamp, but here they rallied and began to fire back from behind the great knobbed trunks of the cypress trees.

Attackers and defenders were evenly matched, about seventy-five on a side, for Humphries's company had skirted too far to the right during their flanking maneuver, ending up on the far side of a sinkhole, and could neither rejoin Newnan nor close with the enemy. For two and a half hours, soldiers and braves, firing from concealment, tried to pick one another off in a shooting match. Newnan tried several times to rout the Seminoles by mounting a charge, and the warriors attempted to flank him, but each charge was repulsed, and the advancing Seminoles ended up running into Humphries's men. As morning wore into afternoon, the opposing lines of musket fire stretched through the forest for half a mile.

From his position near the center of the line, Newnan saw seven of the Seminoles fall wounded, "among whom," he noted, "was their king, Payne." A few of his men, recalling the fate of Smith's couriers and the Patriot Benjamin Armstrong, clambered forward to the bodies of two warriors lying outside the swamp and pared off their scalps. The Seminoles, meanwhile, proved equal to the contest in marksmanship, killing one Volunteer and wounding nine others.

With neither side able to withdraw and powder running low, the shooting gradually subsided, and the forest fell silent for almost five hours, while the braves applied their war paint and the Americans watched and waited. Then, around 6:30 P.M., half an hour before sunset, the swamp and the pine barrens suddenly erupted in a cacophony of noises—grunting alligators, wailing panthers, howling wolves, growling bears, and screeching hawks. It was a war display put on by a much larger party of warriors, including forty or so black auxiliaries out of the maroon villages, that Bowlegs had brought to trap Newnan. In the twilight, the Volunteers caught glimpses of ghostly figures flitting among the tree trunks. The Seminoles and blacks, now comprising a force of some 250, advanced in a body and opened fire. The militiamen held their ground and fired back. As the smoke cleared, two Americans were dead and one wounded, with half a dozen casualties on the other side. Then the warriors withdrew once again into the swamp.

Unable to retreat with such a large enemy force on his trail, Newnan used the night hours to formulate a defense, ordering his men to erect a breastwork of logs and earth and to take refuge inside it with the baggage and munitions. He sent away Captain Whitaker and six other couriers by horse to summon reinforcements.

For the next week, as the provisions ran out, a hundred men huddled inside Newnan's makeshift fort. Outside, the Seminoles kept up a sporadic fire but rarely found a mark. The weather also turned against the detachment. Rising winds foretold the coming of an autumn storm. Throughout Thursday and Friday, cold rain pelted down on the exposed men. Seminole sharpshooters picked off the horses, and Newnan started to butcher the carcasses for food. By Sunday, October 4, many of the Volunteers were at the limits of their endurance. They were trapped, on foot, without provisions, three days' march from safety, and outnumbered by more than two to one. Goaded by Captain Humphries, they insisted on retreat. Newnan argued against it. How far could they get, carrying the wounded? he asked. It was better to stay in a defensible position and await relief. The men overruled him. Yet they went only eight miles that day before some were collapsing with fatigue, and Newnan had to call a halt and build a second breastwork. At evening, he sent off two additional couriers—this time on foot—to find help.

Fierce driving rain and gale-force winds howled all about the men that night, toppling pine trees or snapping them in half at midtrunk, so that by morning the forest resembled a logging camp of felled timber. Wet, chilled, and hungry, the men rallied to make another hard march to the east. After just a few miles, they came to a place thick with the trunks of fallen pine trees, affording good concealment, and here the Seminoles, having outflanked them, sprang an ambush. They shot three men, including Newnan's slave, and scalped a wounded man before his comrades could come to his rescue.

Meanwhile, relief parties sent out by Colonel Smith were scouring the pine barrens for Newnan and could not find him. Only around October 9, after the battered detachment had endured another four days of privation and terror, did Sergeant Major Reese finally arrive with horses and supplies. The exhausted Volunteers told him they had survived by eating alligator, gopher tortoise, and the hearts of palmetto. On October 11, two weeks after first encountering the Seminoles and having retreated for nearly seven days, Newnan and his men finally staggered out of the woods and reached Fort Picolata. Although the colonel estimated Seminole losses at fifty dead, he himself had eight dead, nine wounded, and eight missing.[11]

The battle, and especially the retreat, created another sensation in the American press, where Newnan was lauded as a national hero for his fortitude. Locally, Smith and Mitchell dismissed the action as a near catastrophe saved by luck. "I am much gratified at the return of Colonel Newnan's Detachment with so little loss," commented Mitchell. But he could not resist adding that Newnan had been fortunate, for if the Seminoles had anticipated attack, they would have overwhelmed his men "notwithstanding their gallantry and firmness." Smith, hearing that Newnan blamed him for botching the rescue effort, was less kind and hinted that further slanders on his honor would be resolved at pistol point.[12]

Although Newnan's raid, as it came to be called, was largely a defeat, costing numerous lives without ever reaching the towns in the Seminole heartland, it ultimately dissuaded the Seminoles from further participation in the war. Payne, suffering from a mortal wound, remained uncowed and was in no mood to make peace. Speaking in council, he urged his fellow chiefs to widen their attacks and commence a general uprising of all the Florida tribes. However, Wolf Warrior, leader of the Miccosukees, and the chiefs from other bands of Seminoles declined to involve themselves.

The English were already trying to draw the Creeks into an alliance, and many tribes simply wanted to look after their own affairs and avoid the larger war that was breaking out to the north. Besides, they had already raided most of the hostile plantations of East Florida. Without support, Payne had little choice but to relent and send envoys to Benjamin Hawkins, the Indian agent in Georgia, saying his people were willing to sue for peace and come to terms. A few days after these messages were delivered to Hawkins, the old chief succumbed to his injuries and died. "What a misfortune for me that I could not have died this day instead of you," Bowlegs pronounced during the funeral rites. "What a trifling loss our people would have sustained in my death. How great in yours." Up in Milledgeville, Governor Mitchell welcomed the calls for a truce. As it turned out, though, the Seminoles had not seen the last of the Georgia militia and the Patriots.[13]

Even as Smith worked desperately to extract Newnan's men from the interior, news came from a different quarter that St. Augustine had received more reinforcements and supplies. The Yankee privateers haunting the coast had vanished into the sea mists after the lifting of the siege, opening a safe passage for inward-bound merchantmen and government courier vessels. Another company of black troops was disembarking at the capital, and ships from Fernandina and Cuba were off-loading comestibles and other amenities. "We are now well supplied with provisions for more than two months," wrote a town resident to a friend in Charleston, "and are in hopes that our fate will be decided before they are consumed." In an optimistic mood, Spanish subjects were even beginning to inquire about remuneration and indemnification, hoping the U.S. Congress might offer compensation for the property damages inflicted upon them by the invasion. Letters and propaganda mailed to various American newspaper editors contrasted East Florida's prosperous state before the occupation with its current poverty and ruin.

Although it did not appear in print until late November, Benigo García's sarcastic "History of the Invasion of East Florida" circulated widely, eventually gracing the front page of the *Federal Republican and Commercial Gazette*. García knew that an article published in this newspaper would not only catch the attention of American Federalists but would also be seen in Cuba, where the *Republican* was a popular source of news about the United States. The Patriots, he wrote, were nothing more than a pack of fifty ungrateful Spanish subjects ("not one of them *real*

Spaniards") who had allied themselves with 300 Georgians to overthrow East Florida's legitimate government. Other correspondents dwelled on the devastation of the countryside. "General Mathews, General McIntosh, and I know not how many other Generals, are obliged to halt in their career of conquest," said one angry merchant. "They look around them if not with shame, at least with dismay, on a country ruined by their machinations, and find they have been fools and villains to no purpose." A letter published in the *New York Evening Post* proved oddly prescient when it said that a court of law would one day investigate American complicity in the destruction wrought throughout the colony.[14]

Other matters besides the war also pressed upon Floridians' attentions during October. Spain's Cortes Generales, or National Assembly, had promulgated a new constitution that radically altered the administration of the empire, creating a limited monarchy in place of the absolutist regime of the past, and allowing colonial possessions to send elected representatives to Spain. Kindelán found himself under strict orders to implement the provisions of this constitution by organizing an election. As a subsidiary province of Cuba, East Florida could not directly elect a deputy to the Cortes but instead had to choose a delegate, or *elector provincial*, who would travel to Havana and cast a ballot for a slate of candidates. With all of the disruptions of war, coupled with Florida's small population, Kindelán decided to depart from the guidelines he had been given for election procedures and improvised a procedure of his own. The resulting system had two stages. First, the enfranchised population cast their ballots for eleven commissioners, and then these commissioners met and cast ballots for the *elector provincial*. Only free males who were Catholics and had reached the age of twenty-one were entitled to vote, a restriction on the franchise that evoked bitter protests from loyalist Protestants. After making voluntary contributions to the Spanish war effort and defending the colony as members of the militia, how could they be denied suffrage? they asked. Bound by the dictates of the law, Kindelán did his best to defuse their anger and promised he would address their complaints to the National Assembly. In the meantime, competition for the wholly honorary title of commissioner was heated, with ninety-seven men standing for the eleven openings. Five military officers, two merchants, and four members of the Minorcan community won the distinction and at once fulfilled their obligations by appointing Don Fernando de la Maza Arredondo, the elder, to fill the role of *elector provincial* in Havana.

Of far greater interest to the local population was the second election, which filled the posts of the new town council, or *ayuntimiento*. For the first time, the governor, as *jefe político*, had to share his civil authority with an elected board presided over by a mayor, or *alcalde*. The elevation of Gerónimo Álvarez, a baker turned merchant, to the office of town mayor would fill Governor Kindelán's life with many colorful and frustrating misadventures in the days to come. The two men quarreled constantly, Álvarez portraying Kindelán as a usurper and Kindelán railing against the haughty presumptions of "a rough poor man" blessed with a "natural stupidity." It was a double irony, however, that men like John Houston McIntosh could castigate Spain for its tyranny at the very time when colonial Spaniards were taking these first, sometimes comical steps toward rule by popular sovereignty.[15]

Political changes were also taking place among the Patriots. Under the stresses of war, the unified body that Mathews had tried to forge at St. Marys had broken apart into factions. Increasingly, men with ties to Georgia dominated what was left of the rank and file. William Cone, flush with accolades for his part in the Newnan expedition, and Buckner Harris, an influential leader in the Georgia militia, attracted large followings from among their fellow frontiersmen and also gained the backing of local Floridians such as James Dell and Daniel Delany. Former Patriot leaders, on the other hand, faded from view. William Craig resided quietly at his plantation, no doubt dreading the day when he would have to face Estrada and explain his reasons for becoming a turncoat. Zephaniah Kingsley was already conniving at ways to regain the good graces of the Spaniards without suffering chastisement from his rebel friends. Lodowick Ashley sought refuge with his brother, William, in Georgia.

As for John Houston McIntosh, director of East Florida, he presided over a government that existed only on paper. Mathews, his protector and guarantor, was dead; Smith and Mitchell paid him little heed; and Kindelán, according to rumors, had promised the Seminoles $1,000 if they took his scalp. He had no interest in making war on the Seminoles and placed no faith in promises that the Spanish Regency would grant amnesty to the rebels and their leaders. Hoping to revive the Patriot cause with an infusion of funds, McIntosh pressed Captain Massias to release the proceeds of the customhouse at Fernandina. Massias refused. Then the director tried to impose a tax on the loyalists in Fernandina. Again, Massias opposed him. Devoid of allies, McIntosh retreated to St. Marys, fretting and worrying. Commodore Campbell, never overly sympathetic to the planter, feared he was falling victim to nervous collapse, saying the misfortunes of the Patriots and the confrontation with Massias had "all but deranged his mind, little short of a madness." Drawing on the prestige of his family name and his friendship with Congressman George Troup (a distant relation), McIntosh hounded officials in Washington to make good on their offers of support and take East Florida by force. In October, he asked Monroe to intercede for the Patriots at Amelia Island. The "Anglo-Spaniards" there were "exulting at our misfortunes," he complained, "boasting that the U. States gives protection to their property and persons only, and that they yet expect to possess our Estates under a confiscation. Can we be blamed for wishing to lay them under some contribution?" If necessary, McIntosh said, the Patriots would carry on their fight as guerrillas. He had already warned Governor Kindelán that "if he permitted his motley mercenaries to burn any more of our Houses, I would retaliate by ordering to be burnt as many Houses of his friends on Amelia."[16]

In Georgia, pressure for retaliation was also reaching fever pitch. "The blood of our slaughtered citizens calls aloud for it," said a writer in the *Savannah Republican*. Citizens of St. Marys, disgusted that loyalists on Amelia Island had renewed their shipments of food and provisions to St. Augustine, passed a resolution to defy and punish them. In Savannah, two weeks later, a mob attacked the sloop *Alpha* because the crew was loading cargo for the Spaniards. Five citizens from Camden County, fearing more Indian raids, petitioned Governor Mitchell to save their homes, for "we that are in the front have no guard and our crops are all destroyed and our stock at the discretion of the savage." Even the governor himself was succumbing to his simmering resentments. If the national government tried to recall troops from the province, he told Smith, he would resign as U.S. commissioner. "No!" he stressed. "Satisfaction must be had for the blood already spilt, and that satisfaction must be taken at the point of a bayonet." To Monroe, he wrote with less feeling but greater urgency. "If Colonel Smith was withdrawn or compelled to retire from the province," he warned, "it would be attended with the most fatal consequences to Georgia, and indeed nothing short of the whole military strength of the State being brought to act against the Indians and Negroes would in my opinion save her from the worst Evils imaginable."[17]

On November 3, he brought this same message before the Georgia Assembly. Addressing men of like mind to his own, he pressed them to finance operations against both the British and Spanish. "The present force in St. Augustine," he said, speaking of the black troops, "is of a description we cannot tolerate, and the mode of warfare . . . so savage and barbarous that it is impossible for an American to hear of it without feeling the utmost indignation and resentment against the power that commands it or even permits it." To meet the crisis at the border, he was mobilizing 500 men at Trader's Hill, and he urged his legislators to pass a bill to send Georgia's militia storming into East Florida as an offensive force. In effect, he was asking Georgia to declare war on Florida.[18]

As had been the case in the past, these local attempts to deal with East Florida soon ran afoul of national policy. Even as Georgians cried out for vengeance, James Monroe was flirting with efforts to restore peace in East Florida and achieve through negotiation what had so far eluded resolution by force. Over the summer, the Madison administration had finally recognized Don Luis de Onís as someone who could officially speak for Spain as the legitimate consul of the legitimate government—but this acknowledgment came with an ulterior motive. Onís had offered to broker a transfer of the Floridas from the Spanish Crown to the United States.

President Madison expected nothing from such an overture and discouraged it. Onís, he thought, just wanted to play diplomatic games and enhance his image with his superiors. "Your interview with Onís will, I see, be fruitless," he told Monroe. "His object is to bring himself into importance and to gain time." The secretary of state was not so dismissive, however. He spent two months corresponding with Onís, ignoring a groundswell of support for use of force in East Florida. Even when the talks led nowhere and he resumed a more militant attitude, he paid no heed to the appeals and advice of Governor Mitchell. In fact, Monroe was once again ready to try a new man as the administration's agent for Florida. With the president's approval, he decided to terminate Mitchell's appointment as commissioner and to replace him with Major General Thomas Pinckney. Pinckney, he reasoned, would have far greater ease transferring troops and munitions into East Florida and would bring the faltering invasion back into line with standard military procedures.[19]

Learning of the appointment, General Pinckney expressed some reservations about taking it. A veteran of the American Revolution, he had come out of retirement at age sixty-two specifically to meet the crisis with England and to take charge of the Sixth Military District of the South, which consisted of the Carolinas and Georgia. There was no question that he possessed the credentials for the job. He had spent a year in Spain in 1795, negotiating the Treaty of San Lorenzo, and thus had both military and diplomatic experience in his background. Yet he was also a former Federalist congressman, and his sentiments regarding East Florida differed from those of the president and the secretary of state. In summarizing the administration's expectations, Monroe had tried to drive home justifications for the occupation. "East Florida has become essentially a British province," he said. The Spaniards, it was well known, would only act as England directed. Pinckney disagreed with this appraisal. "My opinion is that we are not justified in withholding any part of the Province . . . upon the ground that the Spanish Government refuses to pardon the offenses committed against it by their subjects." Nevertheless, he could see the military hazards of British intervention and agreed to do the president's bidding, whatever it might be.[20]

This second change in the chain of command in East Florida was just as disruptive as the first. With Governor Mitchell's powers suspended and with Pinckney not yet ready to take over command, military affairs in the province continued to drift aimlessly. During October, Colonel Smith and Major General John Floyd tried to put together an expeditionary force of 170 militiamen and forty regulars to renew the campaign against the Seminoles. Sickness and supply shortages drained away their efforts before the detachment could march. Then, at the end of November, Smith learned that his contingent was being transferred to the war in the North. Initially overjoyed at this news, his joy turned to chagrin when he discovered that only the riflemen and dragoons were going. He was under orders to remain in Florida in command of a small infantry unit.[21]

Governor Mitchell's plans also came to naught. After lengthy deliberation, the Georgia Assembly decided that the state militia could reinforce Colonel Smith in defending occupied territory but that authorization for an offensive war had to come from the federal government. In Florida, the only skirmish of consequence against the Spaniards was an attempted cattle raid on the outskirts of St. Augustine led by Captain Woodruff and sixty men. "The party failed to get hold of the beeves in consequence of their being kept close under the guns of the town and fort. They succeeded in bringing off a Spanish picket guard composed of a corporal and three privates."[22]

The mood and conditions of military life in East Florida during the fall of 1812 were witnessed and reported by a newcomer to the province, twenty-four-year-old William Clay Cumming of Augusta, Georgia, who commanded one of four companies of Georgia militia dispatched to assist Colonel Smith. Ordered south in early November, Cumming wrote home to his parents, relating his hardships and adventures. Even before crossing the border, his men had to endure a grueling trek through Georgia, where, because of the poor condition of the roads, they wore themselves out trying to wrestle their supply wagons through a series of swamps and creeks. "The fatigue parties (which were very large) were frequently obliged to plunge up to the waist in mud & water to extract the wagon," he observed, "& then such shouting & screaming & swearing! I expect the War-whoop will be music to it."[23]

By the time Cumming reached Point Peter, he was already afflicted with a sore throat, the beginnings of a more serious illness. On November 2, gunboats ferried his company across to Fernandina, where they joined the other three units, about 218 men in all. "The inhabitants seem most of them to be of the lowest order & are poor & dirty," he reported. "In short they are much like creatures as the Spanish seegar makers with us." He took no rest in the town, staying up for twenty-four hours straight, first to encamp his men and then to break camp the next morning. His trip down the Amelia and Nassau Rivers turned out to be as unpleasant as the one Colonel Smith had made with the regulars in the previous spring.

> We embarked at a wrong time of tide & continued first when the tide was falling to the Narrows. This is a long narrow shallow passage which separates Amelia and the Main. Our men dragged their boats for miles thro' these abominable narrows & did not reach the Nassau River till late at night, when everyone was about exhausted. Next day we reached the St. Johns, but did not proceed far up the River. The wind & tide were both against us & the men so weakened by fatigue & want of water that we were obliged to land about nine in the evening at a place called the St. Johns Bluff.[24]

Climbing the steep bluff in the dark, the men discovered the abandoned and ransacked remains of the Spanish supply depot of San Vicente de Ferrer. "It had a most gloomy aspect," said Cumming.

> There were eight or ten houses, stores & out-buildings all deserted & the whole place was grown with tall fennel. We groped about in the dark however & at length found the well. One of the party was down

in a moment (the wells in this country are seldom deep) & handed up water to us. Everyone exclaimed it was the best they had drunk since he left home. Our anxiety was then concerning the quantity & you may smile when I tell you, we were exceedingly rejoiced when the man in the well informed us that he was up to his knees in the water. Bad weather detained us the following day at the same place & two Indians or Negroes being descried in the neighboring woods we had an unsuccessful chase for three or four miles in pursuit of them.[25]

On November 9, Cumming's company arrived safely at Camp New Hope. The camp was large, he reported, too large, in fact, for the 400 men who occupied it. It was on the east bank of the river, with a pond of water and a swamp to the south and a morass on the north. The morass extended along the eastern side of the camp until it nearly intercepted the swamp. This afforded strong natural protection. The camp buildings and the hospital were spaced widely apart, however, and Cumming thought this arrangement would make them difficult to defend in the event of attack. "I can give you no information concerning the Enemy. We have no cavalry but a few cowardly Patriots who never ride out of camp but to drive in confiscated and stolen beef."[26]

He had barely been in the province two weeks when he collapsed from sickness, "a severe indisposition which reduced me to a state of the lowest debility." Fatigue kept him from duty for nearly a month, and it was only in mid-January, having "regained both my flesh & strength," that he rejoined the active list. By this time, winter had arrived, and he thanked his mother for sending him worsted stockings. "Some might suppose that the cold can not be a very formidable enemy in Florida but I assure you the weather is often very severe. The oldest inhabitants can not recollect a winter so inclement as the present & while I am writing the fields are all covered with heavy frost."[27]

Relations between the troops and the Patriots remained strained during all this time. Cumming had nothing good to say about the rebels. Upon reporting himself fit, he was assigned to an expedition setting out under Captain Woodruff of the riflemen. Woodruff took his men twenty miles south of Camp New Hope, most likely to the Fatio plantation, "to surprise some Spanish Negroes who were reported to be plundering the cornfield. . . . But the report was groundless and it is believed in Camp was fabricated by some worthy Patriots who designed to plunder the fields themselves but were anxious to frighten away any enemies who might be lurking in the neighborhood before commencing their operations." Echoing the words of some of his predecessors in East Florida, Cumming wrote a postscript to his father: "I should be very glad to obtain an appointment in the Northern Army."[28]

With General Pinckney awaiting clearance to advance and Governor Mitchell stymied from further action, the impetus for prosecuting war against the Spaniards now switched back to the federal government. On Monroe's instructions, Pinckney began to collect a large and better-provisioned army destined for East Florida, with orders to station it at Point Peter. Analyzing the requirements of a major campaign, the general estimated it might take until March 1813 to gather together the horses, artillery, supplies, and men needed to launch an assault against St. Augustine. This posed no problem to the administration. Monroe was canvassing senators and using his new, temporary position as secretary of war to push through another bill in Congress, one that would authorize a direct military seizure of East and West Florida. Remembering the defeat of the previous June, he was taking no chances, emphasizing British threats to the South to make sure the new Congress would back the administration's policy. The editor of the *National Intelligencer* observed that public opinion now favored resolute action, for "the safety of the Southern frontier . . . requires that East Florida should be added to our territorial possessions."[29]

The success of this new initiative depended entirely on Monroe's ability to secure congressional support. Indeed, President Madison desperately wanted a victory in East Florida to offset the embarrassing and demoralizing American defeats at Fort Detroit, Frenchtown, and Queenstown during the 1812 campaigns against Canada. In a detailed analysis of the nation's military needs, Monroe told Congress that the country required 22,000 additional regular troops, with 2,000 assigned to Savannah and East Florida, to guard against a British landing in the South, and with another 2,500 soldiers for New Orleans and the Gulf Coast. He carefully justified action in East Florida as part of an overall war strategy. "While it is held by Spain it will be used as a British province for annoying us in every mode which may be made instrumental to that end. The ascendancy which the British government has over the Spanish Regency secures to Great Britain that advantage while the war lasts. We find that at present the Creek Indians are excited against us, and an asylum afforded to the Southern slaves who seek it there." Determined to press home the acquisition of the Floridas as an extension of war with England, he called upon Andrew Jackson to ready an advance into West Florida, with Pinckney scheduled to move south into the Florida peninsula from Colerain and St. Marys. On January 13, 1813, hopeful of a win in Congress, Monroe told Pinckney to prepare for an attack on St. Augustine.[30]

The second debate on the bill to take possession of East and West Florida began in secret session in the Senate on December 10, 1812, amid growing concerns about setbacks in the war with England. For twelve days, senators reviewed American claims to the Floridas, read over negotiations between the United States and Spain going back fifteen years, and considered other documents submitted by the president. In mid-January, Monroe responded to a plethora of questions regarding American rights to the provinces and the predilections of the settlers there, and then on January 19 debate resumed. A bill was introduced, reading in similar terms to that of the previous June, with five sections, the second of which authorized the president to use military force to take possession of East Florida. On January 26, senators listened to a memorial submitted by the Georgia legislature, recommending an immediate seizure of the province.[31]

President Madison anticipated trouble. "Congress proceed with their usual slowness, even in the most essential subjects," he told Thomas Jefferson on January 27, "and the undercurrent against us is as strong as ever."[32]

The fact that the Senate had already rejected a measure on East Florida once before became a rallying point for renewed opposition. Samuel Smith, President Madison's old foe, made a motion to strip the new bill of all the provisions pertaining to East Florida, leaving only those that dealt with military preparations aimed against West Florida. William Hunter, a respected Federalist from Rhode Island, rose to address the same point. In a long and sometimes impassioned speech of some 10,000 words, he refuted, point by point, the legal and military justifications the administration had advanced for taking aggressive action against East Florida. He suggested, almost at once, that the Senate was wasting its time in even considering the bill. It was substantially the same as the one they had already read, debated, and thrown out in June. Then, too, he wanted to know why there was no motion for a formal declaration of war against Spain. If the United States had legitimate grievances against Spain, let Congress proclaim them, he said. What, after all, were the reasons given for seizing East Florida? That the Spaniards in East Florida defended themselves against rebels? That they repelled invaders at their doors? These were not sufficient reasons for a military occupation. "Next to an English, a Spanish War, is the most disastrous in which this country can be engaged," he proclaimed. "Where is our property?—our commerce?—at Cádiz—at Havanna [sic]—at Lisbon—Do you think that the Spaniards, and the Portuguese, their allies, are dullards and fools? And that they will omit the fair and honest exercise of the rights of reprisal and retaliation?"[33]

Perhaps the most telling sentences in Hunter's speech, however, were contained in his denunciation of the ongoing attacks against the people and government of East Florida. "I say this is not only war, but an offensive war," he told the members, "not only an offensive war, but an unjust war."[34]

A demand for a vote followed immediately upon the conclusion of Hunter's remarks, and some of his points apparently struck home. On February 2, by a ballot of nineteen to sixteen, the Senate removed the crucial section of the bill that related to East Florida. An attempt to restore it the following day also failed. The rest of the measure eventually passed both the Senate and the House to become law on February 12, when President Madison signed it. But it gave him nothing that he wanted. It confirmed American claims to West Florida, yet these had already been stated in previous bills. At the same time, it eliminated, with even greater thoroughness than before, any legal sanction for attacking Spanish forces in East Florida. Once more, the administration saw its ambitions thwarted.[35]

Even as the Senate closed the door on a major invasion of East Florida, matters inside the province were following their own course. The day after Senator Hunter made his speech, 400 men departed Colerain and Camp New Hope to fight the Seminoles. Oblivious to debates in Washington, southern militias were taking matters into their own hands.

Georgians, as it turned out, were not the only people chafing for a chance to avenge Daniel Newnan. In November, Colonel John Williams, adjutant general of the Tennessee militia, hearing of Newnan's raid and retreat, issued a call to his fellow frontiersmen for a punitive expedition against the Indians responsible. By early December, 240 eager recruits were on the move from Knoxville, crossing the snows of North Carolina, and coming down the mountain passes into Georgia. Their arrival took Governor Mitchell by surprise. Though still bloody-minded in regard to the Spanish, he had received numerous overtures from the Seminoles of Alachua, asking for a cessation of hostilities and offering to make restitution for any property or slaves they had taken during their raids. Confident that Georgians required no help in fighting Indians, he rather brusquely told the Tennessee Volunteers to return home. He saw no point in stirring up further animosities with the Seminoles just when they were suing for peace. General Pinckney, however, was on the lookout for additional men and intervened to take charge of the men from Tennessee, adding them to the force he was amassing at Colerain.[36]

All through a chill January, the Tennessee Volunteers champed at the bit, cursing the delays and demanding to advance. For sustenance, they followed the lead of some of the Georgia militia and Patriot rebels living along the St. Marys River and encamped at deserted plantations, taking over James Dell's lands on the border near Trader's Hill. Pinckney was still acting on his mid-January instructions from Monroe, and word about congressional decisions had not reached him. On February 3, the militia forces finally received the orders they wanted to hear, to rendezvous with 220 men under Colonel Smith's command and support him in a strike against the Seminoles. William Cumming was among the officers assigned to accompany Smith. "Today, after dinner, we march against the towns of the Aulochaways," he confided in a letter to his parents.

The force from this place will consist of about two hundred & fifty riflemen and infantry who are to be joined within a few miles of the first Indian Town by about two hundred & seventy mounted infantry & riflemen from Camp Pinkney [sic] on the St. Marys. (These last are the Tennessee Volunteers & about 100 Georgians who have joined them). Col. Smith commands in person & I hope will now obtain some sweet retribution for the mortifications to which he was so long most unjustly subjected. Sixty-five miles is the supposed distance to the first point of attack. We shall have three or four days hard marching through the wilderness by an unbeaten track & at the end of that time (about Sunday morning) we expect to see the flames rising from the wigwams of those scalping butchers. . . . Please let no part of my letter relating to an expedition get to the papers. This request I make in conformity to a general Order.[37]

As planned, the two detachments, marching separately from Camp New Hope and Colerain, headed into north-central Florida and united on Sunday, February 7, about thirteen miles from Payne's Town in the Alachua territory. Colonel Smith then advanced his combined force into this key location. He found it empty. The tribal leaders, forewarned that the troops were coming, had withdrawn their people into swamps and other hiding places.

Surprised but certainly not deterred, Smith remained at Payne's Town while Colonel Williams proceeded some miles farther to the south with the Tennessee Volunteers to investigate the main settlement of Bowlegs. Just before entering the town, his detachment caught sight of two Seminole scouts and opened fire on them, killing one. Like Payne's Town, though, the town of Bowlegs was eerily empty. A search of the houses and sheds turned up only seven men, women, and children, who were detained as prisoners. From them, Williams learned of a maroon village a short distance away, but when he marched upon it, he again found the place abandoned. A few days later, on February 10, his men engaged in a skirmish with a small party of warriors who were quickly beaten off. Alachua, it seemed, was being conceded to the Americans.

Using Payne's Town as a base of operations, Smith ordered his soldiers to scour the surrounding countryside. On the eleventh, they burned the maroon settlement they had previously discovered. During expeditions to other villages, they found the decapitated heads of Newnan's casualties nailed to trees and recovered the scalps of victims. With no one to oppose them, their mission became one of search and destroy. All in all, they set fire to 386 houses, seized between 1,500 and 2,000 bushels of corn, took away 300 horses and 400 head of cattle, and destroyed stockpiles of hides intended for the pelt trade. Some twenty Seminoles were killed, and nine people—women, boys, and runaway slaves—were taken prisoner.

North Florida's winter weather intervened to halt these operations. Three weeks of constant cold drizzles and sharp blustery winds proved a harsher enemy than the Seminoles, leaving the men fatigued and ill from exposure and the horses too languid and feeble for hard service. Lodowick Ashley and James Dell, who had accompanied the detachment as guides, offered to take charge of the cattle, so that the soldiers could march or ride quickly back toward the St. Johns River.

Even with operations cut short, the campaign was a disaster for the Seminoles. Though they preserved their people by evacuating the area, they sacrificed their homeland. At the end of February, the Alachua territory, which they had successfully maintained for some seventy years, was razed earth. Upon the withdrawal of the Americans, Bowlegs returned to survey the destruction and quickly decided to remove his people forty miles westward to the Suwannee River. It was a bitter price to pay for siding with the Spanish. The destruction in the area probably also prompted a southward migration of some maroons, who shortly afterward founded Pilaklikaha (near modern day Bushnell). As for Alachua, though the Seminoles would come and go through the area for many years, from 1813 onward it lay open before the path of white settlement.[38]

On March 7, shortly after the return and dispersal of the Smith and Williams expedition, Secretary of State Monroe bowed to the unavoidable and advised President Madison that American troops would have to leave East Florida. Having received assurances from Luis de Onís that Spain intended to pardon the Patriot rebels, he instructed Pinckney to oversee an evacuation. The decision came too late to spare the Seminoles—and it would not go unchallenged by the Patriots.[39]

The Americans Withdraw

In giving up on the conquest of East Florida, President Madison and James Monroe acceded to congressional will and the fortunes of war—1813 was not a propitious year for dreams of invasion. Quite the opposite, the president and his military advisers were turning their thoughts to defensive warfare, for the news from Europe brought constant reports of French defeats and English victories. The 1812 French campaign into Russia had ended in catastrophe, and a combined British, Portuguese, and Spanish army was pushing Napoleon's forces out of Spain. Soon France would cease to be a distraction to the British—and they would be able to fully focus their war machine on the United States. Already, they were recruiting allies among the Creeks, pressuring the Spanish in West Florida to give them a base at Pensacola, and dispatching more warships to patrol the American coast. The clash of rebels and Spaniards in East Florida was now a minor fracas in a conflict that menaced New England, the Potomac, and the Mississippi River Valley.[1]

The men who had heeded General Mathews's call to arms were suddenly on their own, and their war was quickly diminishing once again into a mere revolt. This time, though, the rebellion was not an orchestrated bit of theater but a struggle for survival against an angry and vengeful East Florida populace. Confused and divided by this state of affairs, some Patriots tested the waters of possible amnesty, while others resolved to defy the Spaniards and fight to the last extremity.

"The order for withdrawing the troops comes like a thunderclap," said one resident of St. Marys to a friend in Philadelphia. "Little expecting such an event, many of the Patriots were planting, in expectation of reaping the products, and now when it is too late to begin elsewhere, they are told you must serve your former task masters and their sable satellites, or fly beggared and disgraced. Certainly no one in his senses can expect to live uninjured by the vindictive government of St. Augustine and their black troops." This sorry business, the writer said, would compel Georgia to keep large garrisons of troops on its frontier and assiduously patrol the mouth of the St. Marys River, where British ships could come and go from Fernandina under protection of alliance with Spain.[2]

The biggest danger facing the Patriots was no longer artillery or Indians or sorties. It was something far more difficult to combat—the offer of pardon that Spain had extended to their ranks. On March 18, exactly one year after American troops had set foot on Spanish soil, people in St. Augustine and Fernandina gathered to hear the town criers proclaim a royal decree, stating that rebels could, without penalty, renew their allegiance to Spain and resume their lives and livelihoods as Spanish subjects. Don Luis de Onís had used a vast amount of influence peddling and diplomatic wheedling to convince Spain's Regency government that amnesty in East Florida was in the best interests of the Crown. Fortunately for him, the Regency was in a mood to exhibit largess, even to the most recalcitrant Spanish subjects. Despite a sense of outrage regarding American actions, the Cortes had no desire for war with the United States. Spain needed American trade and American flour for its war effort in Europe. There were great hopes for a revival of Spanish fortunes in the world. The French had been expelled from Madrid and continued to flee back into France. The king was still a captive, but the Spanish government, imbued with the powers gained under the new constitution, exuded confidence in its enactments. If pardons would regain peace and stability in East Florida without an effusion of blood or a cost to the Real Hacienda, then pardons were good policy.[3]

Governor Kindelán, too, expressed relief about the grant of amnesty. The absolution would save him from the otherwise onerous task of tracking down and bringing to trial scores of rebels. He made sure everyone knew the conditions: "Don Fernando VII, by the grace of God, and by the constitution of the Spanish monarchy, king of Spain, and during his absence and captivity, the Regency of the kingdom . . . to grant an amnesty to the insurgents, who have co-operated in the invasion of the Spanish territory in East and West Florida . . . has determined to grant them a general pardon with oblivion of the past, on condition that in future and after the proclamation of amnesty, they shall demean themselves as good and faithful Spaniards." As Kindelán explained to General Pinckney, the decree allowed rebels a period of four months to take advantage of the provisions for amnesty and merely required them to appear in St. Augustine and swear fidelity to Spain.[4]

It was therefore somewhat of a shock to both Kindelán and Pinckney when a large number of Patriots vehemently rejected, even denounced, the offer of a pardon. What Kindelán saw as generous, they saw as insidious. Amnesty held no attraction at all to Georgians like Buckner Harris and William Cone. It would not restore their lands, because they had none in Florida to begin with, and thus it could only drain away the men at arms they needed to sustain their hold on the province. Prominent rebel leaders—John Houston McIntosh and Daniel Delany, in particular—also dismissed the offer. Whatever promises Kindelán made, they told Pinckney, the greater population would never allow them to return to their properties in peace and tranquility.

Speaking on behalf of the Legislative Council of the Patriot government, Harris, Delany, and McIntosh decried the Spanish proclamation as a ruse. The Regency had never approved a general pardon, they claimed. Governor Kindelán had merely thrown together some high-sounding words, without the backing of law, to lure rebels into St. Augustine so that he could more easily capture them. Nor was there any truth to the scurrilous rumors that American troops would depart East Florida. Think, they told their followers, of the kind of life they would lead if they capitulated to the Spaniards. They would become victims of a colony run by escaped slaves. "Weak must be the mind," wrote McIntosh,

> that can have the least dependence upon a promise so hollow and deceitful. Can any one believe that such a corrupt, jealous, and arbitrary Government will adhere to promises, however sacredly made? Will they not screw every tittle [sic] of your property from you under the pretext of making retribution for damages done to Individuals who have adhered to their oppressions? It is needless to dwell upon the subject. The pardon no doubt has been manufactured in St. Augustine—the Government in Spain knows nothing of it—it is designed to entrap the unwary, thinking that you are depressed by the rumor (however false) that the troops are to be removed. Can

You? Will you! in poverty become the sport of slaves and the ab-
horred army in St. Augustine?[5]

This audacious snub, from men whose destinies teetered on the verge
of defeat and arrest, inaugurated the Patriots' final gambit to remain at
liberty and free from Spanish control. Low morale and a yearning to return to their homes had long ago replaced visions of glory in the hearts of
dozens of rebels. Unless something could be done to reawaken their spirits
and prevent defections, the Patriot movement would collapse, leaving no
place of refuge for those who still supported the cause.

It was at this juncture that the mantle of rebel leadership passed to
General Buckner Harris. Though he had long been one of the powers behind the scenes among the Patriots, Harris now emerged as the true
leader. His resourceful and quick-witted personality helped to sway others
to follow him. Harris was born into the same generation as James Monroe
and, like Monroe, had fought in the American Revolution while in his
teens. Previously, he had made his living in the lumber trade around St.
Marys and was an officer in the Georgia militia. Related by marriage to
both George Mathews and Peter Early (the man who would succeed David
Mitchell as governor of Georgia), Harris had a checkered reputation even
among his own kin. His friendship with John Floyd had been tarnished by
quarrels, and Peter Early, his brother-in-law, once described him as an adventurer who had "absconded from the Laws" to seek refuge in East Florida. Commodore Campbell referred to him as "the notorious General Harris, who took refuge in that country to evade the fate that awaited him in
this, and who is well known to the marshal of the district." Whatever the
sentiments of these men, however, the distraught and increasingly leaderless recruits of the Patriots saw in Harris a means to their salvation and
accorded him the same respect they had given to Mathews. He was a familiar face at Camp New Hope, where he ran the quartermaster's store,
selling off cattle and other livestock he acquired from the Patriot Isaac
Hendricks. Acting as the president of the Legislative Council of the territory of East Florida, Harris dashed off a letter to Governor Mitchell, saying the Patriots would not be beggared and sent in dire want into the
towns of Georgia. They intended to make a stand against Kindelán, and it
was in Georgia's best interests to assist them. To those among the rebels
who would listen, he proclaimed that their rebellion was not lost. Indeed,

it could not be, for they would receive no mercy at the hands of the Spanish. Some were inspired by his words. Others were frightened by his threats of retaliation. Backed by John Houston McIntosh, Harris levied a penalty of property confiscation on any Patriot who accepted the terms of the pardon and sent agents to the homes of the most faint-hearted, warning them that he would burn down their houses if they deserted the ranks. Besides the support of fellow Georgia militiamen like William Cone, he won the confidence of at least a dozen north Florida families, notably the Braddocks, Harts, Hendricks, Loftins, Dells, Fitzpatricks, and Ashleys.[6]

While Harris rallied their spirits, McIntosh, still functioning as the director of East Florida, used his influence and his eloquence in a bid to dissuade General Pinckney and Secretary of State Monroe from carrying out the evacuation. McIntosh was convinced that General Pinckney, like Mathews and Mitchell before him, would take the Patriot side in any dispute with the Spaniards if properly apprised about what was at stake. "Can we as men live in a country where nearly the whole of the Army is composed of blacks and mulattos who already begin to manifest their superiority," he asked the general. "Our Laborers are slaves—they will be enticed to join their Brethren in Color and will be protected by them in any enormity. . . . If the Troops are to be withdrawn—which a merciful and just God forbid!—the military positions ought to be placed into the hands of the Patriots, for from them they were received by the U.S." As further proof that the rebel cause was alive and well, McIntosh forwarded Pinckney a copy of the council's rejection of amnesty, augmented by another appeal for aid from Harris, Delany, D. S. Miller, William Christopher, William and John Braddock, John Houston, George Morrison, and John Lowe.[7]

Contrary to McIntosh's expectations, these petitions had little effect on Pinckney. He had no personal grudge against the Spanish, nor was he plagued by doubts or misgivings about ending the American occupation. Instead, he had struck up a lively and cordial correspondence with Governor Kindelán, ironing out the details of when and how American troops should leave the province, and he intended to carry out an evacuation "on the most amicable footing."[8]

Seeing their doom in this resolve, the rebels continued to badger Pinckney with petitions. On April 9, twenty-eight residents wrote to him from the St. Johns District, asking him to reconsider his orders and to intervene on their behalf and protect their lives and property. Besides the men who had signed earlier pleas, this one included the signatures of Zephaniah Kingsley, the Summeralls, the Loftins, the Harts, and Abner and William Williams. "Now, sir, should it be the policy of the United States to withdraw their troops," they said, "we the Inhabitants in our feeble situation must fall a sacrifice to the ambition of a Band of Black Troops introduced from foreign Countries, and other merciless Savages, or abandon our homes in a forlorn and beggarly situation."[9]

McIntosh was also determined to force the issue. His high-strung temperament, strained once before over the loss of General Mathews, now came close to shattering. "Allow me to remind you of the Spanish character generally," he told the general, "of the losses which many of them have sustained in our contest, of their frequent blood thirsty declarations against us. . . . We beg that you would allow the Troops under your command to protect us until you can represent us to your Government."[10]

Going over Pinckney's head, the planter also wrote directly to Secretary of State Monroe. "We are most cruelly disappointed," he told Monroe with barely suppressed anger. "After all our expectations and hopes, after all the assurances we have received, we are surrendered on the declaration of a crazy imbecile Cortes . . . at the most critical unfortunate period that has existed since we have attempted to throw off oppression." The financial losses McIntosh had sustained in support of rebellion only increased his fury over the government's half-hearted efforts at protection and indemnification. "Genl. Mathews found me with a numerous family, possessed of affluence to give them the best education and to carry them in the most fashionable circles in America. . . . Genl. Pinckney will leave me poor and without the means of living anywhere, but in retirement."[11]

Pinckney sympathized with the Patriots' plight, though he believed the rebels were the authors of their own misfortunes. To McIntosh, he apologetically explained that he had no authority to keep troops stationed in East Florida. He offered to intercede with Governor Kindelán on the Patriots' behalf and to ask Kindelán to widen the latitude of the amnesty, so that rebel inhabitants could remain at their homesteads at least until they harvested their crops and then remove themselves from the province when their affairs were set in order. Repeating the same apologies to the other petitioners, he informed them that evacuation of the province would proceed, according to schedule, around April 28.

True to his word, Pinckney did write immediately to Monroe, alerting him to the objections the rebels had made. The secretary of state was unimpressed. He had fought hard, and expended considerable political capital, to protect the Patriots and obtain their pardon. If they refused it, that was their business.

Kindelán was hardly more sympathetic. Pinckney suggested that many difficulties associated with the removal of the troops could be avoided if the governor gave the rebel subjects more time to depart East Florida.

A number of the most influential men among them have planted their crops and will be greatly distressed if obliged to remove their negroes and relinquish these crops on the approaching evacuation. . . . At the same time, they are unwilling to return permanently to the situation of Spanish subjects. . . . If these persons could then be permitted to reap the crops they have planted, they would be bound by the strong tie of their interest, to demean themselves to the period of that indulgence with propriety. The destruction of their crops would not benefit, but on the contrary must by the diminution of the export be prejudicial to the interests of Florida, and by driving the proprietors to despair, may cause the renewal of scenes which tho' unsupported by any countenance from the Government of the United States, might prevent the restoration of that tranquility in the Province you command.[12]

Kindelán, reading this, was polite but firm in his response. After all the delaying tactics employed by Governor Mitchell, he could only regard this latest overture from Pinckney with suspicion. More than anything else, Kindelán wanted the American army out of his province, and the rebels, in his opinion, had already received greater clemency than they deserved. Hence, his reply to Pinckney, while friendly, was emphatic on two points: he expected the troops at Camp New Hope and Amelia Island to withdraw from the province peacefully and with proper decorum, treating the people and their property with respect, and he likewise expected the rebels to renew their oaths of allegiance to Spain, put down their arms, and retire to their homes. Those who wanted to leave the province and could not conveniently arrange their affairs within the specified time could appoint agents from among the loyal subjects to dispose of their property. As for the Georgians, they had no business in the province and should depart: "I dare to ask that you will exercise your authority, and prevent persons of no character, or vagabonds from the state of Georgia, from agitating among the discontented persons who may yet remain in the province, owing to this new order of things."[13]

With no further room, or any further reason, to negotiate, on April 16 Pinckney issued orders to Major Manning at Camp New Hope for a general withdrawal of the troops. Manning should pull back from the camp on April 29, bringing with him all the ordnance, ammunition, and stores belonging to the United States. "The removal of the troops from East Florida is not to be considered in the light of the evacuation of an enemy's territory," Pinckney emphasized to his subordinate, "but as restoring to a state of neutrality a territory which our Executive deemed expedient to occupy. . . . Therefore in withdrawing the troops, you will prevent the removal or destruction of anything appertaining thereto." As so often in East Florida, orders and actions did not go hand in hand.[14]

In Major Lawrence Manning of the Eighth U.S. Infantry, the Patriots had perhaps their last ally within the American military command structure. As the day for the withdrawal of troops neared, rebels clustered around Camp New Hope, taking advantage of the protection it afforded. Manning did not turn them away. He had been appointed as camp commandant to replace Colonel Smith, who had finally, and much to his satisfaction, been transferred out of East Florida to take on duties in the North with the army of General William Henry Harrison. An energetic officer, Manning, upon taking over command, had privately assured Smith that he would not allow Camp New Hope to fall into Spanish hands. Despite bleak prospects for a lengthy command at the post, he had put his men to work, strengthening the defenses of Camp New Hope by enclosing it in an earthen rampart that was four feet high and twelve feet wide with corner redoubts.[15]

Manning was disinclined to surrender the camp and indifferent to Pinckney's agreements with Kindelán. Military priorities, in his opinion, took precedence over diplomatic niceties. Having given Colonel Smith his solemn pledge to destroy Camp New Hope—a point of honor that superceded other considerations—Manning was equally resolved to destroy the estates of the English settlers who owned lands between the middle St. Johns River and Fernandina. The United States might not be at war with Spain—but it was at war with Great Britain—and Manning had no intention of letting the Republic's enemies return to their estates, or what was left of them, in peace and prosperity. Whether they lived in a Spanish colony or a British one, the English were still foes, serving on the wrong side of a war with his country.

Independent of Pinckney, Manning therefore made his own plans for evacuation. According to the agreement reached with Kindelán, the Americans were to remain at Camp New Hope until Spanish troops arrived and then transfer possession of the camp. Pinckney had already transmitted these arrangements to Manning, and Kindelán, anxious to see them followed, had dispatched his own courier to Camp New Hope with a duplicate copy. The transfer of possession was scheduled for April 29.

Manning, however, did not wait. On April 26, he gathered his men and supplies together and prepared to depart. As the hundreds of men collected their kits and loaded the flatboats and *periaguas* for the voyage down the St. Johns, the major issued commands to burn the camp. Then he announced his intention of leaving several of the British estates in ruins as well: James Hollingsworth's, to begin with, and the neighboring plantation of Farquhar Bethune, that of William Craig at the Cowford, and those of the Atkinsons.

Dr. James Hall and Francisco Roman Sánchez, standing with Manning as he announced his intentions, turned to him in surprise and asked why Craig and Bethune should suffer such punishment. Craig, after all, had assisted the Patriots. And Bethune, a wealthy, soft-spoken men who wore thick spectacles, was widely regarded as harmless, despite his loyalist sympathies. The Patriots had never even bothered to press him into service. "Damn him, he was blind," one rebel had commented, "and could be of no service," for he was so near-sighted he was just as likely to shoot a friend as a foe.

Manning's reply contained all the contempt and anger felt by many of his soldiers. He had only been in command at Camp New Hope for six weeks, yet his first order was to retreat. He was disgusted and said so. There was no choice about the camp buildings, he told Hall and Sánchez, for "he had promised Colonel Smith to lay them in ashes." As for Bethune, "he was a damned Englishman and he would burn his house!" And Craig, by seeking a pardon, deserved no mercy, either, "because he was a Traitor!"[16]

Sánchez later recounted the scene at Hollingsworth's as the soldiers went to work: "They rolled Puncheons of Rice to the River and knocked

the heads out, and so wantonly destroyed even Firkins of Soft Soap. . . .
They had collected 300 bushels of corn from neighboring plantations, into
one House, and destroyed it by Fire. They burned their barracks and
Hollingsworth's Houses caught and were consumed from the conflagra-
tion. . . . [I] saw Col. [sic] Manning apply the torch, with his own hands, at
Camp New Hope. He swore the Spaniards should not have the pleasure of
occupying the Fortifications."[17]

Buckner Harris, also present at Camp New Hope, where he was rounding up his rebel forces to accompany the troops north, heartily approved
of the burnings. A few such examples would show both loyalists and de-
fecting rebels that they could not spurn the Patriots with impunity. This
point was brought home at once to Francisco Roman Sánchez. At news of
the pardon, Sánchez's long-standing allegiance to the Patriots faltered,
and, in hopes of safeguarding some of his property until after the end of
hostilities, he attempted to cross a herd of his cattle over the St. Johns
River and hide them. Hearing of this, Harris issued orders to burn down
Sánchez's San José plantation house. Luck alone saved the structure. The
man detailed to apply the torch went about his task obediently enough
but got lost in the woods and, unable to find Sánchez's house, gave up the
endeavor. Even so, Sánchez understood the point being made. He immediately renewed his pledge to the Patriot cause knowing, as he said later in
life, what the consequences would be if he did not.[18]

Having destroyed Camp New Hope and Hollingsworth's plantation,
Major Manning embarked his men onto the waiting river craft, and
within minutes, as sails unfurled and oars were set into locks, the troops
that had sat in occupation of East Florida for more than a year headed
northward for the border. Sailing or rowing down the wide and placid St.
Johns in a straggling line of boats, the troops undertook their final assign-
ments (see fig. 2). One boat landed at New Ross, Farquhar Bethune's estate immediately north of Camp New Hope, and soon it was engulfed in
flames. Another party of troops stopped at the plantation of William
Craig, on the south bank of the St. Johns River where it turned eastward,
and set fire to his buildings. Then, a little farther on, it was the turn of the
Atkinsons' Isabela estate, then their Precher and Shipyard plantations at
St. Johns Bluff, where Andrew Atkinson and Justo Lopez planted in part-
nership, and so on, up the length of the river. Patriots assisted in the destruction. Joseph S. Sánchez, a sixteen-year-old lad at the time of the
evacuation, witnessed them setting fire to Shipyard. Hitching a ride in

one of the troop transports, Sánchez remembered putting ashore at the bluff in a party of five boats commanded by William Cone. The men from Sánchez's boat all leaped out and disappeared in the direction of the Atkinson plantation house. "They soon returned to the boats," he said, "and we shoved off but as we put off I discovered that the buildings were on fire."[19]

As bitter as the evacuation was for the rebels, it provided them essential cover to withdraw and reorganize their forces. Between the St. Johns and St. Marys Rivers, they still had many friends and several strongholds. At Underwood's Mill, on the St. Marys near Trader's Hill, and at Lodowick Ashley's house, hard by Mill's Ferry, Harris collected some sixty men and secured his defenses, with freedom to move back and forth across the Georgia border. Francisco Roman Sánchez fortified his plantation of San José with a palisade, and rebels also invested the houses of William Fitzpatrick at Cedar Point and James Smith at Sawpit Bluff on the Nassau River. From here, they could harass boat traffic and intercept communications between Amelia Island and St. Augustine.

Far from giving up, Harris was just beginning to fight. And news soon arrived that proved conducive to his plans. Some former Patriots, trying to exercise their rights to a pardon, were discovering they were no longer welcome among their neighbors. Before long, men were presenting themselves before Harris or before Judge William Ashley at St. Marys, swearing out depositions about the harsh treatment they had received from Spanish subjects and black troops.

As the Patriots regrouped, Spanish forces south of the St. Johns River were moving to reoccupy their territory. Marching along the King's Road at the head of a large detachment composed of the Third Infantry Battalion of Cuba and men from the local and Havana militias, Captain Gil José Pascot cast a disdainful glance around at a countryside laid waste. It was chilly and rainy, and his troops, joking and laughing when they first left St. Augustine, had become distressed and subdued by their surroundings. Some among the militia saw the ruins of their homes as they marched past. From Fort Mose and Araquay they turned northwest, passing through Twelve Mile Swamp and into Julington, and then north again to Camp New Hope, where another melancholy scene met their eyes. Arriving around 6 P.M. on April 29 and expecting to find shelters and an American garrison awaiting him, Pascot looked with angry disbelief at an unusable ruin. Fires at Camp New Hope and farther north along the riverside were still burning or smoldering. It was clear at once that the retreating Americans had practiced scorched-earth tactics.

With the light failing, Pascot set his men to salvaging clapboards from wrecked houses and ordered them to erect crude lean-to sheds so they would have some protection against the night mists. Then he dispatched Juan Bautista Witten of the free black militia to reconnoiter the damage in surrounding areas. There was no point in maintaining a post at Camp New Hope, Pascot wrote to Kindelán. Whatever use it had served for the Americans was now gone. It would be better to reinforce posts closer to the border and let this one sink into oblivion.[20]

After a hard transit north, in which they reoccupied Fort San Nicolás and the Cowford and passed by the smoking husks of some of the province's most thriving plantations, Pascot's detachment eventually arrived at Fernandina. Again, there was no elaborate change of flags. Captain Massias and the American troops were absent, having departed on May 6 for Point Peter. Captain Francisco Rivera and forty men took over garrison duty at the town as residents set off cannons to celebrate the return of Spanish rule. On May 8, citizens pledged their fealty to Spain, and Rivera read out a proclamation, stipulating for the first time the provisions and rights enjoyed by Spanish subjects under the Constitution of 1812. It was a deceptively auspicious beginning to a situation that soon proved harder to rectify than anyone had suspected.

Far from quieting down, the border area remained even more restless and dangerous than in the first days of the Patriot rebellion. The reoccupation of the Cowford and Fort San Nicolás did not go smoothly. Eight members of the *moreno* militia of Havana, tired of duty that left them barefoot and hungry, deserted the post and disappeared. It was the first of many such desertions. At Amelia Island, the drinking water was contaminated, and within a few days the soldiers began to fall ill. Pascot himself was incapacitated with a serious case of dysentery. Local physicians suggested dousing the water with rum to relieve the unhealthy humors. A good idea, commented Justo Lopez, except that no one had any rum.[21]

Establishing a civil administration at Amelia Island also proved problematic. Kindelán suspended a portion of constitutional law by denying Fernandina the right to its own elected municipal government. Instead, he appointed men to postings as *capitánes de perdido*, or district heads, responsible directly to him. Fernando de la Maza Arredondo, the younger, and Farquhar Bethune both turned down the appointments. Shattered by the destruction of his property at New Ross, Bethune wanted only to salvage what he could from his plantation and to search for missing slaves. Instead, the office of *capitán* at Amelia went to Philip Yonge, and Francis Philip Fatio Jr. accepted a similar office for the St. Johns District. Immediately, both men began to brief Governor Kindelán on continued disturbances around the province. More reports came in from Captain Tomás Llorente, in charge of a contingent of *moreno* troops at Fort San Nicolás, and from Captain Rivera at Fernandina. The reports were remarkably similar. The *moreno* troops, and other soldiers and militia, were abandoning their posts, sick of making do with poor clothing, bad food, no shoes, and harsh conditions. White residents were uneasy about having so many black soldiers in their midst. A certain General Buckner Harris was ensconced on the St. Marys River, on the Spanish side of the border, with a large contingent of armed men. He was threatening to burn down the properties of Patriots seeking amnesty from the Spanish. Besides this, he had men stationed on the Nassau River, opposite Talbot Island, and they were attacking the Spanish mail boats and making threatening forays to nearby plantations.[22]

These reports became so persistent and alarming that in mid-May, Kindelán decided to come north himself to observe the trouble. The trip was the governor's first opportunity to see the countryside of Spanish East Florida since his last visit to the province in 1795, and the gloomy state of the settlements did nothing to lift his spirits. He had already made a token protest to General Pinckney at what he regarded as the latest instance of American treachery—the deliberate burning of private property. Yet he made no accusations against the United States. He wanted no more trouble from that direction or a resumption of the occupation. The destruction of the barracks at Camp New Hope, he told Pinckney, was "of little consequence . . . were it not for the circumstances of their having consigned also to the flames the machinery and houses of the inhabitants. . . . All countries abound with inconsiderate persons, the unwarrantable proceedings of which class of people very often disconcert the best concerted plans and measures."[23]

Pinckney, for his part, had written to Monroe about the affair. Unwilling to ascribe malicious motives to Major Manning, he nonetheless suggested a formal inquiry into the circumstances behind the burnings. Like Kindelán, he was ready to pass over the matter in favor of other issues.

The United States would need to reinforce its naval patrols on the St. Marys River, he warned Monroe, now that Amelia Island was once again open to British shipping. Georgians were continuing to launch expeditions into the Alachua territory, to seize cattle, and this could also incite trouble. In a more lengthy report, he voiced his opinion that the United States should purchase East Florida. Spain clearly had little use for the province, he said, and with the disruptions of the recent conflict, the government might strike a very good deal.[24]

Kindelán's tour of the province was rapid, for he was needed in St. Augustine, where Mayor Álvarez was challenging his authority. Hence, he spent only enough time at Amelia Island to see it properly reinforced with troops and to instruct Captain Rivera to treat former rebels gently. On the way back to the capital, traveling in company with Joseph M. Hernández, Kindelán remained disconsolate. Hernández later recounted one incident that stood out more than any other in his recollections. The governor's party, crossing the Cowford and taking the King's Road south, had come upon the ruins of the sawmill of Levin Gunby and Abraham (Arbino) Follis, both of them still on the run as rebels. Before the war, the mill had been the wonder of the province. The two lumber merchants had spent a fortune on damming the local creek to provide waterpower for the saws. Several times the dam had burst, but they had fixed and improved it until they had the mill running smoothly. Now there was nothing left. The buildings and lumberyard had been raided of planking to build the Davis Creek blockhouse. "The place was deserted," Hernández remembered, "the houses and fences in ruins, the doors and windows and much of the weather boarding had been abstracted from the dwelling so as to make it uncomfortable even to pass the night there. The Mill was in ruins, indeed, wherever improvements had been made, some effort seemed to have been made to destroy them." The shattered remains of the mill stood at the site until 1815. By that time, though, alligators and otters had burrowed into the base of the dam to make their abodes. The wilderness was reclaiming East Florida from the hands of humans—it was an image that applied to the whole province.[25]

The Patriots, meanwhile, continued to set up their camps along the south side of the St. Mary's River, where men like James Dell and Lodowick Ashley had estates that could serve as strongholds. Soon, Harris had gained additional adherents from among local families—the Higginbothams, the Vinzants, the McCulloughs, the Swearingens, and the Haddocks, among others—and had between 70 and 100 men under arms and passing back and forth between camps.

Other former rebels also rejoined his ranks, having found it difficult, if not impossible, to reintegrate themselves into the community they had betrayed. In St. Augustine and at Fernandina, there was great hostility against those men identified as close consorts of General Mathews or as leaders of the parties that had pillaged property and livestock. Throughout the month of June, a string of petitioners complained to Buckner Harris and William Ashley about threats and reprisals made against them. Ashley began to collect their depositions, forwarding them to Governor Mitchell as an example of why the Patriots deserved further support and protection. Most of the grievances specifically blamed angry loyalist or black soldiers for inciting acts of revenge, something that Ashley knew would catch Mitchell's attention. "The Black Troops are getting very bad, and oppressive on the Inhabitants of East Florida, and from their enmity toward the people of this State, we have no doubt, but they will shortly begin to exercise their influence over our slaves," he said. Since "no measure will be adopted by the U. States in time to remove the impending danger," Ashley concluded, the Patriots would take matters into their own hands, certain that Georgians would fully approve. Daniel Delany traveled north to Milledgeville to make a personal appeal for aid, and Buckner Harris, acknowledging himself as head of the Patriot government, wrote to Governor Mitchell, saying his adherents were "subjected to the painful and degraded epithets of Rebel and Traitor, and exposed to the menaces of free Negroes and the slaves."[26]

One of the first men to testify before Justice Ashley was Abner Broadway, who had disappeared into the cells of the Castillo more than a year before, seized by Spanish pickets on the very day the Patriots' scouts first reconnoitered St. Augustine. He had been kept in a "loathsome Dungeon," he said, until October 6, 1812, and upon his discharge, the people in town had rebelled against Kindelán and had insisted that Broadway be confined again. Having regained his liberty a second time on March 17, nothing could persuade him that the Spanish authorities would protect his rights.[27]

Soon afterward, Dr. James Hall applied to Ashley for protection. The good doctor had been up to his ears in conspiracies ever since being ban-

ished from East Florida in 1810 and had served as a medical doctor with
the rebels throughout 1812, being one of the physicians who treated Marine Captain John Williams. Despite such close association with the Patriots, he was among the first to seek forgiveness, going to St. Augustine on
April 19, about a week before the American evacuation. Kindelán, he said,
had treated him politely and had accepted his pledge of loyalty. But there
were many in the population at St. Augustine who wanted vengeance, he
noted. When he inquired about some slaves who had been stolen away
from his wife, one "man who had considerable influence" told him that no
one was going to restore any property taken off rebels and that they
would bring down the governor if he even considered it. When friends
warned Hall that some soldiers planned to assault him, he left town and
came away to St. Marys.[28]

John Black, also deposing before Ashley, said most of the posts along
the St. Johns River were now garrisoned by black troops and that no one,
not even the Spanish commanders, could fully control them. The blacks
were swearing they would protect fugitive slaves from Georgia, that
former rebels would be under their charge, and that "they would slap any
white man's jaws who would dare to say anything not pleasing to
them."[29]

Jacob Summerlin made a similar complaint directly to Buckner Harris.
Using words that were almost identical to Black's, Summerlin said that
black troops at the Cowford had tried to seize him as a rebel, despite the
offer of pardon, and that they were actively accepting runaway slaves into
their ranks, were boasting that they would rule the country, and were
killing milk cows and stealing property from the residence of Prudence
Plummer. Seeing the state of things, Summerlin had decided to "join the
Patriots again Being the Best Plan Suggisted [sic] to his mind."[30]

Other Patriot collaborators found they had to run a gauntlet of hostile
crowds in St. Augustine, where people jeered at them and insulted them
when they tried to obtain their pardons. Kindelán issued orders to cease
the harassment. He had given his word, he told the townspeople, that
rebels would receive amnesty, and these cases of intimidation were dis-
crediting the honor of his pledge. Mindful that Georgians would never
tolerate black troops at the border area, he also made arrangements to
recall the black militia and the morenos who were serving there. Beyond
this, though, there was little he could do, for the province was still in a

state of upset, with feelings of rancor running high. The presence of many rebels, still under arms, between Trader's Hill and the Nassau River did nothing to calm the situation.[31]

Buckner Harris, in the meantime, had used the months of May and June to what he hoped would be good effect. While McIntosh importuned Pinckney about his impending ruin and sought means of recouping his losses, Harris turned his attention to the Alachua District of the Florida interior. Here, in an area cleared of Indian towns and maroon villages and far from the centers of Spanish military power, he contemplated a true territory of East Florida, one with settlers, homesteads, and a chance of autonomy. The attraction of Alachua was not a new one. As far back as 1810, Harris had recommended that Georgians attempt to subdue and then settle this region. Now he opened his thoughts to Governor Mitchell, asking for money and assistance. Alachua had been won by Newnan's valor, he said. It was only right that those who had aided the colonel should benefit from his achievements.

In response, Mitchell referred Harris to Benjamin Hawkins, saying the Indian agent was already in conference with chiefs from the Tampa Bay area. With Hawkins's assistance and a letter of introduction, Harris, Daniel Delany, and Francisco Roman Sánchez overtook several chiefs as they returned southward to their homelands. Harris proposed a treaty that would cede the Alachua territory to the Patriots. The chiefs listened to the proposal and agreed to meet Harris again, at Underwood's Mill, around July 13.[32]

The overture, however, came to nothing. In July, Harris waited several days for representatives from the Seminoles and other groups to show up. No one came north to treat with him. The chiefs had made the appointment only to be conveniently rid of him.

Neither Pinckney nor Mitchell seemed inclined to help, either. Mitchell, in fact, increasingly concerned that British warships might attack Savannah, was demanding to know why American troops were concentrated at Point Peter, on the Florida border, instead of where they were needed farther north. At the same time, the Spaniards were renewing their efforts to break and rout the Patriots once and for all.[33]

The people of Fernandina were among the most outspoken of Harris's detractors, having grown more and more frustrated at the continued presence of rebels on the Nassau River. In early July, Captain Rivera sent numerous representatives to the house of William Fitzpatrick at Cedar Point, demanding that Fitzpatrick return a boat and some rigging and sail canvas he had confiscated. When Fitzpatrick ignored the demand, Rivera decided to take more decisive action. Sometime around July 9, he dispatched Francisco Estacholy with a contingent of black militia to the Fitzpatrick estate. Fitzpatrick's wife, seeing the approach of black soldiers, screamed out vilifications at them, while Fitzpatrick clambered to the second story of his house, grabbed up a musket, threw open a window, and called down to Estacholy, "Clear off from here right now," loosing off a shot to make his point. Fitzpatrick subsequently testified that Estacholy and "five large Negro men" had tried to arrest him, bringing ropes with which to bind him and telling him they were under orders to take him dead or alive. He nonetheless stood his ground and escaped detention.[34]

Shortly afterward, a group of insurgents visited the plantation of William O'Neill, a prominent loyalist who owned property at Lanceford Creek. They became so threatening that O'Neill decided to transfer his family to Fernandina. In town, he encouraged Rivera and Philip Yonge to launch an expedition against the remaining rebels. With Rivera's approval, they requisitioned the use of an armed schooner, the *Governor Kindelán*, and a small frigate, the *Emperador*, and mustered a force of forty-four volunteers and militiamen. Their goal was to sail up the St. Marys River to Lodowick Ashley's plantation, where some sixty Patriots had fortified the main house and mounted a 6-pound field piece. Their expedition left Fernandina on July 23 under a heavy squall of rain, but when the storms would not abate, they had to scratch the mission as a failure. Conditions were too wet to permit action.[35]

Other confrontations soon occurred. Eber O'Neill, with a party of thirty men, began to keep watch on the Patriots stationed at Ashley's. Then, on Saturday, August 7, Philip Yonge, landing at Lowe's plantation at Bells River with a sergeant and ten men, was ambushed by a squad of rebels. His men killed four of the Patriots and wounded six others before retreating with one man killed and another wounded.[36]

The ambush at Lowe's set the scene for the final denouement between the rebels and the loyalists. Ironically, the last major skirmish of their conflict was destined to take place at almost exactly the point where the rebellion had begun. Aware of the activities of O'Neill's scouts and receiving information from spies on Amelia Island, Harris prepared to meet the coming assault. His men took over the plantation of Eleazar Waterman, located adjacent to Lowe's plantation and situated on Waterman's Bluff, a wide, flat table of land, 200 yards in length and about 8 feet above the water, which commanded a view of the Bells and Jolly Rivers. Here the Patriots maintained a party of advance pickets. Their best information was that the loyalists would come against them at once.

The fight between the Patriot and Spanish forces on Bells River would become the stuff of folk legend. The attack was a tactical blunder on the part of the loyal Spanish subjects. Instead of surprising the rebels under cover of darkness, the expedition set out from Fernandina at 2 P.M. on Sunday, August 8. Two companies of men, totaling about sixty in all, including twelve soldiers, a sergeant, and a lieutenant from the Third Infantry Battalion of Cuba, crossed the Amelia River and prepared to drive the Patriots away. Responding to complaints from the Spanish soldiers and militia, saying they did not want to serve under English-speaking officers, José de la Maza Arredondo and Pedro Pons took charge of one company, and Francis Philip Fatio Jr. and George Atkinson took charge of another. Against the advice of Fatio, the expedition leaders decided to split their forces. Half of their contingent advanced overland to cut off any chance of a rebel retreat from Lodowick Ashley's house, while the other half proceeded up Bells River in four boats. It was a hazardous and unwise maneuver. Out of contact with each other, the two detachments could not coordinate their attack. The attempt at an amphibious landing was also a disaster. Struggling against adverse winds and the ebbing current of Bells River, the oarsmen in the boats strained at their strokes to propel their vessels forward. Progress around a twisting meander at Lowe's plantation was torturously slow. From the mainland, the laden boats, restricted to the narrow channel that wound through the tall marsh reeds, were clearly visible for a quarter mile. As the party rounded a second meander, the boats fell off into a wide and marshy stretch of water. The main channel, cutting through the reeds, curved south to approach the shore at Waterman's Bluff (see fig. 5).

On the bluff, making good use of concealment behind trees and fence railings, Buckner Harris and about thirty Patriots were waiting for them. They had come east from Ashley's to catch the attackers off-guard. The foremost boat, they could see, was packed with black troops—"by far the braver soldiers during the action," Harris later admitted. Fatio was in charge of another boat, with Eber O'Neill serving as coxswain and with Archibald Atkinson also a member of the party. José de la Maza Arredondo had charge of a third boat. Harris hailed the group, calling out across the water and demanding that they surrender. In response, the boats opened fire upon his position with their 6-pounders. Over in the town of St. Marys, directly opposite, Francis Fatio's wife, recently delivered of a baby, and his young daughter, Susan, heard the reverberations of the opening cannon shots and sent one of the house slaves, Frank, racing to the upper story of their lodgings with a telescope to report on the fight.

The firing of the artillery did not shift Harris's widely spaced men. They waited, with the advantage of cover and high ground, as the boats struggled in toward the shore, bringing the occupants within musket and rifle range. Then there was an explosion of gunfire as Harris's men peppered the attackers with shot. Almost at once, forty more Patriots came running onto the bluff from the west and joined their comrades. The men in the boats made excellent targets and, crowded together, with their aim ruined by the swaying and rocking of their transports, could do little harm in return. For fifteen minutes the rebels fired volley after volley into them, with barely a return shot. Those few of the loyalists and soldiers who managed to reach the foot of the bluff and gain the shore, with their heads just below the level of their adversaries' feet, could not hold their ground and were driven back into the boats. In the vessels farther from the bluff, the oarsmen ceased rowing and huddled down behind the bulwarks to shield themselves from the gunfire. Slowly the current pushed the drifting boats back east and away from the battle.

Having routed this assault from the river, the Patriots turned to face the thirty men who were coming by land. These men had been hampered in their advance by a wide expanse of marsh that cut between Lowe's and Waterman's plantations. The obstacle forced them to waste time in a detour to the south and stopped them from falling on the rebels from behind during the first engagement. Now they were outnumbered two to one and were thrown back with little effort. All told, the loyalists had six men killed and another twelve wounded. The Patriots did not take a single casualty.[37]

Harris was elated at the victory, which was significant enough to merit the attention of the *Savannah Republican*. Writing to Governor Mitchell, the Patriot leader expounded on the fighting qualities of his men. They had not only vanquished the loyalists but had killed several individuals against whom they had special grudges. "The action lasted Twenty minutes," Harris reported.

> They had Twenty kild and wounded Besides a number of Negroes which they are unwilling to acknowledge . . . the Patriots received no damages whatever. One amoungst the wounded was W. D. Sheen, that was so very Insolent when you was at St. Marys. He got it through his body, young Mr. Arradunda [Arredondo] through his shoulder, and Mr. Seaton through his intestines. They had seven kild dead, three died the day following, and others Expected to die. The Amelia Gentry sufferd particularly, young Atkerson [Atkinson] was amoungst the dead. The Patriots are now masters of the whole Country on this side of the St. Johns River and those on Amelia are flying for safety.[38]

Philip Yonge's report to Governor Kindelán was far more somber. "I am certain that we were betrayed to the enemy," Yonge wrote, noting how the rebels had been lying in wait. Yet he made no attempt to hide a dismal failure. The rebels had attacked and completely overwhelmed the expedition, he reported. José de la Maza Arredondo and Charles Seton were seriously wounded. Archibald Atkinson and Eber O'Neill were dead.[39]

It was a poor showing by the Spaniards, as foolish in its way as Newnan's attack on the Seminoles had been, and it bolstered, at least for a time, the Patriots' confidence that they could hold their own against the province. Meanwhile, the number of personal vendettas that screamed out for blood vengeance was multiplying. George and Andrew Atkinson implored Governor Kindelán to let them mount a punitive expedition, determined to avenge both the destruction of their plantations and the death of Archibald, George's younger brother.[40]

At the moment, though, Harris was both triumphant and safe. The sting of the defeat at Waterman's Bluff knocked all the fight out of the people of Fernandina. There was no enthusiasm for a second expedition. Some families began moving their furniture and possessions onto ships, certain that the rebels would follow up their victory with an attack on the town itself. Harris, however, was once more thinking of the Alachua territory, a land that beckoned to him like the fabled El Dorado. As long as he remained on the St. Marys River, he could do no more than hold and defend a few plantations. In Alachua, he might build a legacy.

The Last of the Patriots

During the four months following the battle at Waterman's Bluff on August 8, 1813, law and order along the St. Marys River continued to break down, and the name of Buckner Harris became as familiar to Spanish officials as that of George Mathews or John Houston McIntosh. Residents of Fernandina suffered under a reign of raids and robberies committed not only by the rebels but by a new breed of interlopers—bandits and thieves from across the border—while rebel families appealed to magistrates in Georgia, saying they lived in fear for their lives in East Florida and could get no redress from Spanish authorities. All this time, Harris matured his plans to march on the Alachua territory. Along with William Cone and James Dell, he sent overtures to Governor Kindelán, trying to persuade him to cede the Indian territory in return for a cessation of hostilities.

The disturbances in East Florida now fell under the rubric of local affairs. In Georgia, Governor Mitchell and his successor, Peter Early, maintained a lukewarm correspondence with Harris, lured by his visions of a new settlement of southern pioneers in the interior of Florida yet reluctant to involve themselves any further with the Patriots. In Washington, President Madison and Secretary of State Monroe were engineering peace talks with the British, putting out feelers to see if the war might be drawn to a premature close. Russian intermediaries offered to broker an arbitration, and Monroe, ever single-minded when it came to the acquisition of territory, suggested the British might even support a plan to transfer the Floridas from Spain to the United States as part of a political settlement to restore peace. There were still some calls for use of force in East Florida. One citizen of Louisiana, writing to a friend at the capital, expressed the hope that Congress would revive the issue: "At length, as our defeats or victories in Canada either inspired the sentiments of hope or revenge in the British, the war in the south assumes a more decisively ferocious and tragical character. . . . The taking possession of Florida was necessary as a measure of general national defense against the common enemy." Yet with the evacuation completed and hopes rising for a negotiated settlement regarding the Floridas, such sentiments gained few adherents. In the fall, Monroe endured an unpleasant meeting with John Houston McIntosh. The planter lambasted the government for forsaking the rebel cause and raised the issue of reimbursement for expenditures he had made on behalf of the Patriots. Mathews, he reminded Monroe, had promised to indemnify him against pecuniary losses. Rapidly shedding his skin as rebel leader, he was reverting to that of hard-nosed businessman, and he insisted that the Madison administration meet its financial obligations. While the director of East Florida thus counted pennies and carried over decimals, tallying up the monies the United States owed him, the remaining Patriots embarked on the road to their last stand.[1]

William Cone, Buckner Harris, and James Dell followed up their victory at Waterman's Bluff by sending peace overtures to the Spanish, reasoning that it was best to strike a bargain while they were in the ascendancy over their adversaries. Cone, soliciting the mediation of Francis Philip Fatio, Jr., suggested an armistice and a conference to resolve disagreements. If Governor Kindelán would agree to remove all black troops from East Florida and to cede the Alachua country, the rebels would settle themselves in the interior of the province and leave Spanish subjects in peace. Harris and Dell made a similar proposal to Philip Yonge in early September. Let both sides appoint commissioners to negotiate a truce, they said, with terms that would grant the Patriots a reasonable cession of land in East Florida.[2]

As the Patriots dictated these terms, they also entrenched along the border. The district between the St. Johns and St. Marys Rivers was rapidly becoming home to a series of armed rebel camps. In reaction to the affair at Waterman's Bluff, Kindelán had rushed Captain Tomás Llorente to the Cowford and Fort San Nicolás with a contingent of forty black soldiers. These men were busily reconstructing the fort, expanding it into a blockhouse with a moat, drawbridge, and palisade. A formidable armed presence at the ferry station was essential, Llorente reported, for the rebels had already established their own stronghold on Trout Creek.[3]

From Fernandina, Philip Yonge and others kept up surveillance on Harris's followers, noting that the rebels were once again becoming troublesome. They had occupied the plantation of James Smith near

Sawpit Bluff on the Nassau River and also that of William Fitzpatrick at a place called Cedar Point, where Cedar Creek emptied into the St. Johns River (see fig. 2). From there, armed parties were making occasional forays to Talbot Island, where the Houstons and Christophers appeared to be aiding them. They were also intercepting the Spanish mail boats traveling between the Amelia River and the St. Johns and were therefore privy to all the governor's correspondence.[4]

Instead of negotiating with Harris, the Spanish focused their efforts on expelling the Patriots from the province by force. On August 19, 1813, Llorente sent out a detachment of thirty-two men, aided by the Spanish gunboat *Immutable*, to harass rebel encampments. His men discovered some twenty-five insurgents at William Hart's plantation, under the command of Francisco Roman Sánchez, and managed to drive them off. They also displaced a group of armed men from the house of William Fitzpatrick.[5]

On August 28, deciding that the Smith and Fitzpatrick plantations had to be eliminated as sanctuaries for the rebels, the Spaniards attacked in force. Two gunboats sailed up Two Sisters Creek and blasted apart the timbers of the Fitzpatrick house with an artillery barrage. As the occupants fled from the building, a squad of soldiers landed and seized Fitzpatrick. Then the boats proceeded to Sawpit Bluff and shelled the house of James and Mary Smith until the inhabitants came out and surrendered. From Fitzpatrick and Smith, Llorente discovered that Buckner Harris, James Dell, and some thirty other men had left the area just a few hours before the attack for another hideout on the St. Marys River.[6]

These expeditions stopped rebel interference with communications between Fernandina and St. Augustine; however, they failed to suppress other activity. In September, a new menace appeared in the border area in the person of Colonel Samuel Alexander. With a band of handpicked men out of Georgia, Alexander marauded against local plantations, striking from bases at Point Peter and Trader's Hill. Operating independently of the Patriots, though often using their name, he specialized in making slave raids. Over a period of two months, he and his cohorts penetrated deep into East Florida. On November 12, a party of some sixty men robbed the plantation of Farquhar Bethune, already heavily damaged by fire during the American evacuation, and stole away three slaves. They captured three more from George Morrison, John Houston McIntosh's former overseer. Four days later they carried off three slaves from the Fatio plantation south of Julington Creek and drove Edward Wanton off a small landholding called Cook's Place, from which they hauled away seven slaves.[7]

The most notorious of the raids that occurred at this time has sometimes been attributed to Alexander's men and sometimes to a band of rebels working with William Cone. On Sunday, September 19, a group of armed men invaded Amelia Island, targeting an area several miles south of Fernandina, and seized control of Erin Hall, the estate of James Cashen, Amelia's second-wealthiest planter and a prominent supporter of Spanish rule (see fig. 5). Cashen was jerked awake in the middle of the night by the noise of men breaking down his door. They took him hostage, looted the plantation house of its furnishings, and hunted down thirty-six slaves. Before leaving the island, they attacked the plantation of Fernando D. McDonell, one of Cashen's near neighbors, rifling the main house of gilt-framed paintings, looking glasses, mahogany furniture, and an eight-day clock and smashing the pianoforte into pieces. Retreating to Georgia with their booty, the party eventually released Cashen, after selling off his slaves and the furnishings plundered from his house. Upon his return to East Florida, Cashen discovered that rebels had also burned his remaining plantation at Reid's Bluff on the St. Marys River. He later learned that the slaves, whom he identified in great detail in the *Georgia Argus*, were taken into the Carolinas and Tennessee.[8]

These sensational assaults evoked a public outcry at Fernandina, where residents demanded an end to the anarchy. Andrew and George Atkinson pleaded with Captain Rivera and petitioned Governor Kindelán to mount a major expedition against the Patriots and any other Georgia "banditti" still inhabiting the border area.[9]

In Camden County and other parts of Georgia, people were aghast at the depredations but split in their sympathies. A letter in the *Savannah Republican* blamed the Spanish themselves for creating civil war through such bloody-minded expeditions as the one launched against the Fitzpatrick and Smith homesteads. The editor of the *Augusta Chronicle*, on the other hand, characterized Colonel Alexander's brutal instances of pillage as "a burlesque of military operations" and concluded that "no object favorable to them or honorable to us, can possibly result from so polluted and corrupt men [as] are assembled in Florida." Even Peter Early, having recently taken up the office of governor of Georgia, began to receive complaints from Spanish subjects. Francis Philip Fatio, Jr., told him that rebel damages to his plantation represented a loss of $10,000. Joseph Hibberson, of Amelia Island, wanted the state of Georgia to take legal action against any of its citizens committing larceny or pillage in East Florida.[10]

Confronted with additional efforts to dislodge his forces and somewhat discredited by the unfavorable publicity surrounding the adventures of Samuel Alexander, Buckner Harris wrote once more to Kindelán in hopes of reaching an accord. Angry that the governor had never responded to his previous overture, Harris lapsed almost at once into making threats. Perhaps Kindelán was unaware, he said, that British factions in the colony were attempting to disrupt peace between the Spaniards and Patriots for the benefit of their own government. The Patriots could not capitulate to these British interests or to the Negro troops who were burning them out of their homes. "Such menacing conduct may not be particularly known to you," Harris said, "but so far from having a direct tendency to close and settle the disturbances which now Exist, the Patriots have consented to accept of considerable additional military force in their defense." Having stated his reasons for opposing Kindelán's forces, he concluded with a warning: "[I] venture to assure your Excellency, that while the Present Plans are Pursued . . . not one Spanish Subject will ever rest in Peace without the Walls of your Fortifications, and the calamities of War will be severely felt in those places where Negro Troops are quartered."[11]

Other Patriots, trying to resuscitate an outcry in Georgia for retribution against the Spaniards, began to capitalize on one of the most frightening events in the southern war. In August, the Red Sticks, a faction within the Creek confederation, attacked Fort Mims, located a few miles above the mouth of the Alabama River in the Mississippi Territory. Conflict between the United States and Great Britain had plunged the Creeks into civil war, pitting those who advocated neutrality or cooperation with the Americans against those allying themselves with the English. The Red Sticks had already skirmished with American militia at Burnt Corn Creek and decided to target Fort Mims, which sheltered about 300 settlers, soldiers, and friendly Creeks and perhaps 100 slaves. On August 20, 1813, Red Stick warriors overwhelmed the outpost, launching their attack at the noon lunch hour, when the settlers and garrison were distracted and the gates to the fort were wide open. In a three-hour battle, the Red Sticks set fire to the buildings, burning many of the defenders alive. Those who managed to escape later said the warriors scalped women and the injured and swung children around by their feet, smashing their brains out against the stockade. Between 250 and 275 of the fort's occupants either died during the battle or were taken captive.

The savagery of the attack stirred up fear and fury all over the American frontiers. Rumors circulated that the slaves in the fort had joined with the Red Sticks in annihilating the defenders. Spanish and British agents were accused of abetting the attack. With all of southern Georgia still shuddering from this horrible news, several Patriots began to spread rumors that the Seminoles, maroons, and black soldiers in East Florida were plotting a similar spree of slaughter. Spanish sympathizers were helping them, claimed William Hart in a deposition before the magistrates of Camden County, Georgia. John Forbes of Forbes and Company trading house on Amelia Island was hiring a contingent of 300 mulatto soldiers, he said, and was providing them with 150 bloodhounds to hunt down the enemies of Spain. As Hart tried to circulate this story, Cyrus Stow, a ship's captain from Charleston, also appeared before the magistrates. Stow told them he had been accosted by the black troops at Fort San Nicolás during a trip up the St. Johns River. The soldiers had forced him to shout out insults about the inhabitants of St. Marys, Georgia, he said, and one had snapped an unloaded musket at him, while another thrust at him with a bayonet. Angus McEchran, traveling with Stow, had also been attacked and told how soldiers had kicked and beaten him. Fortunately, he said, William Craig's wife came running down from her house to the ferry station and ordered the solders to desist. But soon everyone in Georgia could expect such abuse, Stow warned, because 200 Indians and 300 black soldiers were preparing to march on St. Marys and burn it to the ground.[12]

These statements, conjuring up the specter of a second Fort Mims, failed to elicit much of a response. No one doubted that there was bad blood and a thirst for revenge between the Patriots and the black soldiers garrisoned in East Florida—the two groups had been skirmishing almost daily. As often as not, however, it was the rebels who gained the upper hand in these engagements. On November 12, a group of rebels on the south side of the St. Johns River had repelled an attack by a detachment of Captain Llorente's men. They captured three soldiers and killed three others, with the loss of one of their own men.[13]

Men like Judge Francis Hopkins of McIntosh County, Georgia, therefore paid little heed to fabrications about armies of black mercenaries on the move. Contrary to what the Patriots were claiming, he told Governor Early, black troops at Fernandina "behaved in the most respectful manner, never speaking to or passing a white man without taking off their hats," and the Spanish authorities were assisting residents of Georgia in retrieving runaway slaves. Nor was there any fear of Indian attack in his part of the state. People lived in far greater dread, he said, of the British fleet. Meanwhile, regular troops and Georgia militias were not destined for action in East Florida. Under General John Floyd, they were hurrying westward to hunt down the Red Sticks. Soon Andrew Jackson, leading regulars, Tennessee militia, and friendly Indians, would crush the Red Sticks at Horseshoe Bend and make the first of his forays into Spanish West Florida. East Florida was no longer the focal point of anyone's attention.[14]

By the close of November, the Patriots finally met a defeat that ended their hopes of reviving control over northern Florida—and it came at the hands of a free woman of color. From the earliest days of the hostilities, Zephaniah Kingsley's plantation at Laurel Grove, near Doctor's Lake on the St. Johns River, had served as a stronghold for rebel forces. Although the plantation buildings had been heavily damaged during the Seminole raids of 1812, the dwelling house remained, protected by a seven-foot post-and-clapboard cedar fence. Inside this rebel blockhouse were two 4-pound brass cannons positioned to cover the river. On November 22, 1813, Commander José Antonio Moreno, in charge of the *Immutable*, along with Don Lorenzo Avila of the *Habanera*, launched an assault on the Kingsley house, firing into it with heavy artillery in an attempt to dislodge some seventy rebels and to disable the guns.

Unable to counter this barrage, the house's occupants fled into the woods. Moreno, seeing them go and observing that his cannon fire had damaged the walls of the house, called a halt to his attack and retired to the eastern shore of the St. Johns to confer with a Spanish detachment there. Shortly afterward, a canoe approached from the direction of Laurel Grove. Among the passengers was twenty-year-old Anna Kingsley. Anna had been kidnapped from Senegal, West Africa, in 1806 and sold into slavery. Her owner, Zephaniah Kingsley, eventually became her husband. In 1811, he had freed her and their three children. Anna harbored little sympathy for the rebels or their cause and asked Commander Moreno for sanctuary from them. When he agreed, she recrossed the river and returned with some fifteen men, women, and children of her household. She then informed Moreno that the men investing her husband's plantation had not suffered any casualties and that their cannons were still intact. Offering to help in a strike against them, she led twenty mulatto and free black soldiers back to the dock at Laurel Grove. They were unable to land, however, as the rebels were still close by, ready to repulse them.

Undeterred, Anna made a second offer—to go by herself to Laurel Grove and set fire to the plantation house. With two male slaves to row her canoe, she again set off, finally returning to Moreno at 7 P.M.

The commander was growing increasingly suspicious of Anna. He thought perhaps she was trying to deceive him about her loyalties or lure his men into a rebel ambush. Noting that there was no sign of any flames across the river, he said, "You went to set a fire, and you haven't done anything?" She replied, "Wait a moment."

Surveying the opposite bank of the river again, the commander was astonished to see the Kingsley house suddenly engulfed in flames, which soon became so intense that they set off the cannons. Asked how she had accomplished this, Anna replied that she had started a fire in "a trunk full of combustibles so that it would give her time to move away."

The burning of the house at Laurel Grove destroyed the last Patriot refuge on the St. Johns River and made a local heroine out of Anna. She would later burn down her own small property, immediately opposite her husband's estate, to ensure that the rebels could make no use of it. Moreno praised her in his official report: "[I] cannot help but recommend this woman," he told his superiors, "who has demonstrated a great enthusiasm concerning the Spaniards and extreme aversion to the rebels, being worthy of being looked after, since she has worked like a heroine, destroying the strong house with the fire she set so that the artillery could not be obtained, and later doing the same with her own property." Anna would eventually receive a land grant of 350 acres in compensation for her losses and in recognition of her bravery.[15]

By the close of 1813, the Patriots were rapidly losing interest in the hit-and-run tactics they had employed along the St. Johns and St. Marys Rivers. There seemed little point in remaining in the area, where they could never let down their guard. Joseph Hibberson, of Amelia Island, had written to the U.S. district attorney in Georgia, demanding the removal of Harris and his men. He discounted the allegations of unruly black troops in East Florida, saying that if the Spaniards truly wished to menace Georgia, they could announce a sanctuary policy for slaves and "one half the negroes of your sea coast would be over the St. Marys River in less than a month." Harris, for his part, was ready to leave. He was gathering his men and collecting his resources for his grander vision—an investiture of the Alachua territory.[16]

In the chill winter of 1814, Harris led some seventy fellow adventurers into the backwoods of East Florida. They traveled by way of the King's Road south from Colerain, then branched off westward via a bridle path, the Alachua trail, that skirted around the western bank of the St. Johns River and led into Indian country. It was a domain where the Spanish rarely patrolled. Even so, their departure into the interior did not pass without notice. Kindelán had already been warned by Don Luis de Onís, among others, that a party of Georgians intended to invade Alachua and establish a settlement. He had protested to Peter Early about this incursion, asking the governor of Georgia to intervene. Early pointed out that the men taking part in the expedition were already in East Florida and outside his jurisdiction. If they returned across the border, he said, he would detain them. Otherwise, they were Kindelán's problem.[17]

It was a six-day march from the border down into the old Seminole heartland, for Harris planned to follow the route that had been used by Colonel Smith in his joint operation with the Tennessee Volunteers and headed for Payne's Town, at the center of rich farmlands and pasture. The men who accompanied him, though still designating themselves as Patriots, were significantly changed in composition from the rebels who had first joined George Mathews in 1812. Most of the old leadership was gone. John Houston McIntosh, apart from giving verbal support to the endeavor, took no part in it. William Craig and Zephaniah Kingsley had accepted amnesty and were already trying to rebuild their fortunes and reputations under Spanish rule. Many of the families from along the upper St. Johns and Nassau Rivers—who had stuck close to Harris during the first weeks after the American evacuation—had also given up on revolt and had either renewed their allegiance to Spain or had moved to Georgia. The Braddocks, the Harts, the Loftins, the Higginbothams, the Wingates, the Vinzants, the Swearingens, and the Fitzpatricks—all listed in Spanish records as adherents of Harris who had rejected the general amnesty or who had turned rebel again—were noticeably absent from those heading for Alachua.

Nonetheless, at the core of the group were some men who had long been partisans of the Patriot banner. Abner Broadway joined the expedition, as did Britton Knight, John Uptegrove, Jacob Summerlin, Thomas

Prevatt, and one of the Hollingsworths. The leaders were Harris's most faithful subordinates: Francisco Roman Sánchez, James Dell, and William Cone. This trip to Alachua represented Cone's third journey into Indian country, for he had been with Newnan in 1812 and with Smith and Williams in 1813. James Dell, another participant in the punitive 1813 expedition, was returning to Alachua as head of a family venture, for he brought along his younger siblings, Bennett Maxey Dell and Simeon Dell. Taking McIntosh's place, Harris inherited the title of director of the Republic of East Florida, with Francisco Roman Sánchez as president of the Legislative Council and James Dell as colonel commandant in charge of military affairs. Most of the rank and file, with the exceptions noted above, were men out of Georgia.[18]

No one opposed the men's progress, and they found the vicinity of Payne's Town deserted, as it had been ever since February 1813. Harris's first order of business was to construct a two-story blockhouse inside a twenty-five-foot square, which he named Fort Mitchell, in honor of David Mitchell of Georgia. Having seen to the immediate needs of defense, he then convened a meeting to set forth his plans. It was only a matter of time before the Spaniards or the Seminoles tried to oust his intrepid group of pioneers. They had one sure means of securing a title to the land, and a future for themselves, and that was by getting formal recognition from the American government. It was the one thing the Patriots had never managed to obtain, and now they could not sustain their efforts without it.

On January 25, Harris addressed the Legislative Council, congratulating them on bringing democratic government to "a quarter of the Continent heretofore the Lurking Places of the most inveterate and troublesome Savages." He blamed the Spaniards for most of the bloodshed and looting that had occurred during recent conflicts. We have undergone many privations, he told his followers, our names have been besmirched by allegations of our supposed misdeeds while little is said of our own losses. Now, however, our task is clear: to supply for the common defense, appoint judges of an inferior court to maintain law and order, and send a minister to the U.S. government with an offer to cede this territory to the Republic.[19]

Following Harris's lead, the council, too, commenced its business. It drafted a resolution that recounted the history of the Patriot rebellion and made a proclamation concerning their rights to the Alachua country. The members expressed gratitude to God, the all-wise composer of events, for delivering such a solitary wilderness into their hands. Employing an argument that would be used again in later years, they charged that the Seminoles had forfeited all claim to Alachua by making war upon the Patriots in violation of the treaty negotiated in August 1812. "Aided by the brave Col. Newnan and their kindred in flesh and blood," the Patriots "pursued the enemy into their own Territory," where they were "put to the rout, and with the loss of their blood, their lives and their king fled without the country that we now possess and for which we are bound to contend." In effect, the council was expressing a doctrine that would lay the groundwork for the policy of removal and the Second Seminole War in the 1830s: that Indians were, by nature, uncivilized and had lost their claim to the land by making war upon whites.[20]

Next, the Legislative Council drafted a lengthy petition to Congress, making sure to legitimize their endeavor, after the fashion of the convention held in Baton Rouge in 1810, by setting forth their grievances against Spanish rule and by outlining their apparatus for self-government. As with all past appeals, they requested annexation into the United States. They made no pretense of being in rebellion against Spain, noting only that it was "worthy of remark that at least three of your petitioners, and one of them a native of St. Augustine by birth, have suffered in the hands of the Spanish authority of East Florida in a manner not even conjectured by those who have not personally experienced the distress and calamity incident to a state of Confinement in a close dungeon, and all this for no other reason than a firm attachment to the American government." The Spanish denied them public worship in their faith, armed black troops against them, and furnished weapons to the Indians—reasons enough to justify independence. For this and other reasons, they asked Congress to accept a cession of the Alachua territory and to make it a dependency of the United States. One hundred and five men signed the petition, showing that even during the short spell of time between the commencement of their expedition and the building of the blockhouse, their numbers had increased significantly.[21]

Pursuant to Harris's request, the council appointed Wilson Connor, a Baptist preacher, as their delegate to Washington and sent him north. This representative never reached the federal capital. Two months later, through a series of mishaps, he had proceeded no farther than Louisburg, North Carolina, and there took to bed with fever.[22]

The Alachua District, in the meantime, showed signs of prospering. The settlers managed to provision themselves with supplies from Georgia and from the remaining livestock of the abandoned Seminole towns, began to plow fields and cultivate a crop, and attracted more people. On March 15, 1814, Francisco R. Sánchez's wife, Francisca, became the first woman to give birth in the new settlement, to Alexander Bonaparte Sánchez.[23]

Governor Kindelán, however, had not forgotten about these interlopers into his province. Instead of dispatching troops to confront the settlers, he fell back on a tactic he had used with great effect during the Patriot War and enlisted the aid of the Seminoles, promising them a bounty for killing members of the rebels, Buckner Harris in particular.

The contest to win recognition for the Republic of East Florida also met with scant reward. Benjamin Hawkins inspected the Patriot settlement and counseled Governor Early that this intrusion in Indian territory might stir up the tribes against Georgia. "You can with truth assure the Seminoles," Early said in his reply to Hawkins, "that the government of Georgia gives no countenance to the patriots."[24]

Ultimately, the embassy to Washington fell by the wayside. Connor, unable to make it there in person, forwarded the council's petition to James Monroe, with an explanation of his mission and a request for a reply. On April 19, Monroe wrote back. The American government would not recognize the rebel government, he responded. Moreover, if American citizens were involved in the endeavor, they were violating United States statutes and "will be liable to censure."[25]

This news alone threatened to invalidate and undermine all of Harris's hopes for a stable, permanent settlement. However, the real blow fell in May. There had been little sign of trouble in the area, Harris himself acknowledging, "Our enemies have all fled; our numbers are increasing." This calm proved deceptive. The Seminoles, if not making their presence overtly felt, were still watching and observing the settlement. On May 5, a war party ambushed Harris while he was out exploring the countryside and killed and scalped him. They later turned in his scalp and a small pocketbook of maps and surveys to Governor Kindelán in order to receive the reward placed on his head.[26]

The death of Harris terminated the great experiment of the Republic of East Florida. Though there were other capable military men among the settlers, none could match Harris's charismatic leadership. True to the sentiments of one of his followers, who portrayed Harris as "the sole support of the cause," his death left the Patriots once more leaderless and rudderless. Lacking aid from the U.S. government and the government of Georgia and still exposed to reprisals from the Spanish and the Indians, the settlers lost heart and gradually departed for other lands. The Dells returned to the St. Marys River and swore fealty to the Spanish government. William Cone went back to Georgia to take up arms against the British. Francisco Roman Sánchez returned to St. Augustine to discover that his mother, María Carmen Hill Sánchez, was ill and dying at St. Marys. According to her physician, she died of a broken heart, struck down by the calamities that had destroyed most of the Sánchez properties and haunted by the fact that one of her own sons had taken part in the plunder and looting of the family estates.[27]

The Seminoles and maroons chose to reestablish their villages south of the Alachua area rather than return to the great savanna (Payne's Prairie). Micanopy, Payne's nephew, set up a new town at Okahumpka, about fifty miles south of the old settlements of Payne's Town and Cuscowilla, and a community of maroons took over the hammocks and prairies around Pilaklikaha. By 1823, this latter community had 100 acres of land under cultivation and once again maintained large herds of cattle. For about a year after Harris's death, Colonel Samuel Alexander tried to invest Alachua. However, the next major migration of white settlers into the region would come after East Florida was incorporated into the United States.[28]

Back in St. Augustine and Fernandina, the spring of 1814 brought news that Spanish subjects everywhere had long awaited. Joseph Bonaparte had abdicated the throne of Spain on January 7, 1814. By the end of March, Ferdinand VII had returned to Spain, acknowledged by everyone, including Napoleon, as Spain's legitimate king. His return seemed both momentous and propitious, the dawning of a new enlightened age of constitutional monarchy and renewed vigor for the empire.

It was not to be. On May 2, 1814, Ferdinand, with the backing of Spanish conservatives, renounced the Constitution of 1812, proclaimed himself king by divine right alone, and ordered the arrest of all the liberal members of the Regency who had fought for six years to protect his kingdom and restore him to the throne. He would go on to win notoriety as the worst and most despotic monarch in Spanish history and the one who presided over the disintegration of an empire that had once spanned two hemispheres.[29]

In East Florida, Kindelán was ordered to remove the monument to the Spanish Constitution of 1812 that had been erected during the last days of the siege of St. Augustine. Antonio Álvarez, furious at this betrayal of Spanish liberalism, took the commemorative tablet off the monument and hid it away in his house. In 1821, when Florida became an American territory, Álvarez threw a last snub at King Ferdinand by restoring the tablet to public display.[30]

With the collapse of Buckner Harris's Republic of East Florida in Alachua, the Patriot War came to an end. This was by no means the end of conflicts in the Floridas, however. In May 1814, a squadron of British ships entered the St. Marys River and put landing parties ashore at Amelia Island. For a while, it looked as if the British might replace the Americans as the new military conquerors of Fernandina. Kindelán, however, refused to further endanger the colony by violating Spanish pledges of neutrality and after some tense moments persuaded the British to leave. Soon, British agents were moving west toward the Apalachicola River, the western boundary of East Florida, to plot with the Creeks and with black maroons for an invasion of Georgia, and Admiral George Cockburn commenced operations to harass the coasts and seaports of Georgia. As the British set their sights on an invasion of the South, the Madison administration moved against Mobile, and Andrew Jackson occupied Pensacola to expel an English fleet. After the close of the War of 1812, the United States would slowly dismantle Spanish West Florida, destroy Indian and maroon strongholds along the Apalachicola and Suwannee Rivers, reoccupy Amelia Island, and send troops against the Seminoles of East Florida. The repercussions of George Mathews's unsuccessful filibuster would be far-reaching.[31]

The Patriot War and American History

The introduction to this book set forth several assertions concerning the significance of the Patriot War in American history. It is now time to review these assertions and see how they have held up. In order of presentation, they were that the war marked a transition in the policies and practices of the Jeffersonians in their quest for territorial expansion; that fervor for war in the South, and particularly in Georgia, was grounded in regional grievances; and that the Patriot War illustrates, in a number of ways, the need to reevaluate standard historical precepts about the origins and progress of the War of 1812.

With respect to American foreign policy during the Jefferson, Madison, and Monroe administrations, the attempt to seize Spanish East Florida in 1812 was not an isolated event. It fit into a broader landscape of diplomatic and filibustering initiatives that dated from Jefferson's negotiations for Louisiana. By playing upon political schisms in Europe, Jefferson was able to detach the Louisiana Territory from Spain and France in 1803 and use its acquisition to press for further concessions. He carried this out primarily by exploiting boundary disputes—Louisiana was ill defined on paper—and by insisting on the broadest possible interpretation of the Louisiana Purchase, something that allowed American administrations, at various times, to exert claims over other Spanish possessions, notably West Florida and Texas. While Spain always rejected American pretensions to these areas, the arguments supporting American claims gradually permeated the consciousness of congressmen and the public, serving as justifications for the use of sharper and more intimidating tactics to gain the Spanish borderlands. James Madison and James Monroe (both intimately involved in the original creation of the claims) used them as legalistic props for their own policies on expansion.[1]

Wanjohi Waciuma, in *Intervention in Spanish Floridas, 1801–1813: A Study in Jeffersonian Foreign Policy*, has extensively documented the arguments and philosophies underlying American efforts in this regard. Over three administrations and twenty years, Jefferson, Madison, and Monroe remained remarkably focused in their desire to secure all lands east of the Mississippi River for the United States. Encouraged by their certainty that Americans were preordained to occupy the continent, Jefferson and Madison both became opportunists, seeking chances to pressure Spain for territorial concessions as circumstances permitted. Frank L. Owsley Jr. and Gene A. Smith, in *Filibusters and Expansionists*, describe the Jeffersonians' quest for territory as "varied but relentless." Generally, they chose to follow the path of least resistance. Though desires to gain lands in Canada were as prevalent as desires for expansion in the South and West, Canada was too closely protected by the era's superpower—Great Britain—and by a population that saw no benefits to annexation to the United States. The route to Louisiana, the Floridas, and ultimately Texas was far less fraught with peril and, given Spain's declining power, far easier to forge.[2]

James Madison, through his willingness to back American claims to territory with a minimal employment of armed force, first in Baton Rouge and then in East Florida, moved the nation toward a more aggressive stance in its relations with Spain. In midcareer, as secretary of state, when the United States could still count on amicable relations with France and England, Madison had, in the words of biographer Ralph Ketcham, "adopted a firm, even arrogant attitude toward the weak and declining giant of the new world. He never doubted that all of Florida would some day be part of the United States, and he never doubted that despotic, corrupt Spain was unfit to possess it." This may help to explain why a normally cautious man resorted to coercive methods. The risk, however, was greater than Madison believed, for by 1810 and 1812, when he came to apply force, England was a hostile power allied with Spain, and neither country was easily intimidated. The president, exhibiting another longtime characteristic, had an "inclination to overplay his hand" and was fortunate to escape the invasion of East Florida at the cost of nothing more than mild humiliation. He rarely committed his opinions about the conflict to paper. In assessing Madison's attitude toward Mathews's espionage, it is nonetheless possible to draw certain conclusions. The convolutions of the West Florida Revolution at Baton Rouge undoubtedly encouraged Madison to attempt a filibuster in East Florida. It seems clear, too, that he never intended to commit himself in advance to a government-sponsored coup d'état. Prior to March 1812, he had little reason to suspect that General Mathews would openly employ the U.S. Navy in the capture of Fernandina (though it is hard to conjecture how the State Department missed the many signals that Mathews gave, indicating that he was on a dangerous course of action).

In any case, the use of Mathews as an agent provocateur was not a new or unusual strategy. The general was just one among a number of American agents working in Spanish colonies in the years between 1809 and 1812. William Shaler was in Cuba, assessing Cuban sentiments about a split with Spain. When he was expelled, the Madison administration sent him to Texas to intrigue with the leaders of a liberation movement. Similarly, Madison had employed General James Wilkinson, Governor William C. C. Claiborne, and others as agents in West Florida and had dispatched Joel R. Poinsett as a special agent to Chile, Peru, and Buenos Aires. The role of these men was to gather intelligence and to encourage pro-American allegiances among settlers in the soft underbelly of Spain's empire. It was only when Mathews mounted an invasion of East Florida, poorly concealed behind the screen of the Patriots, that the tactics of his mission became abnormal and took the president by surprise. From that point on, Madison was reacting to events rather than directing them.[3]

As for James Monroe, secretary of state, he came late to the affair. Rembert Patrick, in *Florida Fiasco*, argues that Monroe deliberately gave Mathews a free hand in East Florida, leaving him to his own devices in the hope that he would produce a meretricious delivery of the province. This is certainly plausible. Robert Remini has noted that Monroe adopted a similar tactic during the First Seminole War, letting Andrew Jackson proceed with an invasion of Florida while retaining the option of "disavowal" as a reserve card in case things went badly. The whole affair of East Florida and the Patriots thus comes down to us as an early and poorly managed example of the type of armed diplomacy that would be used with more finesse in later years. Rufus K. Wyllys once observed that it reflected small credit on either the political morality or experience of James Madison or his secretaries of state. While this may be true, some of the inept management of the conflict can be blamed on the fact that a forcible seizure of the province was never formally planned. Unlike the invasion of Canada in 1812, which was always part of the Madison administration's war strategy, Mathews's unexpected seizure of Amelia Island presented the administration with a fait accompli that it was not fully prepared to exploit. At first, Madison and Monroe opted to retain the area to guard against a British flanking maneuver in the South. Subsequently, East Florida became an extension of the administration's plans for Canada. Just as the government hoped to hold Canadian provinces as hostages against a settlement with England, East Florida was to be a hostage against future negotiations with Spain. Both plans fell victim to the misfortunes (and miscalculations) of war. By 1814, they were abandoned, for the United States was no longer waging an offensive war but a defensive one.[4]

It is an irony, then, that the failed conquest of East Florida later resulted in cession of the province. The moral victory in the war may have gone to Spain, but every practical benefit went to the Americans. Though the cession of the Floridas to the United States did not take shape until 1819 and was not finalized until 1821, the devastation wrought by the Patriots went a long way toward convincing the Spanish Crown, and even some of Florida's settlers, that the only viable future for the province was as part of the United States. Hence, in the end, the Patriot War accomplished the one thing that the War of 1812 failed to do—it brought new territory into the American confederation.

In this respect, the Patriot War stands as one of the events that paved the way for the presidential initiatives of James Monroe and his more systematic assertion of American power in the Western Hemisphere. The seizure of Baton Rouge (1810) and Mobile (1813–14), the disruption of Spanish control over East Florida, and the various events that followed signaled the collapse of Spain's Gulf Coast buffer colonies. In 1818, when American troops reoccupied Amelia Island, Monroe used the secret act of 1811, originally intended for Madison, to legally justify his orders to send in troops. During these same years, he, Henry Clay, and other American leaders began to espouse support for Spanish American independence. The end of the War of 1812 and the ascension of Monroe to the presidency inaugurated a new era in American foreign policy, one in which the United States could freely involve itself in the Spanish American independence movements.[5]

Other facets of the Patriot War illustrate the nature of southern warfare during the early years of the Republic. War fever was especially pronounced in the South in 1811, and once war came, southerners carried it forward with vigor. Their motivations owed much to regional concerns—

to a belief in expansion, a desire to quash the power of Native Americans in the Southeast, and calls for an end to Spanish hegemony along the Gulf Coast. These concerns were quite distinct from national grievances against England and influenced southern conceptions of "the enemy." As Frank L. Owsley Jr. has noted, in 1812 and 1813 southerners were generally fighting familiar foes, ones perceived as surrogates for the British— the Spaniards, their militias and Native American allies, and the Red Sticks among the Creeks. There can be little question that the primary motivation behind southern support of the Patriots was a desire to see Spanish power in East Florida crumble and to supplant Spain's banner with the Stars and Stripes. This upwelling of American nationalism (countered by similar patriotism on the Spanish side) was anchored in historically rooted and emotionally charged divisions that already existed along the southern frontiers.[6]

The search for the causes of a conflict is always problematical, and in the case of the Patriot War, previous answers must be revised. Inside East Florida, the Patriots gained support from settlers with grudges against Spanish authority and from others who assumed American forces would emerge as the victors. Arrayed against them were the Spanish military hierarchy, those loyal to Spain, and those who saw no benefits to affiliation with the United States. Numerous studies, glossing Rembert Patrick's *Florida Fiasco*, have fingered "land hungry" southern frontiersmen as the principal instigators of conflict. More recently, Chris Monaco has tried to cast the Patriot leadership in nobler colors, arguing that they "articulated a genuine nationalism that represented the culmination of American expansionist fervor." The truth is a good deal more complicated than either of these interpretations. For instance, it cannot be denied that hunger for land played an important role in Patriot recruitment. Mathews originally gained adherents through his (rather ungenerous) offer of fifty acres. He and the Patriot government then had to sweeten the inducement to 500 acres, while Newnan, to coax his Georgia Volunteers into reenlisting in the autumn of 1812, also had to dangle the prospects of land grants before them. Land, in short, was the currency promised to citizen-soldiers for armed service. At the same time, there is little evidence that land hunger drove Georgia's political leaders, its prowar press, or the bulk of its citizens into a year-long commitment to win the East Florida conflict.

By the same token, an appeal to "nationalism" or "expansionism" puts a label on motives without explaining them. Admittedly, in 1811 and 1812 southerners, and particularly Georgians, were whole-hearted advocates of acquiring the Floridas. "At no very distant day," wrote the editor of the *Georgia Journal*, "it may reasonably be calculated that one million of American citizens will find the possession of Florida essential to their happiness." But such sentiments furnished only an ideology for war, not a motive. Justification for attacking East Florida seems to have rested, instead, on three sources of friction that directly affected life along the southern frontier. First, in the years prior to 1812, there was great resentment against commerce at Fernandina as well as apprehension about potential British intervention there. The town's busy trade mocked the hardships caused by the Embargo Act in Georgia. Its status as a neutral Spanish American port allowed English merchantmen and warships to cruise the southern coasts of the United States. While it would take more study to prove the case, there also seems to have been an element of class warfare in the hostility that frontiersmen in Camden County, Georgia, exhibited toward the affluent English, Irish, Scottish, and Spanish gentry of Amelia Island. With its slave trade, its mix of peoples of different shades and nations, and its ties to British trading interests, Amelia was an affront to many frontier values in 1812. Patriot and American animosity toward the "Anglo-Spaniards" intensified after they rejected "liberation" and after black soldiers and Seminole warriors began to contribute to American military defeats in East Florida. The southern *code duello*, with its demand of blood for blood and satisfaction for dishonor, possibly played some role in the bitter infighting that occurred on Amelia Island, fueling the reprisals that were meted out against loyalist residents throughout 1812 and 1813.[7]

This brings us to a second important factor in the war, the volatile undercurrents of racial animosities that were such a prominent feature in it. Southern expressions of frustration and anger with East Florida as a sanctuary for runaway slaves and a haven for armed maroons and free blacks are too well documented in this narrative to require further explication here. Twice before, during the American Revolution and during the East Florida rebellion of 1795, people on the southern frontiers had defied a European power that contemplated allying itself with slaves and free people of color. Spanish deployment of black soldiers, "the vilest species of troops" in the words of Major General John Floyd, was something that white Georgians had no intention of tolerating. When the Patriots crossed the border, John Houston McIntosh and Lodowick Ashley immediately issued warnings to the Spaniards to disarm the free black militia, and General Floyd advised making strikes against the maroon communities among the Seminoles. Throughout the conflict, Governor Mitchell denounced Estrada and Kindelán for arming free men of color. By late 1812, he, McIntosh, and various citizens groups in Georgia were all petitioning the state and federal governments, expressing their convictions that Spanish military tactics in East Florida would kindle a slave insurrection in the South. In 1813 the Patriots did not play upon land grants or anti-British sentiments in their attempts to get Georgians back into the conflict. Instead, they generated a propaganda machine that alleged East Florida was ruled by black revolutionaries and slaves.

For all these reasons, the Patriot War must be regarded as intrinsically tied to southern attitudes about race and slavery. "Questions of race and servitude," Larry Rivers has recently observed, "played key roles in virtually every event of importance [in Florida] from the 1810s through the Union challenge to Confederate authorities at Pensacola in 1861. The clash between Spanish and Anglos during the Patriot War of 1812 . . . stemmed partly from a difference in attitudes about free and enslaved blacks and their treatment in northeast Florida." Southerners regarded Spanish policies in Florida as antithetical to the supremacy of master over slave. Free people of color living under Spanish rule, on the other hand, and slaves and maroons living among the Seminoles had every reason to resist an American takeover of the province. "The Spaniards would thereby lose their independence," Kenneth Porter reminds us in his study of the conflict, "the Indians their land, but the Negroes would lose at once their independence, their homes, and the very freedom of themselves and their families."[8]

By the same token, it can be noted that the Patriot War, as an ancillary combat to the Creek War, merged with other military endeavors to curb the autonomy of Native American polities in the Southeast. As Frank Marotti has pointed out, "the key to the balance of power in East Florida was the allegiance of the Indians," for it provided the essential prop to Spanish power. In this respect, George Mathews made a serious miscalculation when he dismissed the Seminoles' offers of support in 1812. The Seminoles, in turn, paid a high price for allying with Kindelán. The two expeditions that Colonel Newnan and Colonel Smith launched against Alachua in 1812 and 1813 represented the opening salvos of the region's Seminole wars. Georgia and Tennessee militias entered East Florida primarily to avenge Seminole attacks on American contingents, to force the Indians to withdraw from combat, and to punish Spaniards for using them as military surrogates. In this respect, the war followed up on the American Revolution in reordering the domestic military situation in the South. The Revolution had removed England as a sponsor of tribal autonomy. Spanish representatives stepped into this role, trying to broker influence with Native Americans to bolster the region's allegiance to Crown interests. By 1814, the Spaniards had been rendered impotent as well, and the southern tribes and confederations stood alone against the encroachments of white settlers. Moreover, the breaking of Creek power during the War of 1812 "made it possible to remove all the southern Indians from their lands east of the Mississippi." During the rest of its time as a Spanish colony and during the American territorial period (1821–45), Florida became an arena for additional expeditions against Indians and maroons— in the 1816 attack that eliminated the Negro Fort at Apalachicola, in the expulsion of Luis Aury and his black adherents from Amelia Island in 1818, and finally in the assault on the Seminoles during the First Seminole War (1817–18) and the use of military force to relocate them during the Second Seminole War (1835–42).[9]

All in all, the Patriot War in East Florida turned into a "day of reckoning" directed against everything that alienated Americans from Spaniards along the Georgia-Florida frontier, a clash not only of soldiers but of different methods for settling and securing territory.

An assessment of the Patriot War also calls into question long-accepted precepts about the origins of the War of 1812. J.C.A. Stagg has observed that the War of 1812 was "not so much one war as a series of conflicts." Herein lies the great dilemma for analysis. The war consisted of at least four interrelated arenas of contest: the struggle for the Great Lakes and Canada; the proving of the young American navy against the British fleet; the defense of the South; and the ongoing contest between Native Americans and Americans for control of territory. As both Hickey and Owsley have noted, such a complex conflict can only be attributed to multiple causes.[10]

As already stated, southerners had their own regional motivations for engaging in war in 1812. However, the prosecution of the war in the South was just as regional as its motives. The Madison administration's supervision of affairs in East Florida during 1812 and 1813 was at best haphazard, something that held true for its overall management of southern military affairs. With their attention focused on Canada during 1812 and 1813 and on a defensive war in 1814, Madison, Secretary of State Monroe, and Secretaries of War Eustis and Armstrong for the most part abdicated responsibility in the South to state and territorial governments. This is one reason why the southern campaigns can be thought of as "the other war of 1812." The war in the North was one of policy—a deliberate effort to deprive England of possessions—while the war in the South tended to be reactive—a rearguard action to prevent England from landing troops at Fernandina or Pensacola, to stop the marauding Red Sticks, and to protect New Orleans and the Mississippi Territory. Directives from the War Department, slow in coming, had little impact on actual events as they unfolded on the fields of battle. Thus, while the administration intended to prosecute the Creek War from Georgia, in the end it fell to Andrew Jackson and Tennessee to confront a danger that Georgia could not fully meet. Combat against the Red Sticks proved to be a boon to the American war effort in that it forced the national government to begin addressing the problem of raising, supplying, and training troops in the South, something that prepared the area for its later defense against English invasion. However, in the suppression of British infiltration into Spanish West Florida, Jackson was again operating under only the loosest direction from the War Department. Having reinforced Mobile against a British landing, he wrote to the secretary of war, recommending a strike against Pensacola, which a British fleet was using as a friendly harbor. Without waiting for a reply, he seized the capital of West Florida on November 7, 1814, and forced the British to withdraw. He then stabilized the area before proceeding to the defense of New Orleans.[11]

Here, then, are the key elements of the southern campaigns. War in the South began as a pseudowar against Spain, a British ally, fought largely with the limited military resources of Georgia. In the midst of this conflict, the British gained a foothold in the area through their Native American surrogates, the Red Sticks. By 1814, the British were gearing up for a more direct attack on the South, planning naval expeditions against Georgia, and establishing bases of operation along the Apalachicola and at Pensacola. Their expulsion from these areas led to the final confrontation between American and British forces at New Orleans. On the whole, the South witnessed a series of conflicts directed by governors, militias, and local generals, usually operating in semi-independence from the national government and often hampered by delays in disbursal of funds and supplies. In many ways, the South fought its own War of 1812, and this may be one reason why historians seem to have difficulty in treating the southern theater of battle within the context of the war as a whole. Certainly the difficulty does not stem from a dearth of material. Frank L. Owsley Jr. has written a thorough analysis of the Creek War; Robert Remini has dedicated much of his career to an explication of Andrew Jackson's exploits; and there are now two monographs on the Patriot War. Even so, the southern campaigns have not fared well in general texts. Few studies draw any links between the War of 1812 and the extension of American hegemony over Spanish territory. John Mahon's *War of 1812* remains the only text that integrates the Patriot War, the Creek War, Jackson's moves against Mobile and Pensacola, and the Battle of New Orleans into the overall military picture. Although English maneuvers with regard to East Florida have been summarized by Albert Hazen Wright in *Britain and the American Frontier*, one must go to Owsley's *Struggle for the Gulf Borderlands* or Owsley and Smith's *Filibusters and Expansionists* to find an interpretation of American diplomacy toward Spain and its bearing on the war. Perhaps in a conflict that was regional, analysis is also destined to be regional. Popular reference works on the war seem to be slightly ahead of scholarly studies. *The Encyclopedia of the War of 1812* and Eugene Wait's *America and the War of 1812* have both incorporated the various Florida campaigns into general coverage (although in the case of the latter, with several inaccuracies).[12]

To return for some final comments to the scene of the Patriot War, it should be noted that the War of 1812 continued to affect East Florida even as Governor Kindelán tried to return the colony to a state of neutrality in the contest between England and the United States. Almost as soon as Patriot resistance disintegrated, the British made a play to obtain a base in the province. Paris had fallen on March 30, 1814, and Napoleon with it. By May, an English squadron was patrolling off the St. Marys River, part of a British plan to step up the war effort against the United States, and Georgians scrambled to counter the threat of invasion that loomed along the coast. For the moment, though, British strategy was directed elsewhere. Vice Admiral Alexander Cochrane dispatched Captain George Woodbine to the borders of East and West Florida at the Apalachicola River to treat with the Seminoles and Lower Creeks and entice them into an attack on the southern states. Over the summer, Admiral George Cockburn commenced a campaign in the Chesapeake that led to the capture and burning of Washington on August 24. From Milledgeville, Governor Peter Early pleaded for aid to secure the Georgia coasts, while Kindelán nudged the British away from Amelia Island and refused to consort with their agents. Soon, British attention had switched to West Florida, where Major Edward Nicholls established a beachhead in Pensacola and then sent an expedition against American forces that were occupying Mobile. In response, Andrew Jackson invaded West Florida in November 1814 with a force of 4,100 regulars, militia, and Indians. He took the city of Pensacola without a fight, and the British, realizing the Spanish would not support them, blew up the fort they had confiscated and evacuated their squadron from the harbor.[13]

A campaign against Georgia began in December. Admiral Cockburn's fleet arrived off Cumberland Sound near the mouth of the St. Marys and began to occupy, loot, and burn coastal Georgia towns. Governor Early had to declare martial law at Savannah to keep order among a panicking population. On January 24, 1815, the British burned Point Peter. Then, in February, they sent an expedition to destroy the sawmills of Archibald Clark, George Mathews's friend and ally, at Colerain. In an engagement reminiscent of the Battle of Waterman's Bluff but on a larger scale, the Georgia militia ambushed the men in the boats and cut the expeditionary force to pieces with gun fire. Before the British could retaliate, news came from abroad of the signing of the Treaty of Ghent, establishing peace. Far away in New Orleans, Alexander Cochrane and Andrew Jackson, oblivious to the treaty, were about to fight the single greatest battle of the war.[14]

The immediate aftereffects of the war included chaos and banditry along the Georgia–East Florida border. A good example of the lawlessness that prevailed comes from the colorful history of William Williams, onetime Patriot turned bandit, slave catcher, and murderer. In 1814, at the head of a gang of hooligans, Williams held north Florida in his grip as he launched raids from Georgia, waiting in ambush to waylay travelers on the King's Road. Hearing that one of his more daring escapades, the kidnapping of several slaves, had been mistakenly attributed to another settler, he wrote to Don Tomás Llorente, commander at Fort San Nicolás, to set the dubious record straight. "For my own part I can inform you that it was me and Old Mr. Turner and a man from St. Marys. . . . In six hours I can be over the river laying behind an old pine log within one hundred yard[s] of your garrison and let me tell you Old Mr. Comidant, don't you go so far from your garrison to shit, for it lay in my power to shoot you in what part I chose." Williams's gang, and many others, would continue to disrupt life at the border for another two years.[15]

Other legacies of the war also left their mark. The termination of hostilities halted British intrigues among the Creeks but left a well-stocked and fortified stronghold on the Apalachicola River, East Florida's boundary line with West Florida. In 1815, a large community of runaway slaves and black maroons began to congregate at this outpost, including some slaves who had fled from East Florida during the Patriot War. More than a hundred families lived in and around what became known as the Negro Fort and controlled the hinterlands at the crux of the Florida panhandle. Disconcerted by the presence of this large maroon settlement at the borders, the American government sent angry protests to Juan José de Estrada, who had once again become interim governor of East Florida, demanding that he break up the fort and return the maroons to slavery. Still angry over the Patriot War and unwilling to send an expedition clear across the province, Estrada refused to do anything. Determined to eliminate the fort, the American army dispatched Colonel Duncan Clinch to destroy it, and in an attack on July 27, 1816, Clinch began a barrage of the place with gunboats. One shot, apparently penetrating a powder magazine, obliterated the fort in a massive explosion that killed some 270 defenders.[16]

In 1817, Amelia Island fell victim for a second time to filibusters. Gregor MacGregor, a self-proclaimed advocate of Spanish American independence, captured the town on June 28. The disruptions and disorders that resulted prompted American intervention, and in 1818, during the administration of President James Monroe, American troops invested the town. This time, the United States refused to withdraw and did not return possession of Amelia to Spain.[17]

Also in 1817, continuing conflicts between the army and the various tribes of the Seminoles settled along the Apalachicola and Flint Rivers instigated the First Seminole War. In November, American troops assailed the Indian settlement of Fowltown, and a war party responded by ambushing an American detachment. During the spring of the following year, Andrew Jackson swept south into East Florida, leading an army of Georgia and Tennessee militia, U.S. regulars, and friendly Creeks, and headed for Bowlegs's Town on the Suwannee River. Having attacked and burned other settlements en route, Jackson's forces found Bowlegs's Town deserted and quickly destroyed it. The "war" was very one-sided, more a continuation of the "search and destroy" missions that had occurred in 1813, yet it succeeded in disrupting the Seminoles' abilities to fight and again paved the way for white settlement in north-central Florida.[18]

With Amelia Island under occupation and American troops coming and going freely on the Florida peninsula, the Monroe administration pressed Spain to cede its Florida possessions to the United States. By the Transcontinental, or Adams-Onís, Treaty ratified by the Senate on February 24, 1819, Spain offered to give up the colonies essentially for free. The United States withdrew its claims to Texas and also promised to pay compensation to Spanish subjects in Florida to a total allotment of $5 million for loss of or damage to property. Thus, as president, Monroe accomplished by negotiation—and at very little expense—what he had failed to achieve as secretary of state. The Spanish government dragged its feet about ratifying the treaty, which did nothing but rid Spain of two troublesome colonies, but finally signed off on it in 1821. In that year, in dual ceremonies at the twin capitals of Pensacola and St. Augustine, the Spanish authorities turned over possession of the Floridas to U.S. forces.[19]

Another legacy of the Patriot War was the protracted and complicated court cases that resulted from attempts to gain compensation for losses suffered during the American occupation of East Florida in 1812 and 1813. The ninth article of the Adams-Onís Treaty specifically stated that the United States was obligated to make restitution for damages caused "by the late operations of the American Army in Florida." Although Congress tried to renege on this agreement in the 1820s, after many protests from Spain and from Florida itself the legal path to compensation claims was at last cleared in the 1830s, and between 1836 and 1842 judges in Jacksonville and representatives of the Treasury Department reviewed some 200 cases alleging financial losses from the Patriot War.

The story of the claims is nearly as lengthy and complex as that of the war and equally replete with sorrows and surprises. Judge J. H. Bronson, who, along with Judge Robert Raymond Reid, presided over the adjudication and disposition of the suits, was astonished at the duplicity, bankrupt political policies, and personal vendettas that seemed to have played themselves out in East Florida. "It is an episode in the general history of the nation, which, as an American citizen, I could have wished might remain unwritten," he said. As a moral fable, the claims cases reflected almost as poorly on American justice as the conflict itself, for many destitute families that were genuinely impoverished by the Patriot War received little in the way of restitution, while some of the richest inhabitants of Florida, including those who had been active rebels, ate up the lion's share. By 1840, Bronson, in charge of stipulating the amount of each award, had already settled twenty-three claims for a total compensation of $133,782.50. He still had 132 cases outstanding in which plaintiffs had collectively petitioned for restitution amounting to $1,184,712.10. Altogether, more than 200 families filed suit, practically the entire free population of the province under Spanish rule.[20]

Claimants rarely received more than half of the amount they had assessed as their losses, and those who had political clout or sharp lawyers usually fared better than others, even if their claim to compensation was dubious. The three largest awards went to John Fraser, Zephaniah Kingsley, and John Houston McIntosh. The estate of John Fraser received $157,140 for damages to his Roundabout and Greenfield plantations. Zephaniah Kingsley received $113,410 as compensation for the destruction of Laurel Grove and other losses. The heirs of John Houston McIntosh, the leader of the Patriots, managed to collect $127,580, thus recouping damages from a war their forebear had helped to start.[21]

The Atkinson family, whose plantations were burned down during the evacuation, submitted a claim for $11,299 and were awarded $10,480 for what Bronson described as "unquestionably a meritorious claim." Manuel Solana, estimating that some 1,400 head of his cattle had been butchered or pirated away, put his losses at $20,600 and received $12,700. Francisco and Pedro Pons, submitting for the loss of their ship and bakery destroyed at Fernandina in 1812, requested $3,915.79 and received an award of $2,000. Henry Hartley, the young Mandarin planter forced into Patriot service, asked to be compensated $860 for the destruction of his small plantation and received $380. Edward Wanton, kept in shackles at Camp New Hope and burned out of both his Chancery and Cook's Place holdings, assessed his losses at $12,760 and was awarded $2,650. After the Patriot War, he became instrumental in the founding of the town of Micanopy and in settling the Alachua area during the 1820s. Anna Kingsley, having put her own Mandarin estate to the torch in 1813 to deprive the rebels of its use, received $1,594. Matthew Long, who railed that no amount of money could ever compensate him for the death of his father, requested $6,769 as the cost of the family homestead, livestock, and crops and received $3,915. The Fatio family, whose New Switzerland estate was ransacked by the military, the Seminoles, and Samuel Alexander's raiding party, gave a detailed inventory of their losses totaling $39,784 and won an award of $3,458.08. John Lowe, owner of the plantation where the Patriot War commenced, assessed his losses at $2,370 and received $1,190. The heirs of Eber O'Neill, one of the casualties in the Battle of Waterman's Bluff, won $2,450.[22]

Among the smallest claims and awards were those of Tony Primus, free person of color and member of the black militia, and José and Matilda Pomar, Minorcan farmers. Primus claimed $270 for the destruction of his small farm at Mandarin and was awarded $102. The Pomars received $88.75 for the looting of their tiny holding outside St. Augustine.[23]

As for the principal individuals of the war, John Houston McIntosh went back to his Georgia plantation, appropriately called the Refuge, disgruntled at how harshly and unfairly fate had repaid his efforts to be a great liberator. He found his reputation permanently sullied by his association with the Patriots and spent much of his time trying to exonerate his conduct before public opinion, vehemently denying any responsibility for the ruthless acts committed by the rebel government he had headed. In 1815, when he learned that Juan José de Estrada had granted him permission to return to Florida to settle his affairs, McIntosh wrote back to Estrada—a man he had tried to bribe and overthrow—as if he were a lifelong friend. "I would never have presumed to make this request of another Governor for two reasons," he said. "First there are few who fill the position with more honor and generosity, and second because I am convinced that no other Governor would accede to my petition with more profusion than Your Excellency, who through loyalty to your Government valiantly and successfully defended the Province in its moment of danger, with no other motive than that of honor." He was equally effusive in his flattery for Sebastián Kindelán, someone who had put a price on his head. "I never had the honor of seeing this *Caballero* but always entertained the most gracious memory that his conduct was peaceable and honorable."[24]

In 1823, McIntosh submitted a vindication of his role with the Patriots for publication in the *National Intelligencer*, charging that he was being unfairly slandered and defamed by those who laid the devastation of the war at his doorstep. His exposition took up half a page of the newspaper. "I have not the ambition of the Ephesian incendiary, to have my name handed down to posterity as that of a villain," he complained. "Travellers and others, who have spoken of, or written in newspapers and pamphlets an account of East Florida, and have mentioned anything of the rebellion which took place in that province in the year of 1812, have generally called it 'the rebellion of M'Intosh'—'of the marauder M'Intosh'—'of the marauding conduct of General M'Intosh's followers,' &c, &c. A few, who have had more charity, have termed it, from its unhappy termination, the rebellion of an unfortunate visionary." At great length, he retraced his dealings with General Mathews, maintaining that the Patriots' rebellion was fully justified, that the majority of the people in Florida favored it, that the people of Fernandina "who had surrendered their arms to us, were with their property perfectly secure," and that "any little excesses" that had been committed at the time of the evacuation could not be blamed on him. "I now flatter myself," he concluded, "I shall never again be called either a visionary or a marauder." He was not to get his wish. When Judge Reid and Judge Bronson began to take depositions in the compensations claims, witnesses by the dozens fingered two people—Mathews and McIntosh—as the men who had brought catastrophe crashing down upon their heads. McIntosh was spared this final besmirching of his name. He died in 1836, just as the claims cases began. His son, John Houston McIntosh Jr., and his son-in-law, Duncan Clinch, would both go on to become prominent Floridians.[25]

As for the other Patriot leaders, William Cone lived on to become a kind of Georgia version of Davy Crockett. He served with distinction in the War of 1812, became the center of many tall tales, remained a life-long friend of General John Floyd's, represented Camden County in the Georgia legislature, and eventually moved to Florida in 1842, where he also served in public office. Captain Abraham Massias won renown in the War of 1812 for his defeat of a British raiding party sent up the St. Marys River.[26]

James Dell eventually made his peace with the Spanish authorities and continued to reside in East Florida. He and his brothers returned to the Alachua territory, where they established a settlement that eventually became the town of Newnansville (1828), named after Daniel Newnan. He later became a member of the Territorial Legislature for Alachua County, where one of his brothers, Maxey, was clerk of the court and the other, Simeon, was sheriff. The Dells went on to serve in the area during the Second Seminole War. In 1841, Dell submitted a claim against the U.S. Treasury for the losses he had sustained during the Patriot War. Asked if he had been a Patriot, Dell replied that "he was, and is." Of all the former rebels, Dell was the only man who openly acknowledged to the claims court his support for the Patriot cause. With David Levy Yulee as his attorney, he pressed through a claim for $3,595 and won an award of $2,590. The next year, he won another $1,999 on behalf of his brother, William, killed in the attack at San Pablo in 1812.[27]

Thomas Adam Smith, commander of American forces in East Florida, rose to the rank of brigadier general during the War of 1812. At its conclusion, he took command of the Ninth Military Department in St. Louis and then resigned from the army to become receiver of public monies at New Franklin in 1818. He died in 1844.[28]

Sebastián Kindelán y O'Regan returned to Cuba on June 28, 1814, where, having already reached the rank of brigadier general, he took the post of subinspector of the island's military forces. He lived long enough to see Florida transferred to the United States, dying on July 17, 1822, after a grave illness.[29]

Juan José de Estrada continued for a while as interim governor of East Florida and then in 1815 was promoted to the prestigious post of sergeant major of the Plaza of Havana. Juan Bautista Witten, Benjamín Seguí, Tony Primus, and other officers and members of St. Augustine's free black militia lived on in East Florida, the recipients of various land grants for their services during the war. Antonio Proctor, the slave who tricked General Mathews and brought the Seminoles into the Patriot War, lived to an age in excess of 100 years and remained for a time in the Indian trade before establishing himself as a property owner near Tallahassee. Two of his grandsons served in the Florida legislature in the 1870s and 1880s.[30]

Ana María Williams, the widow of Samuel Williams, soon became Ana María (Williams) Hernández when she married Joseph M. Hernández and united her considerable wealth from the Orange Grove plantation to Mala Compra estate. Joseph Hernández, who was one of the attorneys in the claims cases, would later gain renown as a territorial delegate to Congress and as the officer who carried out General Thomas Jesup's orders to seize Osceola under a flag of truce during the Second Seminole War. The Arredondo family moved away to Cuba in the 1820s, but sent family representatives back to look after their claims for restitution and also to settle matters surrounding one of the largest land grants made in the last years of colonial rule, the Arredondo Grant, encompassing modern-day Micanopy, portions of Paynes Prairie, and Gainesville.[31]

George J. F. Clarke, the loyalist who called for a defense of Fernandina and had to flee East Florida to save his life, eventually became a magistrate for the Amelia Island area and continued as the surveyor general for Spanish East Florida. His fidelity to the Spanish cause reaped further reward in 1817 when Governor José Coppinger granted him 26,000 acres of land. After the transfer of the Floridas to the United States in 1821, Clarke remained one of the best-known men in East Florida, where he was considered a local expert on the period of Spanish rule. He wrote newspaper articles on topics ranging from the proper picking and storage of citrus to the nature of Spain's relations with the Indians and spoke out for the rights of free people of color. He did not live long enough to see the start of the claims for compensation. Nevertheless, his heirs and executors eventually saw a partial restoration of the losses he sustained in 1812 and 1813. In two suits brought on behalf of Clarke's estate, for the destruction of his business at Fernandina, his lumber camps, and his plantation on the Matanzas River, the U.S. Treasury assigned awards of $9,365 and $12,928. Clarke's brother, Charles, lived to testify during the claims cases and won $3,155 in an independent claim.[32]

To the end of his life, George Clarke remained first and foremost a Floridian, having resided in the colony under periods of British, Spanish, and American rule. "East Florida is the land of my nativity," he once said, "it has been the theater of my life, and I expect it to be the repository of my bones." Apparently, this was a sentiment shared by many others, for the descendents of the Pellicers, Solanas, Cosifacios, Maestres, O'Neills, Clarkes, Martinellis, Hartleys, Sánchezes, Harts, Dells, and dozens of other colonial families that survived the Patriot War continue to live in north Florida to the present day.[33]

Notes

Americans vs. Spaniards

1. This account is based on information from "Affairs of E. and W. Florida," Mathews to Robert Smith, n.d., Undated Miscellaneous Letters, Department of State, National Archives (Misc. Let., DS, NA), in Stagg, *Papers of James Madison*, 3: 123–24, and Testimony of Dr. James Hall, Additional Cross Interrogations, Claim of Francis X. Sánchez, No. 74,969, First Auditor, Records of the Accounting Offices of the Department of Treasury, Miscellaneous Division, relating to Claims and Accounts, Record Group 217, Entry 347, National Archives (hereafter First Aud., NA). It is not clear if the men all met together at one time, but they communicated their feelings among themselves.

2. Lovett, *Birth of Modern Spain*, 1: 85–120.

3. "Affairs of E. and W. Florida," in Stagg, *Papers of James Madison*, 3: 123–24; Lopez to White, July 30, 1810, Section 32, East Florida Papers, 1737–1858, Library of Congress (hereafter EFP, LC).

4. The major secondary sources on the Patriot War, in chronological order, are: *Secret Acts, Resolutions, and Instructions under which East Florida was Invaded by the United States Troops, Naval Forces, and Volunteers in 1812 and 1813, together with the official correspondence of the agents and officers of the government; United States, Appellants, v. Francis P. Ferreira, Administrator of Francis Pass, Deceased;* Julius W. Pratt, *Expansionists of 1812;* Isaac J. Cox, "The Border Missions of General George Mathews"; A. H. Phinney, "The First Spanish American War"; Rufus Kay Wyllys, "The East Florida Revolution of 1812–1814"; Paul Kruse, "A Secret Agent in East Florida: General George Mathews and the Patriot War"; Rembert W. Patrick, *Florida Fiasco: Rampant Rebels on the Georgia-Florida Border, 1810–1815;* Wanjohi Waciuma, *Intervention in Spanish Floridas, 1801–1813: A Study in Jeffersonian Foreign Policy;* Joseph H. Alexander, "The Ambush of Captain John Williams, U.S.M.C.: Failure of the East Florida Invasion, 1812–1813"; Joseph B. Smith, *The Plot to Steal Florida: James Madison's Phony War;* Frank L. Owsley Jr. and Gene A. Smith, *Filibusters and Expansionists, Jeffersonian Manifest Destiny, 1800–1821;* and Joseph H. Alexander, "Swamp Ambush in East Florida." For brief

assessments within more general texts, see Glenn Tucker, *Poltroons and Patriots, A Popular Account of the War of 1812*, 127–35; John K. Mahon, *War of 1812*, 194–98; Paul E. Hoffman, *Florida's Frontiers*, 260–68; and William S. Coker and Susan R. Parker, "The Second Spanish Period in the Two Floridas," 162–64.

5. The rebellion and American occupation in the Baton Rouge District of Spanish West Florida are extensively covered in Cox, *West Florida*. See also Waciuma, *Intervention*, 99–200, and Owsley and Smith, *Filibusters*, 7–9.

6. See discussion in Akins, "Georgians," 43–45, and in Tucker, *Poltroons and Patriots*, 131–35. Quote is from the *Savannah Republican*, April 11, 1812.

7. *New York Evening Post*, April 28, 1812.

8. *Augusta Chronicle*, May 15, 1812.

9. Mitchell to Kindelán, July 6, 1812, Letter No. 30, *United States v. Ferreira*, 87–88.

10. Copy of a letter from the governor of St. Augustine to the governor of Georgia, St. Augustine, December 12, 1812, *Weekly Register*, January 16, 1813.

11. *Federal Republican and Commercial Gazette*, November 30, 1812.

12. Byron, *Childe Harold's Pilgrimage*, 54.

13. *United States v. Ferreira*, 40, cites the figure $1.2 million and also reproduces the judge's comment. An itemized list of claimants, reporting the amount awarded by the judge and the amount allowed by the Treasury, can be found as a typescript in the Sánchez Family Papers, Miscellaneous Manuscripts Collection, PKY. It summarizes the former amount as $1,089,747.91 and the latter as $1,024,741.44. The final quote is from "Extract of a Second Letter from St. Marys, to a merchant in this city," *New York Evening Post*, October 16, 1812.

14. General John Floyd to Senator William Crawford, March 21, 1812, Misc. Let., DS, NA.

15. Lieutenant Colonel Thomas Adam Smith to Adjutant General and Inspector, June 4, 1812, Thomas Adam Smith Letterbook, Typescript in the T. Frederick Davis Collection, PKY (hereafter Smith Letterbook). Original in the Western Historical Manuscript Collection, Columbia, Missouri.

16. *United States Gazette For the Country—Extra*, November 24, 1813.

17. Two important collections that did not figure significantly in Patrick's account are the EFP, LC, and the compensation and claims cases contained in First Aud., NA.

18. Owsley and Smith, *Filibusters*, 16–31.

19. In the first half of the twentieth century, debate on causes of the War of 1812 focused on American desires for territorial conquest (Pratt, *Expansionists of 1812*) versus defense of maritime rights (Burt, *United States, Great Britain*). The latter interpretation gained ascendancy in the 1960s and 1970s with such works as Horsman, *Causes of the War of 1812*, and Brown, *Republic in Peril*, 164–73, and was summarized in Coles, *War of 1812*, 27–37. Egan, "Origins of the War of 1812," argued that desire to push aside western and southern Native American tribes was an important but secondary factor in support for war. Perkins, both in his *Prologue to War*, 418–37, and in his edited volume, *Causes*, identified southern expansionism

as one of the regional motives for war. Stagg, *Mr. Madison's War*, proposed that Madison was forced into war because of a lack of reasonable options. See also Hatzenbuehler and Ivie, *Congress Declares War*. Hickey, *War of 1812*, 1–3, 300, concluded that the war had its origins in a variety of economic and political issues, but he did not rank acquisition of territory as a major cause.

20. Akins, "Georgians," 43–55.

Chapter 1. Mr. Madison's Worries

1. Owsley and Smith, *Filibusters*, 16–31; Smith, *Republic of Letters*, 1356–58, 1383–84; Wills, *Madison*, 52.

2. Akins, "Georgians," 1–3; Hickey, *War of 1812*, 19–22; Wills, *Madison*, 50–55.

3. Johnson and Malone, *Dictionary of American Biography*, 184–93; Moore, *Madisons*, 238; Ketcham, *Madison*, 425–27, 441–73; Armstrong, "Madison," 317–25; Ellis, *Founding Brothers*, 82; Willis, *Madison*, 1–8; Smith, *Republic of Letters*, 1566–73; Stagg, *Mr. Madison's War*, 3; Lovett, *Birth of Modern Spain*, 1: 85–120.

4. Wills, *Madison*, 77–79; Waciuma, *Intervention*, 122–45.

5. Cox, *West Florida*, 150–60, 331–57, 388–407; Owsley and Smith, *Filibusters*, 7–8; Waciuma, *Intervention*, 148–62; White, *Folch*, 98–100.

6. Cox, *West Florida*, 397–400; Waciuma, *Intervention*, 178–87; Robert Smith to Governor Claiborne, October 27, 1810, and proclamation on West Florida, in the *National Intelligencer*, December 6, 1810. See also Wills, *Madison*, 77–79.

7. Owsley and Smith, *Filibusters*, 16–31; Ketcham, *Madison*, 425–26.

8. Murdoch, *Georgia-Florida Frontier*, 1–10; Coker and Parker, "Second Spanish Period," 150–66; Brooks, *Diplomacy*, 1–25; Olaechea and Ferrer Benimeli, *Conde de Aranda*, 142.

9. Lovett, *Birth of Modern Spain*, 1: 1–46.

10. Owsley and Smith, *Filibusters*, 10–13, 19–21, 61–64; Murdoch, *Georgia-Florida Frontier*, 3–5; Brooks, *Diplomacy*, 1–10; Patrick, *Fiasco*, 20–28.

11. Lovett, *Birth of Modern Spain*, 1: 21; Waciuma, *Intervention*, 14–98; Ammon, *Monroe*, 233–47; Hickey, *War of 1812*, 17–19; Blake and Lawrence, *Illustrated Companion*, 32–33. See Tucker and Reuter, *Injured Honor*, 41–43, 207–11, on the purchase and on the consequences of the *Chesapeake* affair.

12. Lovett, *Birth of Modern Spain*, 1: 85–179.

13. Hopkins, *Papers of Henry Clay*, 1: 516.

14. Madison to Monroe and Livingston, July 29, 1803, cited in Ketcham, *Madison*, 423; Patrick, *Fiasco*, 11–12. The final quote is from a report that Madison partially authored regarding the need to acquire New Orleans and the Floridas, *Annals of Congress*, 7th Cong., 2nd sess. (December 1802), 371–74.

15. Hickey, *War of 1812*, 18–19; Jefferson to General John Mason, December 1807, in Bergh, *Writings of Thomas Jefferson*, 11: 401–2; Stagg, *Mr. Madison's War*, 9–38; Tucker and Reuter, *Injured Honor*, 18–36.

16. Hickey, "American Trade Restrictions," 517–38; Graebner, "Secretary of State," 258–73; Hickey, *War of 1812*, 20–24; Ketcham, *Madison*, 465–66; Senator

Randolph, April 14, 1808, *Annals of Congress*, 10th Cong., 1st sess. (April 1808), 2136; Senator Bayard, *Annals of Congress*, 10th Cong., 2nd sess. (February 1809), 404.

17. Hickey, *War of 1812*, 20–22; Smith, *Republic of Letters*, 1548–54, 1614–23.

18. Excerpts reprinted in the *National Intelligencer*, December 27, 1810. For additional comments, see ibid., December 25, 1810.

19. *Abridgement*, 251; see also Richardson, *Compilation*, 1: 484.

20. Richardson, ibid., 1: 488; see also *Georgia Journal*, July 17, 1811.

21. Richardson, ibid.

22. Hickey, *War of 1812*, 9–35; Smith, *Republic of Letters*, 1548–54, 1650–58; Stagg, *Mr. Madison's War*, 48–55.

23. Ketcham, *Madison*, 484–85; Rutland, "Presidency," 273–80; Smith, *Republic of Letters*, 1650–58.

24. Hickey, *War of 1812*, 30; Patrick, *Fiasco*, 114–15.

25. Hickey, ibid., 5–6, 21.

26. *Abridgement*, 355; Waciuma, *Intervention*, 201–2; *National Intelligencer*, January 5, 1811.

27. *Abridgement*, 255–61; Waciuma, *Intervention*, 203–4; *National Intelligencer*, January 8, 1811.

28. *Abridgement*, 264.

29. Cited in Waciuma, *Intervention*, 205, and Ford, *Writings of Thomas Jefferson*, 290.

30. Waciuma, ibid., 183; Morier to Wellesley, January 12, 1811, Foreign Office 5/74, PRO.

31. Toulmin to Madison, Private and Confidential, November 19, 22, 28, 1810, January 23, 1811, Mad. Papers, LC; Cox, *West Florida*, 176.

32. Reprinted in the *Georgia Argus*, July 17, 1811; Waciuma, *Intervention*, 174–76.

33. Waciuma, ibid., 209–14.

Chapter 2. A Plot Thickens

1. Singleton, *Story of the White House*, 1: 55–60; Seale, *President's House*, 1: 119–30; Klapthor, *Benjamin Latrobe and Dolley Madison*. On Mathews, see *Dictionary of American Biography*, 403–4, and Patrick, *Fiasco*, 4–6.

2. *Dictionary of American Biography*, ibid.; Patrick, ibid.; *Biographical Directory*, 1298.

3. Senator William Crawford to Robert Smith, November 1, 1810, Colonel Ralph Isaacs to Monroe, July 3, 1814, Misc. Let., DS, NA; Patrick, *Fiasco*, 12–15; Waciuma, *Intervention*, 146–48; Cox, "Border Missions," 310–13.

4. "Affairs of E. and W. Florida," in Stagg, *Papers of James Madison*, 3: 123–24. Years later, Dr. James Hall also implicated McIntosh and Arredondo in an intrigue in 1810, adding that William Craig and George Cook (both of whom became Patriots)

were also involved. Testimony of Dr. James Hall, Additional Cross Interrogations, Claim of Francis X. Sánchez, No. 74,969, First Aud., NA. See also Troup to Madison, June 28, 1811, in Stagg, ibid., 4: 518.

5. "Affairs of E. and W. Florida," ibid.

6. *United States v. Ferreira*, 17.

7. Reference to Floyd is in George Mathews to James Madison, April 16, 1812, in Stagg, *Papers of James Madison*, 4: 328, in which the general reminded the president that he made the recommendation "when I last saw you." The incident about Dr. Hall was reported in William Craig to Governor Estrada, August 5, 1811, Section 32, EFP, LC. See also Lopez to White, July 30, September 2, October 29, 1810, and White to Lopez, October 23, 1810, Section 32, EFP, LC. Mathews was acquainted with Hall and knew his fate. See also DuPree and Taylor, "Hall," 626–27.

8. *Secret Acts*, 3–4; Wyllys, "East Florida," 421; Clay to Caesar A. Rodney and Bill Authorizing Occupation of East Florida, in Hopkins, *Papers of Henry Clay*, 1: 520–22. Clay was a member of the Senate at this time but would shortly join the House as Speaker. Ralph Isaacs later claimed that the $100,000 included bribe money for Governor Folch; Isaacs to Monroe, July 3, 1814, Misc. Let., DS, NA.

9. *Secret Acts*, 4–7; Waciuma, *Intervention*, 212–16; Colonel Ralph Isaacs to Monroe, July 3, 1814, Misc. Let., DS, NA.

10. *Secret Acts*, 4–5; Waciuma, *Intervention*, 213–16; Cox, "Border Missions," 314–15; Robert Smith to George Mathews and John McKee, January 26, 1811, Dom. Let., DS, NA.

11. *Secret Acts*, ibid., emphasis added; John Houston McIntosh later called attention to this phrase, noting that as there was no legal government in East Florida aside from the governor, the reference to an alternative "local authority" clearly meant a rebel government, such as the one he created with Mathews's help. "Communication to the Editors," *National Intelligencer*, July 2, 1823.

12. *Secret Acts*, 4; Smith to Mathews and McKee, January 25, 1811, Dom. Let., DS, NA; Patrick, *Fiasco*, 14–15.

13. Eustis to Thomas Adam Smith, January 26, 1811, Sec. War, NA; Waciuma, *Intervention*, 222–23.

14. Hamilton to Hugh Campbell, January 25, 26, 1811, Sec. Navy, NA; Waciuma, ibid., 216–20.

15. Patrick, *Fiasco*, 16–17.

16. Ibid., 43–45; Reddick, *Camden's Challenge*, 150.

17. Vocelle, *Camden County*, 34–37, 61–63.

18. For commerce and prices, see Patrick, *Fiasco*, 45; Shambaugh, "Development of Agriculture," 65–66; Schafer, "Laurel Grove," 102–5; Kruse, "Secret Agent," 193–218. See also Testimony of Dr. James Hall, Claim of Francis X. Sánchez, No. 74,969, First Aud., NA.

19. *Secret Acts*, 6.

20. The story of the West Florida mission is fully covered in Waciuma, *Interven-*

tion, 224–34; Patrick, *Fiasco,* 30–32; Cox, "Border Missions," 316; Cox, *West Florida,* 520–29; White, *Folch,* 89–105; and McKee to Smith, April 24, 1811, McKee to Monroe, June 5, 1811, TP, NA.

Chapter 3. Georgia and Spanish East Florida, a Clash of Cultures

1. Lovett, *Birth of Modern Spain,* 1: 1–3, 385–90; Anna, "Independence," 60–63; Owsley and Smith, *Filibusters,* 4–15, 41–43; Jensen, *Children,* 1; William Shaler to Robert Smith, Havana, February 20, 1811, Misc. Let., DS, NA.

2. Bushnell, "Peripheral Perspective," 18; Arnade, "Raids," 106–8, 111–14; Hoffman, *Florida's Frontiers,* 176–79, 193–95; Landers, *Black Society,* 35–39.

3. Fabel, "British Rule"; Porter, "Negroes," 12–16; Hoffman, ibid., 202–34; Parker, "Men without God," 21–24; Schafer, "Not so Gay"; Griffin, "Spanish Return."

4. Tanner, *Zéspedes; Augusta Chronicle and Gazette of the State,* January 4, 1794; Murdoch, *Georgia-Florida Frontier,* 4–9.

5. Weber, *Spanish Frontier,* 271–75; Tanner, ibid., 153; *Return of the Whole Number of Persons,* 20; *Aggregate Amount,* 80–81; Akins, "Georgians," 9.

6. Census figures compiled from Johnson, "Spanish St. Augustine"; Landers, *Black Society,* 82; Hoffman, *Florida's Frontiers,* 238–39; Mills, *Florida's First Families,* 111–22; and Tornero, *Relaciones,* 24–63. See also Lockey, *East Florida,* and Griffin, *Mullet.* The postwar population (1814) was 3,081, of whom 1,302 were whites, 128 were free people of color, and 1,651 were slaves.

7. Forbes, *Sketches,* 57; Miller, *Environmental History,* 134, 145–53; Landers, *Black Society,* 103; Parker, "Men without God," 9–18, 47–78; Tornero, ibid., 13–23.

8. Murdoch, *Georgia-Florida Frontier,* 11–37; Murdoch, "Elijah Clarke"; Wright, *Bowles,* 142–58.

9. Coleman, *History of Georgia,* 92, 96, 100, 105–9, 116–26; Saye, *Constitutional History,* 142–45; Akins, "Georgians," 26–27. Quote is from Appleby, *Inheritors,* 65. See also Zelinsky, "Isochronic Map," 191–95; Hodler and Schretter, *Atlas,* 74–76; Wright, *Creeks and Seminoles,* 6–14; Vocelle, *Camden County,* 34–54.

10. Coleman, ibid., 105–9; Saye, ibid., 159–54; Johnson, "State in the Making," 16–17; Heath, "Yazoo Land Fraud," 274–91; Akins, "Georgians," 9; Coulter, *Georgia,* 194.

11. Coleman, ibid., 116–26; Akins, ibid., 6–21.

12. Akins, ibid., 26–28.

13. Harlan, "Military History," 206; Hoffman, *Florida's Frontiers,* 234–60; Estrada to Someruelos, April 16, 1811, Section 2, EFP, LC; Libros de Servicios de los Officiales Sargentos de Primer Clase, y Cadetes de los Tres Batallones de Regimiento de Infantería de la Havana, Sección de Guerra, Archivo General de Simancas, Legajo 7264; Interim Governor to Justo Lopez, January 30, 1812, Section 32, EFP, LC; Corbitt, "Administration, II," 57–67; Hess, "Letters."

14. Bermudez, "Situado," 15–24, 39–59, 66; Tornero, *Relaciones,* 90–121; Cusick,

"Across the Border"; Hoffman, *Florida's Frontiers*, 256; White to Someruelos, February 11, 1811, Estrada to Someruelos, July 4, 1811, Section 2, EFP, LC. Estrada eventually received 128,463 pesos.

15. Tornero, ibid., 195, 197; Ward, "Commerce."

16. Coker and Parker, "Second Spanish Period," 157–58; Rutherford, "Spain's Immigration Policy," 62–72; Griffin, *Mullet*; Landers, *Black Society*, 84, 106, 202–28; Marotti, "Wanton," 460–61.

17. Weber, *Spanish Frontier*, 272; Coker and Parker, "Second Spanish Period," 157–62; Murdoch, *Georgia-Florida Frontier*, 6–7; Estrada to Someruelos, September 16, 1811, Gifts to the Indians, Section 2, EFP, LC; Corbitt, "Papers, II," 81; Corbitt, "Papers, V," 376; Corbitt, "Administration," 64–67; Letter reprinted in the *Philadelphia Gazette and Daily Advertiser*, July 21, 1800.

18. Landers, *Black Society*, 29–60, 205–20. See also Landers, "Traditions," 34; *Georgia Gazette*, September 23, 1790; Simmons, *Notices*, 76.

19. Claims from First Aud., NA, as well as census records suggest this figure of 1,500 to 2,000, depending on the year in question. Schafer, "Laurel Grove," 98–102; Landers, ibid., 81–82, 174–82; Landers, "Traditions," 30; Deposition of William Craig, Don Luis José de François Richard contra Guillermo Dell, January 16, 1810, Section 65, EFP, LC.

20. Landers, *Black Society*, 222.

21. Murdoch, *Georgia-Florida Frontier*, 42–43, 84–92; Bennett, *Florida's "French" Revolution*, 29, 149, 177; Landers, "Rebellion and Royalism," 160–61; Miller, *Quesada*, 125–66; Hoffman, *Florida's Frontiers*, 248–60.

22. Murdoch, ibid., 105, 109–11, 124, 126; Hoffman, *Florida's Frontiers*, 251; Murdoch, "Seagrove-White," 264; Patrick, *Fiasco*, 52; Bennett, *Florida's "French" Revolution*, 117–18.

23. Bennett, ibid., 179, 75–78; Howes, "Frontiers of Georgia," 92.

24. Howes, ibid., 91; Murdoch, *Georgia-Florida Frontier*, 124–33.

25. *Charleston Evening Courier*, August 10, 1798.

26. Christian, *Founders*, 36; White to Governor of Georgia, February 10, 1807, Section 27, EFP, LC; Patrick, *Fiasco*, 53. On the O'Neill case, see Bullard, *Cumberland Island*, 111.

27. Murdoch, "Dr. Daniel Turner," 92.

28. Ward, "Commerce"; Akins, "Georgians," 18–19; Green, "Crawford," 17–27; *National Intelligencer and Washington Advertiser*, February 22, 1809.

29. Mitchell to Floyd, March 14, 1811, GGL, GDAH.

30. Akins, "Georgians," 20–25, 43–45; McCall, *History of Georgia*, 3–6, 98–105; *Georgia Argus*, January 6, 23, February 13, 1811; *Georgia Journal*, September 12, 1810, January 30, 1811.

31. Ketcham, *Madison*, 423; Green, "Crawford," 27–29; *National Intelligencer and Washington Advertiser*, February 22, 1809.

Chapter 4. Intrigues and Discoveries

1. Ammon, *Monroe*, 7–24; Owsley and Smith, *Filibusters*, 29–31, 32–60; Ketcham, *Madison*, 486–91; Biedzynski, "Monroe," 359–62; Stagg, *Mr. Madison's War*, 62–64.

2. Ammon, ibid.; Biedzynski, "Monroe," 359–62; Monroe to Jefferson, November 1, 1805, in Hamilton, *Letters*, 4: 352; Stagg, *Mr. Madison's War*, 63.

3. Monroe to Mathews, June 29, 1811, TP, NA.

4. Patrick, *Fiasco*, 40; Mathews to Monroe, June 28, 1811, TP, NA.

5. *Secret Acts*, 7; Mathews to Monroe, ibid.

6. At this time, there were four American gunboats patrolling the St. Marys River and 200 men at Point Peter, so that Mathews viewed his mission as adequately supported by the military. For his desires regarding a leader, see Patrick, *Fiasco*, 55.

7. Ibid., 19, 52; Johnston, *Houstons*, 345–47.

8. Patrick, ibid., 52; Johnston, ibid.

9. Patrick, ibid., 48; Mathews to Monroe, August 3, 1811, in *Secret Acts*, 7.

10. It is not altogether clear when these men joined their fortunes to Mathews's. Francisco Roman Sánchez and Dr. James Hall, both early adherents of the Patriots, indicated in later testimony that Ashley, Harris, and others associated with St. Marys were part of the plot as it formed in 1811, although Lodowick Ashley claimed he never joined until Mathews was ready to act. See Claim of Francis X. Sánchez, No. 74,969, First Aud., NA. On Harris, see Lopez to White, September 2, 1810, Section 32, EFP, LC. On Ashley, see Vocelle, *Camden County*, 39–42; Christian, *Founders of St. Marys*, 36–44; Burrus, "Confiscated Property."

11. Patrick, *Fiasco*, 52.

12. Mathews to Monroe, August 3, 1811, TP, NA; Pratt, *Expansionists*, 77–78; Wyllys, "East Florida," 423.

13. On timber cutting, see Lopez to Estrada, April 7, June 1, 1811, Section 32, EFP, LC. On troop movements, see Lopez to Estrada, May 2, 13, 20, 1811, Section 32, EFP, LC. On Fernandina, see White to Someruelos, January 17, 1811, Section 2, EFP, LC; Estrada to Lopez, April 26, 29, 1811, Lopez to Estrada, May 6, 1811, Estrada to Lopez, June 8, 1811, Lopez to Estrada, June 17, 1811, Clarke to Estrada, June 23, 1811, Estrada to Clarke, June 26, 1811, Estrada to Lopez, July 24, 1811, Section 32, EFP, LC.

14. Estrada to Someruelos, May 26, 1811, Section 2, EFP, LC; Craig to Estrada, June 23, 1811, Section 32, EFP, LC.

15. McIntosh to Craig, July 23, 1811, Section 32, EFP, LC; Estrada to Someruelos, August 2, 1811, Section 2, EFP, LC.

16. McIntosh to Estrada, forwarded to Onís, July 24, 1811, Section 32, EFP, LC; Testimony of Dr. James Hall, Additional Cross Interrogations, Claim of Francis X. Sánchez, No. 74,969, First Auditor, NA.

17. Craig to Estrada, August 5, 1811, Section 32, EFP, LC. Dr. Hall gave a very different account of the 1810 intrigue. According to Hall, it was headed by Craig, McIntosh, and Arredondo because of a quarrel with Governor White. When Hall

refused to help, he said, these three men cooked up charges against him to get him banished from the colony before he could talk. Testimony of Dr. James Hall, ibid.

18. Estrada to Someruelos, August 2, 1811, Section 2, EFP, LC; Lopez to Estrada, August 16, 1811, Section 4, EFP, LC; Onís to Governor of Florida, August 21, 1811, Section 26, EFP, LC.

Chapter 5. The Diplomacy of Deception

1. Information on the 1810 conspiracy is taken from "Affairs of E. and W. Florida," in Stagg, *Papers of James Madison*, 3: 123–24, and Testimony of Dr. James Hall, Additional Cross Interrogations, Claim of Francis X. Sánchez, No. 74,969, First Aud., NA. Lopez was probably acting as a spy, for he was reporting on American activities throughout 1810 and 1811. The motives of the other men are unknown. Mathews said they were worried about collapse within the Spanish empire. Hall said they were angry with Governor White. Lovett, *Birth of Modern Spain*, 1: 385–414.

2. Johnston, *Houstons*, 366–69; Cusick, "Oaths."

3. Muster Roll, First Company of St. Johns, Section 23, EFP, LC; *United States v. Ferreira*, 18.

4. Craig to Estrada, July 26, 1811, Arredondo to Estrada, July 26, 1811, Estrada to McIntosh, July 26, 1811, Section 32, EFP, LC.

5. Patrick, *Fiasco*, 19, 50–52, 56–58; Testimony of Dr. James Hall, Claim of Francis X. Sánchez, No. 74,969, First Aud., NA; Johnston, *Houstons*, 366–69. See also McIntosh's lengthy statement about his participation in the rebellion in "Communication to the Editors," *National Intelligencer*, July 2, 1823.

6. "Communication to the Editors," ibid.

7. Bernaben to Monroe, June 7, 1811, Span. Leg., DS, NA.

8. Coles, *War of 1812*, 15; Ammon, *Monroe*, 294–96.

9. Hickey, *War of 1812*, 24; Ammon, ibid., 294–96; Monroe to Lord Auckland(?), n.d., in Hamilton, *Writings of James Monroe*, 192.

10. Foster to Monroe, July 2, 1811, *American State Papers*, 126–28; Foster to Wellesley, July 5, 1811, Foreign Office 5/76, PRO; Monroe to Foster, July 8, 1811, *American State Papers*, 128; Ammon, *Monroe*, 296.

11. The encounter is in Ammon, ibid. The quote is from Foster to Wellesley, July 5, 1811, ibid.

12. Ammon, ibid., 289–90, and, quoted material, Foster to Wellesley, August 5, 1811, ibid.

13. Onís to Monroe, September 5, 1811, Span. Leg., DS, NA.

14. Foster to Monroe, September 5, 1811, *American State Papers*, 131; Foster to Wellesley, September 10, 13, 1811, Foreign Office 5/76, PRO.

15. Ammon, *Monroe*, 299; Ketcham, *Madison*, 508–9; Stagg, *Mr. Madison's War*, 78–79.

16. Ammon, ibid., 299–300; Monroe to Foster, November 2, 1811, *American State Papers*, 132–34.

17. *National Intelligencer*, November 9, 1811.

18. Ammon, *Monroe*, 129.

19. *Secret Acts*, 8; Mathews to Monroe, October 14, 1811, TP, NA; Patrick, *Fiasco*, 58–59.

20. Patrick, ibid., 59.

21. Ibid., 64.

22. Ibid., 64–65; Mathews to Madison, April 16, 1812, Mad. Papers, LC; Mathews to Monroe, April 16, 1812, TP, NA; *National Intelligencer*, July 2, 1823.

23. Patrick, *Fiasco*, 56–57.

24. Ibid., 64–65; Claim of Gabriel Priest, No. 82,301, First Aud., NA; Testimony of George J. F. Clark, *United States v. Ferreira*, 18; on Ashley, see Patrick, ibid., 45, 65; Testimony of Archibald Clark, *United States v. Ferreira*, 28–29; Vocelle, *Camden County*, 34; Lopez to Estrada, July 29, 1811, Section 32, EFP, LC; Wyllys, "East Florida," 427; Parker, "Men without God," 161; Burrus, "Confiscated Property." Other early adherents seem to have been George Morrison, the overseer at McIntosh's Ortega estate, and Abner Broadway.

25. Patrick, ibid., 65, 71.

26. Lopez to Estrada, August 5, 12, September 9, 30, October 2, 1811, Section 32, EFP, LC.

27. Estrada to Someruelos, July 4, September 2, 1811, Section 2, EFP, LC; Someruelos to Estrada, October 3, 1811, Section 1, EFP, LC.

28. Lopez to Estrada, October 28, November 4, 25, 1811, Section 32, EFP, LC.

29. Lopez to Estrada, November 25, December 30, 1811, ibid.; Onís to Estrada, November 7, 1811, Section 26, EFP, LC.

Chapter 6. General Mathews Meets a Crisis

1. *National Intelligencer*, December 7, 1811, January 11, 1812; Jefferson to Madison, December 11, 1811, Madison to Jefferson, February 7, 1812, Smith, *Republic of Letters*, 1686–87; Foster to Wellesley, January 13, 1812, Foreign Office 5/84, PRO.

2. *Georgia Journal*, December 11, 1811.

3. Testimony of George J. F. Clarke, Claim of Francisco and Peter Pons, No. 73,347, First Aud., NA; Estrada to Thomson, April 15, 1812, Admiralty 1/502, PRO.

4. Governor of Florida to Apodaca, Review of the Third Infantry Battalion of Cuba, April 12, July 20, 1812, Legajo 1789, 269–81, PC; Militia Muster Rolls, First and Second Company of St. Johns and Third Company of Amelia Island, Section 28, EFP, LC.

5. El Marques de Someruelos to Francisco Max. de San Maxent, January 2, 1812, Legajo 152b, PC.

6. Craig to Estrada, January 6, 1812, Section 32, EFP, LC.

7. Craig to Estrada, February 16, 1812, ibid.

8. Lopez to Estrada, January 28, 1812, ibid.

9. *Secret Acts*, 9; Patrick, *Fiasco*, 66.

10. Campbell to Hamilton, January 11, 4, 1812, CL, NA; Patrick, ibid., 66–67.

11. Patrick, ibid., 68–69; Foster to Wellesley, April 12, 1812, Foreign Office 5/85, PRO.

12. Testimony of Dr. James Hall, answer to Additional Cross Interrogations, No. 2, Claim of Francis X. Sánchez, No. 74,969, First Aud., NA, emphasis added. The "Tan Yard" was probably Isaac Weeks's tanning facility, which lay just beyond María Sánchez Creek on the west side of town; Claim of Isaac Weeks, No. 75,215, First Aud., NA.

13. Testimony of Dr. James Hall, ibid.

14. Ibid.

15. Patrick, *Fiasco*, 70–72.

16. *Secret Acts*, 12.

17. Wyllys to McIntosh, March 10, 1812, TP, NA; Wyllys, "East Florida," 431; *United States v. Ferreira*, 65–66.

18. Mathews to Monroe, March 14, 1812, TP, NA. Both Patrick, *Fiasco*, 87, and Wyllys, "East Florida," 431, indicate that Lopez wrote to the magistrates of St. Marys on March 10 and that this might have prompted the spy's warning. *United States v. Ferreira*, 65–66, gives a transcription of this letter. However, original source material suggests that the date of this letter in secondary sources is wrong and that Lopez did not write until March 15, at which point Mathews's attack was already well advanced.

19. Campbell promptly delivered the muskets to Lieutenant Appling; Mathews to Campbell, March 11, 1812, in *Secret Acts*, 9.

20. *Secret Acts*, 12.

21. Patrick, *Fiasco*, 73–74, and ibid.

22. *Secret Acts*, 12–13; Patrick, ibid.

23. *Secret Acts*, 13; Patrick, ibid., 74.

24. Patrick, ibid., 75; Laval to Mathews, March 12, 1812, TP, NA.

25. Patrick, ibid., 75–76.

26. Ibid., 76–77.

27. Ibid., 77; Testimony of Dr. Hall, Claim of Francis X. Sánchez, No. 74,969, First Aud., NA.

28. Testimony of Dr. Hall, ibid.

29. McIntosh to Troup, March 12, 1812, TP, NA; Patrick, *Fiasco*, 69.

30. Floyd to Crawford, March 21, 1812, TP, NA; Patrick, *Fiasco*, 83–84, gives Friday, March 13, as the date for the public reading of the manifesto. Waciuma, *Intervention*, 248–53, is unclear on this point but says the cession of Rose's Bluff to the United States took place on March 14; Wyllys, "East Florida," 429, states the public reading was on March 14.

31. *Secret Acts*, 10–11.

32. Mathews to Monroe, March 14, 1812, TP, NA, emphasis added; Waciuma, *Intervention*, 254–55.

33. Russell and Stellings to Cashen, March 13, 1812, Section 32, EFP, LC; Estado

de la rendición de Fernandina, by Henry Yonge, March 24, 1812, in Section 28, EFP, LC; Testimony of Charles Clarke, Claim of George J. F. Clarke, of Clarke and Garvin, No. 83,763, First Aud., NA; Clarke, "Surrender," 90–95, and Patrick, *Fiasco*, 87.

34. Laval to Mathews, March 12, 1812, Misc. Let., DS, NA; Patrick, ibid., 78–79. The entire affair with Laval is covered in Patrick, 70–82, and in Waciuma, *Intervention*, 242–58.

35. Campbell to Mathews, March 14, 1811, CL, NA.

Chapter 7. The Fall of Fernandina

1. Testimony of Peter Pons, Claim of George J. F. Clarke, No. 83,177. The Latin in this case is nonsensical.

2. Testimony of George J. F. Clarke, Claim of Pedro and Francisco Pons, No. 73,347, Testimony of John Abernathy, Claim of George J. F. Clarke, No. 83,177, First Aud., NA. Other sources identify Cutchins's gunboat as No. 115; Campbell to Hamilton, April 1, 1812, CL, NA.

3. Wolff, "Fernandina"; Jaccard, *Historic Splendor*, 97–101; Patrick, *Fiasco*, 45–48; Clarke to Estrada, June 23, 1811, Section 32, EFP, LC; "Plano del proyecto para el Nuevo pueblo de Fernandina," 1811, by George J. F. Clarke, Map Division, NA, and reproduced as R1.1811.001.1997.0232, Map Collection, PKY.

4. Wolff, ibid.; Jaccard, ibid.; "Plano del proyecto," ibid., NA.

5. "Carta del espacio entre La Georgia y la Ysla Amalia," 1811, by George J. F. Clarke, Section 47, EFP, LC, and reproduced as R1.1811.002.1997.1507, Map Collection, PKY; "Sketch map of land between Nassau and St. Marys Rivers," by Philip Robert Yonge [Phelipe Yonge], August 3, 1813, Section 34, EFP, LC. See also "Manuscript map of the territory between the St. Marys and St. Johns rivers in East Florida" and "A map given to Major General Andrew Jackson," in Ward, *Old Hickory's Town*, 79, 104–5.

6. Ward, "Commerce"; Merchants of Fernandina to the Governor, October 23, 1811, Section 44, EFP, LC; Knetsch, "Development of Amelia Island," 6–7.

7. Landers, *Black Society*, 174–77; Schafer, "Family Ties," 2.

8. Reported in *Secret Acts*, 9–14, and in Campbell to Hamilton, March 21, 1812, CL, NA.

9. Clarke, "Surrender," 90; Russell and Stellings to James Cashen, March 13, 1812, Section 32, EFP, LC.

10. Estado de la rendición de Fernandina, Section 28, EFP, LC; Claim of Felipe Solana, No. 73,063, First Aud., NA; Lopez to Estrada, March 14, 1812, Section 32, EFP, LC.

11. Clarke, "Surrender," 91; Estado de la rendición de Fernandina, ibid.

12. Lowe to Lopez, March 15, 1812, Section 32, EFP, LC.

13. Claim of John Lowe, No. 73,359, First Aud., NA.

14. Patrick, *Fiasco*, 84–86; Testimony of Samuel Swearingen, Claim of George and Margaret Starratt, No. 78,509, First Aud., NA.

15. Testimony of William McCullough, Claim of Stephen Vanzandt, No. 83,057, First Aud., NA.

16. Testimony of Samuel Russell, Claim of Joseph Higginbotham, No. 82,989, First Aud., NA.

17. Claim of John Lowe, 1837, No. 73,359, First Aud., NA. Some sources report that two advanced pickets were taken. Lopez said it was three; Lopez to Estrada, March 16, 1812, Section 32, EFP, LC.

18. For the Atkinsons, see Murdoch, *Georgia-Florida Frontier*, 5, 71–104; Lopez to Magistrates of St. Marys, March 15, 1812, Letter No. 1, *United States v. Ferreira*, 65. (Original versions, MC-31–2, SAHS, and Hawks Papers, New-York Historical Society.) Spanish versions of all letters in *United States v. Ferreira* are in submissions to the Senate, January 19, 1813, TPSen, NA. See also Patrick, *Fiasco*, 87–95, and Waciuma, *Intervention*, 258–68.

19. Clarke, "Surrender," 90–91; Estado de la rendición de Fernandina, Section 28, EFP, LC; Floyd to Crawford, March 21, 1812, Misc. Let., DS, NA.

20. "Plano del proyecto para el Nuevo pueblo de Fernandina," Map Division, NA.

21. Campbell to Secretary of the Navy, April 11, 1812, CL, NA.

22. Ibid.

23. The general had stipulated that he wanted one gunboat stationed at Rose's Bluff to protect the Patriots; two more at the mouth of Bells River, where their flotilla would emerge; and others opposite Fernandina itself. Mathews to Campbell, March 15, 1812, in *Secret Acts*, 11; Campbell to Secretary of the Navy, April 11, 1812, CL, NA.

24. Testimony of George J. F. Clarke, *United States v. Ferreira*, 18; Claim of George G. F. Clarke, of Clarke and Garvin, No. 83,763, Testimony of John Abernathy, Claim of George J. F. Clarke, No. 83,177, Testimony of George J. F. Clarke, Claim of Pedro and Francisco Pons, No. 73,347, First Aud., NA.

25. Estado de la rendición de Fernandina, Section 28, EFP, LC. Lopez said the sentries arrived between 11 P.M. and midnight; Lopez to Estrada, March 16, 1812, Section 32, EFP, LC.

26. The entire text of this letter was published as McIntosh to Lopez, March 15, 1812, Letter No. 3, *United States v. Ferreira*, 66–67. (Original versions, MC-31–3, SAHS, and Hawks Papers, New-York Historical Society.)

27. McIntosh to Lopez, ibid. McIntosh probably thought Mathews had succeeded in dispatching gunboats to the St. Johns River and hence claimed to be in control of the entire northern district. Lopez also feared there were gunboats on the St. Johns. Lopez to Estrada, March 15, 16, 1812, Section 32, EFP, LC.

28. Testimony of Dr. Hall, Claim of Francis X. Sánchez, No. 74,969, First Aud., NA.

29. Estado de la rendición de Fernandina, Section 28, EFP, LC.

30. Hill, "Clarke"; Landers, *Black Society*, 242–43; Patrick, *Fiasco*, 88.

31. Clarke, "Surrender," 90.

32. Lodowick Ashley to Don Justo Lopez, March 16, 1812, Letter No. 4, *United States v. Ferreira*, 67–68. (Original versions, MC-31-5, SAHS, and Hawks Papers, New-York Historical Society.)

33. Justo Lopez to Commodore Campbell, March 16, 1812, George Atkinson and George J. F. Clarke to Justo Lopez, March 16, 1812, Hugh Campbell to Don Justo Lopez, March 17, 1812, Letters Nos. 9, 10, and 11, *United States v. Ferreira*, 70–77. (Original versions, MC-31-7, MC-31-4, and MC-31-10, SAHS, and Hawks Papers, New-York Historical Society.) José Hibberson and José de la Maza Arredondo to Justo Lopez, March 17, 1812, Letter No. 14, *United States v. Ferreira*, 72–74. (Original versions, MC-31-13, SAHS, and Hawks Papers, New-York Historical Society.) Justo Lopez to General Mathews, and Philip R. Yonge and George Atkinson to Justo Lopez, March 17, 1812, Letters Nos. 15 and 16, *United States v. Ferreira*, 74–76. (Original versions, MC-31-12 and MC-31-14, SAHS, and Hawks Papers, New-York Historical Society.)

34. Estado de la rendición de Fernandina, Section 28, EFP, LC.

35. Patrick, *Fiasco*, 90; Campbell to Secretary of War, April 16, 1812, CL, NA. Tucker, *Jeffersonian Gunboat Navy*, 99–100, discusses the arrangements made between Mathews and Campbell with regard to the gunboats, though he mistakenly reports the surrender of Fernandina as March 18 instead of March 17, 1812.

36. George Atkinson and George J. F. Clarke to Justo Lopez, March 16, 1812, Letter No. 10, *United States v. Ferreira*, 70.

37. Patrick, *Fiasco*, 90–91; Hibberson and Yonge to Lopez, Letter No. 14, *United States v. Ferreira*, 72–74.

38. Hibberson and Arredondo to Justo Lopez, March 17, 1812, Letter No. 14, ibid.

39. Hibberson and Arredondo to Justo Lopez, ibid.; Laval to the Commandant of Amelia Island, March 16, 1812, Letter No. 13, ibid., 72. (Original versions, MC-31-9, SAHS, and Hawks Papers, New-York Historical Society.)

40. Hibberson and Arredondo to Lopez, March 17, 1812, Letter No. 14, and Commandant of Amelia Island to General Mathews, Letter No. 15, ibid., 72–74. See also Patrick, *Fiasco*, 91–92.

41. Hibberson and Arredondo to Lopez, March 17, 1812, ibid., 74, emphasis added.

42. Ibid.

43. Ibid.; Clarke, "Surrender," 92.

44. Testimony of Dr. Hall, Claim of Francis X. Sánchez, Claim No. 74,969, First Aud., NA.

45. This passage is excerpted directly from Patrick, *Fiasco*, 79–80, with the source cited as Personal Papers of Major Jacint Laval, War Records Office, NA. A search for the originals in 2000 failed to locate any collection with this title.

46. Patrick, ibid., 80, 95; Testimony of Winslow Foster, *United States v. Ferreira*, 26; Laval to Secretary of War, March 16, 1812, in *Secret Acts*, 12–13. See also Waciuma, *Intervention*, 256–58.

47. Patrick, ibid., 80.

48. Extracts of a letter from Major Laval to the War Department, *Secret Acts*, 12–13.

49. Patrick, *Fiasco*, 80–82; Extracts of a letter, ibid.

50. Campbell to Lopez, March 17, 1812, included in Campbell to Hamilton, April 11, 1812, CL, NA.

51. Yonge and Atkinson to Lopez, March 17, 1812, Letter No. 16, *United States v. Ferreira*, 75–76, and Testimony of Winslow Foster, ibid., 25. Foster, many years after the fact, described the armaments as six 32-pounders, one long-18, and six 9-pounders, but this does not agree with the officially listed armaments for the boats. See Tucker, *Jeffersonian Gunboat Navy*, 57–58, 62, 191, 195, 197–200, for specifications on the gunboats stationed at St. Marys in 1812, including two that took station before Fernandina. See also Arredondo to Girard, March 21, 1812, TP, NA.

52. "Plano del ataque de Fernandina el 17 de Marzo de 1812," attributed to George J. F. Clarke, enclosed in Juan José de Estrada, May 16, 1812, Legajo 1789, PC. See also Gonzalez, *Catalogo de Mapas y Planos*, 83.

53. All the subsequent material, including the direct quotations, is taken from the report of Yonge and Atkinson to Lopez, March 17, 1812, Letter No. 16, *United States v. Ferreira*, 75–76; Patrick, *Fiasco*, 93–95.

54. Yonge and Atkinson to Lopez, ibid.

55. Ibid.

56. Ibid.

57. Ibid.

58. Lodowick Ashley to Atkinson and Yonge, March 17, 1812, Letter No. 8, *United States v. Ferreira*, 69. (Original versions, MC-31–15, SAHS, and Hawks Papers, New-York Historical Society.)

59. "Plano del ataque," Legajo 1789, PC; Thompson to Girard, March 21, 1812, TP, NA.

60. Testimony of Winslow Foster, *United States v. Ferreira*, 25.

61. Campbell to Hamilton, March 21, 1812, CL, NA.

62. Patrick, *Fiasco*, 96–97. The armaments of gunboat No. 62 are described in Tucker, *Jeffersonian Gunboat Navy*, 191, and the dialogue is from Testimony of Winslow Foster, *United States v. Ferreira*, 26–27. The orders not to fire are from Campbell to Hamilton, March 21, 1812, CL, NA.

63. Estado de la rendición de Fernandina, Section 28, EFP, LC; Testimony of George Clarke, *United States v. Ferreira*, 18; Thompson to Girard, March 21, 1812, TP, NA; Floyd to Crawford, March 21, 1812, Misc. Let., DS, NA. "Plano del ataque," Legajo 1789, PC, shows the oared boats.

64. Testimony of George Clarke, ibid.

65. The rising panic was noted in Clarke, "Surrender," 93; Estado de la rendición de Fernandina, ibid.; Pedro Pons, Claim of George J. F. Clarke, No. 83,177, says there were about 300 men. Other witnesses say between 200 and 270. Clarke, *United States v. Ferreira*, 93, says 276; Lopez, ibid., 77, says 230; Floyd to Crawford, March 21, 1812, TP, NA, says 180.

66. The account is from Clarke, "Surrender," 92–94; extract from the testimony of George Clarke, *United States v. Ferreira*, 17–19; extract from the testimony of Zephaniah Kingsley, ibid., 22–23. The march of the Patriots into town is in Estado de la rendición de Fernandina, Section 28, EFP, LC.

67. Clarke, "Surrender," 93–95. The surrender of Fernandina is also covered in Patrick, *Fiasco*, 83–98, and in Waciuma, *Intervention*, 258–73.

Chapter 8. Reactions

1. Smith to Lieutenant Appling, March 1812, Smith to Secretary of War, March 18, 1812, Smith Letterbook.

2. The account of the ceremony of cession can be found in Floyd to Crawford, March 21, 1812, Misc. Let., DS, NA. See also Clarke to O'Reilly, March 19, 1812, in Clarke, "Surrender," 90; Patrick, *Fiasco*, 100–101. The description of the uniforms is conjectural. It conforms to Chartrand, *Uniforms*, 18–34, 120, 129–36. Marine uniforms are described in Alexander, "Swamp Ambush," 38–42.

3. Quote from Floyd to Crawford, March 21, 1812, Misc. Let., DS, NA; also from Clarke to O'Reilly, March 19, 1812, in Clarke, "Surrender," 90. See also Patrick, ibid.

4. Mathews to Monroe, March 21, 1812, TP, NA; Floyd to Crawford, March 21, 1812, Misc. Let., DS, NA.

5. Lopez to Estrada, March 18, 1812, *United States v. Ferreira*, 77.

6. Patrick, *Fiasco*, 99–100; Smith to Secretary of War, March 18, 1812, Amos Stoddard to Lieutenant Colonel Thomas H. Smith, June 2, 1812, Smith Letterbook.

7. Smith to Laval, March 24, 1812, Smith to Adjutant General and Inspector, April 26, 1812, Smith Letterbook. On seizures of property, see Testimony of George J. F. Clarke, Claim of Francisco and Peter Pons, No. 73,347, Claim of Mary Smith, No. 78,185, Claim of Spicer Christopher, No. 84,647, First Aud., NA.

8. Lopez to Estrada, March 31, 1812, Section 32, EFP, LC; Estrada to Thomson, April 15, 1812, Admiralty 1/502, PRO; Campbell to Hamilton, April 14, 1812, CL, NA; Mathews to Monroe, March 21, 28, 1812, TP, NA; Mooney, *Dictionary*, 7: 550–51.

9. Adgate to Girard, March 20, 1812, Thompson to Girard, March 21, 1812, TP, NA; Applications made to John Steele, February 8, 1813, Let. Marque, NA.

10. Floyd to Senator Crawford, March 21, 26, 1812, Misc. Let., DS, NA.

11. Campbell to Hamilton, April 11, 14, 1812, Mathews to Campbell, April 2, 1812, CL, NA; Patrick, *Fiasco*, 81.

12. Smith to Laval, March 28, 1812, Smith Letterbook; Laval to Adjutant General, May 1, 1812, Personal Papers of Major Jacint Laval, War Records Office, NA, cited in Patrick, ibid.

13. Testimony of Charles Clarke, Claim of Felipe Solana, No. 73,063, First Aud., NA.

14. Testimony of Charles Clarke, Claim of George J. F. Clarke, No. 83,177, First Aud., NA; Testimony of Bartolo Masters and Charles Clarke, Claim of Felipe Solana, No. 73,063, First Aud., NA; Relación de los Negros, n.d., Section 28, EFP, LC; Joseph

Hibberson to Augustus Foster, March 20, 1812, enclosed in Foster to Wellesley, April 2, 1812, Foreign Office 5/85, PRO; Thompson to Girard, March 21, 1812, TP, NA.

15. Craig to Estrada, March 17, 1812, Section 32, EFP, LC.

16. Ibid.

17. Ibid.

18. Estrada to Someruelos, March 26, 1812, Section 2, EFP, LC; Fernando de la Maza Arredondo, el joven, Report to Estrada, March 17–18, 1812, Section 27, EFP, LC.

19. Arredondo, Report to Estrada, ibid. Quote from Craig to Estrada, March 17, 1812, Section 32, EFP, LC.

20. Arredondo, Report to Estrada, ibid.

21. Francisco Solana to Governor of Florida, March 17, 1812, Section 32, EFP, LC; Estrada to Thomson, April 15, 1812, Admiralty 1/502, PRO.

22. Estrada to Someruelos, March 26, 1812, Section 2, EFP, LC.

23. Estrada to Craig, March 19, 1812, Section 32, EFP, LC.

24. Mitchell to Floyd, March 18, 26, 1812, GGL, GDAH.

25. Hickey, *War of 1812*, 32–35.

26. Ibid., 37–39; Patrick, *Fiasco*, 116–20; Hoffman, *Florida's Frontiers*, 261–62.

27. *Charleston Courier*, March 23, 27, 28, 1812; see also March 18, April 1, 1812, cited in Patrick, ibid., 122; *National Intelligencer*, April 7, 1812, and *Niles Register*, April 11, 1812, cited ibid., 123; *Savannah Republican*, March 26, 20, 1812; *Georgia Argus*, March 25, April 15, 1812; *Boston Weekly Messenger for the Country*, April 10, 1812; *New York Evening Post*, April 28, 1812. For impact in Georgia, see Talmadge, "Georgia's Federalist Press," and Akins, "Georgians," 55–61.

28. Madison to Jefferson, April 24, 1812, Smith, *Republic of Letters*, 1693–94; Stagg, *Mr. Madison's War*, 98–99.

29. Troup to Monroe, April 12, 1812, TP, NA.

30. Isaacs to Monroe, July 3, 1814, Misc. Let., DS, NA; Patrick, *Fiasco*, 120–21.

31. Patrick, ibid., 121; Monroe to Mathews, April 4, 1812, *American State Papers*, 9: 44–46.

32. Ammon, *Monroe*, 306–7.

33. Isaacs to Monroe, July 3, 1814, Misc. Let., DS, NA; Patrick, *Fiasco*, 128–30; Waciuma, *Intervention*, 302–8; Ammon, ibid.

34. Patrick, ibid., 128–33; Waciuma, ibid.; Ammon, ibid.

35. Monroe to Mitchell, April 10, 1812, *American State Papers*, 9: 47–48, and May 27, 1812, Misc. Let., DS, NA.

36. Isaacs to Monroe, July 3, 1814, Misc. Let., DS, NA.

37. Ibid.

38. Crawford to Monroe, April 19, 1812, Misc. Let, DS, NA, typescript copy in the T. Frederick Davis Collection, PKY. See also Green, "Crawford," 30.

39. See Patrick, *Fiasco*, 102–4, 107–8, 124, for discussion of the Patriots' numbers and recruitment. Smith to General Hampton, March 27, 1812, Smith Letterbook, put their strength between 300 and 400 men. Estrada indicated 800 men, which was

328   Notes to Pages 141–46

an overestimate. Estrada to Someruelos, March 26, 1812, Section 2, EFP, LC; Mathews to Madison, April 16, 1812, Papers of James Madison, LC; Mathews to Monroe, March 28, 1812, TP, NA; Vocelle, *Camden County*, 67–70.

40. The division of forces is covered in the deposition of Dr. James Hall, Claim of Francis X. Sánchez, No. 74,969, First Aud., NA.

41. Testimony of Tony Primus, Claim of George J. F. Clarke, No. 83,177, and Claim of Tony Primus, No. 84,941, First Aud., NA, which describes his farm as on the Gilbert plantation.

42. Testimony of Tony Primus, Claim of George J. F. Clarke, ibid.

43. Deposition of Dr. James Hall, Claim of Francis X. Sánchez, No. 74,969, First Aud., NA; Sastre, "Picolata," 146–47, 158–61.

44. Estrada to Someruelos, March 26, 1812, Section 2, EFP, LC. See also "Información sobre la Revolución de esta Provincia, Año de1812," Section 65, EFP, LC, beginning with a copy of Estrada to Someruelos, March 26, 1812, and followed by the proceedings against Broadway. Due to the disruptions of the rebellion, the difficulty of finding witnesses, and the illness of the *escribano*, or public scribe, Broadway's case was suspended until October 19, 1812, when Kindelán reopened it.

Chapter 9. At the Gates of St. Augustine

1. McIntosh to Alexander McKin, March 21, 1812, Misc. Let., DS, NA.

2. Even in 1817, in his assessment of St. Augustine's natural defenses, military engineer Francisco de Cortazar thought that the rivers and marshes were among the strongest impediments to an attack. See Engineer F. Cortazar, January 25, 1817, Notícia, Section 38, EFP, LC. As a Spanish administrative center, St. Augustine was a *ciudad* and technically should always be referred to as a city. Spanish-speakers usually employed the word *ciudad*, while English speakers sometimes referred to it as a city and sometimes as a town.

3. Campen, *Augustine*, 35–36; Arana and Manucy, *Building of the Castillo*; Torres-Reyes, *British Siege*, 6; Mitchell to Monroe, September 19, 1812, TP, NA. Although Mitchell estimated forty-six cannons at the Castillo, the Spanish inventory of August 19, 1812, is as stated in text. "Estado que manifiesta la Artillería, Montaje, Municiones, y demás pertrechos que se hallan en el Castillo de San Marcos, y otros puestos de esta Plaza," Section 42, EFP, LC.

4. See, for example, the 1817 map of Francisco de Cortazar, "Plano de la ciudad de San Agustín con las entradas de sus barras," Map No. 77, in Servicio Geográfico de Ejército, *Cartografía de Ultramar*.

5. Late colonial repairs to the defenses are covered in Arana and Manucy, *Building of the Castillo*, 54–58, and are shown in the diagram on the inside back cover of their work. See the 1817 Cortazar map and its key.

6. The southern fortifications are depicted on the 1817 Cortazar map and on Ramón de la Cruz, "Plano del Presidio del Sn. Agustín en la Florida Oriental, con las entradas de sus Barras, Rios, Cañas y Vienegras que lo circuyen," 1821 (original National Archives Record Group 59, photocopy, SAHS, Map 9–12–15).

7. See Sastre, "British Redoubts," 78–86, and the 1817 Cortazar map and the 1821 de la Cruz map. Sastre concluded that only two of these redoubts were actually in use between 1784 and 1812, though Estrada's instructions for defense (see note 8 below) suggest he was employing between three and four of the redoubts to the west and south of the city.

8. Transcription and Translation of a Document by Estrada in MC-63, St. Augustine and Florida History, Box 7, Folder 29, 1812–1815 Defenses, SAHS. The original is "Plan detallado de los puestos que deben guarnecerse en esa Plaza para evitar una sorpresa," March 23, 1812, Section 42, EFP, LC. The caliber of the artillery at the redoubts is not stated. It is likely that Estrada also had men and a gun at Segunda Fería. Later, under Kindelán, when St. Augustine had reinforcements, the western line consisted of a garrison with a 12-pounder at Puente, a detachment with a 4-pounder at Segunda Fería, and another detachment with an 8-pounder at Solana. The redoubts on the Cubo Line had 8-pounders, and the María Sánchez redoubt south of town had a 12-pounder. "Estado que manifiesta la Artillería, etc.," Section 42, EFP, LC.

9. Arnade, "Raids," 100–115.

10. Fort Matanzas Stabilization Team, *Historic Structure Report*, 51–62, 195–96, 457–59; Arana, "Fort at Matanzas Inlet," 20–22.

11. Patrick, *Fiasco*, 104; McIntosh to Estrada, March 26, 1812, Section 28, EFP, LC.

12. Estrada to Thomson, April 15, 1812, Admiralty 1/502, PRO.

13. Annotations, militia muster rolls for the First and Second Company of the St. Johns and the Third Company of Amelia Island, with tally, and also "Relación de los havitantes a la Rivera de San Juan, conocidamente reveldes, con expresión del pasage donde están situados los repectivos plantages," July 19, 1812, Section 28, EFP, LC; Patrick, *Fiasco*, 103. In testimony against Abner Broadway given on October 30, 1812, in "Información sobre la Revolución," Section 65, EFP, LC, Domingo Fernández and Pedro Suarez identified the following individuals as being part of the rebellion: John Houston McIntosh; Lodowick Ashley; Jesse Youngblood; Samuel Russell, the elder; Samuel Russell, the younger; John Russell; William Carney; William Starratt; John Edwards; George Cook; William Christopher; John Christopher; Spicer Christopher, the younger; John Houston; William Braddock; David Braddock; John Lowe; Redin Blunt; William Waller; Samuel Miller; William Lane; William Craig; Zephaniah Kingsley; Timothy Hollingsworth; Diego [James] Hollingsworth; William Hollingsworth; Thomas and Gilbert Manz[?]; David Akens; William Fitzpatrick; James Smith; Robert Piquet; Isaac Carter; Leslie Carter; Henry Carter; Robert Prichard; John Creighton; Nathaniel Hall; and Geliu Spintman[?]. According to Miller, *Quesada*, 163, both Timothy Hollingsworth and William Lane had been implicated and severely punished for taking part in the rebellion of 1795, so that they, like Braddock and Dell, had bitter memories of Spanish legal proceedings and justice.

14. Governor of Florida to Apodaca, Review of the Third Infantry Battalion of Cuba, April 12, July 20, 1812, Legajo 1789, PC, 269–81; Militia Muster Rolls, First

and Second Company of St. Johns and Third Company of Amelia Island, Section 28, EFP, LC; Estrada to Someruelos, March 26, 1812, Section 2, EFP, LC, with enclosure "Noticia de los Individuos que se han incorporado en el tercer Bat^n del Regimiento de Cuba a server," March 27, 1812. The initial militia roll is "Lista que manifiesta los individuos que se hallan en esa Plaza para tomar armas," March 28, 1812, Section 42, EFP, LC. More men would soon turn up to help in the defense.

15. Estrada to Thomson, April 15, 1812, Admiralty 1/502, PRO; Estrada to Someruelos, March 26, 1812, Section 2, EFP, LC.

16. Estrada to Someruelos, March 27, 1812, ibid., enclosure, "Españoles y habitantes unidos en esta Plaza de San Agustín de la Florida Oriental."

17. Patrick, *Fiasco*, 105; on the terms of cession, see Mathews to Monroe, March 21, 1812, in Misc. Let., DS, NA. Lopez to Estrada, March 31, 1812, Section 32, EFP, LC, mentions the quarrel between McIntosh and Mathews.

18. Patrick, ibid., 106. The return journey to St. Augustine was described in Daniel Delany to the Board of Officers, April 3, 1812, Section 28, EFP, LC.

19. Patrick, ibid.

20. Ibid., 106–7. Original in Campbell to Hamilton, April 24, 1812, CL, NA.

21. Ibid., 107; Smith to Secretary of War, April 14, 1812, Smith Letterbook. Smith could have gone either by the road from Fort Picolata or the one from Six Mile Creek. His subsequent correspondence referring to Six Mile Creek as his original line of supply suggests perhaps he went by way of the latter.

22. Estrada to Crespo, March 24, 1812, Crespo to Estrada, March 20, 1812, Section 32, EFP, LC.

23. Crespo to Estrada, March 30, April 7, 1812, ibid.

24. Crespo to Estrada, April 9, 1812, ibid.

25. Crespo to Estrada, April 10, 1812, ibid.; Testimony of Francis Pellicer, Claim of Bernardino and Joseph Sánchez, No. 80,681, First Aud., NA. Some accounts cite Captain John Miller, an officer in Smith's contingent, as the leader of this raid, but Smith did not arrive in the area until April 11. James Dell was in the raid, but it is not clear if he led it. See also the testimony of Ramon Sánchez and José Laderal, Claim of Francis Pellicer, No. 75,214, First Aud., NA, and *Georgia Journal*, June 3, 1812.

26. Estrada to Crespo, April 7, 1812, Crespo to Estrada, April 8, 1812, Estrada to Crespo, April 8, 9, 1812, Crespo to Estrada, April 12, 1812, Section 32, EFP, LC.

27. Estrada to Thomson, April 15, 1812, Admiralty 1/502, PRO; Smith to Secretary of War, April 13, 1812, Smith Letterbook.

28. *Savannah Republican*, April 23, 1812; Estrada to Someruelos, April 13, 1812, Section 2, EFP, LC; Franco, *Conspiración*, 37–56.

29. Estrada to Thomson, April 15, 1812, Admiralty 1/502, PRO; Smith to Secretary of War, April 14, 1812, Smith to General Wade, May 5, 1812, Smith Letterbook. The North River is also sometimes referred to as the Tolomato River.

30. Smith to Secretary of War, ibid.

31. Claim of Francis Pellicer, No. 75,214, First Aud., NA.

32. Marotti, "Enslaved," 39; Testimony of John M. Bowden, Claim of Francis Pellicer, No. 75,214, Testimony of James Pellicer, Claim No. 89,050, First Aud., NA.

33. Depositions of Andreas Papy and Matthew Long, Claim of Francis Pellicer, ibid.; Mills, *Florida's First Families*, 114.

34. Claim of Francis Pellicer, ibid.

35. Marotti, "Enslaved," 39; Dell, "Dell Brothers," 1–10. The story of events at Pellicer's is given in the depositions of Francisco Roman Sánchez, Andreas Papy, José Laderal, Matthew Long, Philip Weedman, and James Dell, Claim of Francis Pellicer, No. 75,214, and Claim of James Dell, No. 82,248, and Testimony of Francis Pellicer, Claim of John Bunch, No. 84,638, First Aud., NA.

36. Depositions of Matthew Long, Philip Weedman, Mateo Lorenzo, and James Dell, Claim of Francis Pellicer, No. 75,214, First Aud., NA; Crespo to Estrada, April 14, 1812, Section 32, EFP, LC.

37. Vice Admiral Sawyer to Lords of Admiralty, May 26, 1812, Admiralty 1/502, PRO; *Savannah Republican*, April 23, 1812.

38. Campbell to Hamilton, April 15, 17, 1812, CL, NA.

39. Ibid.

40. Zephaniah Kingsley to James Hamilton, April 1, 1812, James Hamilton Papers, RBMSCL, Duke University. See also quote of Ambrose Hull in Rutherford, "Spain's Immigration Policy," 71.

41. Smith to Mr. McDougall, April 13, 1812, Smith to Stallings, April 14, 1812, Smith to Mr. McDougall, April 18, 1812, Smith Letterbook. On armaments, see Hickey, *War of 1812*, 78–80.

42. Smith to Secretary of War, April 12, 26, 1812, Smith to Adjutant General and Inspector, April 26, 1812, Smith Letterbook.

43. Smith to Secretary of War, April 26, 1812, Smith to Captain Williams, April 18, 1812, Smith Letterbook. Problems of supply are discussed in Skeen, *Citizen Soldiers*, 52–54. Smith's difficulties were typical, as was the menace of dysentery and other camp diseases that would soon afflict his contingent.

44. Floyd to Crawford, March 26, 1812, Misc. Let., DS, NA.

45. Testimony of Zephaniah Kingsley, Claim of the Estate of James Cashen, No. 82,920, First Aud., NA. This account, which places Kingsley's arrest around April 5, contradicts his letter of April 1 showing he was already on the rebel side. For yet another version, see Testimony of Zephaniah Kingsley, Claim of the Estate of Francis Philip Fatio, Sr., No. 76,455, First Aud., NA.

46. Crespo to Estrada, March 30, May 17, 1812, Section 32, EFP, LC.

47. Testimony of Ana María Hernández Williams and Philip Weedman, Claim of John Bunch, No. 84,638, First Aud., NA. Weedman said the overseer was either Abner or William Williams, but Abner was a landowner from the northern part of the province.

48. Testimony of Ana María Hernández Williams, ibid.

49. Ibid.

50. Claim of the Estate of Samuel Williams, No. 76,042, First Aud., NA; Williams, Diary, 1811–1822, PKY.

51. Testimony of Ana María Hernández Williams and Philip Weedman, Claim of John Bunch, No. 84,638, First Aud., NA; Crespo to Estrada, May 17, 1812, Section 32, EFP, LC.

52. Smith to Secretary of War, April 26, 1812, Smith Letterbook; Patrick, *Fiasco*, 107–9; Mathews to Monroe, April 16, 1812, TP, NA; Mathews to Madison, April 16, 1812, in Stagg, *Papers of James Madison*, 4: 226–328.

53. General McIntosh to Mitchell, April 27, 1812, Miscellaneous Manuscripts Collection, PKY; Testimony of Dr. James Hall, Claim of Francis X. Sánchez, No. 74,969, RG 217/345. Governor Mitchell refused to allow McIntosh to resign from the Georgia militia, and his tenure as leader of the Patriot Army soon ended; see Patrick, ibid., 112–13.

54. Patrick, ibid.; Smith to Adjutant General and Inspector, April 26, 1812, Smith Letterbook; *Athens Express*, May 22, 1812; *Savannah Republican*, May 26, 1812; General John McIntosh to Governor Mitchell, April 27, 1812, Miscellaneous Manuscripts Collection, PKY.

55. Patrick, ibid., 111–12; Estrada to Someruelos, April 20, 1812, Section 2, EFP, LC. Text is from Constituted Authorities to Juan Blas Entralgo, April 10, 1812, with accompanying cover letter, Section 28, EFP, LC.

56. Estrada to Thomson, April 15, 1812, Admiralty 1/502, PRO.

57. Arredondo to Estrada, April 24, 1812, Section 32, EFP, LC; *Savannah Republican*, April 30, 1812.

58. Patrick, *Fiasco*, 123; General McIntosh to Governor Mitchell, May 1, 1812, Miscellaneous Manuscripts Collection, PKY.

59. Smith to Secretary of War, April 26, 1812, Mitchell to Smith, May 4, 1812, Smith Letterbook.

60. Patrick, *Fiasco*, 124; *Savannah Republican*, May 26, 1812; Hickey, *War of 1812*, 76.

61. Patrick, ibid.; *Savannah Republican*, May 14, 1812.

Chapter 10. Governor of Florida vs. Governor of Georgia

1. Major General McIntosh to Mitchell, May 1, 1812, Miscellaneous Manuscripts Collection, PKY; Mitchell to Monroe, September 19, 1812, TP, NA.

2. Patrick, *Fiasco*, 129–32.

3. Mitchell to Eustis, April 20, 1812, GGL, GDAH. See discussion of Mitchell and the militia in Skeen, *Citizen Soldiers*, 73–74.

4. Mitchell to Floyd, March 29, 1812, GGL, GDAH; *Savannah Republican*, April 28, 1812; Mitchell to Smith, May 4, 1812, copy, Smith Letterbook. Georgians later cited British actions during the Revolution as justification for occupying East Florida; Akins, "Georgians," 68–69.

5. Mitchell to Monroe, May 16, 1812, TP, NA.

6. Harden, *Troup*, 116.

7. Mitchell to Monroe, May 16, 1812, TP, NA; see also Mitchell to Monroe, April 19, 1812, ibid., for his tactics.

8. Patrick, *Fiasco*, 110; *Charleston Courier*, April 11, 1812; *Savannah Republican*, April 23, 1812. All the papers deleted the reference to arming the black population.

9. Junta of the Loyal Subjects, May 13, 1812, Section 32, EFP, LC; Notes re: Arredondo family, 60–61.

10. *Savannah Republican*, May 4, 1812; Lopez to Estrada, April 25, 1812, Arredondo to Estrada, April 28, 1812, Section 32, EFP, LC; Patrick, *Fiasco*, 160. The description of gunboat No. 168 is from Tucker, *Gunboat Navy*, 200.

11. *Savannah Republican*, May 21, 1812; *Georgia Argus*, June 3, 1812.

12. Patrick, *Fiasco*, 110–11; Alexander, "Ambush"; Alexander, "Swamp Ambush," 38–42; Arredondo to Estrada, April 21, 1812, Section 32, EFP, LC; Smith to Williams, April 28, 1812, Smith Letterbook.

13. Smith to Massias, April 28, 1812, Smith to Mitchell, May 9, 1812, Smith to Williams, May 9, 1812, Smith Letterbook; *Savannah Republican*, May 9, 26, 1812.

14. Estrada to Mitchell, May 4, 1812, enclosure in Mitchell to Monroe, May 16, 1812, TP, NA.

15. Translation, May 29, 1813, of a report on the attack by Francisco Marin, a participant, accompanied by a roll of the participants, in Patriot War Claims: Anna Madgigine to St. Johns Co., PKY. Marin and others identify the sloop involved as the *Nuestra Señora del Carmen* rather than the *María*, which is the name given in Estrada's orders.

16. The story of the attack was put together from the following sources: Lopez to Kindelán, July 1, 1812, Informe de la Real Contaduría, Crosby to Kindelán, July 1, 1812, Ribera to Kindelán, July 7, 1812, Maestre to Kindelán, July 2, 1812, all enclosed in Kindelán to Apodaca, July 2, 1812, Section 2, EFP, LC; Testimony of Mary Dewees, James Dell, and Catherine Taylor, Claim of the Estate of Benjamin Armstrong, MC-31–45, SAHS; *Federal Republican and Gazette*, August 24, 1812; *Georgia Argus*, June 3, 1812; Translation, May 29, 1813, of a report on the attack by Francisco Marin, Patriot War Claims: Anna Madgigine to St. Johns Co., PKY; Griffin, "Minorcans," 82.

17. Catherine Taylor, Claim of the Estate of Benjamin Armstrong, MC-31–45, SAHS.

18. The slaves were later the subject of a lawsuit between the Bakers, Deweeses, and Solanas. Marin and others argued that the former masters had forfeited their rights to the slaves by becoming rebels. Translation, May 29, 1813, of a report on the attack by Francisco Marin, Patriot War Claims: Anna Madgigine to St. Johns Co., PKY.

19. Claim of Felipe Solana, No. 73,063; Translation, May 29, 1813, of a report, ibid.; Gamble, *Savannah Duels*, 101–2.

20. Maestre to Kindelán, July 2, 1812, enclosed in Kindelán to Apodaca, July 2, 1812, Section 2, EFP, LC.

21. Mitchell to Monroe, May 16, September 19, 1812, TP, NA.

22. *Savannah Republican,* May 21, 1812.

23. Smith to Mitchell, May 16, 1812, Smith to Adjutant General and Inspector, May 21, 1812, Smith Letterbook; Patrick, *Fiasco,* 136–37.

24. Smith to Mitchell, Smith to Adjutant General and Inspector, ibid.

25. Ibid.; Patrick, *Fiasco,* 137–38.

26. Smith to Mitchell, ibid.; Smith to Adjutant General and Inspector, June 4, 1812, Smith Letterbook.

27. Smith to Mitchell, ibid.

28. Ibid.

29. Mitchell to Smith, May 4, 1812, Smith Letterbook; Mitchell to Monroe, September 19, 1812, TP, NA; Harden, *Troup,* 117.

30. Patrick, *Fiasco,* 148; *Augusta Chronicle,* September 11, 1812; *Georgia Argus,* June 17, 1812.

31. Patrick, ibid., 148, 137–38; *Georgia Argus,* June 17, July 1, 1812.

32. Smith to Mitchell, May 27, 30, 1812, Isaacs to Smith, June 5, 1812, Smith to Adjutant General and Inspector, June 4, 1812, Smith Letterbook.

33. Smith to Adjutant General and Inspector, ibid.

34. Smith to Colonel Alexander McComb, June 11, 1812, Smith Letterbook.

35. Landers, *Black Society,* 221–22; Estrada to Lorenzo Boniquet, June 11, 1812, Boniquet to Estrada, June 11, 1812, Section 32, EFP, LC; Kindelán to Apodaca, June 20, 1812, Section 2, EFP, LC.

36. Pezuela, *Diccionario Geográfico;* Santa Cruz y Mallen, *Historia de Familias Cubanas,* 1: 193.

37. Estrada to Boniquet, June 11, 1812, Boniquet to Estrada, June 11, 1812, Section 32, EFP, LC.

38. Patrick, *Fiasco,* 139; Enclosures, Onís to Monroe, Span. Leg., DS, NA, No. 1, Kindelán to the Commander of American Troops, June 11, 1812, No. 2, Smith to Kindelán, June 12, 1812, No. 3, Kindelán to Smith, June 12, 1812. See also copies of these letters and English translations in Smith Letterbook.

39. Copy of a letter to the Governor of St. Augustine, June 13, 1812, Smith Letterbook.

40. Enclosures, Onís to Monroe, Span. Leg., DS, NA, No. 4, Smith to Kindelán, June 13, 1812, No. 5, Kindelán to Smith, June 13, 1812, and English translation of same in Smith Letterbook.

41. Enclosures, Onís to Monroe, Span. Leg., DS, NA, No. 6, Kindelán to Mitchell, June 11, 1812, Smith Letterbook.

42. Enclosures, Onís to Monroe, Span. Leg., DS, NA, No. 7, Mitchell to Kindelán, June 16, 1812, Smith Letterbook.

43. Enclosures, Onís to Monroe, Span. Leg., DS, NA, No. 8, Kindelán to Mitchell, June 23, 1812, Smith Letterbook.

44. This lengthy contest of words has been fully described in Patrick, *Fiasco,* 139–43, and Akins, "Georgians," 59; Landers, *Black Society,* 222; *Weekly Register,* January 16, 1813.

45. For Onís's outlook on the conflict, see Brooks, *Diplomacy*, 18–34. Acknowledgment of amnesty, Pinckney to Kindelán, March 29, 1813, TP, NA.

46. On free black military service, see Landers, *Black Society*, 205–20. The sortie from St. Augustine was reported by Smith in Smith to Mitchell, June 17, 20, 1812, Smith Letterbook.

47. Smith to Tate, June 21, 1812, Smith Letterbook.

48. Patrick, *Fiasco*, 169. Landers, *Black Society*, 362n.100, cites one expedition in July that brought in ninety-five head and three in August that brought in seventy, forty, and ninety-three. See also Kindelán to Apodaca, July 2, August 12, 15, September 15, 1812, Legajo 1789, PC.

49. Smith to Ridgeway, June 20, 1812, Smith Letterbook. Smith to Major Stoddard, July 6, 1812, put Kindelán's forces between 900 and 1,000. Wanton to Estrada, June 3, 1812, Section 32, EFP, LC, put Smith's contingent before St. Augustine at 435.

50. Hickey, *War of 1812*, 42–51; Address and Resolution of the Citizens of Greene County, August 13, 1812, GGL, GDAH. For Georgians' attitude about the war, see also "The Citizens of Milledgeville," n.d., Lockey Collection, April–June 1812, PKY.

51. *National Intelligencer*, December 12, 1811; Campbell to Hamilton, July 18, 1812, CL, NA.

52. *Georgia Journal*, June 2, 1812. See also Akins, "Georgians," 60–62.

53. Resolution of the Citizens of Milledgeville, June 13, 1812, Misc. Let., DS, NA; *Savannah Republican*, June 3, 1812; Akins, ibid., 62.

54. Akins, ibid., 65–66.

55. Mitchell to Monroe, September 19, 1812, TP, NA.

56. Mathews to Monroe, June 23, 1812, and Isaacs to Monroe, July 3, 1813, TP, NA.

57. Patrick, *Fiasco*, 176–77; Harden, *Troup*, 116–17.

58. See Patrick, ibid., 174–78.

59. *Abridgement*, 561; Akins, "Georgians," 62–64; Jefferson to Madison, June 6, 1812, in Smith, *Republic of Letters*, 3: 1697.

60. *Abridgement*, 422–23, 561–65; see Patrick, *Fiasco*, 144–50, and Akins, ibid.; *Federal Republican and Commercial Gazette*, August 24, 1812; Stagg, *Mr. Madison's War*, 49.

61. Akins, ibid., 64; *Georgia Argus*, August 12, 1812; *Georgia Journal*, July 29, 1812, *Georgia Express*, August 28, 1812, *Augusta Chronicle*, July 24, 1812, cited in Akins, ibid., 64–65.

Chapter 11. Life in the Occupied Land

1. Patrick, *Fiasco*, 185; Smith to Lieutenant Stallings, August 9, 1812, Smith Letterbook.

2. Copy of letter to Mr. McDougall, April 19, 1812, copy of letter to Capt. John Williams, May 6, 1812, copy of letter to Secretary of War, May 24, 1812, copy of letter to Doctor Danridge, June 15, 1812, Smith Letterbook; Testimony of John M.

Bowden, Claim of Manuel Solana, No. 73,340, Testimony of Francisco R. Sánchez, Claim of the estate of Manuel Solana, No. 73,340, Testimony of Francisco Roman Sánchez, Claim of Felipe Solana, No. 73,063, Testimony of Roman Sánchez and James Pellicer, Claim of Bernardino and Joseph Sánchez, No. 80,681, Testimony of John Braddock, Claim of Spicer Christopher, No. 84,647, First Aud., NA.

3. Testimony of James Pellicer, Claim of Bernardino and Joseph Sánchez, No. 80,681, Testimony of Francisco Roman Sánchez, Claim of Manuel Solana, No. 73,340, Claim of John and Peter Maestre, No. 74,385, First Aud., NA.

4. Testimony of Charles Clarke, Claim of Felipe Solana, No. 73,063, Testimony of John Moses Bowden, Claim of Manuel Solana, No. 73,340, Testimony of Francisco R. Sánchez, Claim of the estate of Manuel Solana, No. 73,340, Testimony of Francisco R. Sánchez, Claim of Felipe Solana, No. 73,063, Testimony of Roman Sánchez and James Pellicer, Claim of Bernardino and Joseph Sánchez, No. 80,681, Testimony of John Braddock, Claim of Spicer Christopher, No. 84,647, First Aud., NA. See also Parker, "Cattle Trade," 150–63.

5. References to these activities are made throughout the three collections comprising the Patriot War Claims.

6. Smith to Captain John Williams, May 5, 1812, Smith Letterbook; Testimony of Paul Maestre, Claim of Pedro Cosifacio, No. 81,371, Testimony of Francisco Roman Sánchez, Claim of Follis and Gunby, No. 81,613, Claim of Henry Hartley, No. 83,761, First Aud., NA.

7. Testimony of John Moses Bowden and James Plummer, Claim of Henry Hartley, No. 83,761, First Aud., NA.

8. Testimony of James Plummer and Frederick Hartley, Claim of Henry Hartley, ibid.

9. Claim of Abner Williams, MC-31–43, SAHS; Testimony of Matthew Long, James Dell, Jacob Summerlin, and John Moses Bowden, Claim of Francis Pellicer, No. 75,214, First Aud., NA; Marotti, "Enslaved," 30.

10. Griffin, *Mullet*, 150–83; Claim of Andres Lopez, No. 81,961, Claim of Juan Andreas, No. 81,962, Claim of the estate of Juan Ponce, No. 81,963, Claim of Francis Triay, No. 82,859, Testimony of Francis Triay, Claim of Juan Seguí, No. 82,775, First Aud., NA.

11. Claim of Antonio Hindsman, No. 82,629, Claim of Philip Weedman, No. 75,881, First Aud., NA.

12. Testimony of Antonio Maestre and Paul Maestre, Claim of Pedro Cosifacio, No. 81,371, First Aud., NA. Antonio gives a somewhat different account, saying the confrontation took place in midsummer and that the soldiers—twelve or thirteen in number—threatened to strike down Moill with an ax. Then they robbed the corn house and chopped up one of Cosifacio's canoes. Testimony of Antonio Maestre, Claim of Pedro Cosifacio, ibid.

13. Testimony of Paul Maestre, Claim of Juan Seguí, No. 82,775, First Aud., NA.

14. Testimony of Paul Maestre, Claim of Pedro Cosifacio, No. 81,371, Testimony of Paul Maestre, Claim of Juan Seguí, No. 82,775, First Aud., NA.

15. Testimony of Antonio Maestre, Claim of Pedro Cosifacio, No. 81,371, Testimony of Paul Maestre, Claim of Juan Seguí, No. 82,775, First Aud., NA.

16. Testimony of Juan Maestre, Claim of Pedro Cosifacio, No. 81371, First Aud., NA.

17. Testimony of Francis Pellicer and Matthew Long, Claim of Mrs. Samuel Williams, PWC-ML, 1815, SAHS; Claim of Samuel Williams, No. 76,042, Claim of Frances Kerr, No. 73,358, Testimony of Francisco Roman Sánchez and Dr. James Hall, Claim of Prudence Plummer, No. 84,671, Testimony of William Munroe, Claim of Rebecca [Richards] Read, No. 83,831, First Aud., NA.

18. Claim of George J. F. Clarke, No. 83,763, Claim of George J. F. Clarke, No. 83,177, First Aud., NA.

19. Claim of Felipe Solana, No. 73,063, First Aud., NA.

20. Testimony of Charles W. Clarke, Claim of George J. F. Clarke, No. 83,763, Claim of Fernando D. McDonell, No. 73,313, First Aud., NA. Witnesses in this case suggested that Massias was responsible, but the description and time frame fit with Ridgeway's tenure.

21. Claim of Francisco and Pedro Pons, No. 73,347, First Aud., NA. Some witnesses described the vessel as a schooner.

22. Claim of Robert Andrews, No. 83,229, Claim of the Estate of Eber O'Neill, No. 83,467, Claim of William O'Neill, No. 83,762, First Aud., NA. See also O'Neill Family Papers, PKY.

23. Smith to Captain Williams, July 5, 1812, Smith to Captain Massias, August 12, 1812, Smith Letterbook; Patrick, *Fiasco*, 162–63.

24. Schafer, "Family Ties," 2; Schafer, "Laurel Grove," 101; Marotti, "Enslaved," 8, 11–20; Claim of Spicer Christopher, No. 84,647, Claim of the Estate of Francis X. Sánchez, No. 74,969 First Aud., NA; Mills, *Florida's First Families*, 119–49; Testimony of Bartolo Solana, Claim of Gaspar Papy, No. 75,182, Testimony of Francisco Roman Sánchez, Claim of Farquhar Bethune, No. 73,008, Testimony of Francisco Roman Sánchez, Claim of Prudence Plummer, No. 84,671, First Aud., NA.

25. *Universal Gazette*, January 15, 1813; Claim of Samuel Williams, No. 76,042, Claim of Frances Kerr, No. 73,358, Claim of Francis Richards, No. 83,129, Claim of John Bunch, No. 84,638, Testimony of Daniel Vaughn and Ephraim Harrison, Claim of Fernando D. McDonell, No. 73,313, First Aud., NA.

26. Claim of María P. de Burgo, 1838, E. F. Claims, NA; Claim of Spicer Christopher, No. 84,647, First Aud., NA; Marotti, "Black Knights," 15.

27. Claim of Francis Richards, No. 83,129, Testimony of Esteven Arnow, Claim of Peter Capo, No. 82,988, First Aud., NA.

28. Claim of Eleazer Waterman, No. 77,524, Claim of Ramon and Nicolás Sánchez, No. 75,015, Claim of Bartolome Castro y Ferrer, No. 77,832, First Aud., NA; Petition of Matthew Long and Testimony of Francis Pellicer, Matthew Long, Admr. v. United States for the Losses of George Long, 1812, No. 280, PWC-ML, SAHS; Claim of Matthew Long, No. 74,832, First Aud., NA.

Chapter 12. War Even to the Knife

1. Patrick, *Fiasco*, 153; Mitchell to Monroe, July 17, 1812, TP, NA; *Georgia Argus*, July 15, 1812; Citizens of Greene County to President James Madison, August 13, 1812, GEFWF, GDAH, cited in Akins, "Georgians," 69–70.

2. Smith to Major Stoddard, July 6, 1812, Smith Letterbook.

3. Smith to General Floyd, August 21, 1812, Smith to Governor Mitchell, August 21, 1812, Smith to J. H. McIntosh, August 26, 1812, Captain Fiedler Ridgeway to his brother, September 11, 1812, in Patrick, "Letters of the Invaders," 60–61.

4. Patrick, *Fiasco*, 171–72; Smith to Thomas Bourke, August 21, 1812, Smith to Captain William R. Boots, September 4, 1812, Smith Letterbook.

5. William Kinnear to his parents, September 11, 1812, in Patrick, "Letters of the Invaders," 61–63.

6. Newnan to Smith, August 24, 31, 1812, Smith to Thomas Bourke, August 21, 1812, Smith Letterbook.

7. Smith to Mitchell, July 10, 1812, Smith Letterbook.

8. Patrick, *Fiasco*, 165–67; Constitution of East Florida, typescript copy in GGL, GDAH.

9. McIntosh to Monroe, July 30, 1812, TP, NA; Johnston, *Houstons*, 371–72.

10. Kindelán to Apodaca, July 29, 1812, Section 2, EFP, LC; *Niles Weekly Register*, November 7, 1812, cited in Alexander, "Ambush," 289.

11. Covington, *Seminoles*, 28–30; Weisman, "Plantation System," 139, 145–47. The Alligator band, from the vicinity of modern-day Lake City, was also involved in helping the Spaniards; Monaco, "Fort Mitchell," 5–7.

12. Patrick, *Fiasco*, 181; Alexander, "Swamp Ambush," 43; Testimony of Zephaniah Kingsley, Claim of the Estate of Francis Philip Fatio, Sr., No. 76,455, First Aud., NA.

13. Enclosure, Hawkins to Mitchell, September 20, 1812, TPSen, NA; Patrick, ibid., 181, 325.

14. Porter, "Negroes," 9–29.

15. "Extract of a second letter from St. Marys," *New York Evening Post*, October 16, 1812; Patrick, *Fiasco*, 182–83; Kindelán to Apodaca, August 13, 1812, Legajo 1789, PC; Harvey, "Proctor," 47–57.

16. Landers, *Black Society*, 222–25; "East Florida," *Weekly Register*, January 16, 1813, 311.

17. Patrick, *Fiasco*, 182–84.

18. Smith to Thomas Bourke, July 30, 1812, Smith to Stallings, August 9, 1812, Smith Letterbook; Kindelán to Apodaca, August 13, 1812, Legajo 1778, PC; Landers, *Black Society*, 225; Patrick, ibid., 182; Harvey, "Proctor," 50–51.

19. Patrick, ibid., 185.

20. Wanton to Kindelán, July 5, 26, 1812, Section 32, EFP, LC; Landers, *Black Society*, 225; Marotti, "Wanton," 461–64.

21. Smith to Adjutant General and Inspector, July 30, 1812, Smith Letterbook; Mitchell to Monroe, September 19, 1812, TP, NA.

22. Smith to Mitchell, August 21, 1812, Smith Letterbook.

23. Smith to Pinckney, July 30, 1812, Smith Letterbook; Campbell to Hamilton, October 3, 1812, CL, NA.

24. Patrick, *Fiasco*, 184; Schafer, "Laurel Grove," 106–7; *Georgia Argus*, August 25, 1812; Smith to Mitchell, August 21, 1812, Smith Letterbook.

25. Landers, *Black Society*, 223.

26. William Kinnear to his parents, September 11, 1812, in Patrick, "Letters of the Invaders," 61–63; Griffin, "Minorcans," 81–82.

27. Patrick, *Fiasco*, 187–88; Depositions of George Petty, Zephaniah Kingsley, and William E. Brodnay, Claim of the Estate of Francis Philip Fatio, Sr., No. 76,455, First Aud., NA.

28. Smith to General Cushing, August 21, 1812, Smith Letterbook; Campbell to Hamilton, August 29, 1812, CL, NA.

29. Smith to Lieutenant John Armstrong, August 17, 1812, Smith to McIntosh, August 26, 1812, Smith to Newnan, August 30, 1812, Smith to Lieutenant Stallings, August 10, September 2, 1812, Smith Letterbook.

30. Patrick, *Fiasco*, 188–89; "Our Southern Frontier," *National Intelligencer*, October 29, 1812.

31. Smith to Stallings, August 26, 1812, Claim of Edward M. Wanton, No. 80,361, First Aud., NA; Marotti, "Wanton," 456–61, 464.

32. Smith to Captain Fort, August 11, 1812, Smith to Colonel Newnan, August 30, 1812, Smith to Thomas Bourke, July 30, 1812, Smith to Governor Mitchell, September 7, 1812, Smith Letterbook.

33. Newnan to Smith, August 31, 1812, Smith Letterbook.

34. Lieutenant James Ryan to John Ash, September 11, 1812, Lieutenant James Ryan to Lieutenant James Barton, September 11, 1812, Captain Fiedler Ridgeway to his brother, September 11, 1812, in Patrick, "Letters of the Invaders," 58–60; Claim of the Estate of Benjamin Armstrong, MC-31-45, SAHS.

35. Smith to Newnan, September 9, 1812, Smith to Mitchell, September 7, 1812, Smith Letterbook; Patrick, *Fiasco*, 191.

36. Kindelán to Apodaca, July 2, 1812, Section 2, EFP, LC.

37. The number of people in St. Augustine at this point is an estimate. However, it included nearly 1,000 men under arms, settlers, and the slaves who had been brought into town. Kindelán to Apodaca, July 28, 1812, ibid.

38. On supplies, see Testimony of Andreas Papy, Matthew Long, and Ramon Sánchez, Claim of Francis Pellicer, No. 75,214, Claim of Joseph Baya, No. 72,686, Claim of Juan Seguí, Claim 82,775, Testimony of Francis Triay, Claim of the Estate of Juan Ponce, No. 81,963, First Aud., NA; Claim of Benjamin Wiggins, MC-31-75, SAHS; Miguel Porro to Sebastián Kindelán, July 29, 1812, enclosure in Kindelán to Apodaca, July 29, 1812, Legajo 1789, PC; Kindelán to Apodaca, August 13, 1812, Section 2, EFP, LC.

39. Kindelán to Apodaca, July 19, 1812, Legajo 1789, PC.

40. Patrick, *Fiasco*, 164; Kindelán to Apodaca, September 10, 1812, Section 2, EFP, LC.

41. Patrick, ibid.; see also "testimonios," listed in notes 42 and 43 below.

42. Testimonio de la ocurrencia acabesida a la Goleta Española los dos Hermanos, August 12, 1812, and Kindelán to Onís, September 10, 1812, Legajo 1789, PC. A William T. Burch, possibly the man mentioned by Casimiro, had fled from a murder charge in Georgia in 1811, seeking asylum in Florida, which Estrada refused. He stayed, temporarily, at William Craig's house at the Cowford. Estrada to Someruelos, July 9, 1811, Section 2, EFP, LC.

43. Testimonio del Expediente sobre la averiguación del saquéo y robo cometida en la Goleta Española Eugenia, August 23, 1812, Legajo 1789, PC.

44. Kindelán to Apodaca, September 14, 1812, Legajo 1789, PC; Acosta to Kindelán, August 23, 1812, Kindelán to Mulvey, September 7, 1812, Mulvey to Kindelán, September 30, 1812, Section 26, EFP, LC.

45. Kindelán to Apodaca, August 12, 19, 27, 1812, Legajo 1789, PC.

46. Kindelán to Apodaca, August 26, 1812, Section 2, EFP, LC.

47. Kindelán to Apodaca, August 27, 1812, Legajo 1789, PC.

48. Kindelán to Apodaca, September 12, 1812, Section 2, EFP, LC.

49. Testimony of Tony Primus, Claim of George J. F. Clarke, No. 83,177, First Aud., NA.

50. Landers, *Black Society*, 209–27, 233; Altoff, *My Best Men*, 131–38; Marotti, "Black Knights," 24–32.

51. For accounts, see Alexander, "Ambush," and "Swamp Ambush"; Landers, *Black Society*, 226; Patrick, *Fiasco*, 191–93; and Porter, "Negroes," 20–21. See also "Our Southern Frontier, From the Augusta Chronicle," account of General John Floyd, *National Intelligencer*, October 29, 1812; Smith to Captain Massias, September 22, 1812, Smith to General Pinckney, September 22, 1812, Smith to General Cushing, September 22, 1812, Smith to General Flournoy, September 22, 1812, Smith to Mitchell, September 22, 1812, Smith Letterbook; Williams to Lieutenant Colonel Franklin Wharton, September 15, 1812, LRMC, NA.

52. Landers, *Black Society*, 226.

53. Patrick, *Fiasco*, 193; Williams to Wharton, September 15, 1812, RG 127; Smith to Massias, September 21, 1812, Smith Letterbook; *Federal Republican and Commercial Gazette*, October 9, 1812.

54. Patrick, ibid., 197.

55. Kindelán gives the date as September 19, 1812.

Chapter 13. The Price of Victory

1. *National Intelligencer*, October 29, 1812; *Federal Republican and Commercial Gazette*, October 9, 1812; *Georgia Journal*, October 7, 1812, reprinted in the *Boston Repertory and General Advertiser*, October 27, 1812; *Savannah Republican*, Octo-

ber 8, 1812, cited in Alexander, "Ambush," 295; "Our Southern Frontier," *National Intelligencer*, October 29, 1812.

2. Smith to Mitchell, September 22, 1812, Smith to General Floyd, September 30, 1812, Smith Letterbook; Davis, "Troops, III," 138–34.

3. Smith to Mitchell, September 7, 1812, Smith Letterbook; Davis, ibid., 135–36.

4. Smith to Massias, September 22, 1812, Smith Letterbook.

5. Letter, September 2, 1812, in *Federal Republican and Commercial Gazette*, October 9, 1812.

6. "Letter from an Early Adventurer to his friend," *Savannah Republican*, September 22, 1812; Patrick, *Fiasco*, 199.

7. Smith to Mitchell, September 22, 1812; Patrick, ibid., 195.

8. Testimony of George Petty, Zephaniah Kingsley, William E. Brodnay, and Dr. James Hall, Claim of Francis P. Fatio, No. 76,455, First Aud., NA. Quote is from Hall.

9. Patrick, *Fiasco*, 196; Smith to Mitchell, September 26, 1812, Mitchell to Smith, September 21, 1812, copy, Smith Letterbook.

10. Patrick, ibid., 197.

11. For a more complete account of Newnan's raid, see ibid., 195–210, Covington, *Seminoles*, 28–33, and Akins, "Georgians," 71–73. For Newnan's own account, see Davis, "Troops, III," 146–45; Newnan to Smith, October 11, 12, 13, 1812, Mitchell to Smith, November 7, 1812, Smith to Newnan, October 12, 1812, Smith Letterbook. See also Davis, "Troops, IV," 265–66; Burnett, "Colonel Newnan."

12. Mitchell to Smith, November 7, 1812, Smith to Newnan, October 12, 1812, Smith to Mitchell, October 20, 1812, Smith Letterbook.

13. Covington, *Seminoles*, 31; Mitchell to Floyd, April 12, 1813, GGL, GDAH; Patrick, *Fiasco*, 208–10.

14. Letter, October 27, 1812, in *Federal Republican and Commercial Gazette*, November 18, 1812; *New York Evening Post*, October 15, 16, 1812.

15. Quiroga Fernández de Soto, "Military Liberalism," 441–66.

16. Covington, *Seminoles*, 29; Patrick, *Fiasco*, 166–68; McIntosh to Monroe, October 3, 1812, TP, NA; Campbell to Hamilton, October 3, 1812, CL, NA.

17. *Savannah Republican*, October 15, 1812; Petition to Governor Mitchell, October 22, 1812, reprinted in Arnow, "History," September 28, 1951. See Akins, "Georgians," 69–70; Patrick, *Fiasco*, 214–15; Pratt, *Expansionists*, 210; Mitchell to Monroe, October 13, 1812, TPSen, NA.

18. Address to the Georgia Legislature, Executive Department, Milledgeville, November 3, 1812, GGL, GDAH; Akins, ibid., 74–76.

19. Akins, ibid., 73; Patrick, *Fiasco*, 152–53.

20. Heidler and Heidler, *Encyclopedia*, 417–18; *Biographical Directory*, 1414; Pinckney to Monroe, November 14, 1812, TP, NA, and Patrick, *Fiasco*, 219; Monroe to Pinckney, December 8, 1812, Pinckney to Monroe, December 29, 1812, TPSen, NA.

21. Smith to Major Thomas Bourke, October 24, 1812, copy of a letter to Colonel

Joseph Chambers, October 25, 1812, copy of a letter to Governor Mitchell, November 7, 1812, copy of a letter to General Flournoy, November 7, 1812, Mitchell to Smith, November 7, 1812, Smith Letterbook. On transfer of riflemen and dragoons, see Pinckney to Smith, November 25, 1812, ibid.

22. Akins, "Georgians," 75–76; Patrick, *Fiasco*, 212–17; *Universal Gazette* (Washington, D.C.), January 15, 1813.

23. *Universal Gazette*, ibid.; William Cumming to Thomas Cumming, Esq., November 4, 1812, Alfred Cumming Papers, RBMSCL, Duke University.

24. William Cumming to Thomas Cumming, Esq., November 9, 1812, ibid.

25. Ibid.

26. Ibid.

27. William Cumming to Thomas Cumming, Esq., December 23, 1812, February 1, 1813, ibid.

28. William Cumming to Thomas Cumming, Esq., February 1, 1813, ibid.

29. *National Intelligencer*, November 21, 1812; Patrick, *Fiasco*, 220; Pratt, *Expansionists*, 210.

30. Hickey, *War of 1812*, 82–90; Mahon, *War of 1812*, 63–86; Ammon, *Monroe*, 315–16; "Explanatory Observations," enclosed in Monroe to Crawford, December 3, 1812, in Hamilton, *Writings of James Monroe*, 227–28

31. *Annals of Congress*, 12th Cong., 2nd sess. (December 1812–January 1813), Confidential Proceedings of the Senate, 124–34.

32. Madison to Jefferson, January 27, 1812, in Madison, *Letters and Other Writings*, 2: 558.

33. *Annals of Congress*, 12th Cong., 2nd sess., 127–28; Akins, "Georgians," 77–78; Speech of the Hon. William Hunter, *United States Gazette for the Country, Extra*, November 24, 1813; *Biographical Directory*, 1133.

34. *United States Gazette*, November 24, 1813.

35. *Annals of Congress*, 12th Cong., 2nd sess., 130–31; Akins, "Georgians," 77–78; Patrick, *Fiasco*, 249–53.

36. Patrick, ibid., 225–36.

37. Smith to Kingsley, February 2, 1813, Smith Letterbook; Claim of James Dell, No. 82,248, First Aud., NA; William Cumming to Thomas Cumming, Esq., February 1, 1813, Alfred Cumming Papers, RBMSCL, Duke University.

38. See Covington, *Seminoles*, 32–33; Patrick, *Fiasco*, 230–34; Smith to General Flournoy, February 24, 1812, in Davis, "Troops, IV," 271–74; Weisman, "Plantation System," 144.

39. Patrick, ibid., 254.

Chapter 14. The Americans Withdraw

1. Executive Department, Milledgeville, November 3, 1812, GGL, GDAH, and Mitchell to Monroe, October 19, 1812, TP, NA; Lovett, *Birth of Modern Spain*, 2: 735–52; Hickey, *War of 1812*, 119; Patrick, *Fiasco*, 268–69.

2. "Extract of a letter from a gentleman at St. Mary's to his friend in Philadelphia, dated April 14, 1813," *Boston Weekly Messenger*, May 14, 1813.

3. Brooks, *Diplomacy*, 20–25.

4. Amnesty Edict, in Davis, "Troops, V," 26–27.

5. East Florida, a Proclamation, March 30, 1813, TP, NA; Patrick, *Fiasco*, 260–61.

6. Monaco, "Fort Mitchell," 1–25; Patrick, ibid., 258–61; Harris to Mitchell, March 14, 1813, BHC, GDAH; Floyd to Crawford, March 21, 1812, Misc. Let., DS, NA; Early to Governor of Florida, February 23, 1814, GGL, GDAH; Campbell to Hamilton, October 1, 1812, CL, NA; Testimony of Dr. James Hall, Claim of Francis X. Sánchez, No. 74,969, First Aud., NA.

7. McIntosh to Pinckney, March 30, 1813, TP, NA.

8. Pinckney to Kindelán, March 20, 1813, TP, NA.

9. Inhabitants to Pinckney, April 9, 1813, TP, NA.

10. McIntosh to Pinckney, April 13, 1813, TP, NA.

11. Patrick, *Fiasco*, 263–64.

12. Pinckney to McIntosh, April 14, 15, 1813, Pinckney to Monroe, April 17, 1813, Pinckney to residents, April 18, 1813, Pinckney to Kindelán, April 18, 1813, TP, NA.

13. Kindelán to Pinckney, April 16, 1813, in Davis, "Troops, V," 29; Kindelán to Pinckney, April 26, 1813, copy, TP, NA.

14. Pinckney to Major Manning, April 16, 1813, in Davis, ibid., 30–31.

15. For a diagram of the earthwork, see Davis, "Troops, IV," 276, and for the change in command of Smith and Manning, see Davis, "Troops, V," 24–25.

16. Patrick, *Fiasco*, 264–65; Davis, "Troops, V," 24–25; Kindelán to Pinckney, April 28, 1813, TP, NA; Testimony of James Hall and Francisco Roman Sánchez, Claim of Farquhar Bethune, No. 73,008, First Aud., NA.

17. Testimony, Francis Roman Sánchez, Claim of Brettan Knight, No. 80,172, First Aud., NA.

18. Gil José Pascot to Kindelán, May 7, 1813, Section 32, EFP, LC; Testimony of Francisco Roman Sánchez, Claim of the Estate of Francisco Xavier Sánchez, No. 71,838, First Aud., NA.

19. Testimony of Joseph S. Sánchez, Claim of Andrew Atkinson, MC-31–46, SAHS.

20. Pascot to Kindelán, May 2, 1813, Section 32, EFP, LC.

21. Ibid., and translation, Patriot War Claims, Anna Madgigine to St. Johns Co., PKY; Pascot to Estrada, May 11, 1813, Lopez to Estrada, May 13, 18, 1813, Section 32, EFP, LC; Davis, "Troops, V," 34.

22. Governor of Florida to Bethune, May 17, 1813, Bethune to Kindelán, May 18, 1813, Section 32, EFP, LC; Patrick, *Fiasco*, 265. Regarding desertions, see Estrada to Lopez, May 17, 1813, Section 32, EFP, LC. Regarding drinking water, see Pascot to Estrada, May 7, 1813, Lopez to Estrada, May 13, 1813, Lopez to Kindelán, June 10, 1813, ibid. On Harris, see Lopez to Kindelán, June 19, 26, 1813, ibid. On appoint-

ments, see Quiroga Fernández de Soto, "Military Liberalism," 457–58; L'Engle, *Notes*, 31.

23. Kindelán to Pinckney, April 28, 1813, in Davis, "Troops, V," 33–34.

24. Pinckney to Monroe, April 8, 1813 (probably misdated for May 8) and April 29, 1813, TP, NA.

25. Testimony of George Petty, Joseph Lourcey, and General Joseph M. Hernández, Claim of Follis and Gunby, No. 81,613, First Aud., NA.

26. Ashley to Mitchell, June 11, 1813, GEFWF and BHC, GDAH, with enclosure, Deposition of Abner Broadway, June 10, 1813; Harris to Mitchell, May 24, 1813, in Notes and Documents, "East Florida Documents," 154–55.

27. Deposition of Abner Broadway, ibid.

28. Enclosures, depositions of James Hall and John Black before William Ashley, June 11, 1813, GEFWF, GDAF, and James Hall before Archibald Clark, May 5, 1813, TP, NA.

29. Enclosures, depositions of James Hall and John Black, ibid.

30. Deposition of Jacob Summerlin before Buckner Harris, June 16, 1813, GGL and BHC, GDAH.

31. Landers, *Black Society*, 227.

32. Patrick, *Fiasco*, 269–70; Harris to Mitchell, June 8, 1813, BHC, GDAH; Harris to Mitchell, May 24, 1813, Notes and Documents, "East Florida Documents," 154–55.

33. Mitchell to John Mohr McIntosh, June 13, 1813, GGL, GDAH.

34. Rivera to Kindelán, July 17, 19, 1813, Section 32, EFP, LC; Deposition of William Fitzpatrick, n.d., Section 28, EFP, LC.

35. Phelipe Yonge to Governor, July 21, 1813, Rivera to Governor, July 24, 1813, Section 32, EFP, LC.

36. Rivera to Governor, August 8, 1813, ibid.

37. This account of the battle is a composite drawn from Patrick, *Fiasco*, 272–73; *Savannah Republican*, August 17, 1813; L'Engle, *Notes*, 31–33; Harris to Mitchell, August 18, 1813, BHC, GDAH; Phelipe Yonge to Kindelán, August 9, 20, 1813, Section 32, EFP, LC; and "Sketch map of land between Nassau and St. Marys Rivers," by Philip Robert Yonge [Phelipe Yonge] August 3, 1813, Section 34, EFP, LC, copy in the map collection, Map No. R1.1813.002.1997.1386, PKY.

38. Harris to Mitchell, August 18, 1813, GGL and BHC, GDAH.

39. Phelipe Yonge to Kindelán, August 9, 20, 1813, Section 32, EFP, LC; Notes re: Arredondo Family.

40. Inventario por fallecimiento de Don Archibald Atkinson, October 12, 1814, Section 71, EFP, LC.

Chapter 15. The Last of the Patriots

1. Patrick, *Fiasco*, 256–57, 269, 273–74; "Opelousas, Louisiana, 12th Dec., 1813," reprinted in the *National Intelligencer*, March 19, 1814.

2. William Cone to Francis Fatio, August 24, 1813, Harris and Dell to Yonge, September 7, 1813, Section 28, EFP, LC; Patrick, ibid., 277.

3. Governor to Lopez, August 6, 1813, Llorente to Kindelán, August 10, 13, 1813, Section 32, EFP, LC.

4. Phelipe Yonge to Governor, August 14, 1813, Section 34, EFP, LC.

5. Llorente to Kindelán, August 19, 1813, Section 32, EFP, LC.

6. Llorente to Kindelán, August 28, 1813, ibid.

7. *Georgia Argus*, May 4, 1814; Claim of the Estate of Francis Philip Fatio, Sr., No. 76,455, and Claim of Edward Wanton, No. 80,361, First Aud., NA; Patrick, *Fiasco*, 275.

8. Phelipe Yonge to the Governor, September 20, 1813, Section 34, EFP, LC; Claim of the Estate of James Cashen, No. 82,920 and Claim of Fernando D. McDonell, No. 73,313, First Aud., NA; Patrick, ibid.; *Georgia Argus*, January 12, 1814.

9. Andrew Atkinson to Kindelán, September 23, 1813, Section 32, EFP, LC.

10. Patrick, *Fiasco*, 275–77; Spanish translation labeled as an article appearing in the *Republican and Savannah Evening Ledger* [sic], October 5, 1813, Section 27, EFP, LC.

11. Harris to Kindelán, October 23, 1813, Section 34, EFP, LC.

12. Regarding Fort Mims, see Owsley, *Struggle*, 30–42; Deposition of William Hart before John Ross, November 7, 1813, enclosed with John Ross and Abraham Bessent to Peter Early, November 20, 1813, GGL, GDAH; Depositions of Cyrus Stow and Angus McEchran, November 18, 1813, enclosed in same.

13. John Ross and Abraham Bessent to Peter Early, November 20, 1813, ibid.

14. Hopkins to Early, December 14, 1813, ibid.

15. This entire story, in greater detail, is related in Schafer, *Kingsley*, 33–44.

16. Hibberson to Charles Harris, November 19, 1813, in Notes and Documents, "East Florida Documents," 156–58.

17. Kindelán to Early, January 27, 1814, GGL, GDAH; Early to Kindelán, February 23, 1814, Section 27, EFP, LC.

18. Patrick, *Fiasco*, 278–79; Monaco, "Fort Mitchell," 10–11; Dell, "Dell Brothers," 8–11.

19. Harris to the Honorable Legislative Council of the Republic of East Florida, January 25, 1814, TP, NA; Davis, "Elotchaway," 143–55.

20. The Legislative Council of Elotchaway District . . . to wit, January 25, 1814, TP, NA; Davis, ibid., 148–49. The reference to an August treaty is ambiguous. Mathews's negotiations with the Seminoles took place in April, May, and July. Presumably, the council was referring to the uprising against the Patriots in late July 1812 as the example of "oath-breaking."

21. To the Congress of the United States, January 25, 1814, TP, NA; Monaco, "Fort Mitchell," 11–12; Davis, ibid., 150–53.

22. Connor to James Monroe, March 15, 1814, TP, NA; Patrick, *Fiasco*, 280–81.

23. Monaco, "Fort Mitchell," 12.

24. Patrick, *Fiasco*, 281.

25. Ibid., 281–82.

26. Monaco, "Fort Mitchell," 17.

27. Ibid., 17–19; Dell, "Dell Brothers," 5–10; Vocelle, *Camden County*, 67–70; Claim of Francis Xavier Sánchez, No. 74,969, First Aud., NA.

28. Monaco, "Fort Mitchell," 17; Weisman, "Plantation System," 144–45.

29. Lovett, *Birth of Modern Spain*, 2: 550, 811–31.

30. Waterbury, *Oldest House*, 17–19.

31. Patrick, *Fiasco*, 284–90. See ibid., 291–94, for an account of the confrontation between American gunboat No. 168 and the British ship *Erebus*, March 16, 1815, off the mouth of the St. Marys River, one of the last engagements of the War of 1812.

Chapter 16. The Patriot War and American History

1. Brooks, *Diplomacy*, 3–9, 38–43; Waciuma, *Intervention*, 365–71; Owsley and Smith, *Filibusters*, 16–31, 188–90.

2. Waciuma, ibid., 365–66; Owsley and Smith, ibid., 190; Smith, *Republic of Letters*, 1352–62, 1404–12.

3. Ketcham, *Madison*, 423–25; Owsley and Smith, ibid., 45–46; Waciuma, ibid., 122–45; Ammon, *Monroe*, 410.

4. Patrick, *Fiasco*, 121–22; Remini, *Andrew Jackson*, 137–40. See also Ammon, ibid., 415–17; Wyllys, "East Florida Revolution," 415–16; Wills, *Madison*, 97–100.

5. Ammon, ibid., 409–48.

6. Owsley, *Struggle*, 9–17, 186–88. See also Perkins, *Prologue*, 418–27, on southern expansionist ambitions.

7. Patrick, *Fiasco*, 49–54; Monaco, "Fort Mitchell," 16; *Georgia Journal*, January 30, 1811.

8. Floyd is from "Our Southern Frontier," *National Intelligencer*, October 29, 1812. See Wright, *Creeks and Seminoles*, 164–65; Rivers, *Slavery*, 252; Porter, "Negroes," 16.

9. Marotti, "Wanton," 462; Owsley, *Struggle*, 194.

10. Stagg, *Mr. Madison's War*, xii; Hickey, *War of 1812*, 1–3; Owsley, ibid., 186.

11. Akins, "Georgians," 91–108; Mahon, *War of 1812*, 197–202, 235–44, 347–53; Remini, *Andrew Jackson*, 62–85, 94–95; Owsley, ibid., 189–90.

12. See Wright, *Britain*, 154–57. On conduct of war in the South, see Remini, ibid., 62–162; Mahon, *War of 1812*, 350–53; Stagg, *Mr. Madison's War*, 348–86; Heidler and Heidler, *The War of 1812*.

13. Patrick, *Fiasco*, 284–91; Mahon, ibid., 298–301, 339–53; Hickey, *War of 1812*, 204–6. Brown, *Amphibious Campaign*, 163–88, offers another perspective on the campaigns in West Florida and Louisiana. See also Heidler and Heidler, *Encyclopedia*, and Wait, *America*, 35–82. Wait confuses East and West Florida.

14. Patrick, ibid.; Vocelle, *Camden County*, 56–74. See also Bullard, *Cumberland Island*, 118–21.

15. Williams to Llorente, May 6, 1814, Hodge to Llorente, April 20, 1816, Section 32, EFP, LC.

16. Owsley and Smith, *Filibusters*, 103–17; Landers, *Black Society*, 231–35; see also Millett, "Slave Resistance."

17. Owsley and Smith, ibid., 118–40.

18. Wright, *Creeks and Seminoles*, 203–9; Owsley and Smith, ibid., 150–55; Remini, *Andrew Jackson*, 143–62.

19. Ammon, *Monroe*, 426–48; Brooks, *Diplomacy*, 131–214; Warren, "Textbook Writers."

20. Brooks, ibid., 209–10; *United States v. Ferreira*, 41; Decision Compiled, from Patriot War Papers and Patriot War Claims, 1812–1846, MC-31, SAHS.

21. Patriot War Papers and Patriot War Claims, ibid.; Schafer, "Family Ties," 8–9, and "Laurel Grove," 107–8.

22. Claim of Andrew [Andres] Atkinson, MC-31-46 and Claim of Anna Madgigine alias Kingsley, MC-31–58, SAHS. Claim of Manuel Solana, No. 73,340, Claim of Peter and Francisco Pons, No. 73,347, Claim of Henry Hartley, No. 83,761, Claim of Edward Wanton, No. 80,361, Claim of Matthew Long, No. 74,862, Claim of Francis Philip Fatio, No. 76,455, and Claim of the Estate of Eber O'Neill, No. 83,467, First Aud., NA; Marotti, "Wanton," 464–77.

23. Claim of Tony Primus, No. 84,941, Claims of José and Matilda Pomar, Nos. 73,629 and 73,630, First Aud., NA.

24. McIntosh to Estrada, July 22, 1815, PWC-ML, SAHS.

25. "Communication," *National Intelligencer*, July 2, 1823; Johnston, *Houstons*, 388–90.

26. Vocelle, *Camden County*, 67–70.

27. Dell, "Dell Brothers," 14–23; Claim of James Dell, No. 82,248 and Claim of William Dell, No. 83,832, First Aud., NA.

28. Letter of Thomas B. Hall to T. Frederick Davis, in Smith Letterbook.

29. Pezuela, *Diccionario Geográfico*.

30. Estrada to Apodaca, November 25, 1815, Section 2, EFP, LC, and Appointment, December 18, 1815, Section 1, ibid.; Landers, *Black Society*, 101–6, 247; Notes re: Arredondo Family; Harvey, "Proctor," 53–55.

31. Estate of Samuel Williams, No. 76,042, First Aud., NA; E. F. Claims, NA; Notes re: Arredondo Family; *Biographical Directory*, 1092.

32. Claim of George J. F. Clarke, No 83,177, Claim of Clarke and Garvin, No. 83,763, First Aud., NA.

33. Hill, "Clarke," 238–45.

Bibliography

Manuscripts

Manuscript materials are listed by repository. When abbreviations are used in the notes instead of the full title, the abbreviation is given in the left-hand column.

Bryan-Lang Library, Woodbine, Georgia

The major regional library for genealogy and early history of Camden County, Bryan-Lang has biographical files on major families of southern Georgia and northern Florida as well as manuscript and computer files for tracing individuals and Isaac Arnow's historical series in the *Camden County Tribune*.

The Florida Historical Society (FHS)

The Society holds an original copy of the Patriot Constitution as well as the Marie Taylor Greenslade Papers.

The Georgia Division of Archives and History (GDAH)

BHC—Buckner Harris Collection, Georgia Archives Mss. File 2
GEFWF—Georgia, East Florida, West Florida, and Yazoo Land Sales, 1764–1850
GGL—Georgia Executive Department. Georgia Governors' Letterbooks: David Mitchell, 1809–13, Peter Early, 1813–15

Library of Congress (LC)

EFP—The East Florida Papers, 1737–1858. Section 1: Letters from the Captain General; Section 2: Letters to the Captain General; Section 25: Letters to and from Spanish ministers and consuls in the United States; Section 27: Letters to and from the United States; Section 28: Papers of the revolution in East Florida; Section 32: Correspondence between the governor and civil, financial, and military subordinates on the St. Johns and St. Marys Rivers, Matanzas, and other East Florida posts; Section 34: Papers on the District of Fernandina and Amelia Island; Section 38, Criminal Proceedings; Section 42: Inspection Returns of the Third Battalion of the Cuban Infantry Regiment; Section 47, Papers on Fernandina, 1813–17; Section 65, Testamentary Proceedings.

Mad. Papers—Papers of James Madison, Series I

PC—Papeles procedentes de la Isla de Cuba. A collection of photostatic reprints from the originals in the Archivo General de Indias, Seville. Legajos 1569, 1770, 1789, and 1856

National Archives and Record Administration, Washington, D.C.,
and College Park, Md. (NA)

CL—Letters Received by the Secretary of the Navy from Captains, RG 45, M125

Dom. Let.—Domestic Letters of the Department of State, 1784–1906, RG 59, M40

E. F. Claims—Letters Received re: Claims for Losses during the Operation of American Troops in East Florida, 1812–13, and Certified Copies of Documents in Royal Archives of Spain, re: Spanish Land Grants in Florida, 1851, General Records of the Treasury Department, RG 56

First Aud.—First Auditor, Records of the Accounting Offices of the Department of Treasury, Miscellaneous Division, Relating to Claims and Accounts, RG 217, Entry 347

Let. Marque—Letters Received Concerning Letters of Marque, War of 1812 Papers, Department of State, 1789–1815, RG 59, M588

LRMC—Letters Received, Records of the U.S. Marine Corps, Record Group 127

Misc. Let.—Miscellaneous Letters Received by the Department of State, 1789–1906, RG 59, M179

Sec. Navy—Letters Sent by the Secretary of the Navy to Officers, 1798–1868, RG 45, M149

Sec. War—Letters Sent by the Secretary of War Relating to Military Affairs, 1800–1889, RG 107, M6

Span. Leg.—Notes from the Spanish Legation in the United States to the Department of State, 1790–1906, RG 59, M59

TP—Territorial Papers of the Department of State, 1774–1824, RG 59, M116

TPSen—Territorial Papers of the United States Senate, RG 46, M200, "Florida"

U. Misc. Let.—Undated Miscellaneous Letters Received by the Department of State, ca. 1807–20, RG 59

New-York Historical Society

The Hawks Papers contain English translations of the correspondence that passed between the Patriots and Spanish envoys in March 1812. Other copies can be found at the St. Augustine Historical Society and in the Territorial Papers of the United States Senate.

The P. K. Yonge Library of Florida History (PKY)

Copies of many documents from the National Archives, Library of Congress, Georgia Division of Archives and History, and New-York Historical Society can be found in the Joseph Byrne Lockey Collection on the Spanish borderlands. The T. Frederick Davis Collection contains a typescript of Letterbooks One and Two from the Thomas Adam Smith Papers (originals in the Western Historical Manuscript Collection, Columbia, Missouri). The O'Neill Family Papers contain information on an important loyalist family. The Sánchez Family Papers and two letters of Major General John McIntosh (Miscellaneous Manuscripts Collection) also contain information on the war and its aftermath. In addition, the Yonge Library has two collections of miscellaneous materials assembled on microfilm that pertain to the war and the claims suits, gathered and filmed from the St. Augustine Historical Society, the St. Johns County Clerk of the Court, and the National Archives. These are Patriot War Claims: Anna Madgigine to St. Johns Co. (East Florida) and other legal claims and related papers, translated from the original Spanish documents, Microfilm Reels 182 F–G; and Letters Received re: Claims for Losses during the Operation of American Troops in East Florida, 1812–13, General Records of the Treasury Department, Microfilm Reel 95–O.

Public Record Office, London (PRO)

The letters of the British chargé d'affaires, J. P. Morier, Foreign Office 5/74–76 and of the British consul, Augustus J. Foster, Foreign Office 5/83–87, contain significant accounts of American, British, and Spanish disputes over East Florida. Admiralty 1/502 contains an English translation of Estrada's early account of the siege.

Rare Books, Manuscripts, and Special Collections Library,
Duke University (RBMSCL)

Duke University holds two collections of significance to the Patriot War. The first, the James Hamilton Papers, contains correspondence of Zephaniah Kingsley. The second, the Alfred Cumming Papers, includes the notable correspondence of Captain William Cumming to his father about his service in East Florida during late 1812 and early 1813.

The St. Augustine Historical Society (SAHS)

MC-31—Patriot War Papers and Patriot War Claims, 1812–46
PWC-ML—Patriot War Claims and Miscellaneous Letters, 1815

Western Historical Manuscript Collection, Columbia, Missouri

The letterbooks of Thomas Adam Smith are part of the Thomas Adam Smith Papers (1798–1864) (C1029)

Books, Pamphlets, and Articles

Abridgement of the Debates of Congress from 1789 to 1756. Vol. 1. New York: D. Appleton, 1850.
Aggregate Amount of Each Description of Persons within the United States of America, and the Territories Thereof, 1810. New York: Norman Ross, 1990.

Akins, Billy Lee. "Georgians and the War of 1812." Master's thesis, Georgia State University, 1968.

Alexander, Joseph H. "The Ambush of Captain John Williams, U.S.M.C.: Failure of the East Florida Invasion, 1812–1813." *Florida Historical Quarterly* 56 (January 1978): 280–96.

———. "Swamp Ambush in East Florida." *Military History* (March 1998): 38–44.

Altoff, Gerard T. *Amongst My Best Men: African-Americans and the War of 1812.* Put-in-Bay, Ohio: Perry Group, 1996.

American State Papers. State Papers and Publick Documents of the United States from the Ascension of George Washington to the Presidency. 2nd ed. Boston: T. B. Wait and Sons, 1817.

Ammon, Harry. *James Monroe: The Quest for National Identity.* 1971. Reprint, Charlottesville: University Press of Virginia, 1999.

Anna, Timothy. "The Independence of Mexico and Central America." In *The Independence of Latin America,* edited by Leslie Bethell, 49–94. New York: Cambridge University Press, 1988.

Annals of Congress: The Debates and Proceedings of the Congress of the United States. Washington: Gales and Seaton, 1834–56.

Appleby, Joyce. *Inheriting the Revolution: The First Generation of Americans.* Cambridge, Mass.: Harvard University Press, 2000.

Arana, Luis Rafael. "The Fort at Matanzas Inlet." *El Escribano* 17 (1980): 1–32.

———. "Subsection C: The Second Spanish Period or the Disintegration of Fort Matanzas, 1784–1821." In *Historic Structure Report for Fort Matanzas National Monument, St. Johns County, Florida,* 51–81. Denver: National Park Service, Denver Service Center, 1980.

Arana, Luis Rafael, and Albert Manucy. *The Building of the Castillo de San Marcos.* National Park Service, 1977.

Arnade, Charles W. "Raids, Sieges, and International Wars." In Gannon, *The New History of Florida,* 100–116.

Arnow, Isaac F. "History of St. Marys and Camden County, Chapter 30, the War of 1812." *Camden County Tribune,* September 28, 1951.

Bennett, Charles E. *Florida's "French" Revolution, 1793–1795.* Gainesville: University of Florida Press, 1981.

Bergh, Albert E., ed. *The Writings of Thomas Jefferson.* Washington: Thomas Jefferson Memorial Association, 1904.

Bermudez, Ligia Ma. "The Situado: A Study in the Dynamics of East Florida's Economy during the Second Spanish Period, 1785–1820." Master's thesis, University of Florida, 1989.

Biedzynski, James C. "Monroe, James." In Heidler and Heidler, *Encyclopedia of the War of 1812,* 359–62.

Biographical Directory of the American Congress, 1774–1927. Washington, D.C.: Government Printing Office, 1928.

Blake, Nicholas, and Richard Lawrence. *The Illustrated Companion to Nelson's Navy*. London: Stackpole Books, 1999.

Brooks, Philip C. *Diplomacy and the Borderlands: The Adams-Onís Treaty of 1819*. Berkeley: University of California Press, 1939.

Brown, Roger H. *The Republic in Peril: 1812*. New York: Columbia University Press, 1964.

Brown, Wilburt S. *The Amphibious Campaign for West Florida and Louisiana, 1814–1815: A Critical Review of Strategy and Tactics at New Orleans*. University: University of Alabama Press, 1969.

Bullard, Mary R. *Cumberland Island, a History*. Athens: University of Georgia Press, 2003.

Burnett, Gene M. "Colonel Newnan Sidesteps a Massacre." In *Florida's Past, People and Events that Shaped the State*. Vol. 3, 131–34. Sarasota, Fla.: Pineapple Press, 1991.

Burrus, Vivian R. "Jean Ashley's Confiscated Property, 1795–1796." *El Escribano* 12 (October 1975): 134–42.

Burt, Alfred L. *The United States, Great Britain, and British North America from the Revolution to the Establishment of Peace after the War of 1812*. New Haven, Conn.: Yale University Press, 1940.

Bushnell, Amy Turner. "A Peripheral Perspective." *Historical Archaeology* 1, no. 3: 18–23.

Byron, George Gordon. *Childe Harold's Pilgrimage, A Romaunt and Other Poems*. 4th ed. London: T. Davison, 1812.

Cabot, Ramón Romero. "La Defensa de Florida en el Segundo Período Español (1783–1821)." Master's thesis, Universidad de Sevilla, 1983.

Campen, J. T. van. *The Story of St. Augustine, Florida's Colonial Capital*. St. Augustine: St. Augustine Historical Society, 1977.

Chartrand, René. *Uniforms and Equipment of the United States Forces in the War of 1812*. Youngstown, N.Y.: Old Fort Niagara Association, 1992.

Christian, Richard H. *Founders of St. Marys*. Privately printed, n.d.

Clarke, George J. F. "The Surrender of Amelia Island." *Florida Historical Quarterly* 4 (October 1925): 90–95.

Coker, William S., and Susan R. Parker. "The Second Spanish Period in the Two Floridas." In Gannon, *The New History of Florida*, 150–66.

Coleman, Kenneth, gen. ed. *A History of Georgia*. Athens: University of Georgia Press, 1977.

Coleman, Kenneth, and Charles Stephen Gurr. *Dictionary of Georgia Biography*. Athens: University of Georgia Press, 1983.

Coles, Harry. *The War of 1812*. Chicago: University of Chicago Press, 1965.

Corbitt, Duvon Clough. "The Administration System in the Floridas, 1783–1821, II." *Tequesta* 1 (July 1943): 57–67.

————. "Notes and Documents: Papers Relating to the Georgia-Florida Frontier, 1784–1800, II." *Georgia Historical Quarterly* 21 (March 1937): 73–83.

————. "Notes and Documents: Papers Relating to the Georgia-Florida Frontier, 1784–1800, V." *Georgia Historical Quarterly* 21 (December 1937): 373–81.

Coulter, E. Merton. *Georgia: A Short History*. Chapel Hill: University of North Carolina Press, 1947.

Covington, James W. *The Seminoles of Florida*. Gainesville: University Press of Florida, 1993.

Cox, Isaac J. "The Border Missions of General George Mathews." *Mississippi Valley Historical Review* 12 (December 1925): 309–33.

Cox, Isaac Joslin. *The West Florida Controversy, 1798–1813: A Study in American Diplomacy*. Gloucester, Mass.: Peter Smith, 1967.

Cusick, James. "Across the Border: Commodity Flow and Merchants in Spanish St. Augustine." *Florida Historical Quarterly* 69 (January 1991): 277–99.

————. "Oaths of Allegiance." Manuscript on file, P. K. Yonge Library of Florida History, Gainesville, 1990.

Davis, T. Frederick. "Elotchaway, East Florida, 1814." *Florida Historical Quarterly* 8 (January 1930): 143–55.

————. "United States Troops in Spanish East Florida, 1812–1813, III." *Florida Historical Quarterly* 9 (January 1931): 135–55.

————. "United States Troops in Spanish East Florida, 1812–1813, IV." *Florida Historical Quarterly* 9 (April 1931): 259–78.

————. "United States Troops in Spanish East Florida, 1812–1813, V." *Florida Historical Quarterly* 9 (July 1931): 24–34.

Dell, Lawrence Harper. "Dell Brothers, Florida Patriots: A Short History of One Family and Their Involvement in the Beginnings of the State." Manuscript on file, P. K. Yonge Library of Florida History, Gainesville, 2001.

DuPree, Mary M., and G. Dekle Taylor, M.D. "Dr. James Hall (1760–1837)." *Journal of the Florida Medical Association* 61 (August 1974): 626–31.

Edgar, Walter B. *Partisans and Redcoats: The Southern Conflict that Turned the Tide of the American Revolution*. New York: Morrow, 2001.

Egan, Clifford. "The Origins of the War of 1812: Three Decades of Historical Writing." *Military History* 38 (April 1974): 72–75.

Ellis, Joseph J. *Founding Brothers: The Revolutionary Generation*. New York: Alfred A. Knopf, 2001.

Fabel, Robin F. A. "British Rule in the Floridas." In Gannon, *The New History of Florida*, 134–49.

"Fernandina from 1811 until 1821." Typescript on file, P. K. Yonge Library of Florida History, Gainesville, n.d.

Fitzpatrick, John C., ed. *The Writings of George Washington*. Vol. 21. Washington, D.C.: Government Printing Office, 1940.

Forbes, James Grant. *Sketches, Historical and Topographical of the Floridas, more particularly East Florida.* New York: C. S. van Winkle, 1821.

Ford, Paul L., ed. *The Writings of Thomas Jefferson.* New York: G. P. Putnam's Sons, 1897.

Fort Matanzas Stabilization Team. *Historic Structure Report for Fort Matanzas National Monument, St. Johns County, Florida.* Denver: National Park Service, Denver Service Center, 1980.

Franco, José Luciano. *La conspiración de Aponte.* Havana: Consejo Nacional de Cultura, 1966.

Gamble, Thomas. *Savannah Duels and Duelists, 1733–1877.* Savannah: Review Publishing and Printing Company, 1923.

Gannon, Michael V., ed. *The New History of Florida.* Gainesville: University Press of Florida, 1996.

Gonzalez, Julio. "Numero 242, 1812, Plano del ataque de Fernandina el 17 de marzo de 1812 en la isla Amelia, Firmado por Jorge J. Clarke, en colores grises, explicación al pie, toponimia, rosa de los vientos, 260 x 362 mm, con carta del comandante don Justo Lopez, de 13 de mayo 1812." In *Catalogo de Mapas y Planos de la Florida y la Luisiana* 83. Madrid: Dirección General del Patrimonio Artístico, Archivos y Museos, 1797.

Graebner, Norman A. "Secretary of State." In *James Madison and the American Nation, 1751–1836: An Encyclopedia,* edited by Robert A. Rutland, 258–73. New York: Simon and Schuster, 1994.

Green, Philip J. "William H. Crawford and the War of 1812." *Georgia Historical Quarterly* 26 (March 1942): 16–39.

Griffin, Patricia C. "The Minorcans." In *Clash Between Cultures: Spanish East Florida, 1784–1821,* edited by Jacqueline K. Fretwell and Susan R. Parker, 61–83. St. Augustine, Fla.: St. Augustine Historical Society, 1988.

———. *Mullet on the Beach: The Minorcans of Florida, 1768–1788.* Gainesville: University Press of Florida, 1993.

———. "The Spanish Return: The People-Mix Period, 1784–1821." In Waterbury, *The Oldest City,* 125–49.

Hamilton, Stanislaus M., ed. *The Writings of James Monroe.* New York: AMS Press, 1969.

Harden, Edward J. *The Life of George Troup.* Savannah, Ga.: E. J. Purse, 1859.

Harlan, Roger C. "A Military History of East Florida during the Governorship of Enrique White, 1796–1811." Master's thesis, Florida State University, 1971.

Harvey, Karen. "Antonio Proctor: A Piece of the Mosaic." *El Escribano* 17 (1980): 47–57.

Hatzenbuehler, Ronald L., and Robert L. Ivie. *Congress Declares War: Rhetoric, Leadership, and Partisanship in the Early Republic.* Kent, Ohio: Kent State University Press, 1983.

Heath, William Estill. "The Yazoo Land Fraud." *Georgia Historical Quarterly* 16 (December 1932): 274–91.

Heidler, David S., and Jeanne T. Heidler. *The War of 1812.* Westport, Conn: Greenwood Publishing Group, 2002.

———, eds. *Encyclopedia of the War of 1812.* Santa Barbara, Calif.: ABC-CLIO, 1997.

Hess, Barry R. "The Letters of George J. F. Clarke to Judge Joseph L. Smith." Manuscript on file, P. K. Yonge Library of Florida History, Gainesville, 1973.

Hibbert, Christopher. *Redcoats and Rebels: The American Revolution Through British Eyes.* New York: W. W. Norton, 1990.

Hickey, Donald. "American Trade Restrictions during the War of 1812." *Journal of American History* 68 (December 1981): 517–38.

———. *The War of 1812: A Forgotten Conflict.* Urbana: University of Illinois Press, 1989.

Hill, Louise Biles. "George J. F. Clarke, 1774–1836." *Florida Historical Quarterly* 21 (January 1943): 198–253.

Hodler, Thomas W., and Howard A. Schretter. *The Atlas of Georgia.* Athens: University of Georgia Press, 1986.

Hoffman, Paul E. *Florida's Frontiers.* Bloomington: Indiana University Press, 2002.

Hopkins, James, ed. *The Papers of Henry Clay.* Vol. 1, *The Rising Statesman, 1797–1814.* Lexington: University of Kentucky Press, 1959.

Horsman, Reginald. *The Causes of the War of 1812.* Philadelphia: University of Pennsylvania Press, 1962.

Howes, Lillia Mills, ed. "The Frontiers of Georgia in the Late Eighteenth Century, Jones Fauche to Joseph Vallance Bevan." *Georgia Historical Quarterly* 47 (March 1963): 84–95.

Jaccard, Deon Lawrence. *The Historic Splendor of Amelia Island.* Fernandina Beach, Fla.: Amelia Island Museum of History, 1997.

Jensen, Larry R. *Children of Colonial Despotism: Press, Politics, and Culture in Cuba, 1790–1840.* Tampa: University of South Florida Press, 1988.

Johnson, Allen, and Dumas Malone, eds. *Dictionary of American Biography.* Authors' ed. New York: Charles Scribner's Sons, 1937.

Johnson, Amanda. "A State in the Making: Georgia (1783–1798)." *Georgia Historical Quarterly* 15 (March 1931): 1–27.

Johnson, Sherry. "The Spanish St. Augustine Community, 1784–1795: A Re-evaluation." *Florida Historical Quarterly* 48 (July 1989): 27–54.

Johnston, Edith Duncan. *The Houstons of Georgia.* Athens: University of Georgia Press, 1950.

Ketcham, Ralph. *James Madison: A Biography.* 1971. Reprint, Charlottesville: University Press of Virginia, 2001.

Klapthor, Margaret Brown. *Benjamin Latrobe and Dolley Madison Decorate the*

White House, 1809–1811. Washington, D.C.: Smithsonian Institution, Contributions from the Museum of History and Technology, Paper 49, 1965.

Knetsch, Joe. "The Development of Amelia Island in the Second Spanish Period: The Impact." Manuscript on file, P. K. Yonge Library of Florida History, Gainesville, n.d.

Kruse, Paul. "A Secret Agent in East Florida: General George Mathews and the Patriot War." *Journal of Southern History* 18 (May 1952): 193–218.

Landers, Jane. *Black Society in Spanish Florida*. Urbana: University of Illinois Press, 1999.

———. "Black Society in Spanish St. Augustine." Ph.D. diss., University of Florida, 1988.

———. "Free Black Plantations and Economy in East Florida, 1784–1821." In Landers, *Colonial Plantations and Economy in Florida*, 121–35. Gainesville: University Press of Florida, 2000.

———. "Rebellion and Royalism in Spanish Florida: The French Revolution on Spain's Northern Colonial Frontier." In *A Turbulent Time: The French Revolution and the Greater Caribbean*, edited by David Barry Gaspar and David Patrick Geggus, 156–77. Bloomington: Indiana University Press, 1997.

———. "Traditions of African American Freedom and Community in Spanish Colonial Florida." In *The African American Heritage of Florida*, edited by David R. Colburn and Jane Landers, 17–41. Gainesville: University Press of Florida, 1995.

———, ed. *Colonial Plantations and Economy in Florida*. Gainesville: University Press of Florida, 2000.

L'Engle, Susan. *Notes of My Family and Recollections of My Early Life*. New York: Knickerbocker Press, 1888.

Lipscomb, Andrew A., and Albert Ellery Bergh. *Writings of Thomas Jefferson*. Vol. 2. Washington, D.C.: Thomas Jefferson Memorial Association, 1903–4.

Lockey, Joseph Byrne. *East Florida, 1783–1785: A File of Documents Assembled and Many of Them Translated*. Edited by John Walton Caughey. Berkeley: University of California Press, 1949.

Lovett, Gabriel H. *Napoleon and the Birth of Modern Spain*. 2 vols. New York: New York University Press, 1965.

Madison, James. *Letters and Other Writings of James Madison, Fourth President of the United States, in Four Volumes, published by Order of Congress*. Vol. 2, 1794–1815. New York: R. Worthington, 1884.

Mahon, John K. *The War of 1812*. Gainesville: University of Florida Press, 1972.

Marotti, Frank. "Black Knights: The Free Men of Color, the Patriot War, and the Community of Memory in Antebellum East Florida." Manuscript loaned to the author.

———. "Edward M. Wanton and the Settling of Micanopy." *Florida Historical Quarterly* 3 (April 1995): 456–77.

————. "The Enslaved in the Community of Memory: The Formation of Countermentalities in East Florida during the Patriot War of 1812–1813." Manuscript loaned to the author.

Martin, S. Walter. "Book Reviews and Notes." *Georgia Historical Quarterly* 38 (September 1954): 297–98.

McCall, Hugh. *The History of Georgia, Containing Brief Sketches of the Most Remarkable Events up to the Present Day (1784)*. Atlanta: Cherokee Publishing Company, 1969.

Miller, James J. *An Environmental History of Northeast Florida*. Gainesville: University Press of Florida, 1998.

Miller, Janice Borton. *Juan Nepomuceno de Quesada, Governor of Spanish East Florida, 1790–1795*. Washington, D.C.: University Press of America, 1981.

Millett, Nat. "Slave Resistance During the Age of Revolution: The Maroon Community at Prospect Bluff, Spanish Florida." Ph.D. diss., St. Catherine's College, Cambridge University, 2002.

Mills, Donna Rachal. *Florida's First Families: Translated Abstracts of Pre-1821 Spanish Censuses*. Tuscaloosa, Ala.: Mills Historical Press, 1992.

Monaco, Chris. "Fort Mitchell and the Settlement of Alachua County." *Florida Historical Quarterly* 79 (Summer 2000): 1–25.

Mooney, James L. *Dictionary of American Naval Fighting Ships*. Vol. 7. Washington, D.C.: Naval Historical Center, Department of the Navy, 1981.

Moore, Virginia. *The Madisons: A Biography*. New York: McGraw Hill, 1977.

Murdoch, Richard K. "Elijah Clarke and Anglo-American Designs on East Florida, 1797–1798." *Georgia Historical Quarterly* 35 (September 1951): 174–90.

————. *The Georgia-Florida Frontier, 1793–1796: Spanish Reaction to French Intrigue and American Designs*. Berkeley: University of California Press, University of California Publications in History No. 40, 1915.

————. "The Seagrove-White Stolen Property Agreement." *Georgia Historical Quarterly* 2 (September 1958): 258–76.

————, ed. "Collections of the Georgia Historical Society, Other Documents and Notes, Letters and Papers of Dr. Daniel Turner, a Rhode Islander in South Georgia, Part III." *Georgia Historical Quarterly* 54 (Spring 1970): 91–122.

Notes and Documents. "East Florida Documents." *Georgia Historical Quarterly* 13 (June 1929): 154–58.

Notes re: the Arredondo Family. Typescript on file, P. K. Yonge Library of Florida History, Gainesville, n.d.

Olaechea, Rafael, and Jose A. Ferrer Benimeli. *El Conde de Aranda, Mito y Realidad de un Político Aragonés*. Zaragoza: Diputación de Huesca, IberCaja, 1998.

Owsley, Frank L., Jr. *The Struggle for the Gulf Borderlands: The Creek War and the Battle of New Orleans, 1812–1815*. Gainesville: University of Florida Press, 1981.

Owsley, Frank L., Jr., and Gene A. Smith. *Filibusters and Expansionists: Jeffersonian Manifest Destiny, 1800–1821.* Tuscaloosa: University of Alabama Press, 1997.

Parker, Susan R. "The Cattle Trade in East Florida, 1784–1821." In Landers, *Colonial Plantations and Economy in Florida,* 150–67.

———. "Men without God or King: Rural Settlers of East Florida, 1784–1790." Master's thesis, University of Florida, 1990.

Patrick, Rembert W. *Florida Fiasco: Rampant Rebels on the Georgia-Florida Border, 1810–1815.* Athens: University of Georgia Press, 1954.

———. "Letters of the Invaders of East Florida, 1812." *Florida Historical Quarterly* 28 (July 1949): 53–65.

Perkins, Bradford. *Prologue to War: England and the United States, 1805–1812.* Berkeley: University of California Press, 1968.

———, ed. *The Causes of the War of 1812.* New York: Holt Rinehart and Winston American Problems Series, 1962.

Pezuela, Jacobo de la. *Diccionario Geográfico, Estadístico, Histórico, de la Isla de Cuba.* Vol. 3. Madrid: Establecimiento de Mellado, 1863.

Phinney, A. H. "The First Spanish American War." *Florida Historical Quarterly* 4 (January 1926): 114–29.

Porter, Kenneth. "Negroes and the East Florida Annexation Plot, 1811–1813." *Journal of Negro History* 30 (January 1945): 1–29.

Pratt, Julius W. *The Expansionists of 1812.* New York: Macmillan, 1925.

Quiroga Fernández de Soto, Alejandro. "Military Liberalism on the East Florida 'Frontier': The Implementation of the 1812 Constitution." *Florida Historical Quarterly* 79 (Spring 2001): 441–68.

Reddick, Marguerite, comp. *Camden's Challenge: A History of Camden County, Georgia.* Edited by Eloise Bailey and Virginia Proctor. Camden County Historical Commission, 1976.

Remini, Robert. *Andrew Jackson and His Indian Wars.* New York: Viking, 2001.

———. *The Battle of New Orleans.* New York: Viking, 1999.

Return of the Whole Number of Persons within the Several Districts of the United States. Washington: Duane and Son, 1802.

Richardson, James D. *A Compilation of the Messages and Papers of the Presidents, 1789–1897.* Washington, D.C.: Government Printing Office, 1896–99.

Rivers, Larry Eugene. *Slavery in Florida: Territorial Days to Emancipation.* Gainesville: University Press of Florida, 2000.

Rutherford, Robert Erwin. "Spain's Immigration Policy for the Floridas, 1780–1806." Master's thesis, University of Florida, 1952.

Rutland, Robert A. "Presidency." In *James Madison and the American Nation, 1751–1836: An Encyclopedia,* edited by Robert A. Rutland, 273–80. New York: Simon and Schuster, 1994.

Santa Cruz y Mallen, Francisco Xavier de. *Historia de Familias Cubanas.* Vol. 1. Havana: Editorial Hercules, 1940.

Sastre, Cecile-Marie. "The British Redoubts of St. Augustine." Master's thesis, Florida Atlantic University, 1990.

———. "Picolata on the St. Johns: St. Augustine's River Outpost." Ph.D. diss., Florida State University, 1998.

Saye, Albert Berry. *A Constitutional History of Georgia, 1732–1945.* Athens: University of Georgia Press, 1948.

Schafer, Daniel L. *Anna Madgigine Jai Kingsley: African Princess, Florida Slave, Plantation Slaveowner.* Gainesville: University Press of Florida, 2003.

———. "Family Ties that Bind: Anglo-African Slave Traders in Africa and Florida, John Fraser and His Descendants." *Slavery and Abolition* 20 (December 1999): 1–21.

———. "... not so Gay a Town in America as this ... 1763–1784." In Waterbury, *The Oldest City,* 91–124.

———. "Zephaniah Kingsley's Laurel Grove Plantation, 1802–1813." In Landers, *Colonial Plantations and Economy in Florida,* 98–120.

Seale, William. *The President's House: A History.* Washington, D.C.: White House Historical Association, 1986.

Secret Acts, Resolutions, and Instructions under which East Florida was Invaded by the United States Troops, Naval Forces, and Volunteers in 1812 and 1813, together with the official correspondence of the agents and officers of the government. Washington: George S. Gideon, 1860.

Servicio Geográfico de Ejército. *Cartografía de Ultramar.* Vol. 2. Madrid: Servicio Geográfico de Ejército, 1949–57.

Shambaugh, Marion Francis. "The Development of Agriculture in Florida during the Second Spanish Period." Master's thesis, University of Florida, 1953.

Simmons, William H. *Notices of East Florida with an Account of the Seminole Nation of Indians by a Recent Traveller in the Province.* Charleston, S.C.: Privately printed by A. E. Miller, 1822.

Singleton, Esther. *The Story of the White House.* New York: Benjamin Blom, 1969.

Skeen, C. Edward. *Citizen Soldiers in the War of 1812.* Lexington: University Press of Kentucky, 1999.

Smith, James Morton, ed. *The Republic of Letters: The Correspondence between Thomas Jefferson and James Madison, 1776–1826.* Vol. 3, *1804–1836.* New York: W. W. Norton, 1995.

Smith, Joseph B. *The Plot to Steal Florida: James Madison's Phony War.* New York: Arbor House, 1983.

Stagg, J.C.A. *Mr. Madison's War: Politics, Diplomacy and Warfare in the Early American Republic, 1783–1830.* Princeton, N.J.: Princeton University Press, 1983.

———, ed. *The Papers of James Madison, Presidential Series.* Vols. 3 and 4. Charlottesville: University Press of Virginia, 1996.

Talmadge, John E. "Georgia's Federalist Press and the War of 1812." *Journal of Southern History* 19, no. 4: 488–500.

Tanner, Helen Hornbeck. *Zéspedes in East Florida, 1784–1790*. Jacksonville: University of North Florida Press, 1989.

Tornero Tinajero, Pablo. *Relaciones de Dependencía entre Florida y Estados Unidos (1783–1820)*. Madrid: Ministerio de Asuntos Exteriores, 1979.

Torres-Reyes, Ricardo. *The British Siege of St. Augustine, 1740*. National Park Service, 1972.

Tucker, Glenn. *Poltroons and Patriots: A Popular Account of the War of 1812*. New York: Bobbs-Merrill, 1954.

Tucker, Spencer C. *The Jeffersonian Gunboat Navy*. Columbia: University of South Carolina Press, 1993.

Tucker, Spencer C., and Frank T. Reuter. *Injured Honor: The Chesapeake-Leopard Affair, June 22, 1807*. Annapolis, Md.: Naval Institute Press, 1996.

United States Appellants v. Francis P. Ferreira, Administrator of Francis Pass, Deceased. Supreme Court of the United States No. 197, Senate Misc. Document No. 55, 36th Cong., 1st sess. Washington: George W. Bowman, 1860.

Vocelle, James T. *History of Camden County, Georgia*. Privately printed, 1914.

Waciuma, Wanjohi. *Intervention in Spanish Floridas, 1801–1813: A Study in Jeffersonian Foreign Policy*. Boston: Branden Press, 1976.

Wait, Eugene M. *America and the War of 1812*. Commack, N.Y.: Kroshka Books, 1999.

Ward, Christopher. "The Commerce of East Florida during the Embargo, 1806–1812: The Role of Amelia Island." *Florida Historical Quarterly* 68 (October 1989): 160–79.

Ward, James R. *Old Hickory's Town: An Illustrated History of Jacksonville*. Jacksonville, Fla.: Old Hickory's Town, 1985.

Warren, Harris G. "Textbook Writers and the Florida 'Purchase' Myth." *Florida Historical Quarterly* 41 (April 1963): 325–31.

Waterbury, Jean Parker. *The Oldest House*. St. Augustine, Fla.: St. Augustine Historical Society, 1984.

———, ed. *The Oldest City: St. Augustine, Saga of Survival*. St. Augustine, Fla.: St. Augustine Historical Society, 1983.

Weber, David J. *The Spanish Frontier in North America*. New Haven, Conn.: Yale University Press, 1992.

Weisman, Brent R. "The Plantation System of the Florida Seminole Indians and Black Seminoles during the Colonial Era." In Landers, *Colonial Plantations and Economy in Florida*, 136–49.

White, David Hart. *Vicente Folch, Governor in Spanish Florida, 1787–1811*. Washington, D.C.: University Press of America, 1981.

Williams, Carolina Eliza. Diary, 1811–1822. Ledger 53, P. K. Yonge Library of Florida History, Gainesville.

Wolff, George. Fernandina, 1811–1821. Typescript on file, P. K. Yonge Library of Florida History, Gainesville, n.d.

Wright, Albert Hazen. *Our Georgia-Florida Frontier: The Okefinokee Swamp, Its History and Cartography.* Vol. 1. Ithaca, N.Y.: A. H. Wright, 1945.

Wright, James Leitch. *Britain and the American Frontier, 1783–1815.* Athens: University of Georgia Press, 1975.

———. *Creeks and Seminoles, The Destruction and Regeneration of the Muscogulge People.* Lincoln: University of Nebraska Press, 1986.

———. *William Augustus Bowles, Director General of the Creek Nation.* Athens: University of Georgia Press, 1967.

Wyllys, Rufus Kay. "The East Florida Revolution of 1812–1814." *Hispanic American Historical Review* 9 (November 1929): 415–45.

Zelinsky, Wibur. "An Isochronic Map of Georgia Settlement, 1750–1850." *Georgia Historical Quarterly* 35 (June 1951): 191–95.

Index

James G. Cusick is the curator of the P. K. Yonge Library of Florida History, Department of Special Collections, George A. Smathers Libraries, University of Florida. He has previously published an edited volume, *Studies in Culture Contact: Interaction, Culture Change, and Archaeology,* and is currently working with Frank Laumer and the Seminole Wars Historic Foundation to bring out the Second Seminole War journal of Colonel William S. Foster.